THE SMART HOMEOWNER'S RESOURCE KIT AND GUIDE TO EARLY MORTGAGE RETIREMENT

Put Money In Your Pockets

HOW TO RETIRE YOUR MORTGAGE

ON YOUR OWN TERMS

AT A FRACTION OF THE COST

Josh Bruno

This book is designed to provide accurate and authoritative information in regard to the subject matter covered. It is the product of deep and exhaustive research, and a great deal of careful thought. But, the contents should be viewed as general information only. The book is sold with the understanding that it does not render actual legal, accounting, or financial advice of a personal nature. If legal, accounting, or financial advice is required prior to implementing personal financial plans, the reader is encouraged to seek the services of competent professional advisors. This book is not meant to be a substitute for their advice.

The author and the publisher specifically disclaim any liability, loss, or risk incurred as a consequence of the use, either directly or indirectly, of any information or advice given in this book.

Put Money In Your Pockets

How to retire your mortgage on your own terms at a fraction of the cost

Copyright © 1994, 1995 by Josh Bruno

Publisher's Cataloging-in-Publication Data

Put Money In Your Pockets
How to retire your mortgage on your own terms at a fraction of the cost
By Josh Bruno

ISBN 0-9641964-2-5 (pbk)

1. Mortgage Loans - 2. Prepayment of Debts I. Title
332.7'22 -- dc20   94-094531

Published by **Capital Search Systems**
P.O. Box 4518
Hempstead, NY 11550

Printed in the United States of America.

Acknowledgments

My deepest thanks to my family for their loving support and for providing me with a reason to endure the countless hours of solo work during the four years it has taken me to write this book for you, the reader. I thank my wife, Edith, for her patience and for understanding the necessity to defer much of our personal time. I am grateful for our children, David, Ronald, and Vanessa, the greatest kids in the world. Thank you for being there when I needed it the most. I love you all very much.

Many professional people have contributed to this book without knowing it. I'd like to express my appreciation for my friends Betty and Maurice Perkins, the finest real estate appraisers in the business. When he asked me to me help computerize their practice a few years ago, Maurice got me interested in the intricacies of the six functions of a dollar and loan amortization programming. That was only the beginning. I wish to give special thanks to Marc Eisenson, Vijay Fadia, John Avanzini, Warren Boroson, Michael C. Thomsett, Paul R. Goebel, Norman G. Miller, Arthur Kramer, Charles J. Givens, Dr. Tag Powell, John Cummuta, Ann B. Diamond, Robert A. Ortalda, Jr., John R. Dorfman, R. Harry Koenig, and all the other people from whom I've distilled much of the essence of the valuable concepts in this book. They didn't know it, but they were all my mentors and friends, when I studied their fine writings as part of my research. These authors provided diverse perspectives. The resulting synergy let me perceive greater depths of meaning and develop a wealth of practical knowledge that has made a tremendous difference in my own finances. I want to thank Jeff Kause, a true professional, and Sherry Sanderson, a superb coordinator, for their invaluable assistance in getting the book printed.

I would also like to thank you, the reader, because you've made it all worthwhile. Congratulations on a great choice of reading material. By investing in this book, you stand to gain a lot more than your money's worth. *Put Money in Your Pockets* is specially dedicated to you. May you prosper and live well.

Credits

ClipArt Illustrations Courtesy Of:
ClickArt Incredible Image Pak from T/Maker Company
Presentation Task Force from New Vision Technologies, Inc
Powerpoint and **Word for Windows 2.0** from Microsoft Corporation
DrawPerfect from WordPerfect Corporation

About the Author

Josh Bruno

The author, Josh Bruno, holds a BA in Computer and Information Science. During many years as Programmer Analyst in a corporate environment, Mr. Bruno developed extensive application programs in financial systems. As corporate and private microcomputer consultant, Josh developed a high level of expertise in programming and in the use of all types of PC power tools and applications.

As a microcomputer programmer, Mr. Bruno produced a total custom budget management package for microcomputers, when no packages of the type existed. Josh completed several advanced real estate valuation courses. In particular, he designed and programmed a custom PC-based mortgage amortization system for professional real estate appraisers which featured an advanced mortgage amortization function with extensive *what if* analytical capabilities.

In addition to his consulting activities, Mr. Bruno has been an adjunct lecturer in Computer and Information Science for more than a decade. During this time, he matured in the practical application of educational psychology. The author produced many dozens of technical newsletters, articles, and manuals to provide technical *how-to* information in easily digestible format for *non-technical* users.

As a homeowner with a mortgage, Josh felt the need to apply mortgage reduction techniques on a personal level. He successfully eliminated many years from his mortgage term and saved a fortune in interest costs. This book packs insights and techniques resulting from his many years of experience and in-depth work.

QUICK TABLE OF CONTENTS

TABLE OF CONTENTS

TABLE OF CONTENTS
(Continued)

TABLE OF CONTENTS
(Continued)

TABLE OF CONTENTS
(Continued)

TABLE OF CONTENTS
(Continued)

TABLE OF CONTENTS
(Continued)

INTRODUCTION

THE $80,000 HOUSE YOU BOUGHT FOR $252,741.60

When you bought your house, unless you paid cash for it, you probably gave a down payment and financed the balance with a mortgage (or with a *Deed of Trust*). Most people accept comfortably the fact that *any time you finance something it costs more than the purchase price.* So, you may be willing to pay some premium for the convenience of owning a home. But, that ultimate cost can rise way too high without you realizing it. If the term of your mortgage is 20 years or more, *then what you actually pay for your home can dramatically DWARF what you thought you bought the house for.*

The total dollars you shell out on your mortgage can actually reach OVER THREE TIMES the original amount during the course of the mortgage term. At interest rates above 9.25%, if you do nothing about it, your mortgage is going to cost you a whopping *200 percent or more ON TOP of the amount you borrowed.* When you make only the scheduled monthly payments for the full term, *you allow the interest cost to climb.*

After <u>TWENTY TWO</u> years of payments, the *PRINCIPAL* portion will be **LESS THAN** *75 percent* of the *INTEREST* portion in your monthly mortgage payment. For instance, with an $80,000 mortgage for 30 years at 10%, when you make the *264th* monthly amortization payment of $702.06, only *$296.17* goes to pay down *principal,* while the bank collects *$405.89* of *pure interest.*

By the time the borrower pays off the mortgage, the general picture is sort of like this.

What you buy:

What you actually pay for:

Over the 30-year term, the annual interest rate of 10% actually gives the lender a *true* return of 216%. To the borrower, that's a true cost of 216%. The cost skyrockets because monthly interest compounds for a long time on a **large** mortgage principal balance. As a result, you build equity slowly, and interest piles up quickly.

Slow equity buildup hurts in many ways. Here are some of the possible financial aches:

- *During a **major portion** of the mortgage term, there is less money available to back up an equity loan, if you need one.*

- *When you sell early, you get a lot **less money** than you might expect, because from the early years of a mortgage to well past the half way point in the term, all the payments you make mostly feed interest cost.*

- *When you retire and still have **many years left** to pay off your mortgage, you wind up with a **big financial burden.***

- *Even if the mortgage is paid up by the time you retire, you may have no retirement nest egg to speak of, because you lost both the time and the stream of money that could have built it to mortgage payments that paid mostly interest to the lender.*

- *Because you dump a huge amount of money into **unnecessary mortgage interest** payments, you have to stack up more debt to finance other **important events** in your life, and pay out still more interest.*

- *What's particularly painful is that you not only lose most of the money you pay out in unnecessary interest, but you also lose the interest return YOU would receive on it over the same time frame.*

BUT, THERE IS GOOD NEWS!

The fact is you can easily avoid getting hit so hard. You can take easy steps to prevent total mortgage interest from rising to such damaging heights. You can take action to keep most of those hard earned dollars for other important things in your life. There are practical ways to greatly minimize the cost of your mortgage.

> ***The key is to reduce the remaining mortgage balance at a quicker pace.***

This book will tell you how to do that easily and *save a GIGANTIC* portion of the money that you would otherwise pay out as mortgage interest to the bank.

The procedures you find in here apply to all types of mortgage loans with amortized payments.

You learn how to:

√   *Reduce the massive interest cost on your mortgage, and use that substantial money saving to put yourself on easy street.*

√   *Tap six little known sources of extra cash to help pay off your mortgage early.*

√   *Correctly and easily apply a POWERFUL KEY technique that will eliminate ALL your debts at a DAZZLING pace.*

√   *Use four different techniques alone or in combination to **pay your mortgage early** and eliminate a big burden by the time you retire or before.*

√   *Determine exactly **when your mortgage will be paid off** and **how much you'll save** in interest cost for any fixed prepayment amount.*

√   *Determine exactly **how much to prepay** in order to eliminate your mortgage **within a precise number of years** of YOUR choice.*

√   *Activate, automatically and virtually COST-FREE, two forms of bi-weekly mortgage payment handling to disintegrate YEARS off the term and painlessly SAVE a major portion of the interest cost.*

√   *Determine with assurance when it's better to invest rather than prepay.*

√   *Accelerate your equity buildup, not only so you get more money, if you need an equity loan or decide to sell early, but more importantly, so you clear up time and cash flow early in the game to buildup a big cash reserve that will support the retirement lifestyle you choose.*

You also:

√   *Discover the real effects of prepayments on your income taxes and see why you come out ahead by prepaying.*

√   *Find out what prepayment penalties are really about.*

You can achieve those feats painlessly. The following chapters will reveal exactly why and how the process works and how you can make it work for you.

You will find in here a compass to guide you step-by-step in the direction of putting more of your hard-earned money in your pockets. *You'll receive more than you bargained for.*

This text is a practical document that you'll want to make your personal resource kit. Make it a point to absorb and use the guidelines presented in here to help bring your mortgage to an *early closure,* with you laughing all the way *from* the bank.

HOW TO USE THIS BOOK

Put Money In Your Pockets aims to give you practical understanding of the ways to save many thousands of dollars that would otherwise go to the bank's coffers. It offers you some serious tools that you can start using now. The only technical requirement is to be a homeowner or a prospective homeowner who's not afraid to take the simple necessary steps to defend yourself.

Readers from various backgrounds, going from those with very little liking for numbers to those that can solve differential equations in their sleep, will derive great satisfaction and benefits from the fresh insights found in here.

This book does not intend to give you current interest rates or home prices. So, particular mortgage amounts and interest rates you'll find in *examples* and *illustrations* may not be current. But, the book does give mortgage tables that cover a wide range of interest rates and *any* mortgage amounts.

Start With Part One

You should aim to start by reading the four chapters in *Part One* at one sitting. *Chapter Two* explores how *compound interest* works *for* or *against* you using three interesting scenarios. *Chapter Three* looks into why *total interest cost* gets to be so high. *Chapter Four* spells out what happens when you just do nothing to counter the forces that make interest work against you. It also shows you how to make the same forces work for you to actually *reduce* your interest rate *without refinancing!*

While in Part Two

You receive a tremendous amount of information in **Part Two**. This is where you get the low down poop on the methods that will become your friends and *put money in your pockets*. Take a little time to go over **Chapter Six** in particular. It is a fundamental building block that clarifies a big mystery. From that point on, it's basically downhill. You'll have the essence of the prepayment methods in a nutshell.

Study **Chapter Seven** to learn the *Increasing Prepayment* method. Then, get to know the *Fixed Prepayment* method in **Chapter Eight** and **Chapter Nine**. You'll grasp the *Term-Based Prepayment* method in **Chapter Ten** in no time flat, as it's only a special application of the *Fixed Prepayment* method.

Give yourself a small reward, then go on to **Chapter Eleven** and **Chapter Twelve**, *The Extra Annual Payment* method. Here you learn what the *bi-weekly* phenomenon is *really* all about. This is a *crucial* concept that can save you much time and many thousands of *big ones*. All homeowners should know and apply this technique. But, not too many people realize what it is. *Very few* of those that heard about it understand it. That's why a whole slew of companies got into business just to operate the bi-weekly approach for people. Those two chapters will give you a have solid grasp of this method. You'll learn how to effectively use it **on your own** with minimal effort.

While in Part Three

After you've become acquainted with the mechanics of the four prepayment methods, pick one that suits you. You can also use a combination of two methods. Use the resources of **Chapter Thirteen**, **Chapter Fourteen**, *and* **Chapter Fifteen** to work your personal prepayment program. Study **Chapter Sixteen** with no less attention than the previous chapters. Here, you learn how to tap from unsuspected sources of extra cash.

You'll find a real treasure in **Chapter Seventeen**. You should pay *special attention* to this *key* chapter: *it gives you a POWER technique that can disintegrate ALL your debts fast.* Spend some time reviewing the technique, then waste no time in implementing it.

Read the rest of the chapters to get more dynamite information. If you have any concerns about the effects of prepayments on your income taxes and about bank prepayment penalties, zero in fast on **Chapter Eighteen** *and* **Chapter Nineteen**.

Get Acquainted with the Appendices in Part Four

The *Appendices* contain a real tool kit for your use. Get familiar with them.

Fourteen specialized appendices (*Appendix A* through *Appendix N*) pack tremendous resources and information that will give you the ability to perform various procedures easily and get answers quickly.

Appendix A gives a complete table of mortgage constants that support important functions. As a bonus, it supplements the text in showing how to get the answer to the question: *given a monthly payment that you can afford, a term of years, and an interest rate,* **how much money can you borrow?** The procedure gives the answer in a simple way, using the mortgage constant table.

Appendix B shows how to calculate a monthly payment from published tables, and *Appendix C* gives a quick step-by-step procedure to calculate a monthly mortgage payment using a calculator *alone*. This is useful when your situation is so unique that you can't use the tables in appendices *A* and *B*.

Appendix D shows how to **manually** calculate the interest and time savings from just **one** prepayment of any kind.

Appendix E shows how to manually calculate **total** interest and time savings from using the fixed prepayment method with a given prepayment amount. This appendix exclusively **presents a function that uses the mortgage constant table in a novel way.** *Given an interest rate, a balance, and a monthly payment,* which may include a regular payment and a *base prepayment,* **the procedure generates the resulting term duration.**

In particular, *Appendices F, G, H, and I* contain special tables of **great value** to you. These custom tables give you ways to quickly determine interest and time savings to expect from the each of the four methods regardless of your mortgage balance and how long you've had your mortgage.

In *Appendices J* and *K*, you'll find blank worksheets and slips to use in making and tracking your prepayments. *Appendix L* contains blank worksheets to use in the elimination of all your short-term debts. *Appendix M* clears up a popular misconception about mortgage interest and tax deductions.

Appendix N presents a prepayment method combination chart that summarizes how to use a prepayment method on top of another. You'll need to review the information in this chart after you've developed an understanding of the four fundamental methods. Aim to routinely use two methods in combination whenever possible to get maximum savings.

Part One

THE PROBLEM:

HIGH INTEREST COST

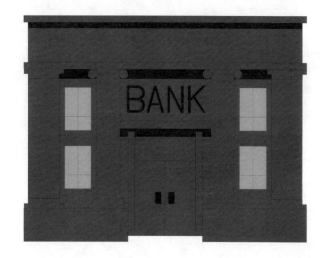

Part One

◊ *Focuses on the problem: high interest cost.*

◊ *Reveals the real cost of your house.*

◊ *Explains in an interesting way how compounded interest works for or against you.*

◊ *Tells why interest cost gets to be so high, and how it hurts when you do nothing.*

◊ *Shows how to virtually reduce your mortgage interest rate without refinancing*

Chapter One

THE REAL COST OF YOUR HOUSE

⇒ *The awful truth:*   *You may pay THREE times the mortgage amount*

The *cost* of your house is not what the *interest rate* might indicate. Not counting the down payment and closing costs, the total payments you make on a 30-year mortgage will probably be ***about THREE TIMES*** the amount of your mortgage. During the life of the mortgage, the magic of compounded interest actually yields a mammoth return to the lender. Depending on the term of your mortgage and the interest rate you negotiated, the total *amount* of *interest* you pay can be more than ***TWO TIMES*** the money you borrowed.

Think about it. *You could be about to pay the same mortgage amount THREE TIMES over!* In effect, you would wind up paying back *three* dollars for *each* dollar you borrowed. That could really hurt you financially in the long run. Unless you paid cash or inherited the house, you are gradually dishing out a huge pile of money that you could use later for other important things.

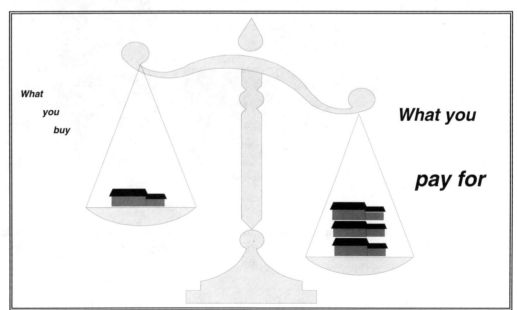

What you buy

What you pay for

Figure 1.1

Let's say you financed your house with a mortgage of $80,000 at 10 percent interest for a term of 30 years. For thirty years, you faithfully remit the required $702.06 plus tax and insurance to the bank every month. When you make the last payment, you've paid off the $80,000-mortgage. Congratulations!? Not so fast. You've just finished forking over an astounding *$252,741.60,* not counting tax and insurance! It is the product of $702.06 times the 360 months in 30 years. That tidy sum is MORE than *three* times the original mortgage balance! You had an interest rate of 10 percent? But, the interest amount came to $172,741.60, the difference between $252,741.60 and the $80,000 you borrowed in the first place. It actually represents an overall profit of *216 percent for the bank, NOT 10%!* Naturally, your lender views this high return as fair compensation for a 30-year risk.

This text uses a symbolic 30-year fixed rate mortgage of $80,000 at 10% to explain how amortized mortgage loans work. This sample mortgage will serve in the demonstration of concepts and methods that can help you keep interest cost down.

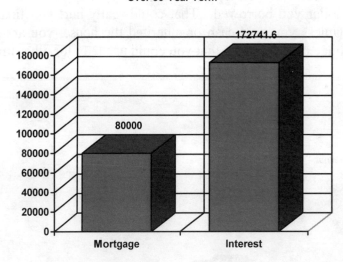

Cash Payments
Over 30-Year Term

Whether the interest rate is high or low, the net result is the same. No matter how much you borrow, if you finance the loan over a long term of years, the interest payout will be tremendous.

Do you think most people would easily agree up front to pay that HUMONGOUS premium for borrowing? Your next-door neighbor probably has no idea how big the interest payout actually gets over thirty years. But, as shocking as it might appear, the size of the interest cost accumulated this way is quite normal. There is no real mystery to it. The whole process rests on the "miracle" of interest compounding.

Chapter Two

HOW COMPOUNDED INTEREST WORKS

⇒ *Three cases that show how interest compounding may work FOR or AGAINST you*
⇒ *Why would a bank care to make mortgage loans, really?*

Even if you're familiar with the inner workings of interest compounding, you may still want to examine these three theoretical cases, as they illustrate some of the *interesting* ways interest compounding can work *for* or *against* you. For simplicity here, let's ignore inflation and taxes.

CASE 1

You invest $1,000 at 10 percent annual interest, compounded monthly, for 30 years. *You defer taxes on the interest, and never make any deposits or withdrawals.*

The monthly interest rate is the annual rate of 10 percent divided by 12. So, in this case, the monthly interest rate is 0.8333333 percent.

Here is what happens: Every month the *interest amount* is calculated by multiplying the *current balance* by 0.008333333. The interest amount is then added to current balance to produce the *new balance.* See (1)

Remember, the *current balance* is $1,000 to start with.

Calculations are actually done with the decimal factor corresponding to the interest percentage. Dividing the percentage by 100 to convert it to a decimal, we're looking at a monthly interest *decimal* factor of 0.008333333.

---

(1) You could also multiply the *current balance* by *1.008333333* to get the *new balance* in one step. Don't let the multiplication by *1.008333333* or by *(1 + 0.008333333)* confuse you. It's just a convenient arithmetic rearrangement that occurs when the common factor *current balance* is factorized in the basic formula. *Here's the plain formula:*

New Balance = Current Balance + Current Balance X 0.008333333

Well, that gives exactly the same result as this rearrangement:

New Balance = Current Balance X (1 + 0.008333333)

So, after the first month, the balance would be $1,000 X (1.008333333) or $1,008.33. The first five months and the last five months would look like this:

From this much

To this much in **30** years!

Month	Balance at Beginning of Month	Interest	Balance at End of Month
1	$1,000.00	$8.33	$1,008.33
2	$1,008.33	$8.40	$1,016.74
3	$1,016.74	$8.47	$1,025.21
4	$1,025.21	$8.54	$1,033.75
5	$1,033.75	$8.61	$1,042.37

356	$19,031.11	$158.59	$19,189.70
357	$19,189.70	$159.91	$19,349.62
358	$19,349.62	$161.25	$19,510.86
359	$19,510.86	$162.59	$19,673.45
360	$19,673.45	$163.95	$19,837.40

*After 30 years, the $1,000 would grow to $19,837.40. You would receive a total interest of $18,803.65, or an effective overall return rate of **1,880 percent!***

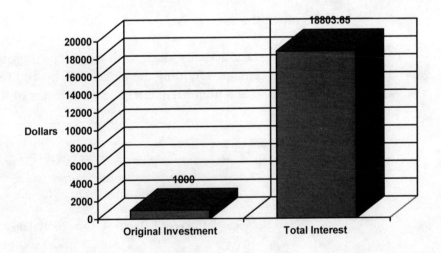

Return at 10% After 30 Years

This is a typical investment model for retirement planning, such as an IRA. *Interest compounding works strongly **for** you in this case.*

CASE 2

In this variation, again you invest $1,000 at 10% for 30 years. ***But, here you decide to take out the interest that accrues each month.***

The monthly interest amount is *$8.33.* Taking out the interest every month causes the balance to be $1,000 *all the time.*

The first five months and the last five months would look like this:

Month	Balance	Interest
1	$1,000.00	$8.33
2	$1,000.00	$8.33
3	$1,000.00	$8.33
4	$1,000.00	$8.33
5	$1,000.00	$8.33

•

•

356	$1,000.00	$8.33
357	$1,000.00	$8.33
358	$1,000.00	$8.33
359	$1,000.00	$8.33
360	$1,000.00	$8.33

Not counting taxes, in 30 years you would receive a total interest of $3,000, or 300 percent.

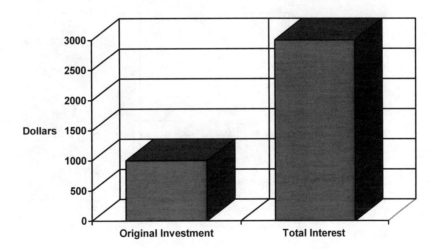

Total Interest Collected at 10% Over 30 Years

You could have a case like that with an investment in tax-free municipal bonds, except that you'd collect the interest every six months or so. *Here also, interest compounding works in your favor.*

CASE 3

Here is one more approach. *You take out BOTH the interest that grows every month AND a portion of the remaining balance.*

In this third theoretical situation, a monthly withdrawal of $8.78 would do the job in such a way that the principal gets smaller and smaller and reaches *$0 exactly at the end of 30 years.* Here are the first five and last five months:

Month	Withdrawal	Interest	Principal	Balance
1	$8.78	$8.33	$0.45	$999.55
2	$8.78	$8.33	$0.45	$999.10
3	$8.78	$8.33	$0.45	$998.65
4	$8.78	$8.32	$0.46	$998.19
5	$8.78	$8.32	$0.46	$997.73

355	$8.78	$0.35	$8.43	$33.45
356	$8.78	$0.28	$8.50	$24.95
357	$8.78	$0.21	$8.57	$16.38
358	$8.78	$0.14	$8.64	$7.74
359	$7.80	$0.06	$7.74	$0.00

You would get your $1,000 back slowly over 30 years and collect a total interest of $2,151.04, or 215 percent.

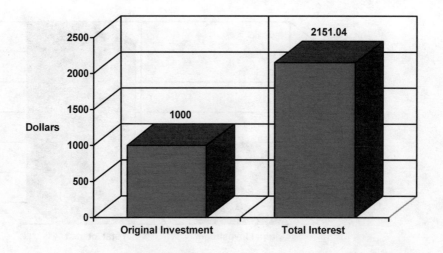

Total Interest Collected at 10% Over 30 Years

Interest compounding works in all three cases to produce a yield. After 30 years, the account balance would be $19,837.40 in the first case, $1,000 in the second variation, and $0 in the third approach. In the first two cases, the principal is still invested. But, in the third case, *the principal is completely withdrawn.*

Case 3 is particularly interesting. It's the pattern in a type of investment where the <u>*bank*</u> "deposits" the principal and receives interest payments. Without a doubt, it is a typical mortgage loan pattern, the familiar scenario you may be playing with the lender on your mortgage loan.

In a mortgage loan, every month until the loan is completely repaid, the borrower pays both interest on the balance and a gradual portion of the principal. Loans of that type are said to be *amortized.* But, in this scenario, unless you're the lender who receives the interest payments, *interest compounding works **against** you in a very BIG way.*

When the scenario in *Case* 3 involves a *mortgage loan,* the picture is exactly the same as when you are the investor. But, here the *bank* receives a payment of $8.78 each month from the *borrower.* Each payment rewards the bank with interest on the remaining balance, and returns a small portion of the loan principal. At the end of the 30 years, the balance reaches $0. We can now put more appropriate titles on the picture so it looks as follows:

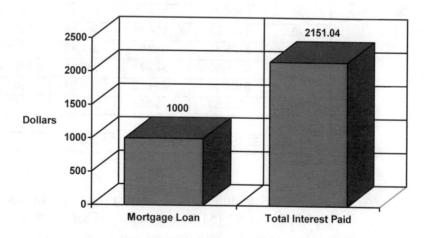

MORTGAGE LOAN MODEL
Total Interest Paid at 10% Over 30 Years

Let's zero in on this specific *mortgage loan model.* We're going to look at the precise damage interest compounding can do here. Then, we'll begin to look at some *truly creative* ways to greatly change the picture.

Here is the complete basic repayment schedule, taken on an annual basis.

Year	Payment	Interest	Principal	Balance
1	$105.36	$99.74	$5.62	$994.38
2	$105.36	$99.16	$6.20	$988.18
3	$105.36	$98.51	$6.85	$981.33
4	$105.36	$97.80	$7.56	$973.77
5	$105.36	$96.99	$8.37	$965.40
6	$105.36	$96.12	$9.24	$956.16
7	$105.36	$95.16	$10.20	$945.96
8	$105.36	$94.10	$11.26	$934.70
9	$105.36	$92.90	$12.46	$922.24
10	$105.36	$91.62	$13.74	$908.50
11	$105.36	$90.18	$15.18	$893.32
12	$105.36	$88.57	$16.79	$876.53
13	$105.36	$86.81	$18.55	$857.98
14	$105.36	$84.87	$20.49	$837.49
15	$105.36	$82.73	$22.63	$814.86
16	$105.36	$80.36	$25.00	$789.86
17	$105.36	$77.74	$27.62	$762.24
18	$105.36	$74.85	$30.51	$731.73
19	$105.36	$71.66	$33.70	$698.03
20	$105.36	$68.13	$37.23	$660.80
21	$105.36	$64.22	$41.14	$619.66
22	$105.36	$59.91	$45.45	$574.21
23	$105.36	$55.17	$50.19	$524.02
24	$105.36	$49.89	$55.47	$468.55
25	$105.36	$44.09	$61.27	$407.28
26	$105.36	$37.68	$67.68	$339.60
27	$105.36	$30.60	$74.76	$264.84
28	$105.36	$22.78	$82.58	$182.26
29	$105.36	$14.12	$91.24	$91.02
30	$95.60	$4.58	$91.02	$0.00
Totals	$3,151.04	*$2,151.04*	$1,000.00	

Just look at the amount of total interest paid over the term. The borrower pays back $1,000 *plus* $2,151.04 in interest. That's a *two-to-one* ratio between the *total interest* and the *loan amount*, where *every single dollar* borrowed costs an additional *$2.15* in interest. That can be painful to know. But, whether or not you're aware of it, the interest cost could hurt you financially.

What can be done about the damage? Well, hang in there. *This is where the magic starts.* We're going to see a couple of fundamental ways to change that ratio dramatically.

You can arrange to pay a **much lower** amount of total interest. One way to do this is to prepay some of the principal **each month.**   The result can be shockingly pleasant when you throw in a little bit extra with each payment.

Watch what happpens when you just pay a measly *$1.22* each month on top of the $8.78. The monthly payment is now $10 *($8.78 plus the $1.22)*.

The first five and last five months give an idea of the month to month changes. Pay particular attention to the month numbers in the last five months.

Month	Withdrawal	Interest	Principal	Balance
1	$10.00	$8.33	$1.67	$998.33
2	$10.00	$8.32	$1.68	$996.65
3	$10.00	$8.31	$1.69	$994.96
4	$10.00	$8.29	$1.71	$993.25
5	$10.00	$8.28	$1.72	$991.53

•
•

212	$10.00	$0.40	$9.60	$38.33
213	$10.00	$0.32	$9.68	$28.65
214	$10.00	$0.24	$9.76	$18.89
215	$10.00	$0.16	$9.84	$9.05
216	$9.13	$0.08	$9.05	$0.00

The last payment pinpoints the end of the loan to month number 216. Because of the monthly prepayments, the repayment schedule shrunk down to *216 payments.*

Now, pay some attention to this *new* repayment schedule in a complete annual form to see the dramatic results.

Year	Payment	Interest	Principal	Balance
1	$120.00	$99.05	$20.95	$979.05
2	$120.00	$96.86	$23.14	$955.91
3	$120.00	$94.44	$25.56	$930.35
4	$120.00	$91.78	$28.22	$902.13
5	$120.00	$88.82	$31.18	$870.95
6	$120.00	$85.56	$34.44	$836.51
7	$120.00	$81.94	$38.06	$798.45
8	$120.00	$77.93	$42.07	$756.38
9	$120.00	$73.54	$46.46	$709.92
10	$120.00	$68.69	$51.31	$658.61

•
•

Continued below

Year	Payment	Interest	Principal	Balance
11	$120.00	$63.32	$56.68	$601.93
12	$120.00	$57.36	$62.64	$539.29
13	$120.00	$50.82	$69.18	$470.11
14	$120.00	$43.58	$76.42	$393.69
15	$120.00	$35.57	$84.43	$309.26
16	$120.00	$26.73	$93.27	$215.99
17	$120.00	$16.95	$103.05	$112.94
18	$119.13	$6.19	$112.94	$0.00
19	$0.00	$0.00	$0.00	$0.00
20	$0.00	$0.00	$0.00	$0.00
21	$0.00	$0.00	$0.00	$0.00
22	$0.00	$0.00	$0.00	$0.00
23	$0.00	$0.00	$0.00	$0.00
24	$0.00	$0.00	$0.00	$0.00
25	$0.00	$0.00	$0.00	$0.00
26	$0.00	$0.00	$0.00	$0.00
27	$0.00	$0.00	$0.00	$0.00
28	$0.00	$0.00	$0.00	$0.00
29	$0.00	$0.00	$0.00	$0.00
30	$0.00	$0.00	$0.00	$0.00
Totals	$2,159.13	$1,159.13	$1,000.00	

Observe that the loan ends in 18 years! That's pretty close to *half* the length of the original term. Also, note that the total interest has been reduced to $1,159.13. Here, every dollar borrowed costs $1.15 in interest. The *total interest-to-loan* ratio is now close to being *one-to-one*.

This new picture is a bit easier to swallow.

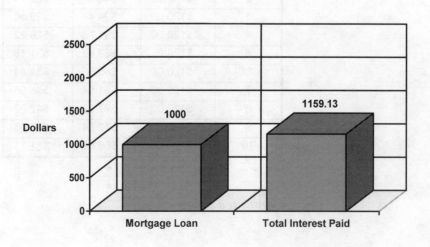

MORTGAGE LOAN MODEL
Total Interest Paid at 10% Over 18 Years With Extra $1.22 Per Month

You can get similar results too. You only have to add an extra amount to your regular monthly payment.

What if you don't have extra cash each month? Do you give up?

But, wait, there's more! You can also cut down the total interest tremendously _WITHOUT_ increasing the monthly payment each month and _WITH NO ADDITIONAL cash out of your pockets every month_!

Another fundamental technique makes that possible. With this second basic method, some money "miraculously" pops out of nowhere every six months. You can use the new found money to reduce the balance a little more. Let's use the same $1,000 loan to examine the effects of this method. Look at the first 12 months and the last 10 months below for a quick preview.

Month	Withdrawal	Interest	Principal	Balance
1	$8.78	$8.33	$0.45	$999.55
2	$8.78	$8.33	$0.45	$999.10
3	$8.78	$8.33	$0.45	$998.65
4	$8.78	$8.32	$0.46	$998.19
5	$8.78	$8.32	$0.46	$997.73
6	$13.17	$8.31	$4.86	$992.87
7	$8.78	$8.27	$0.51	$992.36
8	$8.78	$8.27	$0.51	$991.85
9	$8.78	$8.27	$0.51	$991.34
10	$8.78	$8.26	$0.52	$990.82
11	$8.78	$8.26	$0.52	$990.30
12	$13.17	$8.25	$4.92	$985.38

•
•
•

Month	Withdrawal	Interest	Principal	Balance
249	$8.78	$0.78	$8.00	$85.05
250	$8.78	$0.71	$8.07	$76.98
250	$13.17	$0.64	$12.53	$64.45
250	$8.78	$0.54	$8.24	$56.21
250	$8.78	$0.47	$8.31	$47.90
249	$8.78	$0.40	$8.38	$39.52
250	$8.78	$0.33	$8.45	$31.07
251	$8.78	$0.26	$8.52	$22.55
252	$13.17	$0.19	$12.98	$9.57
253	$9.65	$0.08	$9.57	$0.00

Notice that there are now only **253** payments, compared to 359 in the original scenario. The monthly payment is still the original $8.78. But, see the payment of $13.17 every six months? That's just an additional $4.39 on top of the $8.78, *occuring **twice** each year.* The annual payment is now $114.14, or $105.36 *as in the original schedule* <u>plus</u> an extra $8.78 *($4.39 twice).*

Here's the complete *new* annualized schedule:

Year	Payment	Interest	Principal	Balance
1	$114.14	$99.52	$14.62	$985.38
2	$114.14	$98.00	$16.14	$969.24
3	$114.14	$96.31	$17.83	$951.41
4	$114.14	$94.43	$19.71	$931.70
5	$114.14	$92.39	$21.75	$909.95
6	$114.14	$90.07	$24.07	$885.88
7	$114.14	$87.57	$26.57	$859.31
8	$114.14	$84.79	$29.35	$829.96
9	$114.14	$81.72	$32.42	$797.54
10	$114.14	$78.31	$35.83	$761.71
11	$114.14	$74.59	$39.55	$722.16
12	$114.14	$70.44	$43.70	$678.46
13	$114.14	$65.86	$48.28	$630.18
14	$114.14	$60.78	$53.36	$576.82
15	$114.14	$55.22	$58.92	$517.90
16	$114.14	$49.04	$65.10	$452.80
17	$114.14	$42.22	$71.92	$380.88
18	$114.14	$34.68	$79.46	$301.42
19	$114.14	$26.37	$87.77	$213.65
20	$114.14	$17.16	$96.98	$116.67
21	$114.14	$7.04	$107.10	$9.57
22	$9.65	$0.08	$9.57	$0.00
23	$0.00	$0.00	$0.00	$0.00
24	$0.00	$0.00	$0.00	$0.00
25	$0.00	$0.00	$0.00	$0.00
26	$0.00	$0.00	$0.00	$0.00
27	$0.00	$0.00	$0.00	$0.00
28	$0.00	$0.00	$0.00	$0.00
29	$0.00	$0.00	$0.00	$0.00
30	$0.00	$0.00	$0.00	$0.00
Totals	$2,406.59	$1,406.59	$1,000.00	

With this technique, the loan lasts only 21 years and 1 month. The total interest has been reduced to *$1,406.59,* from the $2,159.26 in the original schedule. Here, every dollar borrowed costs $1.40 in interest. The *total interest-to-loan* ratio is not that far from being *one-to-one.*

This reduction is not as good as the reduction to $1,139.13 that we got with the extra $1.22 out of pocket each month.   But it's a great performance, considering that *the feat was done __WITHOUT__ extra out-of-pocket cash every month!*

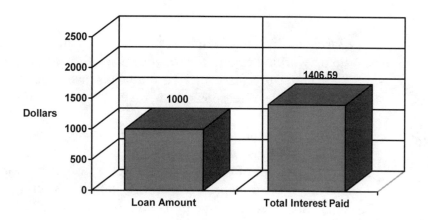

MORTGAGE LOAN MODEL
Total Interest Paid at 10% Over 21 Years and 1 Month
Using Special Interest Reduction Technique

It takes a loan of $1,000 at precisely ***7.04754%*** or approximately ***7.05%*** to eat up $1,406.59 in total interest over ***30 years***.   Because of the ***total interest amount*** they have in common, the interest rate of 10% *with the special method* is truly the *equivalent* of the rate of *7.05%*.   In fact, here the loan at 10% is <u>better</u>, *because it lasts only 21 years and 1 month!*

Both of those fundamental techniques, along with *three more variations,* will be explained and taught in full detail within the chapters to come.

It's appropriate to clarify one point here: *if all homeowners in the country used some techniques to cut down their interest payments, that would not hurt the banks or the economy.* In fact, quite the contrary would occur.

If a bank just invests $80,000 at 10 percent compounded monthly for 30 years, *without touching it the whole time,* the deposit would grow by 1,880 percent to $1,586,991.76!

But, if the bank loans out $80,000 for a mortgage at 10% for 30 years, it "only" gets a yield of 215 percent. In fact, when people use interest reduction techniques *(and they do!),* the bank would collect much less interest.

Clearly, rather than lending you the $80,000, the bank would get a higher return on the money by investing it, as in our theoretical *Case 1.*

A funny question naturally comes to mind at this point:

Rather than make mortgage loans, why doesn't the bank go for investments like *Case 1*?

WHY WOULD A BANK CARE TO MAKE MORTGAGE LOANS, *really*?

Banks do diversify their investments. But, investments of the type in *Case 1* tie up working capital *for the duration of the term*. The money doesn't come back until 30 years later. To the bank, that is not a desirable situation for at least a couple of reasons.

A bank needs to collect money

For one thing, ***banks lend out cash from depositors' accounts.*** Since people tend to withdraw money at random, lending institutions just don't have total control of a lot of principal cash forever. So, a *bank **needs** to collect back a portion of invested principal along with interest every month* to help meet its obligations, recoup some of its investment, reap a little profit, and make more loans.

For another thing, **the bank would run out of investment capital in no time if it kept freezing up its money with that kind of long term investments.** With relatively limited cash, a bank could only make a small number of those investments. In the end, the total return would be low, compared with *a large number of other types of money machines* that feed back dollars **more quickly.**

Mortgages are low-risk investments

On the one hand, the mortgage market is very attractive. ***There are millions of potential home buyers that would pay 10 percent or more per year.*** *Mortgages to those folks are relatively low risk, since real estate provides built-in security.* The interest pay-off is not bad, and the principal gradually trickles back, so the bank can reinvest some of it.

On the other hand, ***there are a lot fewer other LOW-RISK ventures that would pay the same 10 percent or more.*** And even if there were many such ventures available, *there just wouldn't be enough investment cash left over to take advantage of a <u>large</u> number of those ventures.* So, why do banks make mortgage loans? It's simple. *There's a lot of money potential in mortgages,* even if (maybe because) people pay back quicker than scheduled.

In the homeowner's immediate reality, the extravagant accumulation of interest during the life of a mortgage loan is a concrete and cold fact. One of the keys in mastering the remedy is for you to know and *understand the reason why total mortgage interest grows so high.*

Chapter Three

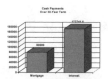

THE REASON WHY TOTAL INTEREST GETS TO BE SO HIGH

⇒ *In a way, you are your banker's bank*
⇒ *Three things a bank does every month*
⇒ *What the interest accrual period is*
⇒ *How total interest gets to be so large*
⇒ *The amortization schedule*

You are your banker's bank

Before we get into understanding the exciting mechanics of paying off your mortgage, let's tackle a fundamental question. Take a look at your mortgage *interest rate*. Do you know of any bank that pays anywhere near that same rate on a *savings* account these days? You certainly do. **YOU ARE IT.** *As far as your mortgage is concerned, you are your banker's bank.* In fact, to the lender, your mortgage appears much better than just a savings account.

The accrual period

The interest *amount* in a monthly mortgage payment usually takes *one* month to build up or *accrue*. This time frame is sometimes called the interest *accrual period or just* **period,** *for short.* Here's how it works.

The bank invests the mortgage balance with you. It calculates the monthly payment you have to make to pay off the total mortgage principal and interest, at the rate and within the term stated in your contract. Then, it collects interest every month and withdraws some of the principal until the balance is paid up.

Three things the bank does

Say you have a 30-year mortgage of $80,000 at a 10 percent annual rate. The monthly payment calculated from a standard amortization factor formula is $702.06. So, every month or *period*, until you completely pay off the mortgage, the bank does these three basic things:

1	Calculate the monthly **interest** amount to be collected.

2	Subtract the monthly **interest** amount from the monthly payment to get the **principal** amount due for the month.

3	"*Withdraw*" the **principal** amount from the **current** total mortgage balance due to get the **new** total balance due.

Here are the three basic things again but with more details:

Calculate the monthly interest amount.

To do this, the bank multiplies the *monthly interest factor* by the entire mortgage balance you owe. The monthly interest factor is the annual interest rate *in decimal form* divided by 12. In this example, the monthly factor is **0.10** divided by 12, which is *0.008333.*

$$\$80,000 \times 0.008333 = \mathbf{\$666.67}$$

So, the month's interest is: **$666.67**. This amount is **LARGE** at the beginning. <u>In fact, most of your money goes to pay interest for many years.</u>

Subtract the monthly interest amount from the monthly payment *(with principal and interest ONLY, no tax and insurance)* to get the principal payment.

$$\$702.06 - \$666.64 = \mathbf{\$35.39}$$

Compared to the interest amount, the principal portion is **really small** at the beginning. *It stays small for a long time.*

"Withdraw" the principal payment from the total mortgage balance due.

$$\$80,000 - \$35.39 = \mathbf{\$79,964.61}$$

The midget principal payments reduce the balance due very slowly. *So, the monthly interest collected on the total balance due will be **large** for a long time.*

> *That's why the total interest amount grows to be so much larger than the original mortgage balance!*

Given the balance, monthly payment, term, and interest rate, the first three payments in the sample mortgage situation would create the following results.

Given:

Starting mortgage balance:	**$80,000**
Annual Interest Rate:	**10 percent or 0.10**
Monthly Interest Factor:	**0.008333333 (0.10 divided by 12)**
Term:	**30 years**
Monthly payment:	**$702.06** *(principal* and *interest ONLY)*

Results:

MONTH	PAYMENT	STARTING BALANCE	INTEREST	PRINCIPAL	BALANCE
1	$702.06	$80,000.00	*$666.67*	**$35.39**	$79,964.61
2	$702.06	$79,964.61	*$666.37*	**$35.69**	$79,928.92
3	$702.06	$79,928.92	*$666.07*	**$35.98**	$79,892.94

The amortization schedule

The above results are a *partial* amortization. A complete **amortization schedule** shows all 360 months or periods. In fact, when you decide to do something about your mortgage, you will need a schedule that applies to your specific situation. But, you won't have to create a complete schedule by hand.

The amortization schedule shows how *interest* and *principal* get paid out over the term. Here's a picture that compares the two amounts on an *annual* basis over thirty years. The "fish tail" area is important. This is where the principal portion in a payment grows larger than the interest portion.

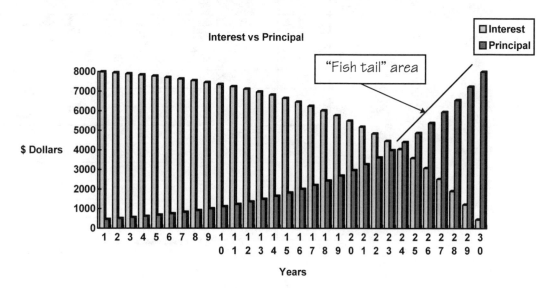

Figure 3.1

The "fish tail" area lasts *six years and eight months* at the 10% interest rate. It lasts *longer* at <u>lower</u> interest rates, and it is *shorter* at <u>higher</u> rates.

When the entries reflect amounts *by year* rather than by month, you're looking at an *annualized* amortization schedule. An amortization schedule that represents the original ***full-term*** repayment plan can be called an *unaccelerated* amortization schedule. Table 3.1 shows the *annualized* amortization schedule over the full 30-year term of the $80,000 mortgage at 10%.

Unaccelerated Amortization Schedule

Year	Payment	Interest	Principal	Balance
1	$8,424.69	$7,979.98	$444.70	$79,555.30
2	$8,424.69	$7,933.42	$491.27	$79,064.03
3	$8,424.69	$7,881.98	$542.71	$78,521.32
4	$8,424.69	$7,825.15	$599.54	$77,921.78
5	$8,424.69	$7,762.37	$662.32	$77,259.46
6	$8,424.69	$7,693.01	$731.67	$76,527.78
7	$8,424.69	$7,616.40	$808.29	$75,719.49
8	$8,424.69	$7,531.76	$892.93	$74,826.57
9	$8,424.69	$7,438.26	$986.43	$73,840.14
10	$8,424.69	$7,334.97	$1,089.72	$72,750.42
11	$8,424.69	$7,220.86	$1,203.83	$71,546.59
12	$8,424.69	$7,094.80	$1,329.89	$70,216.70
13	$8,424.69	$6,955.54	$1,469.14	$68,747.56
14	$8,424.69	$6,801.71	$1,622.98	$67,124.58
15	$8,424.69	$6,631.76	$1,792.93	$65,331.65
16	$8,424.69	$6,444.02	$1,980.67	$63,350.98
17	$8,424.69	$6,236.61	$2,188.07	$61,162.91
18	$8,424.69	$6,007.49	$2,417.19	$58,745.71
19	$8,424.69	$5,754.38	$2,670.30	$56,075.41
20	$8,424.69	$5,474.77	$2,949.92	$53,125.49
21	$8,424.69	$5,165.87	$3,258.82	$49,866.67
22	$8,424.69	$4,824.63	$3,600.06	$46,266.62
23	$8,424.69	$4,447.66	$3,977.03	$42,289.59
24	$8,424.69	$4,031.21	$4,393.48	$37,896.11
25	$8,424.69	$3,571.16	$4,853.53	$33,042.58
26	$8,424.69	$3,062.93	$5,361.76	$27,680.83
27	$8,424.69	$2,501.48	$5,923.20	$21,757.62
28	$8,424.69	$1,881.25	$6,543.44	$15,214.18
29	$8,424.69	$1,196.06	$7,228.62	$7,985.56
30	$8,424.69	$439.13	$7,985.56	$0.00
Totals	$252,740.61	**$172,740.61**	$80,000.00	

Table 3.1

It can hurt *when you do nothing* and just follow the unaccelerated schedule. But, you can accelerate the schedule and *virtually **reduce your interest rate.***

Chapter Four

HOW YOU CAN TAKE AWAY THE HURT

⇒ *After three quarters of a full 30-year term, you've only paid down HALF the balance*
⇒ *The three main things that hurt when you do nothing*
⇒ *You can change the amortization for the better*
⇒ **How to reduce your interest rate WITHOUT refinancing**

After two thirds of the total duration, you've only paid one half of the balance

Make sure you fully appreciate the picture here: *As the years go by, the amount of principal you pay every month increases* <u>*slowly*</u>, *and the interest portion* <u>*slowly*</u> *decreases.* **With an interest rate over 8%, you finally get HALF of the mortgage paid down very late in the life of the mortgage, something like <u>TWENTY-THREE YEARS or more down the road</u>.** The interest portion eventually gets much smaller than the principal portion. Then, the much larger principal payments finish up the mortgage balance at a faster pace during the last five years.

If you follow that typical course and DO NOTHING but pay the stated monthly payments, then you will suffer financially in several ways.

It's worth recapping the major financial aches that you read about in the introduction. First, those pains relate to *slow equity buildup,* which may cause problems early in the game. Second, the unnecessary *time loss* could create a financial burden that opens up another domain of hurt on you later in life. Third, the *hefty interest* you pay, perhaps the worst of those ills, creates a cash drain that's infinitely more damaging than it might look.

HOW IT HURTS WHEN YOU DO NOTHING

1 SLOW EQUITY BUILDUP

Your equity is the *difference between what your house is worth on the market and what you still owe* on your mortgage. Equity is important. *It pays to build a lot of it as quickly as you can.*

The small portion of your monthly payments that reduces the balance due on the mortgage also contributes to your equity in the house. Clearly, the typical mortgage payment routine builds equity very slowly. Slow equity buildup hurts you in the following ways:

- **Leaves less money to back up any secured loans:**

  If you decide to take an equity loan on your house, you can borrow only up to a certain percentage of the current value of the house. The larger your equity, the more money you can borrow against it. *__On the flip side, the less equity you have, the less you can actually borrow.__*

- **Returns less money when you sell early:**

  The larger your equity, the more money you get to keep when you sell the house. If you only make the payments scheduled by the bank, you're going to get hit badly.

  *When you sell the house early, say less than 15 years or so after you bought it, **you keep very little cash based on the small equity your payments built.*** You can't always rely on great market appreciation, you know. Sometimes, there's very little of it. If you improved the house greatly, the market might not bear your asking price.

2 UNNECESSARY FINANCIAL BURDEN

When you retire (willingly or forcibly) **and still have another 10 or more years left on your mortgage,** you have a burden that **WEIGHS HEAVIER NOW** than when you had more income. Even if you manage to finish paying off the *full-term* mortgage before you retire, you have *less* money in your retirement reserve than you could have socked away. All the time spent in sending payments that carried mostly interest cost took care of that.

3 LESS AVAILABLE CASH

The gigantic interest you pay can create a catastrophic lack of funds. The interest cost absorbs money that would contribute to a more prosperous financial future for yourself. It may cause you to have to spiral into more debt, just because the money's not there to fund emergencies or other important events.

If you could have eliminated ten years of monthly mortgage payments of $702.06 **but didn't**, you would **not** lose just **$84,247.20** ($702.06 times 120 payments). If you could deposit the $702.06 every month for ten years into some money fund that pays only 6% a year compounded monthly, *the true loss would appear to be $115,053.13.* Even that is *an illusion.* The actual loss would be **_infinite_**. If you just let it sit for *one* year, this lost sum would grow to $122,149.36, earning **$7,096.23**. It would pay that much **EVERY year**, and that could be enough to handle certain expenses, so you avoid *more* debt.

You've seen what the $80,000-mortgage looks like over 30 years at 10% in Table **3.1** of the previous chapter. The amount of interest paid gets to be over two times the amount borrowed. To be exact, the total interest reached $172,740.16. Just compare that amount to the original principal. Do it arithmetically. Divide the total interest amount by the principal, like this:

$$\frac{\$172,740.16}{\$80,000} = \textbf{\textit{2.159258}}$$

That's a total percentage of *216%,* or a ratio of $2.16 in interest to every $1 of principal. There's more. *Any mortgage amount* at 10% over thirty years will eat up exactly the same proportion of interest money. Different interest rates produce different total ratios. As you might expect, a rate lower than 10%, maintained for thirty years, will produce a total ratio that's less than 216%. On the flip side, as you may also correctly expect, an interest rate higher than 10%, maintained for thirty years, will produce a total ratio that's greater than 216%.

But, at any given interest rate, it is a fact that *any mortgage amount* held for a full thirty-year term will generate the *SAME RATIO of total interest to principal* as any *other* mortgage amount kept at the **same** interest rate for the **same** thirty-year term. For instance, *any* mortgage amount held at 5.75% for thirty years will crank out a constant total interest-to-principal ratio of *110%.* As another example, *any* mortgage amount held at 14.75% for thirty years will hatch a constant total interest-to-principal ratio of *348%.* You get the point.

If you do nothing about it, **you are doomed to pay away the total interest ratio that your** *official* **interest rate spits out over the term of your mortgage.**

HOW TO CUT YOUR MORTGAGE INTEREST RATE WITHOUT REFINANCING

Why do you need to bother with those facts? They're crucial to your understanding of a BIG *secret.* You can actually cut your interest rate *without refinancing.* The way to do that is so simple it's almost *invisible.* It's only a secret because so few people think about it this way. Here's the *BIG* secret:

> **To pay back a mortgage at a virtually LOWER equivalent rate of interest, you only have to cut the total amount of interest DOLLARS you would pay on the mortgage.**

When you plan to cut your total interest, how do you find out what *lower* equivalent interest rate you'll effectively have? That's really very easy to do. But, before you learn how to do that, get acquainted with the key tool: *the table of* **total interest-to-principal** *ratios*.

Table *4.1* shows the ratios of *total interest to principal* paid back over a term of 30 years for *annual* interest rates ranging from *3%* to *16.75%*. The total ratios range respectively from *52%* (for the 3% annual rate) to *406%* (for the 16.75% annual rate). So, here it is. At a glance, you can determine the *total interest-to-principal* ratio or percentage (and, with a simple multiplication, interest *dollars*) that will be paid over 30 years for *any* mortgage amount at a given annual interest rate.

Total Interest-to-Principal Ratios Paid Over a 30-Year Term

Annual Interest Rate (%)	Total Interest-to-Principal Ratio	Total Interest-to-Principal %	Annual Interest Rate (%)	Total Interest-to-Principal Ratio	Total Interest-to-Principal %
3%	0.517775	52%	10%	2.159258	216%
3.25%	0.566743	57%	10.25%	2.225965	223%
3.5%	0.616561	62%	10.5%	2.293061	229%
3.75%	0.667216	67%	10.75%	2.360533	236%
4%	0.718695	72%	11%	2.428364	243%
4.25%	0.770984	77%	11.25%	2.496541	250%
4.5%	0.824067	82%	11.5%	2.565049	257%
4.75%	0.87793	88%	11.75%	2.633875	263%
5%	0.932558	93%	12%	2.703005	270%
5.25%	0.987933	99%	12.25%	2.772427	277%
5.5%	1.04404	104%	12.5%	2.842128	284%
5.75%	1.100862	110%	12.75%	2.912096	291%
6%	1.158382	116%	13%	2.982318	298%
6.25%	1.216582	122%	13.25%	3.052785	305%
6.5%	1.275445	128%	13.5%	3.123484	312%
6.75%	1.334953	133%	13.75%	3.194405	319%
7%	1.395089	140%	14%	3.265538	327%
7.25%	1.455835	146%	14.25%	3.336874	334%
7.5%	1.517172	152%	14.5%	3.408401	341%
7.75%	1.579084	158%	14.75%	3.480113	348%
8%	1.641552	164%	15%	3.551998	355%
8.25%	1.70456	170%	15.25%	3.624051	362%
8.5%	1.768089	177%	15.5%	3.696261	370%
8.75%	1.832121	183%	15.75%	3.768622	377%
9%	1.896641	190%	16%	3.841125	384%
9.25%	1.961632	196%	16.25%	3.913765	391%
9.5%	2.027075	203%	16.5%	3.986533	399%
9.75%	2.092956	209%	16.75%	4.059424	406%

Table 4.1

At this point, rest assured that *in actuality* you don't have to be locked into a particular *official* interest rate. **Without refinancing,** you can change the picture dramatically. For example, we can accelerate the repayment of the old 30-year $80,000-mortgage at 10% so that the *annualized* amortization schedule looks like Table **4.2**.

Accelerated Amortization Schedule

Year	Payment	Interest	Principal	Balance
1	$11,018.22	$7,872.92	$3,145.30	$76,854.70
2	$11,018.22	$7,543.57	$3,474.65	$73,380.05
3	$11,018.22	$7,179.72	$3,838.50	$69,541.55
4	$11,018.22	$6,777.78	$4,240.44	$65,301.11
5	$11,018.22	$6,333.76	$4,684.46	$60,616.65
6	$11,018.22	$5,843.23	$5,174.99	$55,441.66
7	$11,018.22	$5,301.34	$5,716.88	$49,724.78
8	$11,018.22	$4,702.70	$6,315.52	$43,409.26
9	$11,018.22	$4,041.38	$6,976.84	$36,432.42
10	$11,018.22	$3,310.81	$7,707.41	$28,725.01
11	$11,018.22	$2,503.76	$8,514.46	$20,210.55
12	$11,018.22	$1,612.18	$9,406.04	$10,804.51
13	$11,018.22	$627.24	$10,390.98	$413.53
14	*$416.98*	*$3.45*	*$413.53*	*$0.00*
15	$0.00	$0.00	$0.00	$0.00
16	$0.00	$0.00	$0.00	$0.00
17	$0.00	$0.00	$0.00	$0.00
18	$0.00	$0.00	$0.00	$0.00
19	$0.00	$0.00	$0.00	$0.00
20	$0.00	$0.00	$0.00	$0.00
21	$0.00	$0.00	$0.00	$0.00
22	$0.00	$0.00	$0.00	$0.00
23	$0.00	$0.00	$0.00	$0.00
24	$0.00	$0.00	$0.00	$0.00
25	$0.00	$0.00	$0.00	$0.00
26	$0.00	$0.00	$0.00	$0.00
27	$0.00	$0.00	$0.00	$0.00
28	$0.00	$0.00	$0.00	$0.00
29	$0.00	$0.00	$0.00	$0.00
30	$0.00	$0.00	$0.00	$0.00
Totals	$143,653.84	*$63,653.84*	$80,000.00	

Results

> Compared to the **unaccelerated** amortization schedule for the $80,000-mortgage, this schedule shows tremendous savings in **interest** and **time**:
>
> Interest Savings: *$109,086.77*
> Duration: *13 Years 1 Month*
> Time Savings: *16 Years 11 Months*

Table 4.2

What happened here? To really appreciate what happened, you need to compare this schedule with the *unaccelerated* amortization schedule in Table **3.1** (Chapter 3). Here's a summary of the comparison:

	Table 3.1	**Table 4.2**	**Savings** *in Table 4.2*
Term Duration	30 Years	*13 Years 1 Month*	*16 Years 11 Months*
Total Interest	$172,740.61	***$63,653.84***	***$109,086.77***

In Table **4.2**, the term duration is only *13 years and 1 month,* saving 16 years and 11 months. Also, we produced a *new* total interest payment of *$63,653.84,* saving $109,086.77. A combination of two methods produced these savings. ***Chapter Eleven*** tells precisely how to combine two methods to get those savings. For now, let's focus on the impact of the *new* total interest **payment** on the interest **rate.**

In this example, the *official* annual interest rate is 10%, and the *official* term is **30** years. The way we planned it, we'll repay the mortgage over an **unofficial** term of 13 years and 1 month. *If we stuck with the official term,* **it would really take a MUCH LOWER interest rate to produce a total *interest* payment of *$63,653.84* on a balance of $80,000.** So, what's the *30-year equivalent* rate of annual interest here?

This time, let's divide the *new* total interest by the principal to get the ratio:

$$\frac{\$63,653.84}{\$80,000} = 0.795673$$

This total interest-to-principal ratio converts to a percentage of **80%.** Now, to get a *30-year equivalent interest rate,* we just need to:

- **Search the *Total Interest-to-Principal* % column in *Table 4.1* to find a close match for the total interest-to-principal percentage**

- **Look under *Annual Interest Rate* in the *same* row to find the *equivalent rate.***

An exact match would give the exact *equivalent interest rate.* Otherwise, we can just take the next higher percentage in the table and get a *ballpark* estimate for the equivalent interest rate.

In this example, we don't find an exact match for *80%.* But, we do find **82%,** and that corresponds to a *ballpark equivalent* interest rate of *4.5%.* So, in a very real way, you could say that we *unofficially* reduced the annual interest rate on this mortgage from 10% to *under* **4.5%** *without any refinancing.*

The total interest payment in this acceleration (Table 4.2 above) is *less* than the actual total from an amortization at 4.5%. With an interest rate of 4.5%, the total interest payment for a loan of $80,000 over 30 years is $65,642.04. So, the exact equivalent rate is *less* than 4.5%.

You now have the method to estimate the equivalent interest rate when you accelerate your own mortgage. Just divide the *new* total interest in your accelerated amortization schedule by the total principal to get a percentage. Then, find a match for the percentage in Table 4.1 to locate the associated equivalent rate.

For reference and ease of comparison, Figure 4.1 shows here again the *unaccelerated* amortization schedule we discussed in *Chapter Three*.

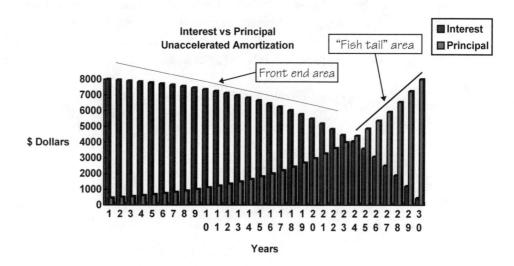

Figure 4.1

Figure 4.2 graphs the *accelerated* amortization data in *Table 4.2*. Observe how it contrasts with Figure **4.1**.

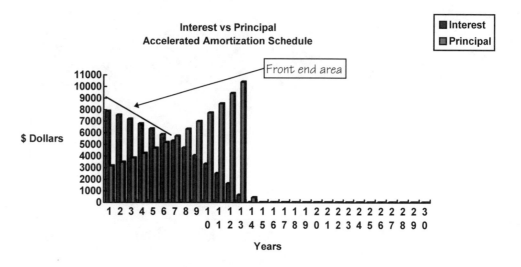

Figure 4.2

Monthly payments in the *front end* area of the amortization service mostly interest cost. Notice that the front end lasts more than twenty-three years in the *unaccelerated* amortization (Figure 4.1). That's why the interest cost is so high. In contrast, the *accelerated* amortization changes the picture so that monthly payments service much more of the principal balance (Figure 4.2). As a result, it also shrinks the *front end* down to *six years*.

The "fish tail" area lasts the *same* number of years in both figures. But, in the *accelerated* amortization, "fish tail" monthly payments carry even *more* principal, and *still* cut down interest cost.

It's clear why interest gets to be so high: *Unaccelerated amortization prolongs the duration of time where monthly payments carry a high interest component and escalate the cost.* The solution is also clear: *Speed up the voyage through the high interest times.* As you do that, you cut a tremendous amount of interest cost, and also naturally wind up with a lower equivalent interest rate. It's up to you to figure out your own equivalent interest rate from your accelerated amortization schedule.

So, on to *Part Two* to get the exact mechanics of the solution.

Part Two

THE SOLUTION:

CUT INTEREST COST

Part Two

◊ *Tells precisely what to do about the problem.*

◊ *Spells out the solution and how to apply it.*

◊ *Gives an unparalleled understanding of your mortgage.*

◊ *Teaches four specific methods to achieve the solution step by step.*

| *Chapter Five* | # WHAT TO DO ABOUT THE PROBLEM |

⇒ *The ticket*
⇒ *What principal prepayment really is*
⇒ *Why principal prepayment works*

I t's now time to get down to specifics. The bank wants you to make its scheduled monthly payments. But, you know the problem with normal unaccelerated repayment: *you wind up paying way too much money in total interest.* Fortunately, it is possible for you to change that situation. By now, **you also know what to do about the problem:** *free yourself from the excessive mortgage interest trap by accelerating the repayment!* How do you do that specifically?

The Ticket

Aim for two objectives:

> • *Cut down the scheduled duration of the mortgage*
> • *Knock off a big portion of the total interest*

You can do both at the same time with *one simple process:*

> ***Reduce the mortgage principal quicker by prepaying small extra amounts systematically as you go.***

Gradual mortgage principal prepayment really works. *That's the ticket.*

WHAT IS PRINCIPAL PREPAYMENT, *REALLY?*

Mortgage principal prepayment is perfectly legal. It is the process of prepaying your mortgage balance with small prepayments you make in addition to the scheduled monthly payments. You see, you can't pay **less** than the mortgage contract specifies for every month. *But, every **month** or every **six months** or every **year**, you can always pay a little more **principal** than what the bank expects.*

Financial experts have defined many approaches to prepayment. Of those approaches, we'll concentrate on the ones with periodic prepayments *that can be planned into an amortization schedule*. They boil down to three basic methods and one offshoot method. These four methods are all mathematically correct and fully reliable. For convenience, it helps to group them as follows:

◊   Methods that require you to have some extra cash every month:

- **Increasing Prepayment**
- **Fixed Prepayment**
- **Term-based Prepayment** *(offshoot from the Fixed)*

◊   Method that produces extra cash "by itself" every six month:

- **Extra-Annual Payment
    or Pseudo Bi-weekly**

Depending on your situation, you can use just one method alone, a variation of one method, or a combination of more than one methods that can work together. Once you grasp the basics, you will have a strong tendency to use one of those plans.

The next several chapters will show you *how* each method works and how **to work** it. They also show you how to choose a method that best fits your particular case and how to apply the four basic techniques. *Appendix N* summarizes how the methods can be combined. But, first, let's consider *why* these methods work.

WHY PRINCIPAL PREPAYMENT WORKS

Every prepayment you make reduces the remaining principal before interest is calculated on it at the end of the next period. That simple action has a double impact. *It **eliminates** an incredible amount of **interest cost** and dramatically **shortens the mortgage term**.*

Remember This!

> *A prepayment is not an extra expense.* It's money that you would have to repay anyway. **You're just repaying it early!**

When you chip off an extra portion of the principal you save a huge chunk of interest *at the same time.* You save on interest because the principal balance is a bit smaller. But, there is another interesting way to look at the saving.

That chunk of interest you save is also the interest that would accrue ***on the actual amount you prepay*** during the periods associated with the prepayment. In fact, that gargantuan amount of interest money would be due in whole or in part at the very next compounding period.

Here is where the magic appears: *You can determine up front how much interest and how many years or months that **any given amount of prepayment** will save for you.*

Given a fixed-term 30-year mortgage for $80,000 at a 10% annual rate, ***a prepayment of $100 with the first payment saves $1,852.32 of interest cost immediately.*** *It also cuts the term by **2 months.***

Quite clearly, you make a fantastic investment with each prepayment. It's like making a small withdrawal that would otherwise gather a whopping interest for the bank over the long term. **You literally spoil the bank's plan to squeeze that jumbo size interest money from you.**

Observe the results of a prepayment of *only $25 per month* on the $80,000-mortgage at 10% for 30 years.

Without prepayments, the borrower pays a total interest of $172,740.61. With the monthly prepayment of $25, *the total interest payout goes down to **$137,988.49**, saving a tidy sum of **$34,752.13.***

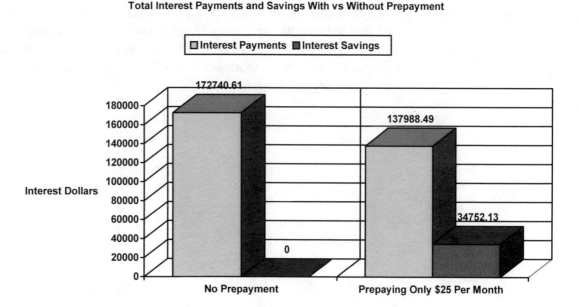

Figure 5.1

Without prepayments, the term lasts the full 30 years. But, if the borrower prepays $25 per month, *the term shrinks to 25 years*, saving **5 years.**

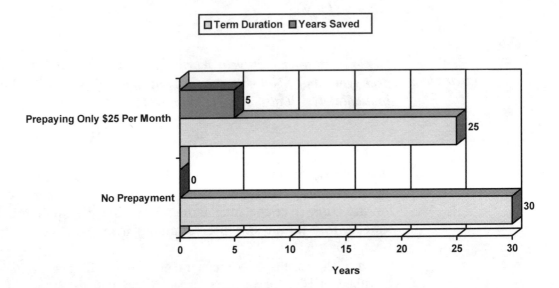

Figure 5.2

The fundamental reason why a prepayment works is because each dollar you prepay reduces the remaining balance and, *as a result, also the interest amount calculated on the balance.* This concept is a basic building block. All prepayment methods work because of it. You'll see it again and again as you go on to further understand your mortgage.

| Chapter Six | ***UNDERSTANDING YOUR MORTGAGE*** |

⇒ *Understanding **ordinary annuity** and **annuity due***
⇒ *Which type is your mortgage?*
⇒ *What the interest in a scheduled payment actually applies to*

A s you know, the payment plan for a mortgage is called an amortization schedule. This schedule does not include insurance and taxes. It shows the series of payments required to pay off the mortgage within the term of years you and the lender agreed upon. Each payment covers a time frame called a period. The period usually lasts one month.

A series of planned regular deposits or payments is called an annuity. Because of the series of regular payments required to pay off the balance, mortgages are annuities. There are basic two categories of annuities, based on the timing of payments.

In the first category, called *ordinary annuity,* a monthly payment occurs *in arrears*, at the end of a period. The other category, called *annuity due,* requires payment for a period *in advance,* at the beginning of that period just like rent for an apartment.

Ordinary Annuity Loan Amortization

Let's consider an ordinary annuity loan for $80,000 at 10% for 30 years. If this loan is effective on January 1st, the time line would look like this:

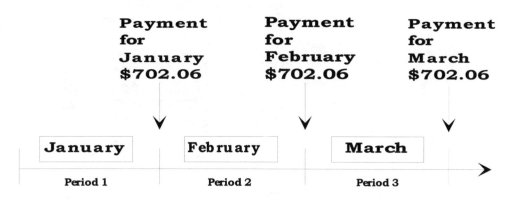

Time Line for payment at end of period

Figure 6.1

The time line shows that the payment for the month of January is due on *February 1st*. So, a payment made at the beginning of a period really covers the period that came *before*. Put another way, your payment for Period 1 is due at the beginning of Period 2, and so on.

*Most mortgages are **ordinary** annuities*

In the ordinary annuity amortization, both the interest and the principal portion of a payment apply to the *preceding* period. The majority of mortgages belong in this category. *Most likely your mortgage has an **ordinary annuity** amortization.*

A certain amount of interest accrues during each one-month time period. The bank collects this interest from the monthly or *periodic* payment. The rest of the payment serves to pay down the principal. The amortization schedule shows the scheduled payment for each period, along with the interest and principal portions in the payment, and the remaining principal balance.

Here is part of an amortization schedule for the ordinary annuity loan of $80,000. Figure 6.2 only shows the first ten months and the last five months of the loan term.

Period	Payment	Interest	Principal	Balance
1	$702.06	$666.67	$35.39	$79,964.61
2	$702.06	$666.37	$35.69	$79,928.92
3	$702.06	$666.07	$35.98	$79,892.94
4	$702.06	$665.77	$36.28	$79,856.66
5	$702.06	$665.47	$36.59	$79,820.07
6	$702.06	$665.17	$36.89	$79,783.18
7	$702.06	$664.86	$37.20	$79,745.99
8	$702.06	$664.55	$37.51	$79,708.48
9	$702.06	$664.24	$37.82	$79,670.66
10	$702.06	$663.92	$38.14	$79,632.52

•
•
•

356	$702.06	$28.54	$673.52	$2,750.69
357	$702.06	$22.92	$679.13	$2,071.55
358	$702.06	$17.26	$684.79	$1,386.76
359	$702.06	$11.56	$690.50	$696.26
360	$702.06	$5.80	$696.26	$0.00

Figure 6.2

Annuity Due Loan Amortization

In an *annuity due* arrangement, a payment for Period 1 is due *at the beginning* of Period 1.

Let's consider a loan of this second type for $80,000 at 10% for 30 years. If this loan is effective on January 1st, payment would be due on *January 1st.* The time line would look like this:

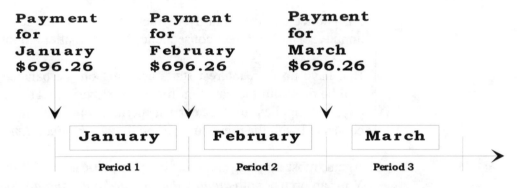

Time Line for payment at beginning of period

Figure 6.3

Here is a portion of the amortization schedule for an $80,000-loan with payments *at the beginning* of all periods:

Period	Payment Due	Interest Due	Principal Due	Balance Due
1	$696.26	$0.00	$696.26	$79,303.74
2	$696.26	$660.86	$35.39	$79,268.35
3	$696.26	$660.57	$35.69	$79,232.67
4	$696.26	$660.27	$35.98	$79,196.69
5	$696.26	$659.97	$36.28	$79,160.40
6	$696.26	$659.67	$36.59	$79,123.82
7	$696.26	$659.37	$36.89	$79,086.93
8	$696.26	$659.06	$37.20	$79,049.73
9	$696.26	$658.75	$37.51	$79,012.22
10	$696.26	$658.44	$37.82	$78,974.40

•

•

356	$696.26	$28.30	$667.96	$2,727.95
357	$696.26	$22.73	$673.52	$2,054.43
358	$696.26	$17.12	$679.13	$1,375.30
359	$696.26	$11.46	$684.79	$690.50
360	$696.26	$5.75	$690.50	$0.00

Figure 6.4

Notice that there is *no interest* in the first payment. That's because *interest does not have time to accrue* for the period. Since it carries no interest, that first payment reduces the whole balance by a big chunk on *day one* of the first period. *So, it's like starting out with a smaller loan.* As a result, this type of mortgage yields a smaller amount of *total interest* to the bank. That's probably one reason why it's not too common. In this example, the *difference* isn't much. But, let's face it, *two thousand dollars* is *two thousand dollars!*

Also notice that the monthly payment here is slightly less than in the ordinary annuity. That's a direct consequence of the smaller amount of total interest.

But, have no fear, interest starts accruing on the balance of $79,303.74 and will be due with the payment for the next period. The principal portion of a payment applies to the current period, but the interest portion is still connected with the preceding period, *in which in had time to accrue.*

Again, most mortgages are ordinary annuities. But, it doesn't matter anyway. You can prepay both *annuity due* and *ordinary annuity* loans the same way.

Putting the two forms of amortization, the *ordinary annuity and the annuity due,* side by side, for easier examination, we get this picture (see Figure 6.5). These are really two independent schedules for the same loan of $80,000 at 10% for 30 years. Total interest is $2,088.76 *more* with *ordinary annuity.*

	Ordinary annuity			*Annuity due*			
Period	Payment	Interest	Principal	Balance	Payment Due	Interest Due	Principal Due	Balance Due
1	$702.06	$666.67	$35.39	$79,964.61	$696.26	$0.00	$696.26	$79,303.74
2	$702.06	$666.37	$35.69	$79,928.92	$696.26	$660.86	$35.39	$79,268.35
3	$702.06	$666.07	$35.98	$79,892.94	$696.26	$660.57	$35.69	$79,232.67
4	$702.06	$665.77	$36.28	$79,856.66	$696.26	$660.27	$35.98	$79,196.69
5	$702.06	$665.47	$36.59	$79,820.07	$696.26	$659.97	$36.28	$79,160.40
6	$702.06	$665.17	$36.89	$79,783.18	$696.26	$659.67	$36.59	$79,123.82
7	$702.06	$664.86	$37.20	$79,745.99	$696.26	$659.37	$36.89	$79,086.93
8	$702.06	$664.55	$37.51	$79,708.48	$696.26	$659.06	$37.20	$79,049.73
9	$702.06	$664.24	$37.82	$79,670.66	$696.26	$658.75	$37.51	$79,012.22
10	$702.06	$663.92	$38.14	$79,632.52	$696.26	$658.44	$37.82	$78,974.40
			•					
			•					
356	$702.06	$28.54	$673.52	$2,750.69	$696.26	$28.30	$667.96	$2,727.95
357	$702.06	$22.92	$679.13	$2,071.55	$696.26	$22.73	$673.52	$2,054.43
358	$702.06	$17.26	$684.79	$1,386.76	$696.26	$17.12	$679.13	$1,375.30
359	$702.06	$11.56	$690.50	$696.26	$696.26	$11.46	$684.79	$690.50
360	$702.06	$5.80	$696.26	$0.00	$696.26	$5.75	$690.50	$0.00
Totals	$252,740.61	**$172,740.61**	$80,000.00		$250,651.85	**$170,651.85**	$80,000.00	

Figure 6.5

Using the comparative tables in Figure 6.5, let's recap the *ordinary annuity* amortization and the *annuity due* amortization from a different angle.

Recap of Ordinary Annuity

To recap, the *ordinary annuity* loan allows the first payment to be made legitimately at the *end* of the first period. Naturally, the first payment will include the interest that accrued during the first period. For example, if the payment for **Period 1** is due on June 1, you know that payment **1** really covers the month of May. Realize also that the interest you pay on June 1 accrued during the period from May 1 to May 31.

Now, here's an important fact. If you prepay the principal amount shown for **Period 1** ($35.39 in Figure 6.5) back on May 1, *you would totally avoid the interest payment shown for Period 1* ($666.67 in Figure 6.5). In fact, if you had the money on May 1, you could prepay the principal for periods **1, 2, 3,** and more, all at once, *and save a small fortune in interest payments.*

Recap of Annuity Due

On the flip side, the *annuity due* loan <u>requires</u> the payment for a period to be made *at the beginning* of the period. There's no time for interest to build before the *very first* period. So, **zero** interest is due in the first payment. *But, the **second** payment will include interest that accrues during the first period.*

In this case, if the payment for **Period 1** is due on June 1, you know that this very first payment includes **zero** accrued interest. *But, the payment for **Period 2** that you'll pay on July 1st will contain interest that accrues during the period of time from June 1 to June 30.* So, if you had enough extra cash, you could prepay all at once the principal amounts for periods **2, 3, 4** or more along with the scheduled payment for **Period 1** on June 1, and save BIG.

Prepay both types the same way

The type of mortgage, bank policy, the point in time the closing occurs during the month, and the amount of money a buyer bring to the closing determine whether a mortgage amortization is of one category or the other. Just the same, every scheduled payment in the *annuity due* amortization shows exactly the same components as a scheduled payment in the *ordinary annuity* amortization. **They both carry a principal payment and an interest charge.** Essentially, you can prepay both categories of loans the *same* way.

From this point on, we'll focus on the **end-of-month** category, since it occurs in most mortgages.

> *The interest portion in an amortized loan payment always applies to the previous period.* **The period <u>preceding</u> a payment is the *interest accrual period.***

There you have it. The idea is really quite simple.

A Common Theme

> *Pay a small portion of the mortgage balance in advance to avoid the interest that would accumulate on it.*

The prepayment methods you're about to learn are all variations on this one theme. *Learn the **minimum** strategy explained below.* Recall the graph in *Chapter Three,* Figure **3.1**, that shows the behavior of principal and interest payments over the term of 30 years. The pattern pivots at a crossover point. That's where the *principal* portion in a monthly payment equals the *interest* portion, and goes on to greatly exceed it until the mortgage is paid off.

At the 10% interest rate, the pivotal spot marks the beginning of the last *six* years and eight months in the loan. In this "fish tail" area, a regular monthly payment packs a lot of punch by itself. Each payment contributes so much principal that the balance now comes down fast. In fact, the regular payment is so strong in this sector that small prepayments don't have spectacular effects on *time* anymore, *although they can still save thousands of dollars.*

For that reason, if you only have five years left to go on your mortgage, using the Fixed Prepayment method, you have to prepay as much as 25% or more of the regular monthly payment to see significant *time* savings. Look at the fixed prepayment savings tables in *Appendix G* to confirm this for yourself.

The Minimum Strategy

Your overall objective should be to keep prepaying all the way to end your mortgage quickly *and to save as much interest cost as possible.* But, the *minimum* strategy is to use the prepayment methods to *speed up your journey through the amortization labyrinth and get you well into the "fish tail" area, inside the **last five years,** as quickly as possible.* Once there, take a break from prepaying and start putting your *prepayment* dollars into other investments. Then, after the mortgage ends, throw in the old *payments* too.

Remember This!

So, if you're ever tempted to stop prepaying, *first make sure you've made it to the "fish tail"!* How do know you're in there? Easy. Just look at your monthly mortgage statement: *The **principal** portion in your **regular** monthly payment* (without any prepayments) *has to be **bigger** than the interest portion.* **Also** make sure that you're within *the last five years of the mortgage.* How? Your current remaining balance should be ***NOT** be greater than* the balance remaining at period number **300** (**120** for a 15-year mortgage) in your *original **unaccelerated*** amortization schedule. You can also look up the scheduled balance in the *loan progress chart* section of a **Consumers Amortization Guide** booklet (available in bookstores). Once you know those two conditions are true, it's OK to switch to your *regular* monthly payment. *Then, focus your **prepayments** on building your nest egg. The full monthly payment will also be available inside **five** years.*

With that background, let's start with the easiest method to understand: *The Increasing Prepayment Method.*

Chapter Seven

THE INCREASING PREPAYMENT METHOD

⇒ *How to tell right away how much you save*
⇒ *The prepayment tracking format you should use*
⇒ *A general **roadmap** for the **increasing prepayment** method*
⇒ *How to do it in **step-by-step** detail*
⇒ *Results from using the increasing prepayment method*

This method cuts a mortgage term dramatically. It saves a whole lot of interest. If you use this method consistently, you'll chop down the remaining term by *one half.* Also, you can easily tell how much interest and time you save with *each* prepayment. That is possible because the amount of principal due is directly associated with the amount of interest due in the same elapsed time.

You know at a glance how much you save

It works like this. The portion of your monthly payment that goes to pay principal is like a mini loan you take out for a month. If you immediately repay this little loan right at the beginning of the period, then you owe no interest. But, if you pay it back at the end of the month, then the interest is due. Think of it as a credit card: you don't get hit with an interest charge if you send in the payment for the purchase right away.

Prepayments gets bigger and bigger

Only one other method combines nicely on top of this one

The portion of your monthly payment that pays principal *gets gradually larger each month.* After a few years, the principal prepayment may get to be more than you can spare. That's the one big drawback of this method. But, when that happens, just switch to the *Fixed Prepayment* method (next chapter) and continue to make constant prepayments at the last level you could afford. If your finances allow you to reconsider this method, *just get an amortization schedule at that point and resume from there.* You should also know up front that only the *Extra-annual* payment method combines <u>conveniently</u> ***on top*** of the *Increasing Prepayment* method. But, on the flip side, *increasing prepayments combine well on top of the other methods.*

The tools you need

To work with this method, you need an amortization schedule for your particular mortgage. You should also use a worksheet to help keep track of your prepayments. A prepayment tracking worksheet can be any piece of paper where you just jot down all your prepayments. Here is a practical prepayment tracking worksheet you might want to use (see figure 7.1 below). Chapters *14* and *15* show exactly how to fill in the details.

MORTGAGE PREPAYMENT TRACKING WORKSHEET

Page ___ of ___

MORTGAGE TYPE	TERM OF YEARS	REMAINING YEARS	ORIGINAL BALANCE	REMAINING BALANCE	INTEREST RATE	EFFECTIVE DATE	MONTHLY PAYMENT

Period No.	Date Paid	Principal Payment Due	Amount Paid	Principal Pre-paid	Interest Saved	Cumulative Interest Saved	Principal Balance	Months Saved	Cumul. Months Saved

Figure 7.1

When you use this worksheet, you realize very quickly that each little prepayment you make is equivalent to putting a pretty nice size sum of money in your savings account every month TAX-FREE. It actually becomes fun to make prepayments. You'll just get a kick out of watching the interest savings accumulate, and you'll relish seeing the big mortgage balance come tumbling down fast.

Let's now dive into the mechanics of increasing prepayments. As you'll see, it's easy to understand the basic idea of this method. These ten entries in *Figure 7.2* will help. They come from the ordinary annuity mortgage of $80,000 at 10% for 30 years.

Period	Payment	Interest	Principal	Balance
1	$702.06	$666.67	$35.39	$79,964.61
2	$702.06	$666.37	$35.69	$79,928.92
3	$702.06	$666.07	$35.98	$79,892.94
4	$702.06	$665.77	$36.28	$79,856.66
5	$702.06	$665.47	$36.59	$79,820.07
6	$702.06	$665.17	$36.89	$79,783.18
7	$702.06	$664.86	$37.20	$79,745.99
8	$702.06	$664.55	$37.51	$79,708.48
9	$702.06	$664.24	$37.82	$79,670.66
10	$702.06	$663.92	$38.14	$79,632.52

Figure 7.2

That partial amortization *shows the BEFORE picture. NO prepayments have been applied yet.* Get ready for what comes next.

UNDERSTANDING THIS METHOD

Remember This!

To eliminate the interest charge for a period, *just prepay the principal portion associated with it.* You can only do that at the very beginning of the *accrual* period or *before*.

Illustration

Using the entries in Figure *7.2*, let's study a situation where Period *1* is due now. Suppose you decide to prepay the *principal portion* from Period *2* with the payment for Period *1*.

Here's what happens:

Period	Payment	Interest	Principal	Balance
1	$702.06	$666.67	$35.39	$79,964.61

To prepay Period 2

| 2 | $702.06 | $666.37 | $35.69 | $79,928.92 |

Just pay an extra $35.69 with Period 1 ⟶ $35.69

Then, you SAVE this much interest ⟶ $666.37

and you actually <u>eliminate</u> this payment ⟶ $702.06

The new balance due is ⟶ $79,928.92

This is the picture after you include a prepayment of $35.69 in the payment for Period 1:

1	$737.75	$666.67	**$71.08**	$79,928.92
2 (3)	$702.06	**$666.07**	**$35.98**	**$79,892.94**
3 (4)	$702.06	**$665.77**	**$36.28**	**$79,856.66**
4 (5)	$702.06	**$665.47**	**$36.59**	**$79,820.07**
5 (6)	$702.06	**$665.17**	**$36.89**	**$79,783.18**
6 (7)	$702.06	**$664.86**	**$37.20**	**$79,745.99**
7 (8)	$702.06	**$664.55**	**$37.51**	**$79,708.48**
8 (9)	$702.06	**$664.24**	**$37.82**	**$79,670.66**
9 (10)	$702.06	**$663.92**	**$38.14**	**$79,632.52**
10 (11)	$702.06	**$663.60**	**$38.45**	**$79,594.07**

*Watch how the original Period **2 amounts** disappear!*

See how the remaining periods (shaded areas) move UP by one month!

Figure 7.3

Notice that the next payment to be made at the end of the *second* period is now *actually* for the old **Period number 3 (shown in parenthesis in Figure 7.3).** The prepayment <u>shortened</u> the term by *one whole* month. *In general, every time you prepay the scheduled principal portion in a period, the term SHRINKS by ONE month at the bottom end.*

It's important to note the difference between the CONTENTS of a <u>scheduled</u> period number and the CONTENTS of an <u>actual</u> period number. Period 2 in Figure 7.2 was the scheduled second period, but Period 2 in Figure 7.3 is the actual second period. The contents of the original Period 2 are gone. But, the next chronological period is <u>STILL the second period</u> or Period 2.

The following results are possible when you start prepaying in **<u>Period 1</u>**:

Each month, if you regularly prepay	*you will cut a 30-year term **<u>down to</u>***
One period	*One half or* **15 years**
Two periods	*One third or* **10 years**
Three periods	*One fourth or* **7.5 years**

If you start prepaying an old mortgage that you've had for a while, *you will still save significantly.* The same proportions of cuts will apply to the remaining term.

Example

Suppose you start this method when you have *sixteen* years left on the mortgage.

√ If you prepay one period every month, you'll cut the remaining term down to *eight* years.

√ If you prepay two periods every month, you'll reduce the rest of the term to *five* years and *four* months.

√ Prepaying three periods every month will shrink the remaining term down to *four* years.

At the end of this chapter, Table **7.2** shows a comparative accelerated amortization schedule resulting from the *Increasing Prepayment* method. Figures **7.7** and **7.8** compare graphically the patterns of interest and principal.

A General Roadmap For The INCREASING PREPAYMENT Method

Do this simple step ONCE before you start

STEP	ACTION
1	*Get a quick estimate of your TOTAL interest and time savings*

Do these four simple steps ONCE a month until you pay off the mortgage

STEP	ACTION
1	*Locate in the amortization schedule the next period to be paid*
2	*Determine how much principal you can afford to prepay*
3	*Figure out the interest and time savings from the prepayment you make this month*
4	*Add all prepayments to the scheduled payment and send in the total payment for the month*

As before, the detailed illustrations and examples that follow will be drawn from the $80,000-mortgage for 30 years at 10%.

HOW TO *QUICKLY* GET YOUR TOTAL INTEREST SAVINGS

Using the special interest savings table in *Appendix F,* you can determine quickly how much total interest you would save with the increasing prepayment method. **Table 7.1** below shows a portion of the data:

INCREASING PREPAYMENT METHOD
30-YEAR FIXED-RATE MORTGAGE INTEREST SAVINGS TABLE

Refer to this table to quickly figure out your interest savings
when you use the *Increasing Prepayment* method

If your Mortgage is	Brand New	5 Years old	10 Years old
The term will last	15 Years	17 Years 7 Months	20 Years
At this Interest rate (%)	Your interest savings factor is	Your interest savings factor is	Your interest savings factor is
6.5	0.636877	0.478777	0.333457
6.75	0.666626	0.502195	0.350618
7	0.696692	0.525919	0.368055
7.25	0.727065	0.549941	0.385762
7.5	0.757737	0.574252	0.403732
7.75	0.788698	0.598843	0.42196
8	0.819941	0.623708	0.440439
8.25	0.851455	0.648836	0.459162
8.5	0.883233	0.674221	0.478122
8.75	0.915266	0.699855	0.497314
9	0.947545	0.725728	0.516731
9.25	0.980062	0.751833	0.536365
9.5	1.012808	0.778163	0.556211
9.75	1.045775	0.804709	0.576263
10	1.078956	0.831463	0.596513
10.25	1.112343	0.858419	0.616955
10.5	1.145926	0.885569	0.637584

If your Mortgage is	Brand New	5 Years old	10 Years old
The term will last	15 Years	17 Years 7 Months	20 Years
At this Interest rate (%)	Your interest savings factor is	Your interest savings factor is	Your interest savings factor is
10.75	1.179701	0.912905	0.658393
11	1.213657	0.940421	0.679375
11.25	1.24779	0.96811	0.700526
11.5	1.28209	0.995964	0.721839
11.75	1.316553	1.023977	0.743308
12	1.35117	1.052143	0.764927
12.25	1.385936	1.080456	0.786692
12.5	1.420844	1.108908	0.808597
12.75	1.455888	1.137496	0.830636
13	1.491062	1.166212	0.852804
13.25	1.526361	1.195051	0.875097
13.5	1.561779	1.224008	0.89751
13.75	1.597311	1.253077	0.920037
14	1.632951	1.282254	0.942674
14.25	1.668695	1.311534	0.965417
14.5	1.704538	1.340912	0.988262
14.75	1.740475	1.370383	1.011203

Table 7.1

Follow these easy steps to find your expected total interest savings.

STEP	ACTION
1	Find the row starting with your interest rate.
2	In that row, go over to the column with your exact mortgage *AGE,* to locate an exact interest savings factor. If you don't find your exact mortgage age, go over to the *first* column that shows *a higher* mortgage *AGE than yours,* to locate an *approximate* factor.
3	To get your total interest savings in dollars, multiply the interest savings factor you find at that location by your *original* mortgage balance. If you're using an *approximate* factor, your *actual* savings will be *MORE* than the approximate interest savings amount you calculate.
4	At the top of the same column, read off how long your term will last. If you're using an *approximate* factor, your *actual* remaining term will be *SHORTER* than the term duration shown in the column.

First Example

Use *Table 7.1* above. Say your *brand new* mortgage balance is $80,000 for 30 years at 10% with a monthly payment of $702.06.

First, look down the *rate* column to find the row starting with *10*. Next, go over to the column with the exact age of your mortgage. Multiply interest savings factor *1.078956* by $80,000 to get your total interest savings of *$86,316.48*. The term would last *15* years.

Second Example

Let's look at another example. It's the same mortgage of $80,000 for 30 years at 10%. But, say you've had the mortgage for *three years.*

First, find the row starting with *10*. Next, go over to the column with the *next higher age* of your mortgage. In this case, it's the *5 Years Old* column. Multiply *approximate* interest savings factor *0.831463* by $80,000 to get your *approximate* total interest savings of *$66,517.04*. Your actual savings would be *MORE* than that amount. The term would last less than *17* years.

HOW TO DO IT IN *step-by-step* DETAIL

Step 1   *Locate the next period to be paid*

The method works to save time and money for you whether you've had your mortgage a while or happen to be at the very beginning of the term.

Determine exactly which period is next to be paid. Call your bank to confirm the exact period number associated with your next payment. Get the exact remaining balance due.

Look at your amortization table. Find the period that matches the balance you confirmed with the bank.

Illustration

Let's say the mortgage is effective on January 1st and the first payment is due on February 1st. Period 1 then corresponds to February 1st.

Let's also say that the current date is February 28th, and there is a remaining balance of $79,964.61. *So, Period 2 is the next one to be paid.* Figure 7.4 shows the first ten periods *before* any payments.

Next to be paid

Period	Payment	Interest	Principal	Balance
1	$702.06	$666.67	$35.39	$79,964.61
2	$702.06	$666.37	$35.69	$79,928.92
3	$702.06	$666.07	$35.98	$79,892.94
4	$702.06	$665.77	$36.28	$79,856.66
5	$702.06	$665.47	$36.59	$79,820.07
6	$702.06	$665.17	$36.89	$79,783.18
7	$702.06	$664.86	$37.20	$79,745.99
8	$702.06	$664.55	$37.51	$79,708.48
9	$702.06	$664.24	$37.82	$79,670.66
10	$702.06	$663.92	$38.14	$79,632.52

Figure 7.4

Step 2

Determine how much principal you can afford to prepay

You can prepay one period or several periods at a time. The more periods you prepay, the quicker you progress toward a balance of zero.

So, the current payment of $702.06 is due for Period 2. Suppose you can spare $80 extra this time. That means you could prepay at least period *3.*

Question is: *How much principal prepayment can this money cover?*

You could be tempted to put the whole $80 into prepaying. But, hold on. The prepayment *must match* **exactly** *the principal amounts* from the amortization schedule. So, first, look at the periods that are eligible for prepayment. Then, starting with the first of those periods, pick the interest amounts until you add up to fit within your extra money amount.

	Period	Payment	Interest	Principal	Balance
Period 1 was already paid	1	$702.06	$666.67	$35.39	$79,964.61
Period 2 is due next	2	$702.06	$666.37	$35.69	$79,928.92
Period 3 is prepayable	3	$702.06	$666.07	*$35.98*	$79,892.94
So is period 4 (since you'd	4	$702.06	$665.77	*$36.28*	$79,856.66
have $44.31 left over)	5	$702.06	$665.47	$36.59	$79,820.07

Figure 7.5

$80 can cover these amounts.

Period 3 is the first one eligible. At this point, you could prepay the principal of $35.98 for <u>Period 3</u> and save $666.07. In fact, since you would have $44.31 extra left, you could also prepay the $36.28 for <u>Period 4</u> and save another $665.77. The total prepayment so far would be $72.26. That's all you can cover with $80. *You'd still have $7.74 worth of change in your pocket.*

Total prepayment: **$72.26**

Figure out the interest and time savings from the prepayment you make this month

When you prepay periods 3 and 4, the actual effect on the amortization schedule is dramatic.

The total payment covers the scheduled interest of $666.67. *But, the principal payment is now $107.95, including the prepayment.* Period **5** moves up to be the next payment due to be paid, with a *starting* balance of $79,856.66. Period **5** becomes the *actual* Period **3**. ***In a strange way, it's like moving forward in time.***

Figure 7.6 shows the first ten periods **after** the payment for *Period 2* was made.

The CONTENTS of the original Periods 3 and 4 vanished. **But, the CONTENTS of period 5 and all the rest moved up by TWO.**

Period	Payment	Interest	Principal	Balance
1	$702.06	$666.67	$35.39	$79,964.61
2	*$774.32*	*$666.37*	*$107.95*	*$79,856.66*
3	$702.06	$665.47	$36.59	$79,820.07
4	$702.06	$665.17	$36.89	$79,783.18
5	$702.06	$664.86	$37.20	$79,745.99
6	$702.06	$664.55	$37.51	$79,708.48
7	$702.06	$664.24	$37.82	$79,670.66
8	$702.06	$663.92	$38.14	$79,632.52
9	$702.06	$663.60	$38.45	$79,594.07
10	$702.06	$663.28	$38.77	$79,555.30

Figure 7.6

Prepaying $72.26 for periods 3 and 4 would save you $1,331.84 right away. It would eliminate the full payments for those two periods. You also save ***one whole month*** for each of the two periods that were prepaid.

Total interest saved: **$1,331.84**   *Total time saved:*   ***2 Months***

Add all prepayments to the scheduled payment *and* send in the total payment for the month

Next, you should add the total prepayment of $72.26 to the regular monthly payment of $702.06, for a total payment of $774.32 to cover **Period 2, Period 3, and Period 4.**

Regular monthly payment	$702.06
Total prepayment	$72.26

Total payment for the month | **$774.32** |

Follow the guidelines in **Chapter Fifteen** to send in the total payment for the month.

When you combine the Extra-annual method on top of this one

If you choose to combine the *Extra-annual* payment method on top of this one, just follow the *Extra-annual* payment guidelines in addition to these steps. This is an advanced combination that requires you to first be familiar with the *pseudo bi-weekly* technique, as explained in chapters eleven and twelve. Basically, you need to deposit *half* of the *total* monthly payment you're going to make in each of the preceding **TWO** *two-week* periods.

You should get a *new* amortization schedule after each *Extra-annual* payment, so you can continue to see the correct principal portions to prepay.

Increasing Prepayment Results

Mortgage Amount: *$80,000*   Term: *30 Years*   Interest Rate: *10%*

Normal Term
No prepayments

Interest Savings: *$0*
Duration: 30 Years
Time Savings: **None**
Monthly Payment: **$702.06**

Accelerated Term
Increasing Prepayments

Interest Savings: **$86,316.50**
Duration: *15 Years*
Time Savings: **15 Years**
Monthly Payment: **Increasing**

Year	Payment	Interest	Principal	Balance	Payment	Interest	Principal	Balance
1	$8,424.69	$7,979.98	$444.70	$79,555.30	$8,894.61	$7,958.64	$935.97	$79,064.03
2	$8,424.69	$7,933.42	$491.27	$79,064.03	$8,998.18	$7,855.93	$1,142.25	$77,921.78
3	$8,424.69	$7,881.98	$542.71	$78,521.32	$9,124.58	$7,730.58	$1,393.99	$76,527.78
4	$8,424.69	$7,825.15	$599.54	$77,921.78	$9,278.83	$7,577.61	$1,701.22	$74,826.57
5	$8,424.69	$7,762.37	$662.32	$77,259.46	$9,467.07	$7,390.92	$2,076.15	$72,750.42
6	$8,424.69	$7,693.01	$731.67	$76,527.78	$9,696.80	$7,163.09	$2,533.71	$70,216.70
7	$8,424.69	$7,616.40	$808.29	$75,719.49	$9,977.16	$6,885.04	$3,092.12	$67,124.58
8	$8,424.69	$7,531.76	$892.93	$74,826.57	$10,319.32	$6,545.72	$3,773.60	$63,350.98
9	$8,424.69	$7,438.26	$986.43	$73,840.14	$10,736.87	$6,131.61	$4,605.27	$58,745.71
10	$8,424.69	$7,334.97	$1,089.72	$72,750.42	$11,255.00	$5,626.20	$5,628.80	$53,116.92
11	$8,424.69	$7,220.86	$1,203.83	$71,546.59	$11,925.99	$5,005.97	$6,920.02	$46,196.90
12	$8,424.69	$7,094.80	$1,329.89	$70,216.70	$12,697.64	$4,246.31	$8,451.33	$37,745.56
13	$8,424.69	$6,955.54	$1,469.14	$68,747.56	$13,639.36	$3,318.57	$10,320.79	$27,424.77
14	$8,424.69	$6,801.71	$1,622.98	$67,124.58	$14,788.63	$2,185.66	$12,602.97	$14,821.80
15	$8,424.69	$6,631.76	$1,792.93	$65,331.65	$15,624.07	$802.27	$14,821.80	$0.00
16	$8,424.69	$6,444.02	$1,980.67	$63,350.98	$0.00	$0.00	$0.00	$0.00
17	$8,424.69	$6,236.61	$2,188.07	$61,162.91	$0.00	$0.00	$0.00	$0.00
18	$8,424.69	$6,007.49	$2,417.19	$58,745.71	$0.00	$0.00	$0.00	$0.00
19	$8,424.69	$5,754.38	$2,670.30	$56,075.41	$0.00	$0.00	$0.00	$0.00
20	$8,424.69	$5,474.77	$2,949.92	$53,125.49	$0.00	$0.00	$0.00	$0.00
21	$8,424.69	$5,165.87	$3,258.82	$49,866.67	$0.00	$0.00	$0.00	$0.00
22	$8,424.69	$4,824.63	$3,600.06	$46,266.62	$0.00	$0.00	$0.00	$0.00
23	$8,424.69	$4,447.66	$3,977.03	$42,289.59	$0.00	$0.00	$0.00	$0.00
24	$8,424.69	$4,031.21	$4,393.48	$37,896.11	$0.00	$0.00	$0.00	$0.00
25	$8,424.69	$3,571.16	$4,853.53	$33,042.58	$0.00	$0.00	$0.00	$0.00
26	$8,424.69	$3,062.93	$5,361.76	$27,680.83	$0.00	$0.00	$0.00	$0.00
27	$8,424.69	$2,501.48	$5,923.20	$21,757.62	$0.00	$0.00	$0.00	$0.00
28	$8,424.69	$1,881.25	$6,543.44	$15,214.18	$0.00	$0.00	$0.00	$0.00
29	$8,424.69	$1,196.06	$7,228.62	$7,985.56	$0.00	$0.00	$0.00	$0.00
30	$8,424.69	$439.13	$7,985.56	$0.00	$0.00	$0.00	$0.00	$0.00
Totals	$252,740.61	$172,740.61	$80,000.00		$166,424.11	$86,424.11	$80,000.00	

Table 7.2

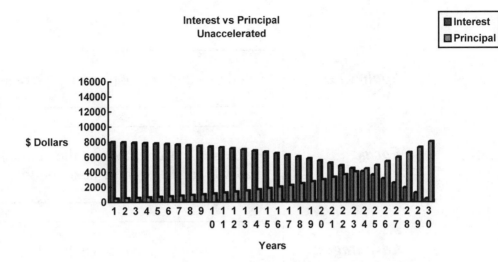

Figure 7.7

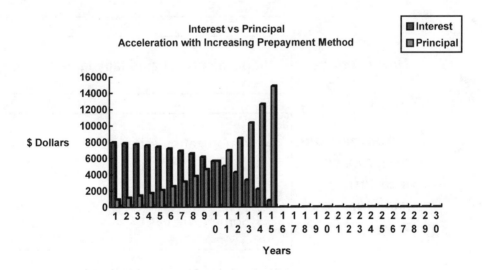

Figure 7.8

KEY POINTS OF THE INCREASING PREPAYMENT METHOD

Applies to:

Fixed rate and adjustable rate mortgages

Focus:

Prepays in current payment the amount of principal that will accrue over the next period.

Advantages:

√ Cuts mortgage term to half or less, when you make regular prepayments.
√ Saves a big chunk of interest payments.
√ You can tell exactly how much each prepayment saves in interests.

Disadvantage:

Prepayments get gradually larger.

Resources you need to work with this method:

⇒ Amortization schedule for your mortgage
⇒ Worksheet
⇒ Some *extra* cash

Other methods to combine with this one:

Extra-annual payment or *pseudo bi-weekly* method

Chapter Eight

THE FIXED PREPAYMENT METHOD

⇒ *HOW IT WORKS: You pick a number, any number*
⇒ *Different ways to use the **fixed prepayment** method: use it alone or in combination with other methods*
⇒ *How to quickly get your **total** interest and time savings*

If your budget is small, this may be the method for you. This approach is particularly flexible and handy.   You just decide on any amount of prepayment you feel comfortable with.   A small, regular amount of prepayment can go a long, long way to cut many years from the term of your mortgage, and save you a lot of money.

Again, let's take the mortgage of $80,000 at 10% for 30 years. Now, examine this next table. See how various fixed prepayment amounts can *save dramatic amounts of interest* and *cut many years off the term.*

If you PREPAY this much per MONTH	You pay this much TOTAL INTEREST	You SAVE this much TOTAL INTEREST	The term lasts		You cut the term by	
			Years	Months	Years	Months
$0.00	$172,740.61	$0.00	30		0	
$10.00	**$156,202.46**	**$16,539.15**	**27**	**8**	**2**	**4**
$15.00	$149,435.37	$23,305.24	26	8	3	4
$20.00	$143,408.44	$29,332.17	25	9	4	3
$25.00	**$137,988.49**	**$34,752.13**	**25**		**5**	
$35.00	$128,591.18	$44,149.43	23	7	6	5
$50.00	$117,155.92	$55,584.69	21	10	8	2
$75.00	$102,727.42	$70,013.20	19	7	10	5
$100.00	$91,937.19	$80,803.43	17	10	12	2
$150.00	*$76,594.66*	*$96,145.95*	*15*	*4*	*14*	*8*
$200.00	$66,027.37	$106,713.24	13	6	16	6

Figure 8.1

Just $10 extra per month will save *$16,539.15* in interest, and cut the 30 year term down to 27 years and 8 months, saving *2 years and 4 months.* Paying only $25 extra per month, *that's about 83 cents a day,* will save $34,752.13 in interest, and cut the term down to 25 years, *saving 5 years*. A prepayment of $150 a month will cut the term in half and save $96,145.95.

You'll learn here how to quickly determine what results *any* prepayment amount will produce for your particular mortgage.

UNDERSTANDING THIS METHOD

How ONE prepayment works

No matter which approach you use, any amount of prepayment you make basically works the same way to save money and time. Let's take a close look at the way *one* given prepayment works. To help with this illustration, we'll use the partial amortization schedule for your mortgage of $80,000 at 10% for 30 years shown in Figure 8.2.

Period	Payment	Interest	Principal	Balance
1	$702.06	$666.67	$35.39	$79,964.61
2	$702.06	$666.37	$35.69	$79,928.92
3	$702.06	$666.07	$35.98	$79,892.94
4	$702.06	$665.77	$36.28	$79,856.66
5	$702.06	$665.47	$36.59	$79,820.07

Figure 8.2

Remember This!

As you saw in chapter seven, the interest *savings* you get with a prepayment always comes from *scheduled* interest amounts in the amortization table. A scheduled *interest* amount is directly associated with the scheduled *principal* payment in the same period. For example, in Period 2, the *scheduled* interest amount of **$666.37** is associated with the *scheduled* principal payment of **$35.69**. Here are more insights on this topic. Prepayment money always covers **scheduled principal** payments. A prepayment amount can be exactly the same as the scheduled principal or it can be different.

If you prepay or **cover** the scheduled principal portion exactly <u>in full</u>, you save a <u>whole</u> month and you eliminate the <u>whole</u> associated interest payment. This prepayment is **"in synch"**.

It could also happen that you decide to prepay a period with a *random* amount of extra money. Most likely, the random amount will be either smaller or larger than the *scheduled* principal payment in the given period. Let's refer to a prepayment in this condition as *being* **"out of synch"**.

If the **out of synch** prepayment is smaller than the scheduled principal, it will only cover part of the principal. Consequently, the interest savings will only be a proportionate part of the scheduled interest in that period. Also, the mortgage term will be reduced by less than a month.

But, if the prepayment is larger than the scheduled principal, it will cover the chosen period in full, and spill over to cover the next period in part. If the prepayment is large enough, it could spill over to cover several of the subsequent periods in full, *plus one more period in part.*

With this understanding, let's see how *one* prepayment of $25 would affect your mortgage of $80,000 at 10% for 30 years.

Let's start at the point where Period 1 is due. So, the current payment of $702.06 is due for Period 1. With your prepayment, the actual payment will be $727.06.

Actual payment is $727.06

Period	Payment	Interest	Principal	Balance
1	**$727.06**	$666.67	**$60.39**	**$79,939.61**
	($702.06 plus **$25**)		($35.39 plus **$25**)	($79,964.61 less **$25**)

As the prepayment of $25 covers only part of the scheduled principal of $35.69 in **Period 2**, it only covers Period 2 in part, so only *part of the interest* is eliminated.

*Extra **$25** only covers **part** of principal in Period 2 (**$35.69 is more than $25**)*

Period			Principal	
2			**$35.69 is more than $25**	

Put another way, the prepayment represents only approximately 70.05% of the principal in Period 2 *(the percentage comes from 100 x 25 / 35.69).*

Therefore, the interest saving is approximately 70.05% of the scheduled interest of 666.37 or about $466.79. (**Note:** The amount $466.79 is an approximation because of rounding errors in the percentage calculation. The exact amount from an amortization schedule is **$466.84**).

*The **total** interest is in fact reduced by **$466.84***

Period		Interest		
2		$666.37 less $466.84		

The mortgage term is reduced by approximately 70.05% of a 30-day month, that is, by about 21 days or three weeks.

What do you get with ONE prepayment of $100?

In this case, the actual payment would be $802.06.

Actual payment is $802.06

Period	Payment	Interest	Principal	Balance
1	**$802.06**	$666.67	**$135.39**	**$79,864.61**
	($702.06 *plus* **$100**)		($35.39 *plus* **$100**)	($79,964.61 **less $100**)

The prepayment of **$100** covers *Periods 2* and *3 in full*, as the scheduled principal amounts in those periods add to $71.67 (less than the $100). There is a prepayment balance of $28.33 *(the difference from $100 - $71.67)* that spills over to cover **Period 4** *in part*.

So then, the prepayment cancels **100%** of the principal amounts in Periods 2 and 3, and **78.09%** of the principal in Period 4.

$35.69 is covered in full ($100 - $35.69 leaves $64.31)
$35.98 is covered in full ($64.31 - $35.98 leaves $28.33)
$36.28 is covered in part by the remaining $28.33

Period			Principal	
2			**$35.69**	
3			**$35.98**	
4			**$36.28**	

The scheduled interest payments from Periods 2 and 3, which stack up to $1,332.44, are eliminated completely. But, the interest saving from **Period 4** is 78.09% of the scheduled interest of 665.77 or **$519.90**. So, the total interest savings from this one prepayment adds up to **$1,852.34**.

Interest Savings
*$666.37 **(fully cut)***
*$666.07 **(fully cut)***
*$519.90 **(partially cut)***

Period		Interest		
2		**$666.37**		
3		**$666.07**		
4		$665.77		

The single $100 prepayment reduces term by two months <u>plus</u> 78.09% of a 30-day month, that is, by two months and 23 days or almost three months.

Effects of a series of **out of synch** random prepayments

When you start out with the original amortization schedule, it's easy to see the effect of the *first* random prepayment. But, after that prepayment, the rest of the *original* amortization schedule becomes useless. It won't give true information about the *next prepayment*. Every time you make a *random* prepayment, the remaining loan balance goes down by the same random amount. Consequently, the remainder of the *regular* amortization schedule gets sort of *reshuffled*. Here is how that happens.

For example, taking the first five periods of the original amortization schedule,

Period	Payment	Interest	Principal	Balance
1	$702.06	$666.67	$35.39	$79,964.61
2	$702.06	$666.37	$35.69	$79,928.92
3	$702.06	$666.07	$35.98	$79,892.94
4	$702.06	$665.77	$36.28	$79,856.66
5	$702.06	$665.47	$36.59	$79,820.07

let's observe what happens when you make a *random* prepayment of $65 in Period 1. The **base** monthly payment is $702.06. (NOTE: A **base** monthly payment is the monthly payment the amortization schedule is based on).

The $65 amount covers Period 2 in full. But, because it only covers part of the scheduled principal portion in Period 3, it's *out of synch* with the schedule.

Here's what the new schedule looks like:

Includes extra $65.

See how the random $65 prepayment in period 1 caused the rest of this schedule to be totally different from the **original** schedule?

Period	Payment	Interest	Principal	Balance
1	$767.06	$666.67	$100.39	$79,899.61
2	$702.06	*$665.83*	*$36.23*	*$79,863.38*
3	$702.06	*$665.53*	*$36.53*	*$79,826.85*
4	$702.06	*$665.22*	*$36.83*	*$79,790.02*
5	$702.06	*$664.92*	*$37.14*	*$79,752.88*

Observe how the remaining balances, interest, and principal portions have changed in Periods 2 through 5. In fact, the original Period 2 was totally eliminated, and the rest of the periods bumped up one. Except for the scheduled payment, *all the remaining values are different from those in the original schedule.*

It is clear that every time you prepay randomly, the rest of the schedule changes randomly. So, *after you've reshuffled the current schedule,* **if you want to track your *random* prepayment activities,** *you have to get a NEW amortization schedule* in order to see exactly what remains ahead.

Here's part of the *original* amortization schedule again.

Watch period 4 before the prepayment.

Period	Payment	Interest	Principal	Balance
1	$702.06	$666.67	$35.39	$79,964.61
2	$702.06	$666.37	$35.69	$79,928.92
3	$702.06	$666.07	$35.98	$79,892.94
4	$702.06	**$665.77**	**$36.28**	**$79,856.66**
5	$702.06	**$665.47**	**$36.59**	**$79,820.07**

Now, observe what would happen if you made a prepayment of *$71.67*. You may realize that this particular amount is *in synch* with the original amortization schedule, because it prepays exactly the *scheduled* principal portions in *Periods 2 and 3*. It's the exact sum of *$35.69* and *$35.98*.

See how period 4 pulled up to position 2?

Period	Payment	Interest	Principal	Balance
1	**$773.73**	$666.67	$107.06	$79,892.94
2	$702.06	*$665.77*	*$36.28*	*$79,856.66*
3	$702.06	*$665.47*	*$36.59*	*$79,820.07*
4	$702.06	*$665.17*	*$36.89*	*$79,783.18*
5	$702.06	*$664.86*	*$37.20*	*$79,745.98*

Notice how the original Periods 2 and 3 have been eliminated. But, look at the other result. The original Periods 4 and 5 have been pulled up to positions 2 and 3. In fact, *the remainder of the modified schedule is identical with the original schedule,* except for the fact that all periods moved up by two months. The point should be clear. *If you keep your prepayments **in synch** with the amortization schedule you're using, you don't have to get a new amortization schedule after each prepayment.*

Obviously, it's important to keep things as simple as possible. So, you should aim to work the Fixed Prepayment method *in synch* with an amortization schedule. That way you don't have to churn out so many *new* amortization schedules.

Two types of prepayment with this method using only one amortization schedule

You can apply two types of prepayment with the *Fixed Prepayment* method using *the same* amortization schedule throughout the term:

1. Stick with a *constant* prepayment amount all the way to the end and get a *new* amortization schedule to go with it

2. Make **ADDITIONAL** *random* prepayments *in synch* with the **new** schedule, as you go. Those random *in-synch* prepayment amounts can be large or small depending on your financial situation at the time.

Constant Amount

Start your prepayment program with a fixed prepayment amount and stay with it the whole time, *no matter what.* It's easier to settle on one amount because you get used to it. You won't even miss the money.

For example, let's say you decide to prepay $100 every month. If you run an amortization schedule to reflect this prepayment, you'd now have a *base prepayment of $100*. Your *new* *base* monthly payment would be $802.06 (the original *$702.06 plus the $100.00 base prepayment*). So then, from the beginning to the end of the term, you would go on to prepay $100 each and every month.

When you decide to use the same small amount of prepayment every month, you can determine *up front,* with precision, how many years and how much interest money you will save *in total*. There are several ways to determine the new term for any given amount of prepayment. *Appendix E* shows how to find the savings in time and interest "long-hand" style. Or, quicker still, you can use the *special savings tables* in this book to get the *new* term and interest savings. You'll get the details on those processes a little further on.

One more time, consider this portion of the original amortization schedule.

Period	Payment	Interest	Principal	Balance
1	$702.06	$666.67	$35.39	$79,964.61
2	$702.06	$666.37	$35.69	$79,928.92
3	$702.06	$666.07	$35.98	$79,892.94
4	$702.06	$665.77	$36.28	$79,856.66
5	$702.06	$665.47	$36.59	$79,820.07

Now, you decide to prepay a constant $35 permanently. So, you get a ***new*** amortization schedule for the new base monthly payment of **$737.06** (*$702.06 plus $35*). You're obligated ***by contract*** to make the $702.06 payment to your lender. But, the extra $35 *base prepayment* is an obligation to yourself.

When you start with the new schedule, *YOU MUST CONTINUE TO MAKE THIS $35 PREPAYMENT every month*. If you skip a $35-prepayment just *ONCE* or prepay a different amount *out of synch,* your new amortization schedule becomes **USELESS**, and you have to get **another** one.

Here's part of the *new* amortization schedule (first five and last five periods).

Period	Payment	Interest	Principal	Balance
1	$737.06	$666.67	$70.39	$79,929.61
2	$737.06	$666.08	$70.98	$79,858.63
3	$737.06	$665.49	$71.57	$79,787.05
4	$737.06	$664.89	$72.17	$79,714.88
5	$737.06	$664.29	$72.77	$79,642.11

279	$737.06	$29.96	$707.10	$2,887.83
280	$737.06	$24.07	$713.00	$2,174.83
281	$737.06	$18.12	$718.94	$1,455.90
282	$737.06	$12.13	$724.93	$730.97
283	$737.06	$6.09	$730.97	$0.00

Figure 8.3

This new base payment chops off ***$44,149.13*** from the total interest cost, and peels away ***6 years and 5 months*** from the mortgage term, bringing it down to 23 years and 7 months. Clearly, you can determine how much your *total* savings in time and interest will be from making the new *base* prepayment throughout the *new* term. But, can you figure out how much you save with any one *small* prepayment? Yes. To see the effects of one small prepayment, you need a *partial* amortization schedule. If you don't have a PC with a good amortization program, you could use a calculator to easily generate a *partial* amortization with up to three or four periods. *Chapter Three* spells out the technique under *Three things the bank does.* But, when you make **large** single prepayments now and then, it's worth getting a *complete* amortization schedule. Whether partial or complete, starting with the <u>current</u> balance *before the prepayment,* the amortization **must be based** on the *original* monthly payment. Once you have the amortization data, use the procedure in *Appendix D* to find the time and interest savings from any *single* prepayment.

Random Amounts In Synch

As your financial situation changes, you can also change to a larger or smaller amount of *base* prepayment, **and stay with the new amount for a while.** That way you keep a steady flow of prepayment, whether cash is scarce or aplenty. *But, remember, you need to get an updated amortization schedule every time you change the **base** prepayment amount.*

You now know the routine. Every time you switch to a new *base* prepayment amount, you need to get a new amortization schedule based on the current balance and the *new* total monthly payment. But, you must realize that this new schedule will give you an accurate picture of your total savings *only if you stay with the **new** prepayment level to the end of the term.*

If you change to a new fixed amount only once in a long while, recreating your amortization schedule is OK. But, if you bounce up and down real often, it gets laborious and sort of impractical. You want to be able to make random prepayments *often*, without having to re-do the amortization schedule. Random prepayment amounts **in synch** allow you to vary the size of *extra* prepayments, while keeping the same *modified* amortization schedule.

You can do it after you've settled on an absolute minimum prepayment that you can make *invariably*, **every month**. This can be $10, $15, or higher. Again, this constant amount is now your *fixed prepayment base.* You can easily do this with pocket change money that you hardly miss. Get an amortization schedule for the *new monthly payment that includes this minimum prepayment.* This is your *modified* working amortization schedule.

Combining the Increasing Prepayment Method On Top of the Fixed Method

Now, as your circumstances permit, you can make additional prepayments **on top** of this new monthly payment. Every time you run into some extra cash to spare for this, use it as *in synch* prepayment by *temporarily* applying the **INCREASING PREPAYMENT METHOD on top of the established fixed prepayments.** That means your extra prepayment will match exactly the scheduled principal portions shown in your modified amortization schedule. Of course, this will **save even MORE time and money** for you.

For example, you might decide to prepay a minimum of $20 every month. Here's part of your **NEW** amortization schedule with a built-in *base* prepayment of $20. If you stay with this new base payment of $722.26, you save **$29,332.17 in interest payments**, and cut **4 years and 3 months** from the term, reducing it to 25 years and 9 months.

Period	Payment	Interest	Principal	Balance
1	$722.26	$666.67	$55.59	$79,944.41
2	$722.26	$666.20	$56.06	$79,888.35
3	$722.26	$665.74	$56.52	$79,831.83
4	$722.26	$665.27	$56.99	$79,774.83
5	$722.26	$664.79	$57.47	$79,717.36
6	$722.26	$664.31	$57.95	$79,659.42
7	$722.26	$663.83	$58.43	$79,600.99
8	$722.26	$663.34	$58.92	$79,542.07
9	$722.26	$662.85	$59.41	$79,482.66
10	$722.26	$662.36	$59.90	$79,422.75

Figure 8.4

Let's say that, after doing this for two months, your financial situation allows you to spare $120 at the end of the third month. So, you now prepay from the $120.

Caution

> **But, prepay <u>only</u> as much of this new extra money** *as will exactly match one or more scheduled principal portions.*

Your strategy here is to take only *$114.46* from the $120, and add that to the current base payment for Period 3, for a total payment of $836.72. You're in effect prepaying Periods 4 and 5 **in full** *(principal portions $56.99 and $57.47)*. Buy yourself something nice with the $5.54 that stays in your pocket. You'll have the pleasant "surprise" to see that, with this *one* prepayment of *$114.46*, you saved an ADDITIONAL *$1,330.36* and cut *two MORE months* from the term. But, there's more. *You can continue to use the SAME amortization schedule.* Do you see why? Examine the results in Figure *8.5* below. Focus on *Period 4.* Then, compare it with *Period 6* in Figure *8.4* (above).

Period	Payment	Interest	Principal	Balance
1	$722.26	$666.67	$55.59	$79,944.41
2	$722.26	$666.20	$56.06	$79,888.35
3	$836.72	$665.74	$170.98	$79,717.37
4	$722.26	$664.31	$57.95	$79,659.42
5	$722.26	$663.83	$58.43	$79,600.99
6	$722.26	$663.34	$58.92	$79,542.07
7	$722.26	$662.85	$59.41	$79,482.66
8	$722.26	$662.36	$59.90	$79,422.76
9	$722.26	$661.86	$60.40	$79,362.35
10	$722.26	$661.35	$60.91	$79,301.45

Figure 8.5

Did you observe that the *old* Period 6 moved to position 4? All remaining periods moved up by *two*. You eliminated two periods and saved *$1,330.36* in interest. But, except for those two periods, *the tail end of the modified schedule is the same as before.*

From $120 extra a month, you can keep prepaying *two* periods each month for the next three months or so. But, a couple of months later, suppose you find that $45 is all the *new* extra money you can come up with. At that point in the schedule, notice that the principal portion in any given period *is already more than the $45*. As it's not enough to cover a principal portion in full, this extra money is *out of synch* with the schedule. So, what do you do?

As long as you'll keep having that extra prepayment money, don't miss the opportunity to use it and save. Here's what you do. Just go to a *higher fixed prepayment base*, and get a new working amortization schedule. It's your call to decide on the exact amount to add on.

Remember:

You can use other methods with this one

When you've been using the **Increasing Prepayment** method for a number of years, if you find that the increasing prepayments have gotten to be more than you can afford, you can switch to this method as a change of the guard so to speak. It lets you continue to make prepayments at a level you can handle.

But, more importantly, while you use the *fixed prepayment method* as a primary method, you can use the *increasing prepayment* method in combination with it, as you've seen. The *Extra-annual* payment method fits in nicely with this one too.

In chapters eleven and twelve, you'll get details on combining the *Extra-Annual Payment* method on top of fixed prepayments. But, before jumping that far, go on to *Chapter Nine* for the roadmap and detailed procedures of the *Fixed Prepayment* method. At the end of *Chapter Nine,* Table **9.2** shows a comparative accelerated amortization schedule resulting from the *Fixed Prepayment* method with a base prepayment of only $50. Figures **9.3** and **9.4** show graphically how the patterns of interest and principal compare.

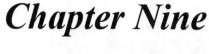

Chapter Nine

THE FIXED PREPAYMENT METHOD

ROADMAP AND DETAILED PROCEDURE

⇒ *A general **roadmap** for the **fixed prepayment** method*
⇒ *How to do it in **step-by-step** detail*
⇒ *How to quickly determine the total savings in interest and time that a prepayment will deliver*
⇒ *Results from using the fixed prepayment method*

This chapter carries the discussion of the *fixed prepayment* method to the step-by-step detailed level. The general roadmap you find here explains how you can make this method work for you.

Before you start prepaying on a monthly basis, you should decide on a minimum **base** prepayment amount. You can pick any affordable amount. But, choose this amount as a *percentage* of the regular monthly payment. Using this percentage and a *special savings table* in this book, you can very quickly determine the *total* savings in interest and time that the prepayment will deliver during the *new* term. The special savings table gives accurate answers for a specific set of prepayment percentages and mortgage ages.

If you don't find an exact match for your mortgage age, you can still get a good approximation of your expected savings. For exact figures instead of an approximation, use the procedure in *Appendix E* to calculate the *total* interest and time savings that a **constant** base prepayment amount would deliver over the new term.

Once you've settled on the base prepayment amount, you should get a new amortization schedule that reflects the *new* total monthly payment. At this point, you're ready to start your monthly prepayment routine. As you go, whenever you come across some more *extra* cash that you wish to use for prepayment, the roadmap shows you how to keep the prepayment *in synch* with the *new* schedule and determine your *extra* savings in interest and time.

A General Roadmap
For The FIXED PREPAYMENT Method

Here is how to get this method working for you:

Prepare for it by taking these four steps NOW.

STEP	ACTION
1	*Decide how much to prepay as a MINIMUM every month*
2	*Quickly determine your expected TOTAL savings in interest and time*
3	*Get a new amortization schedule based on the new monthly payment*

Do these three steps ONCE a month until you pay off the mortgage

STEP	ACTION
1	*Decide how much EXTRA to prepay*
2	*If you make an EXTRA prepayment, determine your EXTRA savings in interest and time*
3	*Send in the NEW monthly payment*

HOW TO DO IT IN *step-by-step* DETAIL

The Three Preparation Steps

Perform these preparation steps once, at the time you decide to prepay using the Fixed Prepayment method.

Decide how much to prepay as a MINIMUM every month

This is a personal decision that only you can make. It depends on your budget. If you can comfortably swing a minimal piece of change every month, it is to your advantage to use the cash for a habitual, constant prepayment.

In spite of rough times, most people could afford an extra $15 to $25 a month routinely and without sweating. Even when it looks like you couldn't spring a dime, it is still possible to painlessly cough up $15 or more bucks each month, just by using a little common sense.

It's easy to do. By drinking *one* less cup of coffee, or planning lunch better, you can pile up quite a few nickels. It's not even necessary to make those little sacrifices every day, just every now and then. You know best what you have to do. But, do decide on a *minimum* amount that you'll automatically prepay for the life of the loan. Read *Chapter Sixteen* to learn about *six* powerful ways to generate additional cash that you can use to prepay your mortgage.

For illustration purposes:

> Let's say you decide to prepay a *minimum of* **$35** permanently.

This $35 is about **5%** of the original monthly payment of $702.06. ***Step 2*** below shows you how to quickly figure out a good estimate of the total interest and time savings you should expect when you keep this prepayment all the way to the end.

Step 2

Quickly determine your expected TOTAL savings in interest and time

Using the special interest savings table in *Appendix G,* you can determine quickly how much total interest you would save with the *Fixed Prepayment* method. Table 9.1 below shows a portion of the table:

FIXED PREPAYMENT METHOD
30-YEAR FIXED-RATE MORTGAGE SAVINGS TABLE

Refer to this table to quickly figure out your ***total*** interest and time savings when you use the *Fixed Prepayment* method

If your Mortgage is	Brand New				If your Mortgage is	Brand New		
and you prepay each month	5% of the regular monthly payment				and you prepay each month	5% of the regular monthly payment		
At this Interest rate (%)	Your interest savings factor is	You'll **save** this many years	and this many months		At this Interest rate (%)	Your interest savings factor is	You'll **save** this many years	and this many months
6.5	0.194608	3	10		10.75	0.664562	7	0
6.75	0.212123	4	0		11	0.704587	7	3
7	0.230748	4	2		11.25	0.74601	7	6
7.25	0.250523	4	4		11.5	0.788817	7	9
7.5	0.271485	4	6		11.75	0.832987	7	11
7.75	0.29367	4	8		12	0.878499	8	2
8	0.317111	4	10		12.25	0.925329	8	5
8.25	0.341839	5	0		12.5	0.973448	8	8
8.5	0.367883	5	2		12.75	1.022827	8	10
8.75	0.395268	5	4		13	1.073432	9	1
9	0.424016	5	7		13.25	1.12523	9	4
9.25	0.454147	5	9		13.5	1.178185	9	7
9.5	0.485676	6	0		13.75	1.232259	9	9
9.75	0.518615	6	2		14	1.287414	10	0
10	0.55297	6	5		14.25	1.343611	10	3
10.25	0.588748	6	7		14.5	1.40081	10	6
10.5	0.625946	6	10		14.75	1.458971	10	8

Table 9.1

Follow these easy steps to find your expected total interest savings.

STEP	ACTION
1	Find the column with your exact mortgage *AGE* and the *percentage* you want to prepay each month. If you don't find your exact mortgage age, go over to the *first* column that shows *a higher* mortgage *AGE than yours,* to locate an *approximate* factor.
2	Under that column, find the row starting with your interest rate, to locate an interest savings factor.
3	To get your total interest savings in dollars, multiply the interest savings factor you find at that location by your *original* mortgage balance. If you're using an *approximate* factor, your *actual* savings will be *MORE* than the approximate interest savings amount you calculate.
4	In the same row, read off how long your term will last. If you're using an *approximate* factor, you'll *actually* save *MORE* than the number of years and months shown in the row.

First Example

Say your *brand new* mortgage balance is $80,000 for 30 years at 10% and you want to prepay 5% of the monthly payment.

Use Table 9.1 above. First, go over to the column with the exact age of your mortgage that shows 5% prepayment. Next, look down the *rate* column to find the row starting with *10*. Find the interest savings factor in that row. Multiply interest savings factor *0.55297* by $80,000 to get your total interest savings of *$44,237.60*. You would also *SAVE 6* years and *5* months.

Second Example

It's the same mortgage of $80,000 for 30 years at 10%. You've had the mortgage for *three years* and you want to prepay 5% of the monthly payment.

Use the tables in *Appendix G*. First, go over to the column with the *next higher age* of your mortgage. In this case, it's the *5 Years Old* column. Next, find the row starting with *10*. Multiply *approximate* interest savings factor *0.338029* by $80,000 to get your *approximate* total interest savings of *$27,042.32*. Your actual savings would be *MORE* than that amount. You'd *save MORE than 4* years and *2* months.

Step 3

Get a new amortization schedule based on the new monthly payment

Once you've settled on an absolute minimum prepayment amount, your new monthly payment is also decided on. It's the sum of the contractual monthly payment that the lender expects and the minimal prepayment that you commit to.

Now, get an amortization schedule that features the new monthly payment, starting with the current loan balance.

Illustration

To illustrate, let's stay with your mortgage of $80,000 at 10% for 30 years. The contractual monthly payment is $702.06. You decided to prepay $35 permanently.

> So, your new *base* monthly payment is **$737.06** (*$702.06 plus $35*).

You get a new amortization schedule based on the new regular monthly payment of **$737.06**. Here are the first seven and last five periods.

Period	Payment	Interest	Principal	Balance
1	$737.06	$666.67	$70.39	$79,929.61
2	$737.06	$666.08	$70.98	$79,858.63
3	$737.06	$665.49	$71.57	$79,787.05
4	$737.06	$664.89	$72.17	$79,714.88
5	$737.06	$664.29	$72.77	$79,642.11
6	$737.06	$663.68	$73.38	$79,568.74
7	$737.06	$663.07	$73.99	$79,494.75
⋮				
279	$737.06	$29.96	$707.10	$2,887.83
280	$737.06	$24.07	$713.00	$2,174.83
281	$737.06	$18.12	$718.94	$1,455.90
282	$737.06	$12.13	$724.93	$730.97
283	$737.06	$6.09	$730.97	$0.00

Figure 9.1

The Three Monthly Action Steps

Perform the first two steps *only* when you're making an **extra** prepayment ON TOP of the new base prepayment. When a good amount of cash comes your way, like a bonus or a tax refund, feel free to use the money to make larger prepayments *in synch* with your amortization schedule.

When cash wears thin, skip the first two steps. Just jump to Step 3, and stay at normal "cruising" speed *with the minimal* base prepayment.

Step 1   *Decide how much EXTRA to prepay*

Regardless how much extra money you have in your hands, *use only as much as will cover **EXACTLY** the principal portion in one or more periods taken together in a row.* That's how to keep the *extra* prepayment **in synch** with the *new* amortization schedule.

Illustration

Let's say the current period due is Period 4. That means you could apply prepayment money starting with the principal in Period 5. Referring to this extract from Figure 9.1, notice that the scheduled principal in Period 5 is **$72.77**.

Period	Payment	Interest	Principal	Balance
4	$737.06	$664.89	$72.17	$79,714.88
5	$737.06	$664.29	**$72.77**	$79,642.11
6	$737.06	$663.68	$73.38	$79,568.74

Suppose you have an extra $95 cash money to play with. You only have enough money to cover Period 5. So, take $72.77 from the available cash and add that to your base monthly payment of $737.06. Spend or, better still, *save* the remaining $22.23 as you like.

Your total monthly payment for Period 4 is now ***$809.83*** ($737.06 *plus* $72.77).

Step 2

Determine your EXTRA savings in interest and time

You should *always* make these *extra* prepayments *in synch* with the amortization schedule. If you do that, you will always eliminate the *whole* scheduled interest payment associated with each period you prepay. You will also save *one month* for *each* prepaid period.

Illustration

With the Extra prepayment of $72.77 in Period 4, you cut out $664.29 in interest and *shortened the loan term by one month.*

Extra Prepayment	**$72.77**	*Extra Interest Savings*	**$664.29**	*Extra Time Savings*	**One Month**

You can, of course, continue to use the same amortization schedule. Just cross out the "old" Period 5 values. Figure **9.2** shows comparative amortization schedules. Notice in that, starting at *Period 5,* all remaining periods moved up by one *as a result of the **extra** prepayment in Period 4.*

	Amortization WITHOUT **extra** prepayment in Period 4				Amortization WITH **extra** prepayment in Period 4			
Period	Payment	Interest	Principal	Balance	Payment	Interest	Principal	Balance
1	$737.06	$666.67	$70.39	$79,929.61	$737.06	$666.67	$70.39	$79,929.61
2	$737.06	$666.08	$70.98	$79,858.63	$737.06	$666.08	$70.98	$79,858.63
3	$737.06	$665.49	$71.57	$79,787.05	$737.06	$665.49	$71.57	$79,787.05
4	$737.06	$664.89	$72.17	$79,714.88	*$809.83*	$664.89	*$144.94*	$79,642.11
5	$737.06	$664.29	$72.77	$79,642.11	$737.06	*$663.68*	*$73.38*	*$79,568.74*
6	$737.06	$663.68	$73.38	$79,568.74	$737.06	*$663.07*	*$73.99*	*$79,494.75*
7	$737.06	$663.07	$73.99	$79,494.75	$737.06	*$662.46*	*$74.60*	*$79,420.15*
8	$737.06	$662.46	$74.60	$79,420.17	$737.06	*$661.83*	*$75.23*	*$79,344.92*
9	$737.06	$661.83	$75.22	$79,344.95	$737.06	*$661.21*	*$75.85*	*$79,269.07*
10	$737.06	$661.21	$75.85	$79,269.10	$737.06	*$660.58*	*$76.49*	*$79,192.58*
280	$737.06	$24.07	$713.00	$2,174.83	$737.06	*$18.12*	*$718.94*	*$1,455.90*
281	$737.06	$18.12	$718.94	$1,455.90	$737.06	*$12.13*	*$724.93*	*$730.97*
282	$737.06	$12.13	$724.93	$730.97	$737.06	*$6.09*	*$730.97*	*$0.00*
283	$737.06	$6.09	$730.97	$0.00				

Figure 9.2

Step 3

Send in the monthly payment

If you do make an EXTRA prepayment, send in the new *base* monthly payment ***plus the extra prepayment.***   But, if you do not use extra cash, just send in the new *base* monthly payment.   Consult *Chapter Fifteen* for guidelines on sending in the prepayment check.

For example, as in the illustration where you send an Extra prepayment, the monthly payment you send in for Period 4 would be *$809.83*.   But, if you had decided not to use the extra cash, you would just send in *$737.06*.

Fixed Prepayment Results

Mortgage Amount: *$80,000* Term: *30 Years* Interest Rate: *10%*

Normal Term
No prepayments

Interest Savings: **$0**
Duration: 30 Years
Time Savings: **None**
Monthly Payment: **$702.06**

Accelerated Term
Fixed Prepayment $50/month

Interest Savings: **$55,586.01**
Duration: *21 Years 11 Months*
Time Savings: **8 Years 1 Month**
Monthly Payment: **$752.06**

Year	Payment	Interest	Principal	Balance	Payment	Interest	Principal	Balance
1	$8,424.69	$7,979.98	$444.70	$79,555.30	$9,024.72	$7,951.70	$1,073.02	$78,926.98
2	$8,424.69	$7,933.42	$491.27	$79,064.03	$9,024.72	$7,839.35	$1,185.37	$77,741.61
3	$8,424.69	$7,881.98	$542.71	$78,521.32	$9,024.72	$7,715.23	$1,309.49	$76,432.12
4	$8,424.69	$7,825.15	$599.54	$77,921.78	$9,024.72	$7,578.10	$1,446.62	$74,985.50
5	$8,424.69	$7,762.37	$662.32	$77,259.46	$9,024.72	$7,426.62	$1,598.10	$73,387.40
6	$8,424.69	$7,693.01	$731.67	$76,527.78	$9,024.72	$7,259.28	$1,765.44	$71,621.96
7	$8,424.69	$7,616.40	$808.29	$75,719.49	$9,024.72	$7,074.42	$1,950.30	$69,671.66
8	$8,424.69	$7,531.76	$892.93	$74,826.57	$9,024.72	$6,870.19	$2,154.53	$67,517.13
9	$8,424.69	$7,438.26	$986.43	$73,840.14	$9,024.72	$6,644.57	$2,380.15	$65,136.98
10	$8,424.69	$7,334.97	$1,089.72	$72,750.42	$9,024.72	$6,395.35	$2,629.37	$62,507.61
11	$8,424.69	$7,220.86	$1,203.83	$71,546.59	$9,024.72	$6,120.02	$2,904.70	$59,602.91
12	$8,424.69	$7,094.80	$1,329.89	$70,216.70	$9,024.72	$5,815.85	$3,208.87	$56,394.04
13	$8,424.69	$6,955.54	$1,469.14	$68,747.56	$9,024.72	$5,479.87	$3,544.85	$52,849.19
14	$8,424.69	$6,801.71	$1,622.98	$67,124.58	$9,024.72	$5,108.65	$3,916.07	$48,933.12
15	$8,424.69	$6,631.76	$1,792.93	$65,331.65	$9,024.72	$4,698.61	$4,326.11	$44,607.01
16	$8,424.69	$6,444.02	$1,980.67	$63,350.98	$9,024.72	$4,245.62	$4,779.10	$39,827.91
17	$8,424.69	$6,236.61	$2,188.07	$61,162.91	$9,024.72	$3,745.18	$5,279.54	$34,548.37
18	$8,424.69	$6,007.49	$2,417.19	$58,745.71	$9,024.72	$3,192.33	$5,832.39	$28,715.98
19	$8,424.69	$5,754.38	$2,670.30	$56,075.41	$9,024.72	$2,581.60	$6,443.12	$22,272.86
20	$8,424.69	$5,474.77	$2,949.92	$53,125.49	$9,024.72	$1,906.93	$7,117.79	$15,155.07
21	$8,424.69	$5,165.87	$3,258.82	$49,866.67	$9,024.72	$1,161.59	$7,863.13	$7,291.94
22	$8,424.69	$4,824.63	$3,600.06	$46,266.62	*$7,635.48*	*$343.54*	*$7,291.94*	*$0.00*
23	$8,424.69	$4,447.66	$3,977.03	$42,289.59	$0.00	$0.00	$0.00	$0.00
24	$8,424.69	$4,031.21	$4,393.48	$37,896.11	$0.00	$0.00	$0.00	$0.00
25	$8,424.69	$3,571.16	$4,853.53	$33,042.58	$0.00	$0.00	$0.00	$0.00
26	$8,424.69	$3,062.93	$5,361.76	$27,680.83	$0.00	$0.00	$0.00	$0.00
27	$8,424.69	$2,501.48	$5,923.20	$21,757.62	$0.00	$0.00	$0.00	$0.00
28	$8,424.69	$1,881.25	$6,543.44	$15,214.18	$0.00	$0.00	$0.00	$0.00
29	$8,424.69	$1,196.06	$7,228.62	$7,985.56	$0.00	$0.00	$0.00	$0.00
30	$8,424.69	$439.13	$7,985.56	$0.00	$0.00	$0.00	$0.00	$0.00
Totals	$252,740.61	$172,740.61	$80,000.00		$197,154.60	$117,154.60	$80,000.00	

Table 9.2

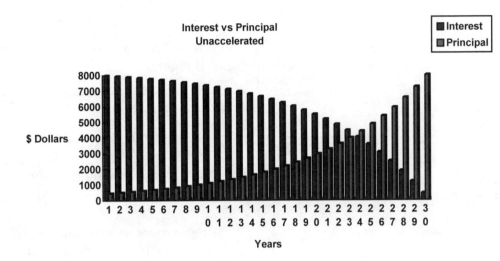

Figure 9.3

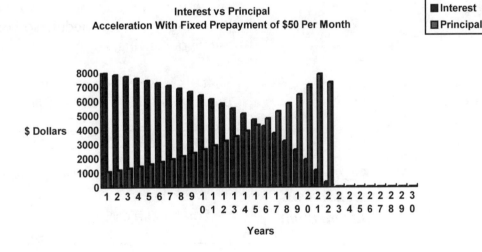

Figure 9.4

KEY POINTS OF THE FIXED PREPAYMENT METHOD

Applies to:	Any type of mortgage

Focus:	Prepays a fixed amount of principal according to your budget.

Advantages:	√ You determine the exact amount to prepay. √ You can tell exactly how much your prepayments save in interest and time. √ Prepayment amount may vary up or down, but you can keep it constant for all periods. √ You can stop and resume *extra* prepayments at will.

Disadvantage:	Every time you make a random prepayment *out of synch* with the current amortization schedule, you have to get a new schedule so you can continue to track your savings. That is also necessary if you skip any *base prepayments* built into your amortization schedule.

Resources you need to work this method:	⇒ Amortization schedule for your mortgage ⇒ Worksheet ⇒ Some *extra* cash

Other methods to combine with this one:	• Increasing Prepayment method • Extra-annual payment or *pseudo bi-weekly* method

Chapter Ten

THE TERM-BASED PREPAYMENT METHOD

⇒ *You choose the term*
⇒ *It's like automatically refinancing for fewer years **at the same interest rate***
⇒ *It's better than a 15-year mortgage: **you can adjust the term as you go***
⇒ *A general **roadmap** for the **term-based prepayment** method*
⇒ *How to do it in **step-by-step** detail*
⇒ *Results from using the **term-based** prepayment method*

This chapter will show you how to calculate the exact prepayment amount you would need to bring your mortgage to conclude within a term of years you choose. When you have the ability to make the required prepayment, the term-based prepayment method puts you completely in the driver's seat. That is usually possible after your salary has gone up a bit, or after you've eliminated other debts.

> **The TERM-BASED prepayment method is actually a special application of the FIXED prepayment method.**

You choose the term of years

(shorter than the original term)

*With the **term-based** method, **you can choose the specific term of years in which to eliminate your mortgage.*** If you decide to cancel your 30-year mortgage in a much shorter term, such as twelve, seven, or five years, *this method will do it for you.* Possibly, some significant event in your future could prompt you to end your mortgage *a **given** number of years **earlier** than scheduled. Well, you're about to learn how to do just that.

Consider these two examples, involving a 30-year mortgage at 10% with a monthly payment of $702.06. *After you've seen the step-by-step procedure later on, come back to these and try to derive the answers on your own. Do that before you look at the answers at the end of the chapter.*

First Example

You have 25 years and a balance of $77,259.46 left on your mortgage. But, you plan to retire within 15 years. Naturally, you wish to cancel the mortgage within the SAME time frame, *while you have a paycheck.* **How much should you prepay, <u>starting now</u>, in order to pay off the balance in 15 years?**

Second Example

You've had your mortgage for 11 years, with 19 years to go. The balance is $71,546.59. It turns out that your estimated retirement is about *19* years down the road. You'd like to build a nice size nest egg by the time you retire. *Something you can use to help pay your real estate taxes,* after you stop working.

You figure that, rather than feed money to the bank, if you were to *invest* $702.06 *every month* at 6% for 10 years before you retire, you'd have a tidy sum of *$115,053.13*. When you invest that sum at only 6% *tax-free*, you would get a return of *$7,096.23* per year, *every* year.

Following this thinking, you plan to retire the mortgage in 9 years, so you can continue to make the $702.06 monthly payment *TO YOURSELF* for 10 years. **What prepayment do you need to make, <u>starting now</u>, to knock off the mortgage in 9 years?**

UNDERSTANDING THIS METHOD

Given an interest rate and a mortgage balance, the required monthly payment to amortize the loan depends on the term of years. The longer the term, the smaller the payment. Conversely, the shorter the term, the larger the payment.

You can terminate your mortgage within a precise number of years of *your choice,* earlier than the remaining number of years on the amortization schedule. You can do this regardless how many years you've had the loan and no matter how many years you have left on the loan.

*It's like **automatically** refinancing for fewer years at the same rate of interest*

Once you know the remaining number of years and the balance due, you can find the exact monthly prepayment required to retire the mortgage in a shorter term of years that you choose. *It's like refinancing the balance for **fewer** years at the **same** interest rate.* Certainly, the monthly payment is a bit higher. But, you wind up saving time and a big bundle of interest money.

You'll find the required monthly payment either *in published mortgage tables booklets* or by *calculating it yourself.* The calculation is easy, thanks to special tables and procedures you'll find here.

You can combine the other methods with this one

As it's only a more focused version of the *Fixed Prepayment* method, you can combine the *Term-Based* method with the *Increasing Prepayment* and the *Extra-Annual Payment* methods in the same ways. But, it doesn't stop there.

You can even combine the *Fixed Prepayment* method itself on top of the *Term-Based.* That's easy to do. When you have *more* surplus cash, just throw in additional fixed prepayments on top of the *base* prepayments.

The regular **base** prepayment you need to make is just the *difference* between the monthly payment for your chosen term and the monthly payment you make now.

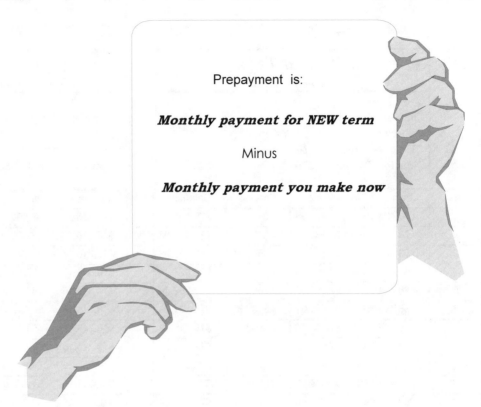

Prepayment is:

Monthly payment for NEW term

Minus

Monthly payment you make now

What About a 15-year Mortgage?

You may have heard some hype about taking a 15-year mortgage instead of a 30-year mortgage. True, a 15-year mortgage saves a good deal of interest, in addition to ending the mortgage in half the time. But, *you should consider the downside seriously.* Aside from the fact that it is harder to get because of the higher monthly payment, there are reasons to think twice even if you can afford it.

The **Down** Side

With a 15-year mortgage, you are obligated to pay the higher monthly payment regularly to the bank. In fact, you are stuck with that payment amount for 15 years, regardless what happens. People have been known to lose their homes, when sudden downturns, such as layoffs, make it unfeasible to keep up that level of payment. There's no flexibility.

A 30-year term is **BETTER** than a 15-year term

In contrast with the 15-year mortgage, a 30-year mortgage for the *same* balance has a *lower* required monthly payment. Using this method, *you can pay down a 30-year mortgage at a 15-year pace.* But here, you have the option to stop the extra payments for a while, should things ever turn sour economically for you. You can always resume with slightly higher prepayments later, when conditions improve. *It's totally up to you.*

Table 10.1 below illustrates the spectacular results you can get with the Term-Based Prepayment method, compared with a full-term schedule.

Term-based Prepayment Results

Mortgage Amount: *$80,000*   Term: *30 Years*   Interest Rate: *10%*

Normal Term
No prepayments

Interest Savings: **$0**
Duration: 30 Years
Time Savings: **None**
Monthly Payment: **$702.06**

Accelerated Term
Term-based Prepayment: $157.62

Interest Savings: **$97,996.39**
Duration: *15 Years*
Time Savings: **15 Years**
Monthly Payment: **$859.68**

Year	Payment	Interest	Principal	Balance	Payment	Interest	Principal	Balance
1	$8,424.69	$7,979.98	$444.70	$79,555.30	$10,316.16	$7,890.85	$2,425.31	$77,574.69
2	$8,424.69	$7,933.42	$491.27	$79,064.03	$10,316.16	$7,636.89	$2,679.27	$74,895.42
3	$8,424.69	$7,881.98	$542.71	$78,521.32	$10,316.16	$7,356.33	$2,959.83	$71,935.59
4	$8,424.69	$7,825.15	$599.54	$77,921.78	$10,316.16	$7,046.38	$3,269.78	$68,665.81
5	$8,424.69	$7,762.37	$662.32	$77,259.46	$10,316.16	$6,704.00	$3,612.16	$65,053.65
6	$8,424.69	$7,693.01	$731.67	$76,527.78	$10,316.16	$6,325.77	$3,990.39	$61,063.26
7	$8,424.69	$7,616.40	$808.29	$75,719.49	$10,316.16	$5,907.92	$4,408.24	$56,655.02
8	$8,424.69	$7,531.76	$892.93	$74,826.57	$10,316.16	$5,446.32	$4,869.84	$51,785.18
9	$8,424.69	$7,438.26	$986.43	$73,840.14	$10,316.16	$4,936.38	$5,379.78	$46,405.40
10	$8,424.69	$7,334.97	$1,089.72	$72,750.42	$10,316.16	$4,373.05	$5,943.11	$40,462.29
11	$8,424.69	$7,220.86	$1,203.83	$71,546.59	$10,316.16	$3,750.71	$6,565.45	$33,896.84
12	$8,424.69	$7,094.80	$1,329.89	$70,216.70	$10,316.16	$3,063.22	$7,252.94	$26,643.90
13	$8,424.69	$6,955.54	$1,469.14	$68,747.56	$10,316.16	$2,303.75	$8,012.41	$18,631.49
14	$8,424.69	$6,801.71	$1,622.98	$67,124.58	$10,316.16	$1,464.75	$8,851.41	$9,780.08
15	$8,424.69	$6,631.76	$1,792.93	$65,331.65	*$10,317.98*	*$537.90*	*$9,780.08*	*$0.00*
16	$8,424.69	$6,444.02	$1,980.67	$63,350.98	**$0.00**	**$0.00**	**$0.00**	**$0.00**
17	$8,424.69	$6,236.61	$2,188.07	$61,162.91	**$0.00**	**$0.00**	**$0.00**	**$0.00**
18	$8,424.69	$6,007.49	$2,417.19	$58,745.71	**$0.00**	**$0.00**	**$0.00**	**$0.00**
19	$8,424.69	$5,754.38	$2,670.30	$56,075.41	**$0.00**	**$0.00**	**$0.00**	**$0.00**
20	$8,424.69	$5,474.77	$2,949.92	$53,125.49	**$0.00**	**$0.00**	**$0.00**	**$0.00**
21	$8,424.69	$5,165.87	$3,258.82	$49,866.67	**$0.00**	**$0.00**	**$0.00**	**$0.00**
22	$8,424.69	$4,824.63	$3,600.06	$46,266.62	**$0.00**	**$0.00**	**$0.00**	**$0.00**
23	$8,424.69	$4,447.66	$3,977.03	$42,289.59	**$0.00**	**$0.00**	**$0.00**	**$0.00**
24	$8,424.69	$4,031.21	$4,393.48	$37,896.11	**$0.00**	**$0.00**	**$0.00**	**$0.00**
25	$8,424.69	$3,571.16	$4,853.53	$33,042.58	**$0.00**	**$0.00**	**$0.00**	**$0.00**
26	$8,424.69	$3,062.93	$5,361.76	$27,680.83	**$0.00**	**$0.00**	**$0.00**	**$0.00**
27	$8,424.69	$2,501.48	$5,923.20	$21,757.62	**$0.00**	**$0.00**	**$0.00**	**$0.00**
28	$8,424.69	$1,881.25	$6,543.44	$15,214.18	**$0.00**	**$0.00**	**$0.00**	**$0.00**
29	$8,424.69	$1,196.06	$7,228.62	$7,985.56	**$0.00**	**$0.00**	**$0.00**	**$0.00**
30	$8,424.69	$439.13	$7,985.56	$0.00	**$0.00**	**$0.00**	**$0.00**	**$0.00**
Totals	$252,740.61	$172,740.61	$80,000.00		$154,744.22	**$74,744.22**	$80,000.00	

Table 10.1

Important Tip! | Rather than getting a 15-year mortgage from your lender, *you are better off with a 30-year mortgage.* You can then use the *Term-Based Prepayment* method to virtually make the term what you wish for it to be. At your own choice and leisure, *you may make your mortgage last 15 years, or even less,* depending on your pocketbook.

You may recall that the *Increasing Prepayment* method also terminates a 30-year mortgage in 15 years. That fact brings an interesting question to mind.

When used at a 15-year pace, how does the *Term-Based Prepayment method* compare with *the Increasing Prepayment method?*

Since both methods lead to a closure in 15 years, the differences concerns *interest savings* and *your particular financial situation.*

Increasing Prepayment Method Takes Lower Budget To Start

On the one hand, the *Increasing Prepayment* method accommodates people starting out a mortgage on a low budget. The smaller prepayments at the beginning of the mortgage cut less of the large principal balance, and naturally make smaller dents in the large initial monthly interest payments. *But, those small initial prepayments may be more affordable.*

Term-Based Prepayment Method Gives Larger Interest Savings

On the other hand, you may correctly conclude that *the Term-Based Prepayment method wins out because it saves more interest.* That's not surprising, when you realize that the steady prepayments are larger right at the beginning. So, right up front, where monthly interest payments tend to be very large, the larger prepayments knock off more of the principal. Consequently, they reduce more of the large monthly interest payments.

Also, It Lets You Adjust The Term As You Go

You can change the targeted term duration at any time, as you go. For instance, after prepaying at a 15-year pace, if you decide to shorten the remaining term some more, just increase the prepayment accordingly. You can do this whenever you materialize extra cash that you can commit to the job. *See **Table 10.2** below for a direct comparison of the two methods.*

The *General Roadmap* shows you how to determine the precise prepayment that will cut any given balance within the time frame you desire. *Figures* **10.2** and **10.3**, at the end of the chapter, depict graphically how the *Term-based* amortization at a 15-year pace compares with the unaccelerated amortization.

Term-based Prepayment Results
Compared With Increasing Prepayment Method

Mortgage Amount: $80,000   Term: 30 Years   Interest Rate: 10%

Accelerated Term		*Accelerated Term*	
Increasing Prepayments		*Term-based Prepayment: $157.62*	
Interest Savings:	**$86,316.50**	Interest Savings:	**$97,996.39**
Duration:	15 Years	Duration:	15 Years
Time Savings:	**15 Years**	Time Savings:	**15 Years**
Monthly Payment:	**Increasing**	Monthly Payment:	**$859.68**

Year	Payment	Interest	Principal	Balance	Payment	Interest	Principal	Balance
1	$8,894.61	$7,958.64	$935.97	$79,064.03	$10,316.16	$7,890.85	$2,425.31	$77,574.69
2	$8,998.18	$7,855.93	$1,142.25	$77,921.78	$10,316.16	$7,636.89	$2,679.27	$74,895.42
3	$9,124.58	$7,730.58	$1,393.99	$76,527.78	$10,316.16	$7,356.33	$2,959.83	$71,935.59
4	$9,278.83	$7,577.61	$1,701.22	$74,826.57	$10,316.16	$7,046.38	$3,269.78	$68,665.81
5	$9,467.07	$7,390.92	$2,076.15	$72,750.42	$10,316.16	$6,704.00	$3,612.16	$65,053.65
6	$9,696.80	$7,163.09	$2,533.71	$70,216.70	$10,316.16	$6,325.77	$3,990.39	$61,063.26
7	$9,977.16	$6,885.04	$3,092.12	$67,124.58	$10,316.16	$5,907.92	$4,408.24	$56,655.02
8	$10,319.32	$6,545.72	$3,773.60	$63,350.98	$10,316.16	$5,446.32	$4,869.84	$51,785.18
9	$10,736.87	$6,131.61	$4,605.27	$58,745.71	$10,316.16	$4,936.38	$5,379.78	$46,405.40
10	$11,255.00	$5,626.20	$5,628.80	$53,116.92	$10,316.16	$4,373.05	$5,943.11	$40,462.29
11	$11,925.99	$5,005.97	$6,920.02	$46,196.90	$10,316.16	$3,750.71	$6,565.45	$33,896.84
12	$12,697.64	$4,246.31	$8,451.33	$37,745.56	$10,316.16	$3,063.22	$7,252.94	$26,643.90
13	$13,639.36	$3,318.57	$10,320.79	$27,424.77	$10,316.16	$2,303.75	$8,012.41	$18,631.49
14	$14,788.63	$2,185.66	$12,602.97	$14,821.80	$10,316.16	$1,464.75	$8,851.41	$9,780.08
15	$15,624.07	$802.27	$14,821.80	$0.00	*$10,317.98*	*$537.90*	*$9,780.08*	*$0.00*
16	$0.00	$0.00	$0.00	$0.00	$0.00	$0.00	$0.00	$0.00
17	$0.00	$0.00	$0.00	$0.00	$0.00	$0.00	$0.00	$0.00
18	$0.00	$0.00	$0.00	$0.00	$0.00	$0.00	$0.00	$0.00
19	$0.00	$0.00	$0.00	$0.00	$0.00	$0.00	$0.00	$0.00
20	$0.00	$0.00	$0.00	$0.00	$0.00	$0.00	$0.00	$0.00
21	$0.00	$0.00	$0.00	$0.00	$0.00	$0.00	$0.00	$0.00
22	$0.00	$0.00	$0.00	$0.00	$0.00	$0.00	$0.00	$0.00
23	$0.00	$0.00	$0.00	$0.00	$0.00	$0.00	$0.00	$0.00
24	$0.00	$0.00	$0.00	$0.00	$0.00	$0.00	$0.00	$0.00
25	$0.00	$0.00	$0.00	$0.00	$0.00	$0.00	$0.00	$0.00
26	$0.00	$0.00	$0.00	$0.00	$0.00	$0.00	$0.00	$0.00
27	$0.00	$0.00	$0.00	$0.00	$0.00	$0.00	$0.00	$0.00
28	$0.00	$0.00	$0.00	$0.00	$0.00	$0.00	$0.00	$0.00
29	$0.00	$0.00	$0.00	$0.00	$0.00	$0.00	$0.00	$0.00
30	$0.00	$0.00	$0.00	$0.00	$0.00	$0.00	$0.00	$0.00
Totals	$166,424.11	$86,424.11	$80,000.00		$154,744.22	*$74,744.22*	$80,000.00	

Table 10.2

A General Roadmap
For The TERM-BASED PREPAYMENT Method

Here is how to get this method working for you.

Prepare for it by taking these two steps NOW

STEP	ACTION
1	*Decide how many years you want the mortgage to last (or how many years you want to cut from the term)*
2	*Quickly determine BOTH the PREPAYMENT required to cancel the mortgage within the desired term* **and** *the TOTAL interest savings you get with the prepayment*

 Do this step ONCE a month until you pay off the mortgage

STEP	ACTION
1	*Send in the ADJUSTED monthly payment*

HOW TO DO IT IN *step-by-step* DETAIL

The Two Preparation Steps

Perform these preparation steps once, at the time you decide to prepay using the Term-based prepayment method.

Step 1

Decide how MANY years you want the mortgage to last (or how many years you want to cut from the term)

Your decision must be based on your personal situation. The reason can just be your desire to be debt-free by a certain point in time. Or, it could emerge out of a necessity to better synchronize events in your life.

If your mortgage is now scheduled to end before you retire, you should still try to cancel it as early as you can. Project your future in your mind's eye. Get a sense of different possible events that could occur, at some future point, to compete with your mortgage holder for your dollars.

You must determine exactly how many years remain on the current term as of now. Most likely, you have a pretty clear idea how many years you've had the mortgage. But, as you might have made some form of prepayment in the past, the remaining years may not be what you think. In any event, it is best to get this exact information from the bank.

Call your lender to get accurate figures. Find out, as per the bank's records, <u>how many years</u> are still ahead of you. While you're at it, you also need to confirm the exact *remaining* mortgage balance.

Once you have the correct information, decide on a specific number of years. *Be certain you know **why** you settle on a particular time frame.*

Step 2

Quickly determine BOTH the PREPAYMENT required to cancel the mortgage within the desired term and the TOTAL interest savings

Using the special interest savings table in *Appendix H,* you can determine quickly how much total interest you would save with the *Term-Based Prepayment* method. Table 10.3 below shows a portion of the table:

TERM-BASED PREPAYMENT METHOD
30-YEAR FIXED-RATE MORTGAGE SAVINGS TABLE

Refer to this table to quickly figure out your interest savings
when you use the *Term-based Prepayment* method

If your Mortgage is	Brand New	
and you want to CUT the term by	1 year	
Find your Interest rate below (%)	Then prepay by this factor each month	To get this interest savings factor
6.5	0.011304	0.050985
6.75	0.010772	0.053517
7	0.010262	0.056076
7.25	0.009773	0.05866
7.5	0.009304	0.061266
7.75	0.008855	0.063894
8	0.008424	0.066541
8.25	0.008012	0.069206
8.5	0.007617	0.071887
8.75	0.00724	0.074583
9	0.006879	0.077293
9.25	0.006534	0.080014
9.5	0.006205	0.082747
9.75	0.00589	0.085488
10	0.00559	0.088237
10.25	0.005303	0.090994
10.5	0.00503	0.093756

If your Mortgage is	Brand New	
and you want to CUT the term by	1 year	
Find your Interest rate below (%)	Then prepay by this factor each month	To get this interest savings factor
10.75	0.00477	0.096523
11	0.004522	0.099294
11.25	0.004285	0.102067
11.5	0.00406	0.104843
11.75	0.003846	0.10762
12	0.003642	0.110397
12.25	0.003448	0.113173
12.5	0.003264	0.115949
12.75	0.003089	0.118723
13	0.002922	0.121495
13.25	0.002764	0.124265
13.5	0.002614	0.127031
13.75	0.002471	0.129794
14	0.002336	0.132553
14.25	0.002207	0.135308
14.5	0.002086	0.138058
14.75	0.00197	0.140804

Table 10.3

Follow these easy steps to find your expected total interest savings.

STEP	ACTION
1	Find the column with your exact mortgage **AGE** and the *number of years* by which you want to CUT the term. **If you don't find your exact mortgage age, use the *next higher* mortgage age. The factors you find will give you approximate results.**
2	Under that column, find the row starting with your interest rate, to locate a *prepayment* factor.
3	To get your *required monthly prepayment* in dollars, multiply the *prepayment* factor you find at that location by your **original** monthly payment (**not including tax and insurance**).
4	Next in the same row, locate the interest savings factor.
5	To get your total interest savings in dollars, multiply the interest savings factor you find at that location by your **original** mortgage balance.

Example

Use Table 10.3 above. Say your *brand new* mortgage balance is $80,000 for 30 years at 10% with a monthly payment of $702.06. Say also that you want to CUT the term by *1* year.

First, go over to the column with the *exact* age of your mortgage that specifies a *1-year CUT*. Next, look down the *rate* column to find the row that starts with *10*. Find the *prepayment* factor right next to the interest rate. Multiply *prepayment* factor *0.00559* by $702.06 to get your *required* prepayment of *$3.92*.

Move to the right to find the interest savings factor in that row. Multiply interest savings factor *0.088237* by $80,000 to get your total interest savings of *$7,058.96*.

Second Example

It's the same mortgage of $80,000 for 30 years at 10%, but you've had it for *eight years*. Say also that you want to CUT the term by *15* years. Use a table in *Appendix H.*

First, go over to the column with the *next higher age* of your mortgage that specifies a *15-year CUT*. In this case, it's a *10 Years Old* column. Next, find the row starting with interest rate *10*. Find the *prepayment* factor right next to the interest rate. Multiply *prepayment* factor *1.201717* by $702.06 to get your *necessary* **prepayment** of *$843.67*.

Move to the right to find the interest savings factor in that row. Multiply interest savings factor *0.946873* by $80,000 to get your total interest savings of *$75,749.84*. If you start prepaying now, you will save MORE than that amount and end the mortgage in LESS than *FIVE* years from the point the mortgage is 10 years old.

At this point, you should have the new term you want, the current balance, and the prepayment required to terminate the mortgage within the new term. But, if for some reason you can't determine the required prepayment with the special table, you can still calculate it easily.

To calculate the required **prepayment**, first you must determine the *necessary new monthly payment* required to amortize the balance within the new time frame. Then, you just need to subtract the current monthly payment *(without tax and insurance components)* from the *new* monthly payment. With that information, you can follow the procedure in *Appendix E* to manually figure out the expected *total* interest savings.

There are three different ways to go about getting the ***necessary new monthly payment***.

You can:

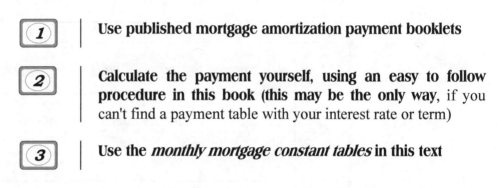

1 | **Use published mortgage amortization payment booklets**

2 | **Calculate the payment yourself, using an easy to follow procedure in this book (this may be the only way,** if you can't find a payment table with your interest rate or term)

3 | Use the ***monthly mortgage constant tables*** in this text

The first approach is fairly simple. If you have a mortgage payment booklet, you can sometimes find a monthly payment just by doing a lookup and a simple addition. But, usually you have to do a little interpolating. That involves some arithmetic. You'll find the way to go about it in *Appendix B*.

The second way calls for a little calculation. But, you don't need any booklets. A very convenient procedure in *Appendix C* takes you painlessly through each step. This approach might turn out to be the only way left for you to use, if your particular interest rate or mortgage is not in any of the tables. So, a calculator will come in handy.

At your leisure, later, just refer to Appendices B and C for more details on those two procedures.

The third approach is the easiest. It is very straightforward. You only need to look up a special number called a *mortgage constant,* then do is a simple multiplication. You'll find a complete table of mortgage constants in *Appendix A.*

Here's the simple way to do it, using mortgage constants.

Using Mortgage Constants To Find The Monthly Payment Required For The New Term

You can find a required monthly payment quickly and easily, using mortgage constants. You don't need mortgage payment books, thanks to the monthly mortgage constant table in *Appendix A*. All you have to do is to multiply your remaining balance by the *mortgage constant* that corresponds to your desired term at the given interest rate.

Refer to the partial table below, Figure 10.1, for the discussion in this section. But, see Appendix A for the complete table of monthly mortgage constants.

Use this procedure with the Monthly Mortgage Constant table to derive your own monthly payment.

HOW TO FIND MONTHLY PAYMENT USING MORTGAGE CONSTANT TABLES

STEP	ACTION
1	*Look across the top row and find the term of years you desire.*
2	*Go down the column under the desired term to locate the monthly mortgage constant that's in the same row as your interest rate.*
3	*Multiply your **remaining balance** by the **mortgage constant** to get the monthly payment.*

Terms (years)	8	9	10	11	12	13	14
Rates (%)							
7	0.013634	0.012506	0.011611	0.010884	0.010284	0.009781	0.009354
7.5	0.013884	0.012761	0.01187	0.011148	0.010552	0.010054	0.009631
8	0.014137	0.013019	0.012133	0.011415	0.010825	0.010331	0.009913
8.5	0.014392	0.013279	0.012399	0.011686	0.011101	0.010612	0.010199
9	0.01465	0.013543	0.012668	0.011961	0.01138	0.010897	0.010489
9.5	0.014911	0.013809	0.01294	0.012239	0.011664	0.011186	0.010784
10	0.015174	0.014079	0.013215	0.01252	0.011951	0.011478	0.011082

Figure 10.1

Practice Problem

You've had your 30-year mortgage for 10 years. The interest rate is 10%. Your scheduled monthly payment is $702.06. The bank confirmed that your remaining balance is $72,750.42. There are 20 years to go. But, you decide to terminate the mortgage in 12 years. *What monthly prepayment will amortize the loan within 12 years?*

Solution

Referring back to Figure 10.1, go through these three steps to get the necessary monthly payment for this situation.

HOW TO FIND MONTHLY PAYMENT USING MORTGAGE CONSTANT TABLES

STEP	ACTION
1	**Look across the top row and find the term of years you desire.** *Example: Given the data from the problem above, the term of 12 years is in the fifth column.*
2	**Go down the column under the desired term to locate the monthly mortgage constant that's in the same row as your interest rate.** *Example: The constant under column **12** and on the same row as interest rate **10** is **0.011951***
3	**Multiply your remaining balance by the constant to get the monthly payment.** *Example: The balance $72,750.42 multiplied by the constant 0.011951 gives a necessary monthly payment of **$869.44**.*

The necessary monthly payment is $869.44. Naturally, the required *prepayment* is the *difference* between the necessary *monthly payment* and the *current* monthly payment. So, in this problem, the required prepayment is ***$167.38***.

Check-up

Now, see if you can get the answers for the two examples at the beginning of this chapter. Compare your answers to those at the bottom of the next page.

The One Monthly Action Step

Send in the ADJUSTED monthly payment

The adjusted monthly payment is the sum of the required *prepayment* and the normal monthly payment you make now.

> *Adjusted Monthly Payment* = *Current Monthly Payment* + *Required Prepayment*

That's actually the same as the *necessary monthly payment* you got from , the second preparation step above. Since you already have that figure, you really don't have to do this addition.

Follow the guidelines in *Chapter Fifteen* to send in the adjusted payment.

• • • • • •

Check-up Solutions

Here are the solutions to the two example situations presented at the beginning of this chapter. An original mortgage of $80,000 for 30 years at 10% with a *current monthly payment* of $702.06 is given for both cases.

To get the answers, you only need to find the appropriate *mortgage constant* for each situation and multiply it by the *given balance* to get the required monthly payment. Then, subtract the *current monthly payment* from the *required payment* to get the necessary **prepayment**.

Answers:

	Desired Duration (Years)	Mortgage Constant	Given Balance	Required Payment	*Necessary Prepayment*
First Example	15	0.011054	$77,259.46	$854.02	*$151.96*
Second Example	9	0.014079	$71,546.59	$1,007.30	*$305.34*

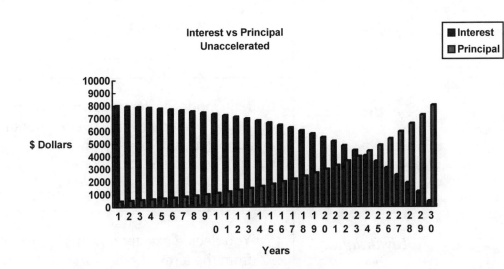

Figure 10.2

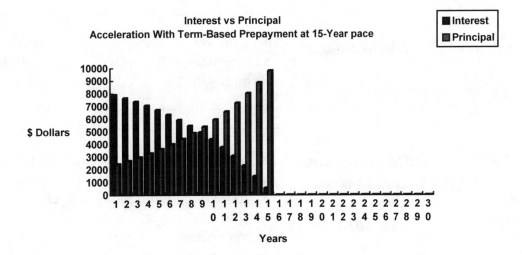

Figure 10.3

KEY POINTS OF THE TERM-BASED PREPAYMENT METHOD

Applies to:

> Any type of mortgage

Focus:

> Cutting mortgage term down to a specific shorter duration by prepaying every month the exact amount that will pay off the mortgage within the specific time frame you choose.

Advantages:

> √ You decide exactly how many years to eliminate from the term.
>
> √ You know the exact amount to prepay.
>
> √ Prepayment stays constant each period.

Disadvantage:

> If you have decided on *a particularly short* mortgage term, the prepayments might feel a bit stiff at the beginning.

Resources you need to work with this method:

> ⇒ Mortgage payment tables, calculator
> ⇒ *Current mortgage balance, interest rate, remaining number of years, current monthly payment*
> ⇒ Worksheet
> ⇒ Some *extra* cash

Other methods to combine with this one:

> • Increasing Prepayment method
> • Fixed Prepayment method
> • Extra-annual payment or *pseudo bi-weekly* method

Chapter Eleven

THE EXTRA ANNUAL PAYMENT METHOD

⇒ *How you mysteriously materialize a **WHOLE MONTH'S** payment as free EXTRA cash*
⇒ *The difference between true "bank" bi-weekly and **pseudo bi-weekly** mortgage*
⇒ *Why you don't need **extra** prepayment cash every month with this method*
⇒ *The BIG **extra** bonus*

When your budget doesn't seem to allow ANY extra cash that you can use for prepayment, does that mean you're condemned to repay *THREE* dollars for *every single* dollar you borrowed? When you don't have money, why should you repay back so much more than you borrowed?

How you mysteriously materialize a whole month's payment as FREE extra cash

A tight budget is the very situation that necessitates a remedy. You need to keep more of your hard-earned money, especially when you don't have that much. The *Extra Annual payment method* offers a painless way for you to accumulate extra cash to prepay with. Using this technique, *without feeling any pinch whatever,* you materialize at the end of the year an extra cash amount equal to a **whole month's** worth of mortgage payment. Then, you can apply this money completely to principal prepayment.

With this method, you make the regular monthly payment each of the twelve months of the year. But, in the process, you manage to accumulate a sum equal to a monthly payment amount. At the end of the year, *you then use this extra cash to make an additional payment FOR PRINCIPAL ONLY.*

At a 10% interest rate, when you apply *a full monthly* payment to cover only principal at the end of the year *every year,* starting with the first year, *you can shorten the duration of a 30-year mortgage down to **21 years and 4 months**.* The interest savings will also be **tremendous.**

A variation of this technique applies TWO prepayments during the year and achieves even *GREATER* savings. One prepayment occurs at mid-year to reduce principal by an amount *half* the size of a monthly payment. The other prepayment, also the size of half of a monthly payment, reduces the loan balance once again at the end of the year.

You can combine this method with any of the other three. In fact, because it doesn't require extra cash for prepayment, you should set up the *Extra Annual Payment* method as a routine measure. Then, whenever possible, use one of the other methods <u>on top</u> of it.

For instance, if you set a goal to cut six years from your mortgage term, you would be using the *term-based* method. But, along with that, you can also use the pseudo bi-weekly approach routinely. Depending on the age of your mortgage, you would cut more than six years and save even more interest than you expected with the *term-based* method alone.

UNDERSTANDING THIS METHOD

This method is commonly known as the "Bi-weekly" method. But, the name *pseudo bi-weekly* fits better. It is a technique that appears to be a form of the little-known "*Bank Bi-weekly*" mortgage. However, the two approaches are definitely <u>not</u> the same.

Bank Bi-weekly

The bank bi-weekly mortgage is a type of mortgage that is set up by the bank. The amortization schedule calls for payment every two weeks. That means, the payments made every two weeks contain BOTH interest and principal components. *Interest compounds every two weeks.* Naturally, the term is shorter than 30 years, and the amount of total interest you pay is less than what the lender would collect on a conventional 30-year mortgage. But, in fact, this is a formal loan where the bank *requires* you to make regular payments every two weeks.

This type of loan is not common. Banks discourage it, because of the more frequent paperwork, payment processing, and possible mailings. That's overhead to a bank. Also, lenders feel that people have a tendency to pay late more often when payments are spaced every two weeks.

Pseudo Bi-weekly

The pseudo bi-weekly method does **not** involve a true bi-weekly mortgage. It's not a *type* of mortgage. It's a method that the customer can adopt to pay back a conventional mortgage. The name "bi-weekly" here applies to the fact that money is *put aside* on a bi-weekly basis or *every two weeks*. The mortgage involved can be *any* mortgage where interest compounds on a *monthly* basis. Payments are due to the bank every month. *The lender only sees a monthly payment.* So, the borrower is obligated to make *twelve* scheduled payments during any year.

The "payments" you make every two weeks are *in fact **deposits*** into a bank account. Every month, *money comes from that account* to meet the regular monthly obligation to the mortgage lender. The monthly payment to the lender contains *monthly* interest and principal components. It does **not** have to include a prepayment.

You don't need extra cash every month

So, what's the hype about?   This method has a special appeal: at the end of every year, *it materializes an **extra sum** the size of a full monthly payment.* You can use that extra money to *prepay* principal. Yet, *you don't have to have extra cash every month.*

Where does the magic of the pseudo "bi-weekly" method come from?

It works this way. There are TWELVE months in the year. But, there are FIFTY TWO weeks in the year. If you put money aside every two weeks, you will have a total of **26 deposits** (that's just the number of *2-week periods* in a year, or *52* divided by *2*).

If you deposit *HALF* of the monthly mortgage payment every two weeks, you'll have 26 *half payments*. But, 26 half payments make up **13 FULL payments** (just like 26 *half dollars* add up to 13 *dollars*). So, after you make the twelve required payments, there is **a thirteenth** full payment amount left at the end of the year. That money is YOURS to use as you please. However, *you choose to use the **whole** amount to prepay PRINCIPAL **only**.*

The logic behind this method follows the fact that most people are paid on either a weekly or bi-weekly basis. So, when the paycheck comes in, it's easy at that time to put aside *half* of the mortgage payment automatically. That's not extra money, since a full payment must be accumulated for the monthly payment anyway.

Key Point

The monthly mortgage payment you actually make probably *includes ADDITIONAL money for INSURANCE and property TAX.* Naturally, the half-payment deposits you make should reflect that.

Basically, just apply half of whatever you actually pay the bank each month. There is a big EXTRA bonus hidden in the included insurance and tax money. Can you guess what it is?

The Basic Cycle

Deposit a half payment two weeks before the current payment is due. If you don't have two weeks before the current payment, start the basic cycle by depositing a half payment two weeks *after* making the current monthly payment.

Two weeks after the first deposit, deposit the second half payment. The two deposits now total a full payment. Make a regular monthly payment with that money. *The **two deposits followed by the monthly payment** constitute the basic cycle.*

The Basic Cycle

SUN	MON	TUES	WED	THUR	FRI	SAT
					Deposit 1/2 Payment	
					Deposit 1/2 Payment	
		Send in Monthly Payment				

The BIG EXTRA Bonus

The illustrative monthly payment below does NOT include insurance and tax. But, your actual monthly payment usually does. So, your actual prepayment for the year *will be larger than a plain amortization monthly payment amount.* As a result, *your overall savings will be much greater and the actual term will be much shorter* than what you would expect.

You can proceed two different ways with the basic cycle. You can just run the process as a single 52-week segment with one prepayment, or you can break it up into two 26-week segments with a total of two prepayments. Either way, *if you want to track your savings,* you should *get a regular amortization schedule before you start.* For comparison and planning purposes, you should also get a one-time *pseudo bi-weekly* amortization schedule that shows the acceleration of your mortgage over the shorter term.

One Prepayment

This approach requires minimal discipline. Doing the process in one segment is almost a hands-free operation. Here's how it works.

After you start the process, perform the basic cycle continuously twelve more times for a total of **twenty six** times or 52 weeks. An extra full-payment sized loot pops up all of a sudden at the end of the year. The money emerges apparently out of nowhere, as if by magic. But, there's no real magic. The deposits you make in the *last two weeks* make up the EXTRA money that you can use for *PRINCIPAL* reduction.

Send in an EXTRA separate check for the *full-payment* sized amount. Specify on this check **FOR PRINCIPAL ONLY.**

When you prepay the principal with this surprise leftover money, you literally pull up the tail end of the loan to an earlier termination point. To determine exactly your savings in interest and time, you need the current year's amortization schedule.

After the prepayment, the remaining balance is smaller, and there are fewer periods left. The rest of your loan payout is now different from what the current schedule shows. *Consequently, if you need to see the exact new picture, you have to get an updated amortization schedule.* This **new** current schedule will also serve to determine your exact savings at the end of the **next** year.

Illustration of the One-Prepayment Approach

Illustration

Using the $80,000-mortgage for 30 years at 10%, let's look at the picture we'd get over one year. The monthly payment is $702.06, due on the first of the every month. We'll assume this is an existing mortgage. The process can start anytime during the year. But, for convenience, again we'll start in January, right at the beginning of the year.

You make a regular monthly payment on January 1st. ***Now the basic cycle starts.*** Two weeks later, on January 15th, deposit $351.03, a half payment. On January 29th, make the second half payment. You now have on deposit $702.06. Make the February 1st payment with this money.

Repeat this basic payment cycle until you've made *twelve full payments.* Then, do the cycle one more time. But, this time BOTH the 51st and the 52nd half payments, on December 16th and December 30th, will be *EXTRA* money that will reduce your balance due. You've completed the full annual cycle. Use the *extra* deposit of $702.06 to prepay principal.

Here's an example of the *One-Prepayment* flow over one year *(your dates may be different)*:

Month	Day	Deposit	Payment		Extra
January	1				
January	15	351.03			
January	29	351.03	**$702.06**	*#1*	
February	12	351.03			
February	26	351.03	**$702.06**	*#2*	
March	11	351.03			
March	25	351.03	**$702.06**	*#3*	
April	8	351.03			
April	22	351.03	**$702.06**	*#4*	
May	6	351.03			
May	20	351.03	**$702.06**	*#5*	
June	3	351.03			
June	17	351.03	**$702.06**	*#6*	
July	1	351.03			
July	15	351.03	**$702.06**	*#7*	
July	29	351.03			
August	12	351.03	**$702.06**	*#8*	
August	26	351.03			
September	9	351.03	**$702.06**	*#9*	
September	23	351.03			
October	7	351.03	**$702.06**	*#10*	
October	21	351.03			
November	4	351.03	**$702.06**	*#11*	
November	18	351.03			
December	2	351.03	**$702.06**	*#12*	
December	*16*	*351.03*			*$351.03*
December	*30*	*351.03*			*$351.03*
				Total Extra:	**$702.06**

Send the EXTRA *$702.06* that accumulates here as a prepayment on December 30.

Two
Prepayments

Doing the process in two segments takes a little more attention and work, but it saves you more money and time. Here's what you do.

After the first pass, repeat the basic cycle five more times for a total of 26 weeks. By the 26th week, about six months down the road, when thirteen 2-week periods have gone by, you've made thirteen deposits. With *twelve deposits o*ut of those, you've made six *full* payments. But, you now have a *thirteenth* deposit left over, worth a half-payment. *You can use this money for PRINCIPAL reduction only.* Just send in a separate check for the half-deposit amount. Specify on this check "FOR PRINCIPAL ONLY".

Determine your interest and time savings now. *Get an updated amortization schedule after this check clears,* so you can determine your interest and time savings when you make the *second* prepayment at the end year.

Start the second segment with the fourteenth deposit. Repeat the basic cycle for another 26 weeks. The same thing happens over the second six-month period. On the 26th week, *which will really be the **52nd week** at the end of the year,* you wind up with a *second* deposit the size of a half payment. Just send in another separate check for the half-deposit amount. Again, specify on this check *"FOR PRINCIPAL ONLY".*

Once more, determine your interest and time savings. *Get a NEW amortization schedule after this second prepayment check clears,* so you can determine your interest and time savings when you make the first *semi-annual* prepayment in the **next** year.

It doesn't matter when you start applying this technique. The same pattern will occur and it works the same way.

Illustration of the Two-Prepayment Approach

Illustration

Using the $80,000-mortgage for 30 years at 10%, let's look at the picture we'd get over one year. The monthly payment is $702.06, due on the first of the month every month.

The process can start anytime during the year. But, for convenience, we'll start in January, right at the beginning of the year. It goes like this. You make a regular monthly payment on January 1st. ***Now the basic cycle starts.*** Two weeks later, on January 15th, deposit $351.03, a half payment. On January 29th, make the second half payment. You now have on deposit $702.06. Make the February 1st payment with this money.

Repeat this basic payment cycle until you've made *six full payments.* The 13th half payment, on July 1st, will be *EXTRA* money that will accumulate toward your prepayment fund. Send in a check for *principal only*. *Determine your INTEREST and TIME savings*, using the current amortization schedule. You've completed the first six-month cycle. *You need to get an updated amortization schedule from the bank, after the extra payment check clears.*

Perform the second six-month cycle, starting with the half-payment deposit on July 15th. The 26th half-payment deposit on December 30 will be another *extra* deposit of $351.03. Send in a second check for *principal only*. Determine your INTEREST and TIME savings, *using the updated amortization schedule*.

Now, get a NEW updated amortization schedule, after the extra payment check clears. Use this new version to determine your interest and time savings when you make the first *semi-annual* prepayment in the *next year*.

Here's an example of the *Two-Prepayment* flow over one year *(your dates may be different)*:

Month	Day	Deposit	Payment		Extra
January	1				
January	15	351.03			
January	29	351.03	**$702.06**	*#1*	
February	12	351.03			
February	26	351.03	**$702.06**	*#2*	
March	11	351.03			
March	25	351.03	**$702.06**	*#3*	
April	8	351.03			
April	22	351.03	**$702.06**	*#4*	
May	6	351.03			
May	20	351.03	**$702.06**	*#5*	
June	3	351.03			
June	17	351.03	**$702.06**	*#6*	
July	*1*	*351.03*			*$351.03*
July	15	351.03			
July	29	351.03	**$702.06**	*#7*	
August	12	351.03			
August	26	351.03	**$702.06**	*#8*	
September	9	351.03			
September	23	351.03	**$702.06**	*#9*	
October	7	351.03			
October	21	351.03	**$702.06**	*#10*	
November	4	351.03			
November	18	351.03	**$702.06**	*#11*	
December	2	351.03			
December	16	351.03	**$702.06**	*#12*	
December	*30*	*351.03*			*$351.03*
				Total Extra:	**$702.06**

Make a prepayment of *$351.03* on July 1, using the EXTRA money that appears here.

Make a prepayment of *$351.03* on December 30, using the EXTRA money that appears here.

You can determine the interest and time savings from each semi-annual or annual prepayment as you make it. To give you an idea of the tremendous results you can get from just *one annual prepayment,* observe the picture *before* a prepayment and the result afterwards.

Figure 11.1 below shows the first 30 scheduled payments in the initial amortization schedule for the $80,000-mortgage for 30 years at 10% *before* any prepayment. The shaded periods in Figure **11.1** will be chiseled by an annual prepayment in Period 12.

PERIOD	PAYMENT	INTEREST	PRINCIPAL	BALANCE
1	$702.06	$666.67	$35.39	$79,964.61
2	$702.06	$666.37	$35.69	$79,928.92
3	$702.06	$666.07	$35.98	$79,892.94
4	$702.06	$665.77	$36.28	$79,856.66
5	$702.06	$665.47	$36.59	$79,820.07
6	$702.06	$665.17	$36.89	$79,783.18
7	$702.06	$664.86	$37.20	$79,745.99
8	$702.06	$664.55	$37.51	$79,708.48
9	$702.06	$664.24	$37.82	$79,670.66
10	$702.06	$663.92	$38.14	$79,632.52
11	$702.06	$663.60	$38.45	$79,594.07
12	$702.06	$663.28	$38.77	$79,555.30
13	$702.06	$662.96	$39.10	$79,516.20
14	$702.06	$662.64	$39.42	$79,476.78
15	$702.06	$662.31	$39.75	$79,437.03
16	$702.06	$661.98	$40.08	$79,396.95
17	$702.06	$661.64	$40.42	$79,356.53
18	$702.06	$661.30	$40.75	$79,315.78
19	$702.06	$660.96	$41.09	$79,274.68
20	$702.06	$660.62	$41.43	$79,233.25
21	$702.06	$660.28	$41.78	$79,191.47
22	$702.06	$659.93	$42.13	$79,149.34
23	$702.06	$659.58	$42.48	$79,106.86
24	$702.06	$659.22	$42.83	$79,064.03
25	$702.06	$658.87	$43.19	$79,020.84
26	$702.06	$658.51	$43.55	$78,977.29
27	$702.06	$658.14	$43.91	$78,933.37
28	$702.06	$657.78	$44.28	$78,889.10
29	$702.06	$657.41	$44.65	$78,844.45
30	$702.06	$657.04	$45.02	$78,799.43

Figure 11.1

With an annual *prepayment* of $702.06, the actual payment associated with Period *12* was $1,404.12. AFTER the prepayment, an updated amortization schedule shows the astounding result. *Sixteen full periods (13 through 28) and part of one period (29) get eliminated.* The prepayment also CUT forever ***$11,090.36*** in interest. Notice the effect in Figure **11.2** The ***new*** Period 13 ***starts out*** with the new balance of *$78,853.24.*

Figure **11.2** below shows the first 24 periods in the <u>updated</u> amortization schedule *after* the prepayment.

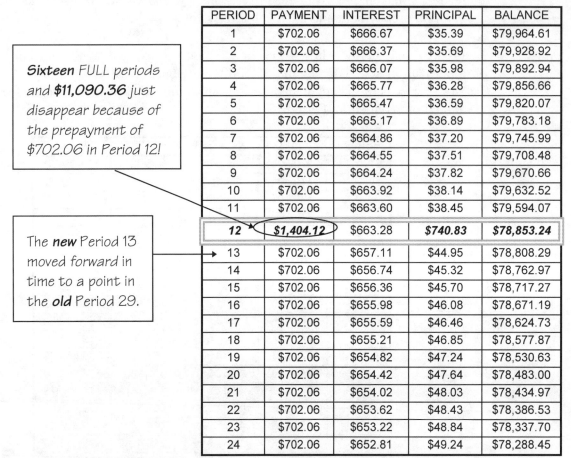

Sixteen FULL periods and **$11,090.36** just disappear because of the prepayment of $702.06 in Period 12!

The **new** Period 13 moved forward in time to a point in the **old** Period 29.

PERIOD	PAYMENT	INTEREST	PRINCIPAL	BALANCE
1	$702.06	$666.67	$35.39	$79,964.61
2	$702.06	$666.37	$35.69	$79,928.92
3	$702.06	$666.07	$35.98	$79,892.94
4	$702.06	$665.77	$36.28	$79,856.66
5	$702.06	$665.47	$36.59	$79,820.07
6	$702.06	$665.17	$36.89	$79,783.18
7	$702.06	$664.86	$37.20	$79,745.99
8	$702.06	$664.55	$37.51	$79,708.48
9	$702.06	$664.24	$37.82	$79,670.66
10	$702.06	$663.92	$38.14	$79,632.52
11	$702.06	$663.60	$38.45	$79,594.07
12	*$1,404.12*	$663.28	*$740.83*	*$78,853.24*
13	$702.06	$657.11	$44.95	$78,808.29
14	$702.06	$656.74	$45.32	$78,762.97
15	$702.06	$656.36	$45.70	$78,717.27
16	$702.06	$655.98	$46.08	$78,671.19
17	$702.06	$655.59	$46.46	$78,624.73
18	$702.06	$655.21	$46.85	$78,577.87
19	$702.06	$654.82	$47.24	$78,530.63
20	$702.06	$654.42	$47.64	$78,483.00
21	$702.06	$654.02	$48.03	$78,434.97
22	$702.06	$653.62	$48.43	$78,386.53
23	$702.06	$653.22	$48.84	$78,337.70
24	$702.06	$652.81	$49.24	$78,288.45

Figure 11.2

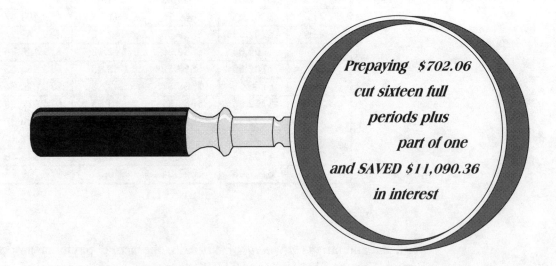

Prepaying $702.06 cut sixteen full periods plus part of one and SAVED $11,090.36 in interest

You'll find an easy step-by-step procedure, complete with an illustration and a blank form, in *Appendix D*. The procedure shows how to calculate interest and time savings from *any ONE* semi-annual or annual prepayment.

If you have the extra cash each month, you can use a different plan to prepay a full monthly payment size amount over the course of a year. You only have to prepay one twelfth of the monthly payment each month, using the *Fixed Prepayment* method. For instance, with the $80,000-mortgage at 10% for 30 years, just divide the monthly payment of $702.06 by 12 to get the monthly prepayment of *$58.51*. You would then have an adjusted monthly payment of **$760.57.**

When you use the *Fixed Prepayment* method this way, the net overall savings are in the same general ballpark, but a little better, than the savings from the bi-weekly approach. Over the life of the loan, you could expect to *save* about **$2,000** more with the *fixed prepayments.*

There's a good reason for the improved results. Because the fixed prepayments reduce the principal balance a bit more every month, you wind up paying *even less* total interest (meaning you *save even more*) with this variation. There's only one stipulation for the *fixed prepayment* route:

> *You have to have some extra cash **each month** for principal prepayment.*

If you can come up with the required amount every month for the whole duration, stay with fixed prepayments. On the other hand:

> *With the pseudo bi-weekly approach, you don't need EXTRA cash every month*

There's no need to do any special budgeting. You can get the results with practically *zero extra* cash input in addition to your normal monthly payments. Depending on how you choose to conduct this method, you may have some small bank fees for fund transfers, but that's all. That's what makes the *pseudo bi-weekly* approach worth considering, if you plan to do it yourself.

Why not combine the two?

What if you can afford some extra cash, like the $58.71, every month? Well, use the extra cash to make fixed prepayments every month. But, do it in a "pseudo bi-weekly" way. That will pack *extra punch* in your prepayments and accumulate savings ON TOP of what you're already getting.

Just deposit *half of the extra cash* on top of your bi-weekly deposits. Then, make a monthly payment that includes the extra cash. The annual prepayment (or semi-annual prepayments together) will be bigger *by the full extra cash amount.* **What's more, the total savings will be much GREATER still.**

Combining for maximum savings

It's simple. When you can apply extra cash to prepay principal every month, no matter how much, just add the *extra* money to the original monthly payment due. *That establishes a new monthly amount of your own.* Then, use the pseudo bi-weekly method with that new amount.

For maximum savings, combine the pseudo bi-weekly's *two-prepayment approach* with the *term-based prepayment method.* That's easy to do. First, determine the prepayment required to close your mortgage within 15 years or less. At this point, consider that your regular monthly payment will put you on course for a 15-year term or less. Then, *apply the pseudo bi-weekly's* **two-prepayment** *technique to this* **new** *monthly payment.*

For instance, examine how two prepayment methods, taken alone and in combination, operate on the $80,000-mortgage at 10% for 30 years. Used alone, the *term-based* prepayment method, aimed at 15 years, *saves $97,996.39 of interest and 15 years.* Refer back to **Table 10.1** on page 86 in *Chapter 10* to observe this.

Used alone, the *pseudo bi-weekly* method, with the two-prepayment approach, *saves $59,988.42 of interest.* It cuts the term down to 21 years and 2 months, *saving 8 years and 10 months.* You'll see that in **Table 12.5** of the next chapter on page 130. But, watch what happens to the same mortgage when you apply a combination of the two-prepayment *pseudo bi-weekly* and the *term-based* prepayment method targeted for 15 years. Here are the *combined* results from **Table 12.7** of the next chapter on page 132:

> √   The total interest savings is now *$109,086.77.*
>
> √   The term only lasts 13 years and 1 month, with a saving of *16 years and 11 months.*

In *Chapter Twelve,* tables **12.2** through **12.7** give detailed comparative amortization tables. *Figures* **12.5** and **12.6** show the comparative results graphically. *Similar tremendous results may be possible with your mortgage.*

In the same way, you can combine the *Increasing Prepayment* and the *Fixed Prepayment* methods on top of the *Extra-Annual* payment method. Since you would know what the prepayment is going to be in either method, during the TWO preceding two-week periods, *just deposit HALF of the **total** monthly payment you're going to make that month.* When combined with the *Increasing Prepayment* method, the *Extra-Annual* payment method requires **close** personal management. The *increasing* monthly prepayment is going to be different every month. A new amortization schedule is **required** after each annual or semi-annual prepayment.

At this point, you're ready to go on to *Chapter Twelve* for the roadmap and detailed procedures of the *Extra-Annual Payment* method.

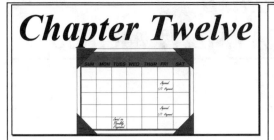

Chapter Twelve

THE EXTRA ANNUAL PAYMENT METHOD

ROADMAP AND DETAILED PROCEDURE

⇒ *How to determine your savings: for the whole term in* **TOTAL** *or for every annual prepayment*
⇒ *A general* **roadmap** *for the* **extra annual payment** *method*
⇒ *How to do it in* **step-by-step** *detail*
⇒ *Results from using* **extra annual payment** *method*

The step-by-step application of the *extra annual payment* method is actually easy to do. You should get acquainted with the following general roadmap and use it to make this interesting method save many thousands of dollars for you.

Start by getting a current amortization schedule. Next, open a bank account dedicated to your mortgage payments. Then, choose either the *one-prepayment* or the *two-prepayment* approach, whichever suits you.

Right off the bat, use the special savings table to very quickly determine the *total* savings in interest and time that you'll enjoy with this method during the *new* term. You get exact answers when you find an exact match for your mortgage age in the special savings table. Otherwise, you can get a pretty good approximation of the savings.

It's possible to run this method manually, making the deposits and payments yourself. But, it's even more efficient to put the banking machinery to work for you. Just monitor the process and direct the bank to make all payments and prepayments automatically for you. Information in this chapter shows you how to do that.

A General Roadmap
For The EXTRA ANNUAL PAYMENT Method

**When you decide to use this method,
prepare for it by taking these four steps**

STEP	ACTION
1	*Get a current amortization schedule*
2	*Set up a bank account dedicated to your mortgage payments only*
3	*Select either the One-Prepayment approach or the Two-Prepayment approach*
4	*Determine your TOTAL savings in interest and time*

The ONE-PREPAYMENT approach

Repeat ALL the following when specified until you've paid off the mortgage

Every TWO weeks

STEP	ACTION
1	*Deposit half of the monthly payment into the dedicated account*

ONCE a month, *after the two deposits*

STEP	ACTION
1	*Send in the REGULAR monthly payment*

At the end of the year, AFTER the *26th* **deposit**

STEP	ACTION
1	*Send in one extra FULL monthly payment TO PAY PRINCIPAL ONLY*
2	*Determine your savings in interest and time from this prepayment*
3	*Get an updated amortization schedule*

The TWO-PREPAYMENT approach

> ### *Repeat ALL the following when specified until you've paid off the mortgage*

Every TWO weeks

STEP	ACTION
1	**Deposit half of the monthly payment into the dedicated account**

ONCE a month, *after the two deposits*

STEP	ACTION
1	**Send in the REGULAR monthly payment**

At MID-YEAR, AFTER the *13th* deposit

STEP	ACTION
1	**Send in HALF a monthly payment TO PAY PRINCIPAL ONLY**
2	**Determine your savings in interest and time from this prepayment**
3	**Get an updated amortization schedule**

At END of year, AFTER the *26th* deposit

STEP	ACTION
1	**Send in HALF a monthly payment TO PAY PRINCIPAL ONLY**
2	**Determine your savings in interest and time from this prepayment**
3	**Get an updated amortization schedule**

HOW TO DO IT IN *step-by-step* DETAIL

The Three Preparation Steps

Perform these preparation steps once, at the time you decide to prepay using the *Extra Annual* payment method.

Get a current amortization schedule

Get a current amortization schedule either from the lender or by other means, such as your personal computer or a specialized service. Call the lender or write to ask for a complete history report to show what you've paid so far.

Set up a bank account dedicated to your mortgage payments only

Beware of outfits that claim to handle your "bi-weekly mortgage" for you. There may be bonded fiduciary organizations that provide a service. But, even with those companies, you need to be aware of some possible pitfalls, and get certain answers.

First of all, they don't set up a true "bank" bi-weekly mortgage. They <u>manage</u> a *pseudo* bi-weekly method for you. For this service, you pay an up-front start-up fee of 1% or more of your expected savings. *For instance, if you're expected to save $70,000, that's $700 you have to pay up front to the company.*

Frankly, that's a fair price to pay for that kind of savings, *if they manage the plan for you the whole time.* The problem is, there is no real assurance they will be around for twenty-two years to service your mortgage. But, there is always a faint possibility for a shadowy company to suddenly go out of business, *and even vanish with some of your bi-weekly money. How do you continue with another company without a start-up fee all over again?*

The arrangement calls for you to authorize the company to electronically transfer half of your mortgage payment every two weeks *into <u>their</u> "escrow" account.* So, with your money in their own account, they make the monthly payments and the annual or semi-annual prepayments for you: *but, who gets to keep the "measly" daily interest that may accumulate on your (and others') deposits?*

Lastly, the bank usually charges a minimal fee for each electronic transfer. Consequently, the company charges you a bi-weekly service fee of about **$5.00** every month. The question is, *do you pay exactly what the bank charges?*

You can set up and manage the plan yourself, *with no big up-front fees*.

Setting Up the plan for yourself

Two weeks after the current payment, open a new <u>statement</u> savings *(not a passbook)* account at your favorite bank. Choose a type of account with a *low minimum required balance* of about $500 or less, and with *a low maintenance charge* when the balance falls below the required minimum. Use the new savings account ONLY for mortgage payments.

Unless an individual or some institution other than a bank owns your mortgage, *open the account at the very same bank that holds your mortgage. THEN, DIRECT THE BANK TO AUTOMATICALLY TAKE THE MONTHLY PAYMENTS FROM THE ACCOUNT. Instead of receiving cash from you, the bank just accepts the payments from the savings account at no charge to you.* You may get another benefit from having the savings account at the same bank as your mortgage: *reputable banks tend to treat accounts set up for mortgage payments as "courtesy" accounts and waive all maintenance charges.*

Figure 12.3 shows the flow of money in the basic setup.

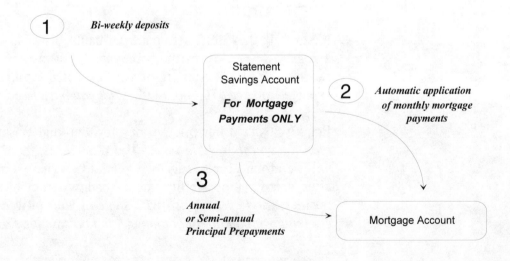

Figure 12.3   Basic Setup of Personal Pseudo Bi-weekly Plan

Setting Up the plan for yourself

(Continued)

<u>Start the account with the *first* bi-weekly deposit</u>. The bi-weekly deposit is just *half the amount* of the monthly mortgage payment, ***including*** what you pay in taxes and interest. Two weeks after that first deposit, <u>make the *second* bi-weekly deposit</u>. You must always ensure that the full monthly payment amount exists in the account prior to the due date. Otherwise, if there is an insufficient balance for whatever reason, you get hit with extra bank charges. Once the account has been set up, you need to make the regular bi-weekly deposits.

Figure 12.3 above gives the general idea of the basic setup. But, there is more. You can in fact optimize the basic concept so the system works smoothly with minimal involvement on your part.

You can certainly work this plan "manually" by making every bi-weekly deposit yourself. But, why not let the banking system work for you. Here's how to make sure the bi-weekly deposits go in regularly in "auto-pilot" mode. Examine Figure 12.4 for a preview.

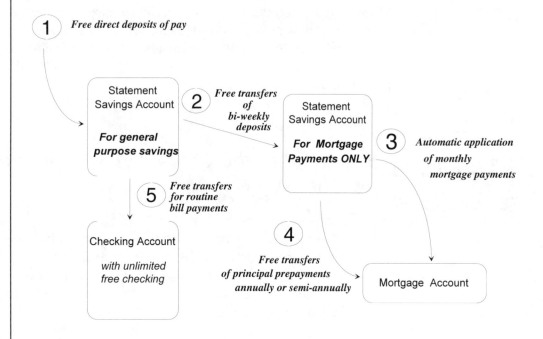

Figure 12.4   Optimal Setup of Personal Pseudo Bi-weekly Plan

Set up a second statement savings account at the same bank, with the same features as the *dedicated* account. Use this second savings account for general purpose savings goals. Deposit your regular paychecks in there. Better still, if your employer offers this facility, *have your paychecks direct-deposited into this second account, at no cost to you.*

Setting Up the plan for yourself

(Continued)

Once a month, or less frequently, you can direct the bank by mail to transfer the bi-weekly deposits from the *general purpose* savings account to the *dedicated* savings account *for you every two weeks*. That easy process gives you *an almost hands-free operation*. You'll find detailed directions below, under **Working with the ONE-PREPAYMENT Approach.**

Lastly, open a checking account with unlimited free checking at the same bank. Get the bank to associate this checking account with your *general purpose* savings account. You pay no maintenance charges as long as the average combined balance in the two accounts remains above the minimum required ($500) in any given month. Use the checking account for routine bill payment and, if you like, also for the annual or semi-annual principal prepayments. Consider making both accounts accessible by automated teller machine (ATM), so you can manage them easily at times convenient to you. There should be no ATM charges.

If your mortgage holder is not a bank, the only difference is that you won't have automatic *free* transfers of the monthly mortgage payments. Even when your mortgage account is *elsewhere*, you would still have the *other three* accounts at your favorite bank. In that case, you would just have your bank transfer the monthly payments and the prepayments to the checking account, free of charge of course. Then, you would simply write the customary checks.

Select either the One-Prepayment approach or the Two-Prepayment approach

With the Single-Prepayment approach, you only have to send in one prepayment check at the end of the year, every year. The advantage of this approach lies in the minimal amount of work it takes to get great savings. Even if you consider yourself to be less than moderately disciplined, you definitely don't need someone else to run this plan for you.

The Two-Prepayment approach requires you to monitor the flow of things a little more closely. This approach calls for two prepayments: the first prepayment occurs half way into the year and the second one at the end of the year. But, the greater savings are worth the extra discipline. *Reducing the balance by half a monthly payment every six months gives greater savings than reducing by just ONE full monthly payment every year.*

Select one of the two approaches according to your own inclinations. *Both approaches are based on the* ***optimal*** *setup.*

Determine your TOTAL savings in interest and time

After you choose either approach, you can quickly determine how much total interest and time you would save with the *Extra Annual Payment* method. Use the special interest savings table in *Appendix I* for that purpose. Table 12.1 below shows a portion of the information. Learn how to do it on the next page.

EXTRA ANNUAL PAYMENT METHOD
30-YEAR FIXED-RATE MORTGAGE SAVINGS TABLE

Refer to this table to quickly figure out your interest savings
when you use the *Extra Annual Payment* method

If your Mortgage is	Brand New			If your Mortgage is	Brand New		
and you prepay every 12th month	One FULL-Size monthly payment			and you prepay every 12th month	One FULL-Size monthly payment		
At this Interest rate (%)	Your interest savings factor is	You'll *save* this many years	and this many months	At this Interest rate (%)	Your interest savings factor is	You'll *save* this many years	and this many months
6.5	0.2798	5	8	10.75	0.8666	9	4
6.75	0.3036	5	11	11	0.9129	9	7
7	0.3285	6	0	11.25	0.9608	9	11
7.25	0.3549	6	3	11.5	1.0078	10	0
7.5	0.3823	6	5	11.75	1.0602	10	3
7.75	0.4113	6	7	12	1.1116	10	7
8	0.4416	6	11	12.25	1.1643	10	11
8.25	0.4732	7	0	12.5	1.2176	11	0
8.5	0.5064	7	3	12.75	1.2725	11	3
8.75	0.541	7	7	13	1.3281	11	6
9	0.5767	7	11	13.25	1.3844	11	8
9.25	0.6142	8	0	13.5	1.4419	11	11
9.5	0.6528	8	2	13.75	1.5003	12	1
9.75	0.6928	8	5	14	1.5596	12	4
10	0.7341	8	8	14.25	1.6199	12	7
10.25	0.7769	8	11	14.5	1.6805	12	11
10.5	0.8211	9	1	14.75	1.742	13	0

Table 12.1

Follow these easy steps to find your expected total interest savings.

STEP	ACTION
1	Find the column with your exact mortgage **AGE**. If you don't find your exact mortgage age, go over to the **first** column that shows **a higher** mortgage **AGE than yours,** to locate an *approximate* factor.
2	Under that column, find the row starting with your interest rate, to locate the *interest savings* factor.
3	To get your total interest savings in dollars, multiply the interest savings factor you find at that location by your **original** mortgage balance. If you're using an *approximate* factor, your *actual* savings will be **MORE** than the approximate interest savings amount you calculate.
4	In the same row, read off how many years and months you'll save. If you're using an *approximate* factor, you'll *actually* save **MORE** than the number of years and months shown in the row.

First Example

Use table 12.1 above. Say your *brand new* mortgage balance is $80,000 for 30 years at 10% and you want to prepay ONCE *annually*.

First, go over to the column with the exact age of your mortgage. Next, look down the *rate* column to find the row starting with **10**. Find the interest savings factor in that row. Multiply interest savings factor *0.7341* by $80,000 to get your total interest savings of *$58,728*. You would also **SAVE 8** years and **8** months.

Second Example

Use a table in *Appendix I*. It's the same mortgage of $80,000 for 30 years at 10%. Suppose you've had the mortgage for *three years*.

First, go over to the column with the **next higher age** of your mortgage. In this case, it's the **5 Years Old** column. Next, find the row starting with **10**. Multiply *approximate* interest savings factor *0.4633* by $80,000 to get your *approximate* total interest savings of *more than $37,064*. Your actual savings would be *MORE* than that amount. You would also **SAVE MORE THAN 6 years.**

Working with the ONE-PREPAYMENT Approach

The Bi-Weekly Step: Do this every two weeks

Deposit half the monthly payment into the dedicated account

Two weeks after the last deposit, arrange to move an amount equal to exactly half of your mortgage from your *general purpose* savings account into the **dedicated** *savings account*. You can go to the bank and personally withdraw the money from one account and deposit it in the other. But, it's better to *use a money transfer slip and get the bank to transfer the money for you.*

When the client requests it, *a bank will move money between accounts at the same bank free of charge.   The bank only requires signature verification to do this.*

The procedure for transferring funds between accounts at a bank is routine. Most banks have their own standard forms available to their clients. You can direct your bank in writing to move money from one account to another. In fact, you may request that the bank move a certain amount at regular intervals throughout the year. It is clearly your responsibility to ensure that the money to be moved is always available in the source account. But, you can automate that part also. Recall the *Optimal Setup* concept (refer back to Figure 12.4). If you get your employer to deposit your checks directly into the source savings account, then the money will always be available for the bank to move.

When you are certain that the money will be there, just ask the bank to transfer half of the monthly payment from the source account to the account dedicated to your mortgage payments. You can either request a **single transfer** every two weeks, or make a request for **multiple transfers** once every so often. Here's specifically how to request a bank transfer.

Bank Transfer

To request a single transfer, fill out a **bank** money transfer slip, sign it, and submit it. You can submit a slip in person *or you can mail it to the bank.*   In fact, you can request that the transfer be done on a *specific date.* **You can even submit one request for multiple transfers to occur on different dates.**

> **Submit requests for *multiple transfers* for your bi-weekly deposits.**

Bank Transfer
(Continued)

To request a single transfer, fill out a *bank* money transfer slip, sign it, and submit it. You can submit a slip in person *or you can mail it to the bank.* In fact, you can request that the transfer be done on a *specific date. You can even submit one request for multiple transfers to occur on different dates.*

Submit requests for *multiple transfers* for your bi-weekly deposits.

To request *multiple* transfers in *one* request, use your *own* form as follows:

- For each transfer, *list the date, amount, from and to account numbers*
- Write in your **name** as the *title* of the account
- Write in your **social security number** and your **address**
- Sign the request note
- Submit a *copy* of the request to the bank.

The transfer form can be a simple letter that lists the dates, amounts and accounts for the transfers. Here's an example:

To: MYBANK   January 3, 1993

Please effect the following transfers *on the DATES specified below:*

DATE	AMOUNT	FROM ACCOUNT	TO ACCOUNT
1/14/93	$351.03	254367-78	254368-74
1/28/93	$351.03	254367-78	254368-74
2/11/93	$351.03	254367-78	254368-74

Title of Account: JOSH KELSICK
Address: 36 Prince St
                         Mytown, NY 11150

Social Security No: 224-56-7786   **Signature:** Josh Kelsick

Technically, you should list *as many* different transfers in the one request as your bank will let you include at one time. Most banks will allow you to list *three transfers* at one time without a fuss. If you request three transfers at one time, then you can submit a request every *six* weeks. Keep a simple log.

The Monthly Step: Do this every month

Step 1   *Send in the REGULAR monthly payment*

Paying by Check	If you want to do this personally, simply transfer the appropriate monthly amount from the dedicated savings account to the checking account. Then, write a check every month from the checking account for the *full monthly payment PLUS any combined monthly prepayments.*

Paying by Bank Transfer	***You should consider paying by bank transfer.*** *You make the request only once.* Just go to the mortgage department, and fill out the required form to direct the bank to *automatically* take the monthly payment from the *dedicated* savings account. The bank keeps on taking the money from that account automatically every month, *until you direct otherwise.*

NOTE: The bank may agree to retrieve only the *regular monthly payment* in this automatic way. If you want to combine *any additional prepayments* on a monthly basis, then **you should write a check for the additional amount to principal.** See *Chapter Fifteen* for guidelines.

The Yearly Steps: Perform these three steps once a year, AFTER the 26th deposit

Send in one extra FULL monthly payment to pay PRINCIPAL ONLY

Two weeks after you make the twelfth and last regular payment for the year, you deposit a half payment. At this point, you will have cash available a full month's payment. Write a check for the full amount to prepay principal only. Send in the check and update the prepayment tracking worksheet as shown in *Chapter Fifteen.*

Determine your savings in interest and time from this prepayment

The general idea is to compare the annual prepayment amount with principal portions starting with the next period to determine how many principal portions are covered. So, with the current amortization schedule, use the procedure in *Appendix D* to find the savings in interest and time.

Get an updated amortization schedule

Allow a couple of weeks or so for the bank to process the prepayment. After the prepayment check clears, get a new amortization schedule. The new schedule will give you the correct data for figuring your savings next year.

Extra-Annual Payment Results
One Annual Prepayment

Mortgage Amount: *$80,000*   Term: *30 Years*   Interest Rate: *10%*

Normal Term
No prepayments

Interest Savings: **$0**
Duration: 30 Years
Time Savings: **None**
Monthly Payment: **$702.06**

Accelerated Term
Extra Annual Prepayment $702.06

Interest Savings: **$58,743.90**
Duration: *21 Years 4 Months*
Time Savings: **8 Years 8 Months**
Monthly Payment: **$702.06**

Year	Payment	Interest	Principal	Balance	Payment	Interest	Principal	Balance
1	$8,424.69	$7,979.98	$444.70	$79,555.30	$9,126.78	$7,979.97	$1,146.81	$78,853.19
2	$8,424.69	$7,933.42	$491.27	$79,064.03	$9,126.78	$7,859.90	$1,266.88	$77,586.31
3	$8,424.69	$7,881.98	$542.71	$78,521.32	$9,126.78	$7,727.23	$1,399.55	$76,186.76
4	$8,424.69	$7,825.15	$599.54	$77,921.78	$9,126.78	$7,580.69	$1,546.09	$74,640.67
5	$8,424.69	$7,762.37	$662.32	$77,259.46	$9,126.78	$7,418.80	$1,707.98	$72,932.69
6	$8,424.69	$7,693.01	$731.67	$76,527.78	$9,126.78	$7,239.94	$1,886.84	$71,045.85
7	$8,424.69	$7,616.40	$808.29	$75,719.49	$9,126.78	$7,042.38	$2,084.40	$68,961.45
8	$8,424.69	$7,531.76	$892.93	$74,826.57	$9,126.78	$6,824.11	$2,302.67	$66,658.78
9	$8,424.69	$7,438.26	$986.43	$73,840.14	$9,126.78	$6,582.98	$2,543.80	$64,114.98
10	$8,424.69	$7,334.97	$1,089.72	$72,750.42	$9,126.78	$6,316.61	$2,810.17	$61,304.81
11	$8,424.69	$7,220.86	$1,203.83	$71,546.59	$9,126.78	$6,022.34	$3,104.44	$58,200.37
12	$8,424.69	$7,094.80	$1,329.89	$70,216.70	$9,126.78	$5,697.27	$3,429.51	$54,770.86
13	$8,424.69	$6,955.54	$1,469.14	$68,747.56	$9,126.78	$5,338.14	$3,788.64	$50,982.22
14	$8,424.69	$6,801.71	$1,622.98	$67,124.58	$9,126.78	$4,941.44	$4,185.34	$46,796.88
15	$8,424.69	$6,631.76	$1,792.93	$65,331.65	$9,126.78	$4,503.17	$4,623.61	$42,173.27
16	$8,424.69	$6,444.02	$1,980.67	$63,350.98	$9,126.78	$4,019.03	$5,107.75	$37,065.52
17	$8,424.69	$6,236.61	$2,188.07	$61,162.91	$9,126.78	$3,484.19	$5,642.59	$31,422.93
18	$8,424.69	$6,007.49	$2,417.19	$58,745.71	$9,126.78	$2,893.33	$6,233.45	$25,189.48
19	$8,424.69	$5,754.38	$2,670.30	$56,075.41	$9,126.78	$2,240.62	$6,886.16	$18,303.32
20	$8,424.69	$5,474.77	$2,949.92	$53,125.49	$9,126.78	$1,519.54	$7,607.24	$10,696.08
21	$8,424.69	$5,165.87	$3,258.82	$49,866.67	$9,126.78	$722.96	$8,403.82	$2,292.26
22	$8,424.69	$4,824.63	$3,600.06	$46,266.62	$2,334.33	$42.07	$2,292.26	$0.00
23	$8,424.69	$4,447.66	$3,977.03	$42,289.59	**$0.00**	**$0.00**	**$0.00**	**$0.00**
24	$8,424.69	$4,031.21	$4,393.48	$37,896.11	**$0.00**	**$0.00**	**$0.00**	**$0.00**
25	$8,424.69	$3,571.16	$4,853.53	$33,042.58	**$0.00**	**$0.00**	**$0.00**	**$0.00**
26	$8,424.69	$3,062.93	$5,361.76	$27,680.83	**$0.00**	**$0.00**	**$0.00**	**$0.00**
27	$8,424.69	$2,501.48	$5,923.20	$21,757.62	**$0.00**	**$0.00**	**$0.00**	**$0.00**
28	$8,424.69	$1,881.25	$6,543.44	$15,214.18	**$0.00**	**$0.00**	**$0.00**	**$0.00**
29	$8,424.69	$1,196.06	$7,228.62	$7,985.56	**$0.00**	**$0.00**	**$0.00**	**$0.00**
30	$8,424.69	$439.13	$7,985.56	$0.00	**$0.00**	**$0.00**	**$0.00**	**$0.00**
Totals	$252,740.61	$172,740.61	$80,000.00		$193,996.71	$113,996.71	$80,000.00	

Table 12.2

Extra-Annual Payment Results
One Annual Prepayment Combined With Fixed Monthly Prepayments

Mortgage Amount: *$80,000*   Term: *30 Years*   Interest Rate: *10%*

Normal Term
No prepayments

Interest Savings: **$0**
Duration: 30 Years
Time Savings: **None**
Monthly Payment: **$702.06**

Accelerated Term
Extra Annual Prepayment $702.06
Combined with $50 /Month

Interest Savings: **$82,421.26**
Duration: *17 Years   7 Months*
Time Savings: **12 Years   5 Months**
Monthly Payment: **$752.06**

Year	Payment	Interest	Principal	Balance	Payment	Interest	Principal	Balance
1	$8,424.69	$7,979.98	$444.70	$79,555.30	$9,726.78	$7,951.70	$1,775.08	$78,224.92
2	$8,424.69	$7,933.42	$491.27	$79,064.03	$9,726.78	$7,765.83	$1,960.95	$76,263.97
3	$8,424.69	$7,881.98	$542.71	$78,521.32	$9,726.78	$7,560.48	$2,166.30	$74,097.67
4	$8,424.69	$7,825.15	$599.54	$77,921.78	$9,726.78	$7,333.66	$2,393.12	$71,704.55
5	$8,424.69	$7,762.37	$662.32	$77,259.46	$9,726.78	$7,083.06	$2,643.72	$69,060.83
6	$8,424.69	$7,693.01	$731.67	$76,527.78	$9,726.78	$6,806.25	$2,920.53	$66,140.30
7	$8,424.69	$7,616.40	$808.29	$75,719.49	$9,726.78	$6,500.42	$3,226.36	$62,913.94
8	$8,424.69	$7,531.76	$892.93	$74,826.57	$9,726.78	$6,162.55	$3,564.23	$59,349.71
9	$8,424.69	$7,438.26	$986.43	$73,840.14	$9,726.78	$5,789.35	$3,937.43	$55,412.28
10	$8,424.69	$7,334.97	$1,089.72	$72,750.42	$9,726.78	$5,377.05	$4,349.73	$51,062.55
11	$8,424.69	$7,220.86	$1,203.83	$71,546.59	$9,726.78	$4,921.59	$4,805.19	$46,257.36
12	$8,424.69	$7,094.80	$1,329.89	$70,216.70	$9,726.78	$4,418.40	$5,308.38	$40,948.98
13	$8,424.69	$6,955.54	$1,469.14	$68,747.56	$9,726.78	$3,862.56	$5,864.22	$35,084.76
14	$8,424.69	$6,801.71	$1,622.98	$67,124.58	$9,726.78	$3,248.48	$6,478.30	$28,606.46
15	$8,424.69	$6,631.76	$1,792.93	$65,331.65	$9,726.78	$2,570.13	$7,156.65	$21,449.81
16	$8,424.69	$6,444.02	$1,980.67	$63,350.98	$9,726.78	$1,820.74	$7,906.04	$13,543.77
17	$8,424.69	$6,236.61	$2,188.07	$61,162.91	$9,726.78	$992.87	$8,733.91	$4,809.86
18	$8,424.69	$6,007.49	$2,417.19	$58,745.71	$4,964.09	$154.23	$4,809.86	$0.00
19	$8,424.69	$5,754.38	$2,670.30	$56,075.41	$0.00	$0.00	$0.00	$0.00
20	$8,424.69	$5,474.77	$2,949.92	$53,125.49	$0.00	$0.00	$0.00	$0.00
21	$8,424.69	$5,165.87	$3,258.82	$49,866.67	$0.00	$0.00	$0.00	$0.00
22	$8,424.69	$4,824.63	$3,600.06	$46,266.62	$0.00	$0.00	$0.00	$0.00
23	$8,424.69	$4,447.66	$3,977.03	$42,289.59	$0.00	$0.00	$0.00	$0.00
24	$8,424.69	$4,031.21	$4,393.48	$37,896.11	$0.00	$0.00	$0.00	$0.00
25	$8,424.69	$3,571.16	$4,853.53	$33,042.58	$0.00	$0.00	$0.00	$0.00
26	$8,424.69	$3,062.93	$5,361.76	$27,680.83	$0.00	$0.00	$0.00	$0.00
27	$8,424.69	$2,501.48	$5,923.20	$21,757.62	$0.00	$0.00	$0.00	$0.00
28	$8,424.69	$1,881.25	$6,543.44	$15,214.18	$0.00	$0.00	$0.00	$0.00
29	$8,424.69	$1,196.06	$7,228.62	$7,985.56	$0.00	$0.00	$0.00	$0.00
30	$8,424.69	$439.13	$7,985.56	$0.00	$0.00	$0.00	$0.00	$0.00
Totals	$252,740.61	$172,740.61	$80,000.00		$170,319.35	$90,319.35	$80,000.00	

Table 12.3

Extra-Annual Payment Results
One Annual Prepayment Combined With *15-Year* Term-Based Prepayments

Mortgage Amount: $80,000   Term: *30 Years*   Interest Rate: *10%*

Normal Term	*Accelerated Term*
No prepayments	***Extra Annual Prepayment $702.06*** ***Combined with $157.62 /Month***
Interest Savings: **$0** Duration: 30 Years Time Savings: **None** Monthly Payment: **$702.06**	Interest Savings: **$108,629.56** Duration: 13 Years 1 Month Time Savings: **16 Years 11 Months** Monthly Payment: **$859.68**

Year	Payment	Interest	Principal	Balance	Payment	Interest	Principal	Balance
1	$8,424.69	$7,979.98	$444.70	$79,555.30	$11,018.22	$7,890.85	$3,127.37	$76,872.63
2	$8,424.69	$7,933.42	$491.27	$79,064.03	$11,018.22	$7,563.37	$3,454.85	$73,417.78
3	$8,424.69	$7,881.98	$542.71	$78,521.32	$11,018.22	$7,201.59	$3,816.63	$69,601.15
4	$8,424.69	$7,825.15	$599.54	$77,921.78	$11,018.22	$6,801.94	$4,216.28	$65,384.87
5	$8,424.69	$7,762.37	$662.32	$77,259.46	$11,018.22	$6,360.43	$4,657.79	$60,727.08
6	$8,424.69	$7,693.01	$731.67	$76,527.78	$11,018.22	$5,872.72	$5,145.50	$55,581.58
7	$8,424.69	$7,616.40	$808.29	$75,719.49	$11,018.22	$5,333.90	$5,684.32	$49,897.26
8	$8,424.69	$7,531.76	$892.93	$74,826.57	$11,018.22	$4,738.68	$6,279.54	$43,617.72
9	$8,424.69	$7,438.26	$986.43	$73,840.14	$11,018.22	$4,081.14	$6,937.08	$36,680.64
10	$8,424.69	$7,334.97	$1,089.72	$72,750.42	$11,018.22	$3,354.74	$7,663.48	$29,017.16
11	$8,424.69	$7,220.86	$1,203.83	$71,546.59	$11,018.22	$2,552.27	$8,465.95	$20,551.21
12	$8,424.69	$7,094.80	$1,329.89	$70,216.70	$11,018.22	$1,665.75	$9,352.47	$11,198.74
13	$8,424.69	$6,955.54	$1,469.14	$68,747.56	$11,018.22	$686.45	$10,331.77	$866.97
14	$8,424.69	$6,801.71	$1,622.98	$67,124.58	$874.19	$7.22	$866.97	$0.00
15	$8,424.69	$6,631.76	$1,792.93	$65,331.65	**$0.00**	**$0.00**	**$0.00**	**$0.00**
16	$8,424.69	$6,444.02	$1,980.67	$63,350.98	**$0.00**	**$0.00**	**$0.00**	**$0.00**
17	$8,424.69	$6,236.61	$2,188.07	$61,162.91	**$0.00**	**$0.00**	**$0.00**	**$0.00**
18	$8,424.69	$6,007.49	$2,417.19	$58,745.71	**$0.00**	**$0.00**	**$0.00**	**$0.00**
19	$8,424.69	$5,754.38	$2,670.30	$56,075.41	**$0.00**	**$0.00**	**$0.00**	**$0.00**
20	$8,424.69	$5,474.77	$2,949.92	$53,125.49	**$0.00**	**$0.00**	**$0.00**	**$0.00**
21	$8,424.69	$5,165.87	$3,258.82	$49,866.67	**$0.00**	**$0.00**	**$0.00**	**$0.00**
22	$8,424.69	$4,824.63	$3,600.06	$46,266.62	**$0.00**	**$0.00**	**$0.00**	**$0.00**
23	$8,424.69	$4,447.66	$3,977.03	$42,289.59	**$0.00**	**$0.00**	**$0.00**	**$0.00**
24	$8,424.69	$4,031.21	$4,393.48	$37,896.11	**$0.00**	**$0.00**	**$0.00**	**$0.00**
25	$8,424.69	$3,571.16	$4,853.53	$33,042.58	**$0.00**	**$0.00**	**$0.00**	**$0.00**
26	$8,424.69	$3,062.93	$5,361.76	$27,680.83	**$0.00**	**$0.00**	**$0.00**	**$0.00**
27	$8,424.69	$2,501.48	$5,923.20	$21,757.62	**$0.00**	**$0.00**	**$0.00**	**$0.00**
28	$8,424.69	$1,881.25	$6,543.44	$15,214.18	**$0.00**	**$0.00**	**$0.00**	**$0.00**
29	$8,424.69	$1,196.06	$7,228.62	$7,985.56	**$0.00**	**$0.00**	**$0.00**	**$0.00**
30	$8,424.69	$439.13	$7,985.56	$0.00	**$0.00**	**$0.00**	**$0.00**	**$0.00**
Totals	$252,740.61	$172,740.61	$80,000.00		$144,111.05	$64,111.05	$80,000.00	

Table 12.4

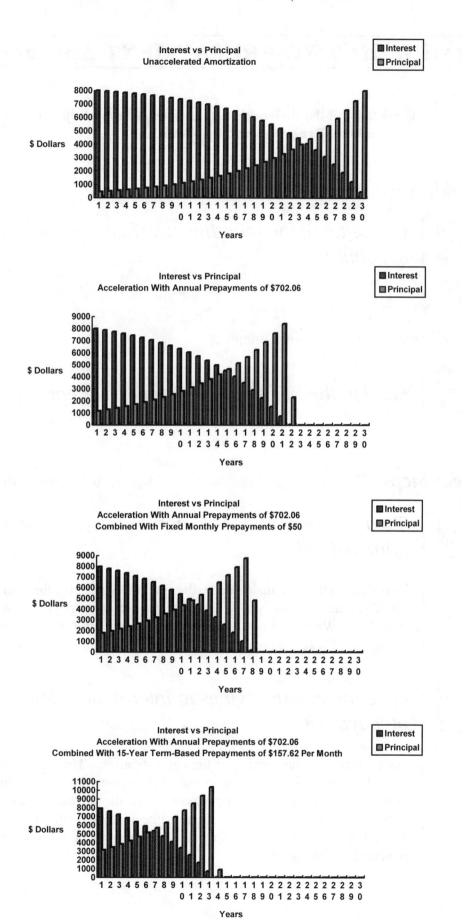

Figure 12.5

Working with the TWO-PREPAYMENT Approach

The details for the *Bi-Weekly Step* and the *Monthly Step* are *exactly the same as in* the **One-Prepayment approach.**

The Bi-Weekly Step: Do this every two weeks

Deposit half the monthly payment into the dedicated account

The Monthly Step: Do this every month

Send in the REGULAR monthly payment

The Mid-Year Steps: Perform these three steps at mid-year, AFTER the 13th deposit

Send in one extra HALF monthly payment to pay principal only

Two weeks after you make the sixth regular payment for the year, you deposit a half payment. Now, you will have a *half* monthly payment's worth of cash available. Write a check for this amount and send it in as prepayment of principal.   Make the prepayment as indicated in *Chapter Fifteen.*

Determine your savings in interest and time from this prepayment

Locate precisely the number of the current period. Then, refer to *Appendix D* to find the procedure for you to use to determine the savings in interest and time from your mid-year prepayment. Use the detailed procedure with the current amortization schedule. The same method works on any amount of prepayment at any time. Update the prepayment tracking worksheet as indicated in *Chapter Fifteen.*

Step 3

Get an updated amortization schedule

Allow a couple of weeks or so for the bank to process the prepayment. After the prepayment check clears, get an updated amortization schedule. The new schedule will provide you with the correct data for figuring your savings at the end of the year.

The Yearly Steps: Perform these three steps once a year, AFTER the 26th deposit

Step 1

Send in one extra HALF monthly payment to pay principal only

Two weeks after you make the twelfth and last regular payment for the year, you deposit a half payment. Now, you will have *another* half monthly payment's worth of cash available. Write a check for the half payment amount and send it in as prepayment of principal. Make the prepayment as indicated in *Chapter Fifteen*.

Step 2

Determine your savings in interest and time from this prepayment

Locate the current period precisely. Then, refer to *Appendix D* to find the procedure for you to use to determine the savings in interest and time from your *year-end* prepayment. Use the detailed procedure with the current amortization schedule. Update the prepayment tracking worksheet as indicated in *Chapter Fifteen*.

Step 3

Get an updated amortization schedule

After the prepayment check clears, get another updated amortization schedule. You'll need this new schedule to figure out your savings at the next *mid-year* point.

Extra-Annual Payment Results
Two Semi-Annual Prepayments

Mortgage Amount: $80,000   Term: 30 Years   Interest Rate: 10%

Normal Term
No prepayments

Interest Savings: **$0**
Duration: 30 Years
Time Savings: **None**
Monthly Payment: **$702.06**

Accelerated Term
Semi-Annual Prepayments $351.03

Interest Savings: **$59,988.42**
Duration: 21 Years 2 Months
Time Savings: **8 Years 10 Months**
Monthly Payment: **$702.06**

Year	Payment	Interest	Principal	Balance	Payment	Interest	Principal	Balance
1	$8,424.69	$7,979.98	$444.70	$79,555.30	$9,126.78	$7,962.04	$1,164.74	$78,835.26
2	$8,424.69	$7,933.42	$491.27	$79,064.03	$9,126.78	$7,840.08	$1,286.70	$77,548.56
3	$8,424.69	$7,881.98	$542.71	$78,521.32	$9,126.78	$7,705.34	$1,421.44	$76,127.12
4	$8,424.69	$7,825.15	$599.54	$77,921.78	$9,126.78	$7,556.53	$1,570.25	$74,556.87
5	$8,424.69	$7,762.37	$662.32	$77,259.46	$9,126.78	$7,392.11	$1,734.67	$72,822.20
6	$8,424.69	$7,693.01	$731.67	$76,527.78	$9,126.78	$7,210.46	$1,916.32	$70,905.88
7	$8,424.69	$7,616.40	$808.29	$75,719.49	$9,126.78	$7,009.79	$2,116.99	$68,788.89
8	$8,424.69	$7,531.76	$892.93	$74,826.57	$9,126.78	$6,788.10	$2,338.68	$66,450.21
9	$8,424.69	$7,438.26	$986.43	$73,840.14	$9,126.78	$6,543.22	$2,583.56	$63,866.65
10	$8,424.69	$7,334.97	$1,089.72	$72,750.42	$9,126.78	$6,272.69	$2,854.09	$61,012.56
11	$8,424.69	$7,220.86	$1,203.83	$71,546.59	$9,126.78	$5,973.82	$3,152.96	$57,859.60
12	$8,424.69	$7,094.80	$1,329.89	$70,216.70	$9,126.78	$5,643.66	$3,483.12	$54,376.48
13	$8,424.69	$6,955.54	$1,469.14	$68,747.56	$9,126.78	$5,278.94	$3,847.84	$50,528.64
14	$8,424.69	$6,801.71	$1,622.98	$67,124.58	$9,126.78	$4,876.03	$4,250.75	$46,277.89
15	$8,424.69	$6,631.76	$1,792.93	$65,331.65	$9,126.78	$4,430.91	$4,695.87	$41,582.02
16	$8,424.69	$6,444.02	$1,980.67	$63,350.98	$9,126.78	$3,939.20	$5,187.58	$36,394.44
17	$8,424.69	$6,236.61	$2,188.07	$61,162.91	$9,126.78	$3,395.98	$5,730.80	$30,663.64
18	$8,424.69	$6,007.49	$2,417.19	$58,745.71	$9,126.78	$2,795.89	$6,330.89	$24,332.75
19	$8,424.69	$5,754.38	$2,670.30	$56,075.41	$9,126.78	$2,132.98	$6,993.80	$17,338.95
20	$8,424.69	$5,474.77	$2,949.92	$53,125.49	$9,126.78	$1,400.62	$7,726.16	$9,612.79
21	$8,424.69	$5,165.87	$3,258.82	$49,866.67	$9,126.78	$591.62	$8,535.16	$1,077.63
22	$8,424.69	$4,824.63	$3,600.06	$46,266.62	$1,089.81	$12.18	$1,077.63	$0.00
23	$8,424.69	$4,447.66	$3,977.03	$42,289.59	**$0.00**	**$0.00**	**$0.00**	**$0.00**
24	$8,424.69	$4,031.21	$4,393.48	$37,896.11	**$0.00**	**$0.00**	**$0.00**	**$0.00**
25	$8,424.69	$3,571.16	$4,853.53	$33,042.58	**$0.00**	**$0.00**	**$0.00**	**$0.00**
26	$8,424.69	$3,062.93	$5,361.76	$27,680.83	**$0.00**	**$0.00**	**$0.00**	**$0.00**
27	$8,424.69	$2,501.48	$5,923.20	$21,757.62	**$0.00**	**$0.00**	**$0.00**	**$0.00**
28	$8,424.69	$1,881.25	$6,543.44	$15,214.18	**$0.00**	**$0.00**	**$0.00**	**$0.00**
29	$8,424.69	$1,196.06	$7,228.62	$7,985.56	**$0.00**	**$0.00**	**$0.00**	**$0.00**
30	$8,424.69	$439.13	$7,985.56	$0.00	**$0.00**	**$0.00**	**$0.00**	**$0.00**
Totals	$252,740.61	$172,740.61	$80,000.00		$192,752.19	$112,752.19	$80,000.00	

Table 12.5

Extra-Annual Payment Results
Two Semi-Annual Prepayments Combined With Fixed Monthly Prepayments

Mortgage Amount: *$80,000*   Term: *30 Years*   Interest Rate: *10%*

Normal Term
No prepayments

Interest Savings: **$0**
Duration: 30 Years
Time Savings: **None**
Monthly Payment: **$702.06**

Accelerated Term
Semi-Annual Prepayments $351.03
Combined with $50 /Month

Interest Savings: **$83,222.80**
Duration: *17 Years   6 Months*
Time Savings: **12 Years 6 Months**
Monthly Payment: **$752.06**

Year	Payment	Interest	Principal	Balance	Payment	Interest	Principal	Balance
1	$8,424.69	$7,979.98	$444.70	$79,555.30	$9,726.78	$7,933.79	$1,792.99	$78,207.01
2	$8,424.69	$7,933.42	$491.27	$79,064.03	$9,726.78	$7,746.05	$1,980.73	$76,226.28
3	$8,424.69	$7,881.98	$542.71	$78,521.32	$9,726.78	$7,538.62	$2,188.16	$74,038.12
4	$8,424.69	$7,825.15	$599.54	$77,921.78	$9,726.78	$7,309.49	$2,417.29	$71,620.83
5	$8,424.69	$7,762.37	$662.32	$77,259.46	$9,726.78	$7,056.37	$2,670.41	$68,950.42
6	$8,424.69	$7,693.01	$731.67	$76,527.78	$9,726.78	$6,776.75	$2,950.03	$66,000.39
7	$8,424.69	$7,616.40	$808.29	$75,719.49	$9,726.78	$6,467.83	$3,258.95	$62,741.44
8	$8,424.69	$7,531.76	$892.93	$74,826.57	$9,726.78	$6,126.61	$3,600.17	$59,141.27
9	$8,424.69	$7,438.26	$986.43	$73,840.14	$9,726.78	$5,749.59	$3,977.19	$55,164.08
10	$8,424.69	$7,334.97	$1,089.72	$72,750.42	$9,726.78	$5,333.13	$4,393.65	$50,770.43
11	$8,424.69	$7,220.86	$1,203.83	$71,546.59	$9,726.78	$4,873.07	$4,853.71	$45,916.72
12	$8,424.69	$7,094.80	$1,329.89	$70,216.70	$9,726.78	$4,364.82	$5,361.96	$40,554.76
13	$8,424.69	$6,955.54	$1,469.14	$68,747.56	$9,726.78	$3,803.37	$5,923.41	$34,631.35
14	$8,424.69	$6,801.71	$1,622.98	$67,124.58	$9,726.78	$3,183.09	$6,543.69	$28,087.66
15	$8,424.69	$6,631.76	$1,792.93	$65,331.65	$9,726.78	$2,497.87	$7,228.91	$20,858.75
16	$8,424.69	$6,444.02	$1,980.67	$63,350.98	$9,726.78	$1,740.92	$7,985.86	$12,872.89
17	$8,424.69	$6,236.61	$2,188.07	$61,162.91	$9,726.78	$904.69	$8,822.09	$4,050.80
18	$8,424.69	$6,007.49	$2,417.19	$58,745.71	$4,162.55	$111.75	$4,050.80	$0.00
19	$8,424.69	$5,754.38	$2,670.30	$56,075.41	$0.00	$0.00	$0.00	$0.00
20	$8,424.69	$5,474.77	$2,949.92	$53,125.49	$0.00	$0.00	$0.00	$0.00
21	$8,424.69	$5,165.87	$3,258.82	$49,866.67	$0.00	$0.00	$0.00	$0.00
22	$8,424.69	$4,824.63	$3,600.06	$46,266.62	$0.00	$0.00	$0.00	$0.00
23	$8,424.69	$4,447.66	$3,977.03	$42,289.59	$0.00	$0.00	$0.00	$0.00
24	$8,424.69	$4,031.21	$4,393.48	$37,896.11	$0.00	$0.00	$0.00	$0.00
25	$8,424.69	$3,571.16	$4,853.53	$33,042.58	$0.00	$0.00	$0.00	$0.00
26	$8,424.69	$3,062.93	$5,361.76	$27,680.83	$0.00	$0.00	$0.00	$0.00
27	$8,424.69	$2,501.48	$5,923.20	$21,757.62	$0.00	$0.00	$0.00	$0.00
28	$8,424.69	$1,881.25	$6,543.44	$15,214.18	$0.00	$0.00	$0.00	$0.00
29	$8,424.69	$1,196.06	$7,228.62	$7,985.56	$0.00	$0.00	$0.00	$0.00
30	$8,424.69	$439.13	$7,985.56	$0.00	$0.00	$0.00	$0.00	$0.00
Totals	$252,740.61	$172,740.61	$80,000.00		$169,517.81	$89,517.81	$80,000.00	

Table 12.6

Extra-Annual Payment Results
Two Semi-Annual Prepayments Combined With *15-Year* Term-Based Prepayments

Mortgage Amount: *$80,000*   Term: *30 Years*   Interest Rate: *10%*

Normal Term
No prepayments

Interest Savings: *$0*
Duration: 30 Years
Time Savings: ***None***
Monthly Payment: ***$702.06***

Accelerated Term
Semi-Annual Prepayments $351.03
Combined with $157.62 /Month

Interest Savings: **$109,086.77**
Duration: *13 Years   1 Month*
Time Savings: **16 Years 11 Months**
Monthly Payment: **$859.68**

Year	Payment	Interest	Principal	Balance	Payment	Interest	Principal	Balance
1	$8,424.69	$7,979.98	$444.70	$79,555.30	$11,018.22	$7,872.92	$3,145.30	$76,854.70
2	$8,424.69	$7,933.42	$491.27	$79,064.03	$11,018.22	$7,543.57	$3,474.65	$73,380.05
3	$8,424.69	$7,881.98	$542.71	$78,521.32	$11,018.22	$7,179.72	$3,838.50	$69,541.55
4	$8,424.69	$7,825.15	$599.54	$77,921.78	$11,018.22	$6,777.78	$4,240.44	$65,301.11
5	$8,424.69	$7,762.37	$662.32	$77,259.46	$11,018.22	$6,333.76	$4,684.46	$60,616.65
6	$8,424.69	$7,693.01	$731.67	$76,527.78	$11,018.22	$5,843.23	$5,174.99	$55,441.66
7	$8,424.69	$7,616.40	$808.29	$75,719.49	$11,018.22	$5,301.34	$5,716.88	$49,724.78
8	$8,424.69	$7,531.76	$892.93	$74,826.57	$11,018.22	$4,702.70	$6,315.52	$43,409.26
9	$8,424.69	$7,438.26	$986.43	$73,840.14	$11,018.22	$4,041.38	$6,976.84	$36,432.42
10	$8,424.69	$7,334.97	$1,089.72	$72,750.42	$11,018.22	$3,310.81	$7,707.41	$28,725.01
11	$8,424.69	$7,220.86	$1,203.83	$71,546.59	$11,018.22	$2,503.76	$8,514.46	$20,210.55
12	$8,424.69	$7,094.80	$1,329.89	$70,216.70	$11,018.22	$1,612.18	$9,406.04	$10,804.51
13	$8,424.69	$6,955.54	$1,469.14	$68,747.56	$11,018.22	$627.24	$10,390.98	$413.53
14	$8,424.69	$6,801.71	$1,622.98	$67,124.58	$416.98	$3.45	$413.53	$0.00
15	$8,424.69	$6,631.76	$1,792.93	$65,331.65	$0.00	$0.00	$0.00	$0.00
16	$8,424.69	$6,444.02	$1,980.67	$63,350.98	$0.00	$0.00	$0.00	$0.00
17	$8,424.69	$6,236.61	$2,188.07	$61,162.91	$0.00	$0.00	$0.00	$0.00
18	$8,424.69	$6,007.49	$2,417.19	$58,745.71	$0.00	$0.00	$0.00	$0.00
19	$8,424.69	$5,754.38	$2,670.30	$56,075.41	$0.00	$0.00	$0.00	$0.00
20	$8,424.69	$5,474.77	$2,949.92	$53,125.49	$0.00	$0.00	$0.00	$0.00
21	$8,424.69	$5,165.87	$3,258.82	$49,866.67	$0.00	$0.00	$0.00	$0.00
22	$8,424.69	$4,824.63	$3,600.06	$46,266.62	$0.00	$0.00	$0.00	$0.00
23	$8,424.69	$4,447.66	$3,977.03	$42,289.59	$0.00	$0.00	$0.00	$0.00
24	$8,424.69	$4,031.21	$4,393.48	$37,896.11	$0.00	$0.00	$0.00	$0.00
25	$8,424.69	$3,571.16	$4,853.53	$33,042.58	$0.00	$0.00	$0.00	$0.00
26	$8,424.69	$3,062.93	$5,361.76	$27,680.83	$0.00	$0.00	$0.00	$0.00
27	$8,424.69	$2,501.48	$5,923.20	$21,757.62	$0.00	$0.00	$0.00	$0.00
28	$8,424.69	$1,881.25	$6,543.44	$15,214.18	$0.00	$0.00	$0.00	$0.00
29	$8,424.69	$1,196.06	$7,228.62	$7,985.56	$0.00	$0.00	$0.00	$0.00
30	$8,424.69	$439.13	$7,985.56	$0.00	$0.00	$0.00	$0.00	$0.00
Totals	$252,740.61	$172,740.61	$80,000.00		$143,653.84	$63,653.84	$80,000.00	

Table 12.7

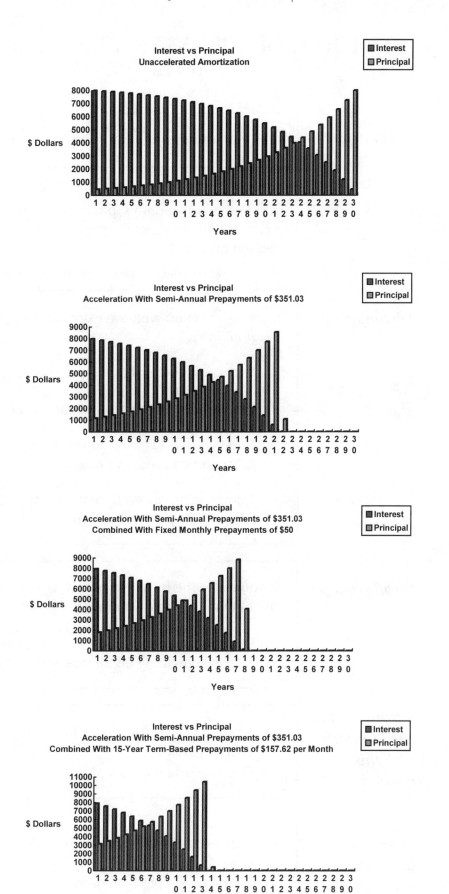

Figure 12.6

KEY POINTS OF THE EXTRA ANNUAL PAYMENT METHOD

Applies to:

> Any type of mortgage

Focus:

> Applies a full month's payment at the *end of the year* or half a month's payment *twice a year* to reduce principal.

Advantages:

> √ You come up with the extra cash *without noticing* it.
>
> √ You know the exact amount to prepay.
>
> √ Prepayment stays constant each year.
>
> √ You can use this method *even if you can't afford any extra cash out of pocket every month.*
>
> √ Combines easily with methods that feature *monthly prepayments* to greatly boost savings.

Disadvantage:

> If you make the bi-weekly deposits yourself, you might tend to skip a deposit.
>
> You need *discipline* to resist spending the *extra* money on something else at the end of the year.

Resources you need to work with this method:

> ⇒ Amortization schedule for the current year
> ⇒ Worksheet
> ⇒ Dedicated savings account

Other methods to combine with this one:

> • Increasing Prepayment method
> • Fixed Prepayment method
> • Term-based Prepayment method

Part Three

GET GOING:

THE PROCESS OF PREPAYING

Part Three

◊ *Introduces the general prepayment procedure and spells out the two phases in implementing it.*

◊ *Reveals how to find cash to prepay with.*

◊ *Teaches an extremely powerful technique that can eliminate ALL your debts in record time.*

◊ *Alleviates your concerns about mortgage tax deduction and bank prepayment penalties.*

◊ *Pinpoints considerations that determine whether you should definitely consider prepaying.*

Chapter Thirteen

Cover the basics
Select a method
Get preliminary info
Make prepayments
Keep records

THE GENERAL PREPAYMENT PROCEDURE

⇒ *The preparation steps you should take **before** starting a prepayment program*
⇒ *The steps you need to repeat every month until your mortgage vanishes*

At this point, you may have made a decision to prepay your mortgage. This chapter offers you a *general procedure* to follow throughout the prepayment process. It's important to develop a good understanding of the concept here. The powerful overall plan, shown in a nutshell on the next page, is in two phases.

Phase one is just preparation you do only once. The details are laid out in *Chapter Fourteen.* Essentially, here you learn how to cover the basics of family finance, select a prepayment method, and collect preliminary information you will need for *phase two.*

This phase prompts you to examine your budget and define your prepayment goals. Get a good handle on the basic prepayment methods. *You can always refer back to previous chapters to rehash specific how-to details about the prepayment methods.* When you have a well-defined goal and understand each method, then you can pick the method that is most appropriate for your situation. *Step 2* gives an easy guide for choosing a prepayment method. Use your chosen prepayment method to determine your prepayment amount and when to pay it. That's the amount you want to plug into *Step 4* in *Phase two.*

Phase two, covered in detail in *Chapter Fifteen,* includes the steps you need to *repeat until the balance is paid off.* Here you find out precisely how to send in a prepayment, confirm the balance, keep records together, and check for any rate changes that might affect your mortgage. Unless you have a *variable rate* mortgage, a fixed rate mortgage *with temporary buydown rates,* or just *refinanced* your old mortgage, *you'll only be concerned with steps 4, 5, and 6.* (For an explanation of buydown rates, see the note included with the details of *Step 7* on page 157.)

As you'll see, these steps are easy to understand and perform.

In a nutshell, here is the

GENERAL PREPAYMENT PROCEDURE

PHASE ONE   *Take these steps before you start prepaying*

STEP	ACTION
1	***Cover the basics of family finances***
2	***Select a prepayment method***
3	***Get preliminary information to include: the current period number, current mortgage balance, and your current mortgage amortization schedule***

PHASE TWO   *Repeat these steps every period until the balance is paid off:*

STEP	ACTION
4	***Make a prepayment, using your chosen method***
5	***Confirm the updated balance***
6	***Keep any written lender acknowledgment, canceled check, or receipt together with the worksheet***
7	*ONLY FOR ADJUSTABLE RATE MORTGAGE, FIXED RATE MORTGAGE WITH TEMPORARY BUYDOWN, OR **REFINANCED** MORTGAGE:* **If the mortgage rate changes beginning the next period,** then *start a new worksheet **and*** get a new amortization schedule that reflects the new rate in effect.

Chapter Fourteen	**THE PREPARATION PHASE**

⇒ *The basics that you should cover*
⇒ *How to select a prepayment method*
⇒ *The preliminary information you need and how to get it*

Perform steps 1 through 3 as a preparation phase before you start prepaying.

STEP	ACTION
1	**Cover the basics of family finances**
2	**Select a prepayment method**
3	**Get preliminary information and materials to include: the *current period number, current mortgage balance,* and your CURRENT *mortgage amortization schedule***

Step 1

COVERING THE BASICS

If you decide to use the pseudo bi-weekly method, **this step becomes optional**

If you've decided to use the *pseudo bi-weekly* method, *jump right into Step 3.* Otherwise, before going ahead with *extra* prepayment plans, you need to review your short term and long term financial picture. Take a hard look at your current budget, if you have one. If you don't have a budget, it's time to **take control** of your finances. Determine your approximate NET WORTH.

Your *net worth* is the **difference** *between the total values of* your *assets (what you* **own**) *and your liabilities (what you* **owe**). Your *assets* include savings, retirement accounts, stocks, bonds, gold and silver coins, the equity in your house, in short anything you possess that has a *known* and immediate cash value. Your *liabilities* include all your loan balances and credit card debts.

On a good day, when you're full of energy, take a few minutes and list all your assets and liabilities right off the top of your head. You'll naturally refine the list as you go. Put a dollar value on each item. Total the assets. Total the liabilities. Subtract the liabilities from the assets. The difference is your *net worth*.

Some people find this a boring exercise. Probably the real reason people are reluctant to get this done is because they think it could be a rude awakening. But, it could be a kick in the pants that sends you in an upward direction. Think of it as a sketch of your current financial position. *Think of it as an exciting game.* In fact, *it will be one*, as you start to maneuver to get from where you are to where you want to be financially. Your net worth is a snapshot of your financial health at the time you calculate it. What do you do with the net worth figure once you have it? Use it as a control gauge. If it's *negative,* that's bad news. You need to get rid of some debts to get out of the hole. As you'll see a bit further, even in this situation, prepaying your mortgage is not out of the question.

With a positive net worth you may still not be in the clear. Compare it to your annual income. If your annual income is more than *twice* your net worth, you need to fix things in your financial life. Get to <u>know</u> your personal and family dollar inflows and outflows. Understand where your money is **coming from** and where it is **going**. Make it a point to track the cash that comes in, goes out, and stays in on a month-to-month basis, so you can be familiar with your financial movements. Definitely plan to prepay your mortgage.

You should recalculate your net worth every year. Compare it to your net worth from a year ago. Are you doing better or worse than last year? **You really never stand still.** *You're either growing your assets or digging a deeper liability hole.* **<u>Be tough and curb spending habits that don't contribute to your goals.</u>** In addition to food, clothing, and shelter, you also need to make sure that you have covered some other basic essentials for your family. Live well, but avoid unnecessary frills.

Get appropriate life insurance coverage. Rather than whole life, stay with *term insurance*. It gives you the same coverage for a lot less. Cancel insurance policies you don't need. Let's face it, your favorite pet doesn't really need to be insured, unless it somehow provides you with a stream of income that could need replacement. **Use the extra cash to build an emergency fund, and a fund for the education of your children.** While you're at it, you could use some of that money to *beef up your IRA*.

The cash you use to prepay your mortgage becomes part of your equity. *If you should need some of that money* **and don't want to sell the house, the only way to get back a portion of equity money in liquid form is to take out an equity loan of some sort. Because you risk losing the house, if you can't keep up the payments (which include interest, of course),** *an equity loan is usually not a good idea.* **When you prepay, think of that additional equity the same way you'd think of your IRA. It's money you don't want to disturb for a while. That's why you should build a pool of emergency money up front.**

See that you have these in place:

> *1.* **Proper life, medical, disability, homeowners, and automobile insurance coverage**
>
> *2.* **At least three months' income in the bank to cover emergencies**
>
> *3.* **Suitable retirement planning investments *(IRA, 401k, etc.)***
>
> *4.* **Funding for the education of your children**

After you take care of those basics, clarify your personal long term goals for retiring your mortgage. Do you know exactly when your current mortgage is **scheduled to be paid off with no prepayments**? How old will you be then?

Would you like to retire your mortgage while you're still young and *long before you retire yourself? Set a target date in the future when you want to be free of your mortgage burden.*

Example

Alice and Earl Kelsick bought a house three years ago with a 30-year mortgage. He's 37 years old and plans to retire by age 62, in exactly 25 years. At that point in time, the Kelsicks will have 2 more years to go on the mortgage.

But, the prospect of being saddled with mortgage payments until age 64 is extremely unappealing to Earl. So, they decide to do whatever it takes to finish off the mortgage by the time Earl is 52. That means the Kelsicks aim to cut the mortgage term by 12 years. **The outside target date is December 1st of the year of Earl's 52nd birthday.**

Using this plan, the Kelsicks will be able to pay **themselves** rather than the bank after ending the mortgage. **They can invest the same old monthly payment amount for ten years right up to Earl's retirement at age 62.**

If your net worth is about the same or *better* than your annual income, that indicates a good state of financial health. You may have some extra money floating around. So, you could be wondering whether to invest the money or prepay your mortgage with it. Here's a guiding thought.

Make sure there is no LOW-RISK investment available to you now that has a LASTING **after-tax** rate that is substantially higher than your *after-tax* mortgage interest rate. The type of investment that applies here must be capable of holding the higher rate for the same length of time it would take to retire your mortgage by prepaying. A bond fund is one of the very few candidate investments. See ***Chapter Twenty*** for a procedure to calculate *after-tax* rates.

Compare your mortgage rate to the current interest rates available on the bond fund market. *When evaluating the rates of tax-free bonds, be sure to compare those rates with the AFTER-TAX interest rate of your mortgage.* Are those rates 3 or more points **higher** than your mortgage rate? If they are, then look for **some low-risk bond instrument.** That instrument must be able to pay those rates FOR THE DURATION **your mortgage would last if you were prepaying.** It should also give you the option to invest small amounts of money **on a monthly basis over the same period of time.**

But, if your mortgage rate is about the same or **higher** than current rates, it pays to go ahead and take the *monthly* prepayment plunge. When you decide it makes sense for you to prepay, let your goals dictate your choice. Your current financial circumstances may be a poor guide.

If it looks like you have no cash available for prepayments, you might just be witnessing a lie. ***Look beyond your apparent limitations for possibilities that may not be visible, but yet may exist.*** Take a peek at things from different angles. You could be pleasantly shocked at your *real* present financial capabilities. See *chapter sixteen* for details on how to dig out some cash.

SELECTING A PREPAYMENT METHOD

There are many approaches to prepaying. Most are variations, extensions, or combinations of basic themes. When you get to know the basics, you might even cook up your own combinations.

Again, all the tactics you might read about in different books boil down to the four basic methods introduced in previous chapters. Here they are again:

> ⇒   *Increasing Prepayment*
> ⇒   *Fixed Prepayment*
> ⇒   *Term-based Prepayment*
> ⇒   *Extra-annual Payment*

Those methods may also be known by other names. That's not important. There are no particular standard names for those. *Focus on the way they work.* In deciding on a prepayment method, you can adopt one of two general guidelines based on your pocketbook.

You can do either of these:

> **Let a tight budget dictate what you can afford to prepay**
>
> *or*
>
> **Go by the time you want to save.**

Let your particular objectives guide your selection. Of course, if your circumstances change, you can switch from one guideline to the other.

GOING BY BUDGET

When you work with a small budget, you have to decide exactly how much you can afford to prepay. You can then find out how much interest each small prepayment can save for you. If you have a fixed-rate mortgage, you can determine approximately how many years a given amount of prepayment can knock off the original term, and how much total interest it can save over the reduced term.

If your budget is really tight at first, do not despair. After trimming down some of your "financial sponges", you can probably still afford to put aside $10, $15, $20, or more each month. *It is better to prepay small amounts than to make no prepayments at all.* In this case, you can use the *Fixed Prepayment* method to get wonderful results.

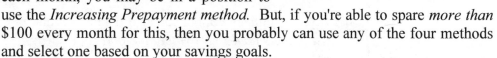

If you have little or no extra cash, *consider the Extra-Annual Payment method.* If you can scrape up around $100 of spare cash each month, you may be in a position to use the *Increasing Prepayment method.* But, if you're able to spare *more than* $100 every month for this, then you probably can use any of the four methods and select one based on your savings goals.

The idea is to have a plan at work for you. Keep it simple. As long as you're prepaying *something*, it doesn't matter if you're not too sure at first which method you should be using. **Start prepaying now.**

Special Tip

Use the *Extra-Annual* payment method while you decide on a monthly prepayment plan. When you do decide, *then use the monthly prepayment plan AS A SECOND METHOD ON TOP of the Extra-Annual Payment method. **The two methods in combination will wipe out your mortgage balance in no time flat and save you MORE money than you could ever imagine.***

Here is an easy guide for selecting a method based on your ability to prepay.

IF YOU CAN PREPAY	CONSIDER THIS METHOD
$0	EXTRA-ANNUAL PAYMENT
$10 to $50	FIXED PREPAYMENT
$50 to $150	INCREASING PREPAYMENT
$150 up	TERM-BASED PREPAYMENT

Table 14.1

Table 14.1 is intended to give you a ballpark idea. The table is only a general starting point that offers suggestions for you to consider first. You decide.

To Recap

- If you want to do something now, but can't come up with regular extra cash, apply the *Extra-Annual Payment* method.

- If you're undecided, but can afford some regular pocket change, *start using the Fixed Prepayment method right away.*

- If you can afford $50 to $150 or so, you should go for the *Increasing Prepayment* method.

- With $150 or more a month, you might also be able to afford the *Term-Based Prepayment* method.

- When you decide on a monthly prepayment method, *use it ON TOP of the Extra-Annual Payment* method.

GOING BY TIME TO SAVE

On the other hand, when you have a larger budget to play with, then you have wider options. You can decide on the term of years within which you want to pay off the mortgage, or set a total amount of interest savings you desire to achieve. Then, it becomes a matter of determining the best prepayment method and the minimum prepayment amount that give those results.

The exact technique to use in determining the minimum prepayment amount depends on the method you choose. The type of mortgage you have may also influence your choice of a method. You can use any method with just about any type of mortgage. But, if you have an adjustable-rate mortgage, then you need to re-evaluate the prepayment amounts every time the interest rate changes. If the rates goes up, you should adjust the prepayment amount up. *However, if the interest rate goes **down**, you should keep the SAME prepayment level.*

Here is a look at the prepayment methods based on what you want to do.

IF YOU WANT TO	*USE THIS PREPAYMENT METHOD*
Reduce the mortgage term to about two thirds of the original schedule	*Extra-annual Payment*
Cut the mortgage term by several years	*Fixed Prepayment*
Cut the mortgage term in half	*Increasing Prepayment*
Cut the mortgage term down to a specific shorter term	*Term-based Prepayment*

Table 14.2

GETTING PRELIMINARY INFORMATION

<u>Before</u> you start prepaying your mortgage, be sure to:

Get a current amortization schedule for your mortgage

The amortization schedule contains valuable information. As you know, it shows payment periods, the associated interest and principal payments, and the declining balance. It is a useful tool to help you plan and manage your prepayment strategy.

If you have access to a personal computer, you can use a spreadsheet program to generate an amortization schedule yourself. You can also use an inexpensive off-the-shelf personal finance program with mortgage amortization functions.

If you don't have access to a PC, contact your bank. You might find someone in your bank's mortgage department who would give you amortization printouts for free. But, these days, a bank will tend to charge a minimal fee ($15-$20) to generate a regular schedule for you. Again for a fee, you could get a regular amortization schedule from accountants, real estate appraisers, or other financial professionals.

If your local resources fail to produce the schedule you need, turn to the product information sheet at the back of this book for details on a variety of amortization products you can order from Capital Search Systems. Use the product order form and attach an amortization information sheet to your order. Be sure to also fill out and send in the book buyer's registration form to be entitled to discounts on those schedule runs.

Determine the current period or payment number

Call your lender to ask for the current payment number. That should be a period number in the amortization schedule. *Record the payment number in the worksheet (see Figure 14.1 below).*

Confirm the current mortgage balance due

Get a quote of the current balance due. You can either get it direct from the bank or read it off the last monthly mortgage statement. *Record the remaining mortgage balance in the worksheet,* as it is the starting point of reference to use in tracking the effects of your prepayments.

Review and confirm your exact type of mortgage. Reconfirm the interest rate and the term. *Jot down the interest rate and the original term of your mortgage in the worksheet.*

If your mortgage includes a *temporary* buydown, ask your lender or the seller for **the buydown rate schedule.** If you have an adjustable rate mortgage (ARM), get the **current rate, ARM adjustment period, index, margin, and cap.** Write down this information.

Get the bank's concurrence for you to prepay without problems

You should consider it your right to prepay. First, look at your mortgage contract. If it specifically prohibits prepayments on the principal, that might be illegal. In such an unusual case, you should consider shopping around for a better bank to refinance your mortgage with.

Most lenders accept prepayments automatically as a normal occurrence. If you have any doubts, inform your lender of your plan to make regular principal prepayments. You want to clear the way right off the bat.

If the bank wants to charge you for prepaying (not the same as a prepayment penalty), that could be illegal and you do have recourse to higher authority. Ask to see where in the mortgage contract such charges are defined for small prepayments. You can ask to refer this to the attention of the bank president. If necessary, you can even complain in writing to your state's banking commission.

Your bank might not want to give you a hard time, but may still want to limit your prepayments to just the exact principal amount due each month or some other amount. If a bank takes a funny position like that, you should discuss things with a representative to understand what they mean. You may be able to negociate a favorable arrangement. *Always remember that you have a fundamental right to gradually prepay your debt.*

The majority of banks really don't mind your prepayments.

Here's the worksheet format to use in tracking your prepayments. In *Appendix J,* you will find a full-size blank that you can copy for your personal use.

MORTGAGE PREPAYMENT TRACKING WORKSHEET

Page ___ of ___

MORTGAGE TYPE	TERM OF YEARS	REMAINING YEARS	ORIGINAL BALANCE	REMAINING BALANCE	INTEREST RATE	EFFECTIVE DATE	MONTHLY PAYMENT

Period No.	Date Paid	Principal Payment Due	Amount Paid	Principal Pre-paid	Interest Saved	Cumulative Interest Saved	Principal Balance	Months Saved	Cumul. Months Saved

Figure 14.1

In Figure 14.1, the *bottom* section of the worksheet (starting with **Period No.**) is the prepayment tracking log you should consider using. The data you log in will quickly show where you stand. *Chapter Fifteen* illustrates exactly how to fill out the tracking details. You'll find a guide on page 156.

You can use this *same* worksheet for any kind of mortgage you're prepaying. Get started by filling in the basic facts about your mortgage in the top section of the worksheet. Specify the mortgage type, term of years, remaining years, original balance, remaining balance, interest rate, effective date, and scheduled monthly payment.

Refer to the guide on the following page for an explanation of the items in the *header* section of Figure 14.1.

MORTGAGE PREPAYMENT TRACKING WORKSHEET
Explanation of Header Entries

MORTGAGE TYPE

The type of your mortgage
Example: Fixed rate, Adjustable rate

TERM OF YEARS

The original term of years
Example: 30

REMAINING YEARS

Number of years remaining to pay off the mortgage
Example: 30 (if you're at the very beginning of the term)

ORIGINAL BALANCE

The original amount of the mortgage loan
Example: $80,000

REMAINING BALANCE

The balance due at the time you start using this worksheet
Example: $80,000 (if you're at the very beginning of the term)

INTEREST RATE

The interest rate you're currently paying
Example: 10%

NOTE: *If the interest rate changes for whatever reason, such as a new adjustable rate, a new buydown rate change, or refinancing, **just get a new amortization schedule and start a new worksheet.***

EFFECTIVE DATE

The effective date of the interest rate you're currently paying. If there were no rate changes, this date is the same as the mortgage origination date.

Example: 1/1/93

MONTHLY PAYMENT

The scheduled monthly payment specified in the mortgage contract (*not including taxes and insurance*).

Example: $702.06

Here is a sample worksheet for the fixed rate 30-year mortgage of $80,000 at 10% using the illustration data from **Chapter Seven**, Step *1* in the section *How To Do It In step-by-step Detail.*

MORTGAGE PREPAYMENT TRACKING WORKSHEET

Page __1__ of ___

MORTGAGE TYPE	TERM OF YEARS	REMAINING YEARS	ORIGINAL BALANCE	REMAINING BALANCE	INTEREST RATE	EFFECTIVE DATE	MONTHLY PAYMENT
Fixed rate	30	30	$80,000	$79,964.61	10%	1/1/93	$702.06

Period No.	Date Paid	Principal Payment Due	Amount Paid	Principal Pre-paid	Interest Saved	Cumulative Interest Saved	Principal Balance	Months Saved	Cumul. Months Saved

Figure 14.2

Chapter Fifteen

THE REPEAT ACTION PHASE

Until your mortgage is paid up, repeat steps 4 through 7 once every month, or whenever you make a prepayment.

STEP	ACTION
4	**Make a prepayment,** using your chosen method
5	**Confirm the new balance**
6	**Update the worksheet** and keep all written lender acknowledgments, canceled checks, and receipts together with the worksheet

STEP 7 *is ONLY for adjustable rate mortgages, fixed rate mortgages with temporary buydown, or newly refinanced mortgages.*

7	**If the mortgage interest rate changes beginning the next period,** then get a new amortization schedule that reflects the new rate *and start a new worksheet.*

Step 4

MAKING A PREPAYMENT

For maximum assurance that your prepayment will be applied to principal only, *write a separate check.* The second check can serve as its own payment slip. Be sure to specify on this check the *mortgage number* and the caption ***"For Principal ONLY".***

The bank's payment slip usually contains an entry *for principal only.* Specify the amount you're prepaying in this area also. Send both checks together attached to the payment slip.

Here's an example using *two* checks.

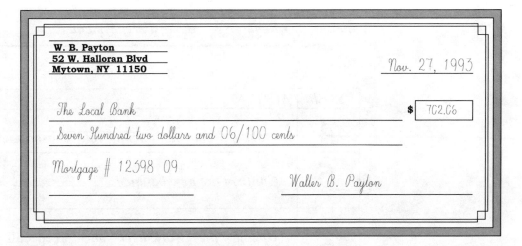

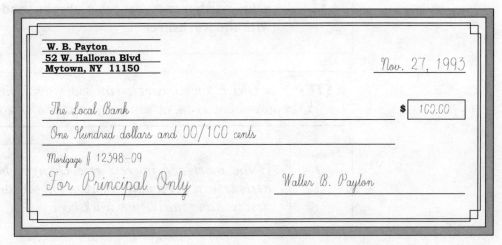

You can also put the prepayment amount in the same check that pays the regular payment. In this case, specify clearly in the memo section of the check the *mortgage number* and the *amount you're prepaying* with the note "*For Principal ONLY*".

Here's an example using *one* check.

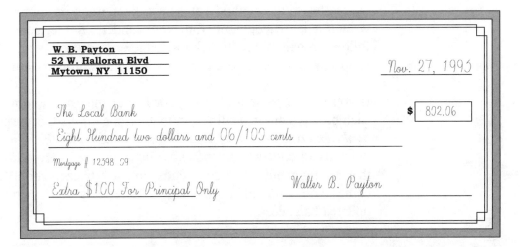

When you include the prepayment in the regular payment check, also attach a payment slip. Make sure you specify the amount you're prepaying in the area on the payment slip reserved *for additional principal*.

Here's an example of a bank payment slip that reflects both payment and prepayment.

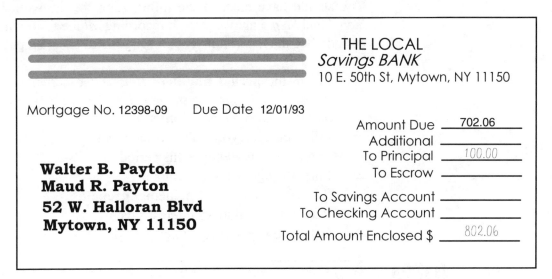

Plan to make and use your own supply of custom mortgage payment slips. They really come in handy, especially when you don't have one from the bank. You'll find a blank that you can copy for your personal use in *Appendix K*.

CONFIRMING THE UPDATED BALANCE

No matter which method you select, keep track of your prepayments and get a written acknowledgment from your lender. Some lenders may automatically follow-up with a note to acknowledge each prepayment. But, others won't. It is up to you to make sure each prepayment is properly credited.

If you have a payment book, your lender may not automatically acknowledge each prepayment in writing. In that case, call, visit, or write to *request that the bank send a statement of your balance once a month.* You should actually ask the bank to *convert your payment book to a monthly billing statement.* With that arrangement, the bank sends you a bill each month. The monthly bill comes with a detailed statement that reflects your payments and shows the updated balance.

UPDATING THE WORKSHEET
AND KEEPING RECORDS TOGETHER

You should have most of the information for the worksheet entry, based on *Step 4* and *Step 5* above. Finish recording *all* the following data for the current period. See the *Explanation of Detail Entries* sheet on page 156.

⇒   Fill in the **period number** *(this is the actual period currently up for payment; it may also indicate the next scheduled period in the amortization schedule printout)*
⇒   Fill in the *date* you make the payment
⇒   Enter the *principal due* this period
⇒   Enter the total payment amount
⇒   Record the amount of **principal prepaid**
⇒   Record the amount of interest saved
⇒   Calculate *cumulative* interest saved

To get the *Cumulative Interest Saved* for a given line in the worksheet, add **Interest Saved** in the *same* line to **Cumulative Interest Saved** from the *previous* line -- (**Note:** *In the very first prepayment line, as there's no previous line, Cumulative Interest Saved is the same as Interest Saved*). The same process applies to *Cumulative Months Saved and Months Saved.*

⇒   Write in the unpaid *principal balance*

⇒   Write in the *Months Saved*

⇒   Write in the unpaid *Cumulative Months Saved*

Continuing with the illustration data from **Chapter Seven**, Steps **1** through **4** in the section *How To Do It In step-by-step Detail* (pages 54 to 57), your worksheet would now look like this:

MORTGAGE PREPAYMENT TRACKING WORKSHEET

Page _ 1 _ of ___

MORTGAGE TYPE	TERM OF YEARS	REMAINING YEARS	ORIGINAL BALANCE	REMAINING BALANCE	INTEREST RATE	EFFECTIVE DATE	MONTHLY PAYMENT
Fixed rate	30	30	$80,000	$79,964.61	10%	1/1/93	$702.06

Period No.	Date Paid	Principal Payment Due	Amount Paid	Principal Pre-paid	Interest Saved	Cumulative Interest Saved	Principal Balance	Months Saved	Cumul. Months Saved
2	3/1/93	35.69	774.32	72.26	1,331.84	1,331.84	79,856.66	2	2

Figure 15.1

Since the original periods 3 and 4 have been prepaid, their contents have been eliminated. So, you should just draw a line through periods 3 and 4 *in the original amortization schedule* paper printout. In that paper schedule, the next scheduled period is period number *5*. But, that is really the *third interest accrual period* or the **actual** Period **3**.

The worksheet can reflect *both* the actual and the scheduled period numbers. Write the *actual* period number in the next row (it's the always next chronological period number). Then, right next to the actual period number, also write in the *scheduled* period number within parentheses just for reference.

Still using Figure 7.6 (page 56) as an example, the principal portion of *$36.89* of the new Period 4 (scheduled Period 6) can be prepaid in the next monthly payment due for actual Period 3. The worksheet entry would then be:

3 (5)	4/1/93	36.59	738.95	36.89	665.17	1,997.01	79,783.18	1	3

After that prepayment, you would then cross out *scheduled* period number **6** in the *original* amortization schedule printout. The *scheduled* period 7 would then become *actual* Period 4, and so on.

The guide on the following page explains the bottom section of Figure 15.1 in more detail.

> **MORTGAGE PREPAYMENT TRACKING WORKSHEET**
> *Explanation of Detail Entries*

PERIOD NO.

The period number corresponding to the payment due. The first period number is extracted from the amortization schedule. Subsequent actual period numbers are **derived from the last worksheet entry.** Corresponding *scheduled* period numbers should be entered in parentheses for reference.
Example: 2
          3 (5)

DATE PAID

The date on the prepayment check
Example: 3/1/93

PRINCIPAL PAYMENT DUE

Scheduled principal portion of the current payment due
Example: $35.69

AMOUNT PAID

Total amount paid including prepayment.
This may be just the prepayment amount if you're sending a separate check.
Example: $774.32

PRINCIPAL PRE-PAID

Amount of principal *prepayment*
Example: $72.36

INTEREST SAVED

Amount of interest saved as a result of the prepayment
Example: $1,331.84

CUMULATIVE INTEREST SAVED

Total interest saved to date. *This is the sum of the current interest saved and the cumulative interest saved in the **last** entry.*
Example: $1,331.84

PRINCIPAL BALANCE

Balance due *after the current total payment*
Example: $79,856.66

MONTHS SAVED

Months saved as a result of the prepayment
Example: 2

CUMULATIVE MONTHS SAVED

Number of months saved to date. *This is the sum of the current months saved and the cumulative months saved in the **last** entry.*
Example: 2

It is important to keep your prepayment tracking worksheets, amortization schedules, all written acknowledgments, and canceled mortgage payment checks in a *dedicated folder.*

CHECKING FOR INTEREST RATE CHANGES

If you have an adjustable rate mortgage, *a fixed rate mortgage with a buydown rate schedule*(see *Note* below) *or if you refinance* stay on the alert.

Key Point

When a new interest rate kicks in, **start a new tracking worksheet.** *You may need to adjust your prepayment level.*

If the rate goes up, your prepayment should also go up proportionately. If the rate goes down, then a smaller prepayment should get the results you want, depending on the method you're using. *However, with a lower interest rate, it's a good idea to keep the same prepayment level.* Obviously, the *same* prepayment with a lower interest rate will result in greater interest savings and an even shorter term.

A *buydown* is a special arrangement that allows a seller to give an incentive to buy. The *seller*, particularly a housing developer, offers a monthly payment based on a lower interest rate than what the lender actually gets on the loan. *As a result, the monthly payment is lower than normal.* With lower payments, **the buyer can afford a mortgage that would normally be out of reach.** That's the main advantage here.

To compensate the lender for the shortage in interest, the seller pays a certain number of *points (a **point** is 1% of the loan balance).* So, the lender gets the full amount expected with the normal interest rate. But, the seller doesn't lose out on the deal. The seller makes up for the *cost* of the buydown either in volume sales or by somehow working this special cost into the *price* of the property.

A buydown can be either *permanent* or *temporary.* A permanent buydown keeps the lower monthly payments for the life of the loan. The buyer gets to stay with the lower interest rate throughout the term. *(Continued on next page)*

Continued

But, a temporary buydown only holds the low payments for the first few years. There is no *negative amortization,*[1] because the seller paid the interest shortage in points. The interest rate usually starts out at 3% *lower than normal* and climbs by 1% per year until it reaches the normal rate.

The temporary buydown is the type that concerns us here. When you're at the beginning of your mortgage term, *if you're not sure whether you have a temporary buydown, just check with your lender or examine your mortgage contract.*

[1] Negative amortization is a phenomenon where the principal balance gets bigger after a monthly payment. That happens when the payment is too small to cover all the *interest* due. The *interest* **shortage** then becomes part of the principal balance due.

Chapter Sixteen

HOW TO FIND THE CASH TO PREPAY WITH

⇒ *How to get cash out of six "sponges"*

You may not yet realize it, but you can actually cough up cash you didn't know you had. You can materialize extra cash now by saving money when you shop for groceries, clothing, appliances, and transportation.

If you make it a habit to record your expenses every day, you will become aware of other areas that absorb your dollars unnecessarily. Every little bit you save adds to your available cash.

With a little thought, you might pull in a precious sum from several areas that may be soaking up more dollars from you than necessary. Those financial "sponges" may include your:

1 Homeowner's insurance

2 Mortgage life insurance

3 Car insurance

4 Property taxes

5 Mortgage escrow account

6 Relatively high mortgage interest rate

Let's isolate the specific actions you can take to plug up those cash "soakers".

"SPONGE" # | 1 | HOMEOWNER'S INSURANCE

You need to examine your home insurance policy details.

Look for the possibility to reduce the premium by INCREASING THE BASIC DEDUCTIBLE. You might go from the usual $250 to $500 or more and save at least 10% on the total annual premium. Check the coverage. It should not cover the value of the WHOLE PROPERTY including the land.

> *Make sure that the coverage is for the amount to replace the HOUSE only.*

Consult with your insurer and ask for details about the various discounts that may be available to you. If you don't smoke, you may qualify for a *non-smoker's discount. You could get a safety device discount,* if your house is equipped with smoke detectors and a burglar alarm system. Those items can add up to a substantial reduction in your total premium.

HOMEOWNER'S INSURANCE REDUCTION
ACTION STEPS

1	*Increase the basic deductible.*
2	*Cover the house for replacement value only.*
3	*Get all the discounts you qualify for.*
4	*Get only the coverage you need.*

"SPONGE" # 2   MORTGAGE LIFE INSURANCE

Right off the bat you would save a tremendous bundle by dumping mortgage life insurance if you have it. This is one type of insurance you definitely don't need. It is excessively expensive.

The way it works, you pay exactly the same premium for the duration of your mortgage. But, the mortgage balance goes down with every principal payment.   So, eventually you wind up paying a lot of premium for a mortgage balance that's next to nothing.

For instance, when your balance is $3,000, the death benefit is $3,000, even if the original mortgage amount covered was $100,000.   What's even worse, the death benefit is paid out to the bank, not to your inheritors.

Special Tip

When you get right down to it, mortgage life insurance is really like an expensive *decreasing term* policy where the bank is the benefitor, not your heirs. *So, you're a lot better off getting a __real__ term life insurance policy to cover your mortgage balance for as much as 65% to 70% less in cost.*

You would do even more for your heirs, if you specify in your will that the death benefit amount be invested so that the income is enough to continue the monthly mortgage payments. That way, you're also guaranteeing a perpetual source of income for your people when the mortgage is paid up.

MORTGAGE LIFE INSURANCE REDUCTION
ACTION STEPS

1 | *Find out if you have mortgage life insurance.*

2 | ***Get a term life insurance policy for the mortgage balance*** *(or add the mortgage balance to your present term insurance).*

3 | *Cancel the mortgage life insurance policy.*

"SPONGE" # 3   CAR INSURANCE

Review your car insurance policy. What is the resale value of your car? ***You could reduce your premium by as much as 20 percent*** just by <u>INCREASING the deductible amounts on comprehensive and collision coverages.</u> Chances are you have a deductible of about $100 on both comprehensive and collision. If you have a little cushion money, raise those deductibles to $500. If you can manage it, go to $1,000.

In fact, if your car is worth less than $1,500 or so on the market, it would make sense to eliminate the comprehensive and collision coverages altogether. Call your insurance company and get the total premium amounts that the different amounts of deductible would produce.

On the flip side, you can also reduce the maximum liability coverage amounts in your policy, as long as the amounts you choose are in line with your state's minimum requirements. Your insurer can tell you what the state minimums are.

Key Point

#1

The important thing here is that you don't let the insurance company determine your total liability coverage. Do work with your insurance agent to whatever extent you feel he or she is willing to advise you with impartiality. But, after carefully weighing all the facts, <u>decide for yourself</u>.

Find out what premium amounts apply to the minimum and the maximum liability coverage amounts *per accident*. As a general rule, adjust your total liability coverage *per accident* to be about twice your net worth.

Avoid making claims for minor acts of vandalism on your car. If some thug busts up the car's door lock, breaks the glass, or damages the dashboard trying to take the factory radio, *just fix it at your own expense.* Any claim you make goes into a central database that most companies have access to. When you're identified as a frequent claim maker *(it only takes **three** claims to do that),* you could be classified as a high risk. That can cost you a few big ones.

Key Point

#2

Shop around. Do this routinely even if you think you have adequate coverage.

Get quotes from several companies. Different insurers have different cost structures. Some manage to cut tremendous marketing overhead and can afford to pass the savings on to their customers. You could save hundreds of dollars a year for the same coverage just by switching to another company.

Here are some things to bear in mind when you talk to an insurance agent:

- *If you habitually park your car in a garage, or even in your driveway, stress that fact.* It makes a big difference in your favor.

- *The number of miles you drive each year counts big.* You make out well for anything up to *7,500 miles per year.* Anything above that, watch out.

- *If you own a radar detector,* most insurance companies might not want you as a customer.

Aim to pinpoint specifically all the discounts that each company allows. These items may qualify you for discounts:

◊ *Passive restraints* (seat belts or air bags)
◊ *Multi-car* (two or three cars in the family covered by the same policy)
◊ *Multi-policy* (car and homeowner's policies with the same insurer)
◊ *Good driver status* (Are you a good driver? Get this discount)
◊ *Anti-theft alarms*
◊ *Car pooling to work*
◊ *Mature driver* (if you're over 50)
◊ *Driver's education* (take a state-approved defensive driving course)
◊ *Being a non-smoker.*

CAR INSURANCE REDUCTION
ACTION STEPS

---

1   *Shop for better prices - they're available!*

2   *Increase the deductibles on comprehensive and collision.*

3   *Decide for yourself how much coverage to get above the minimum state liability coverage requirements.*

4   *If your car is old (worth less than $1,500 or so), just drop the coverages on comprehensive and collision altogether.*

5   *Get all the discounts you qualify for.*

6   *Get only the coverage you need (get rid of optional coverages).*

"SPONGE" # $\boxed{4}$ **PROPERTY TAXES**

One reason the escrow portion of your mortgage payment is high is because your property taxes are relatively high. In fact, your property taxes could be out of line with reality. You could be a victim of a very common phenomenon: *unfair assessment.*

Is it worth pursuing a reduction? The amount of reduction you can get depends on your particular situation. But, look at it this way. If your annual property taxes get reduced by only $600, right there *that's $50 per month LESS on escrow. You can use the $50 to prepay your mortgage, month after month, year after year.*

Unfortunately, most people aren't even aware of the possibility that their homes may be badly assessed, causing them to pay higher taxes. Unbeknownst to the public, a majority of local tax assessors are not *professionally prepared* for the job. As a result, the majority of assessments are unfair. Studies actually show that 60% of all houses deserve a reduction in their assessments.

On the other hand, if you determine that your assessment is flawed, **you can easily get a reduction**. More than 70% of those who protest their assessment get a reduction.

But, very few people ever question their assessments. It turns out that mostly big real estate investors are aware of the necessity to stay on top of real estate taxes. However, the little guy also stands to gain by having an assessment corrected. *A reduction will save you money for many years to come.*

Bear in mind that your local tax assessor sets the real estate tax you pay. Contrary to income taxes, your property taxes are determined for you by someone else. You have a right to know the facts behind your taxes. So, get to know the process used to establish the assessed value of your house and your taxes.

Take the time to look into your property card down at the local assessor's office. Check the data for correctness. Find out what went in as the basis for your assessment. Get the readings on the following:

| 1 | *Recorded market value of your house and other comparable houses in the area* |

| 2 | *Assessment ratio currently in use* |

| 3 | *Assessed value of your house* |

| 4 | *Dimensions of your property shown in the assessor tax records* |

Over Assessment

Analyze the information. Compare the market value of your house to the values of similar houses in the neighborhood. Ask how the market value of your house was derived. *Is the value higher than going market values? If it is, then the assessment based on this market value will be too high.* In this case, you have an ***over assessment*** on your hands.

Ask about when the assessment ratio was calculated. Is it a new ratio? An old ratio?

Illegal Assessment

Do this simple test. Divide the assessed value of your house by the market value to get a ratio. If this ratio is larger than the ***legal*** assessment ratio *currently in use*, that means your house was actually assessed at a *higher* percentage. Consequently, the assessed value is higher than it should be relative to the market value, and the taxes will be too high. Here you have a case of ***illegal assessment.***

Unequal Assessment

Compare the assessed value of your house to the current market value. If the assessed value is larger than the current market value of the house, then confirm whether the law requires assessed values to be set at no more than market values.   If the law requires it, then your assessment should be reduced, because you have a case of ***unequal assessment.***

Scrutinize the data in the assessor's tax records for your property.   Look for errors in calculations, transcription, or  completeness. If you identify an error, again you have reason to look for a reduction. *When the current market value of your house is **greater** than the value used to assess the house, **if you proceed further, you might wind up with an INCREASE in your taxes.***

If you have any of the above grounds for a reduction, ***carefully document everything.*** Get appropriate forms from the assessor's office and fill them out. Determine what your tax should be and put it down on paper. ***At this point, you may not need a formal appeal.*** <u>You could get things cleared up just by having a discussion with the local assessor.</u>

Call or visit your local county clerk's office to get the exact schedule of events. There is a timetable for a preliminary public review and grievance period during which you can get things fixed by the assessor without going further. *That's what you want to aim for.* It happens only once a year, usually at the end of the year, so try not to miss it. ***Stick to the schedule, otherwise you may have to wait another year.***

While you're at it, make sure you are getting any exemptions you filed for. A veteran's exemption could be worth $50 or so a year (nothing to spit at). So, if you haven't done so yet, file for exemptions you qualify for. Remember, every little bit helps.

If the assessor disagrees with your reasons, **then** you want to prepare a formal appeal. Be prepared to proceed to the next step of filing an appeal within the scheduled period. *In fact, you should expect to have to file the appeal.*

Important Tip!

> **There may be experts in your town that can work to get your taxes reduced. If you need one,** *seek only those who would charge you a percentage of the savings.*
>
> **But, sometimes professionals who take small cases have unimpressive credentials.** *The fact that these experts do this often and for pay* **may cause the appeal board to have reservations about their sincerity. Choose cautiously.**

If you have all the facts to support your appeal, it may be better to present your case for examination to the review board personally. The board may react more favorably to your original sincerity and candor. So, even before your case comes up, plan to attend actual appeal sessions as a spectator, just to get familiar with the procedures. Take notes on the formalities and requirements.

When the time comes to have your case examined by the tax review board, have your complete documentation ready. It should include the forms you filled out to indicate the nature of your grievance. Attach a listing of any errors you found, any exemptions you filed for but did not receive.

Remember This!

> Your documentation should specify the amount to which you want to reduce your assessment and your reasons for it. Use clear visual aids that stress your points. Bring copies for every one. Make your presentation in a persuasive way. *Above all don't give the impression you're questioning the assessor's sincerity or competence.*

If the review board also disagrees with you, you still have recourse to a higher court. Very few complaints go this far. But, if you want to go all the way, hire an expert lawyer who will handle the whole thing and charge you only if you get a reduction.

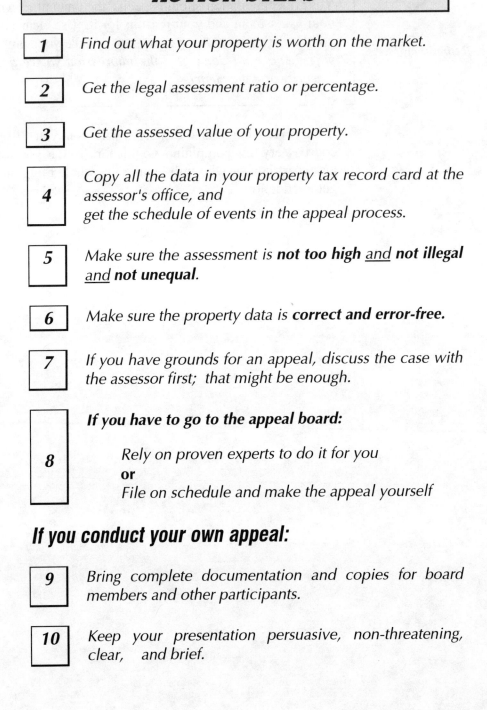

PROPERTY TAXES REDUCTION
ACTION STEPS

1   *Find out what your property is worth on the market.*

2   *Get the legal assessment ratio or percentage.*

3   *Get the assessed value of your property.*

4   *Copy all the data in your property tax record card at the assessor's office, and get the schedule of events in the appeal process.*

5   *Make sure the assessment is **not too high** and **not illegal** and **not unequal**.*

6   *Make sure the property data is **correct and error-free**.*

7   *If you have grounds for an appeal, discuss the case with the assessor first; that might be enough.*

8   **If you have to go to the appeal board:**

     Rely on proven experts to do it for you
     or
     File on schedule and make the appeal yourself

If you conduct your own appeal:

9   *Bring complete documentation and copies for board members and other participants.*

10   *Keep your presentation persuasive, non-threatening, clear, and brief.*

"SPONGE" # ⬚5⬚   MORTGAGE ESCROW ACCOUNT

The type of escrow money we're discussing here involves money the bank may require from you as part of your monthly payment, *in addition to your amortization payment,* to pay for *real estate taxes and homeowner's hazard insurance.*

If your mortgage comes with a monthly escrow deposit requirement, then *some of your money might be sleeping at the bank.* **That could happen after you get your real estate taxes reduced, or after you get less expensive insurance.** It's definitely happening *if your bank holds MORE of a cushion than your mortgage calls for.* When your mortgage requires NO cushion and the bank *insists on holding a cushion balance,* your money could be dozing off and you may be entitled to a refund.

Over a one-year period, the ***lowest end-of-month balance*** in your escrow account should not be GREATER than the cushion amount required in your mortgage contract. *If it is, then some of the balance is dormant money that could prepay some of your mortgage principal.*

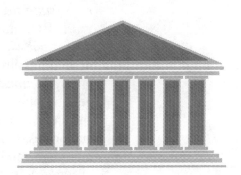

When your mortgage contract comes with an escrow cushion requirement (VA and FHA mortgages usually call for escrow accounts), the contract requires that a minimum balance be kept in reserve in the account *at all times.* That small cushion balance is often stated as a fractional part of the total payments expected from the account in any given year. Your mortgage agreement should state the specific fractional guideline. If you're not sure, then ask the bank for exact details. *You need to know the fractional reserve requirement and determine* **what the cushion amount has to be** *throughout the year.* That's your frame of reference for evaluating the lowest *end-of-month* balance in the account. The strategy is to target a year and find the lowest ending monthly escrow balance reached during that year. You can do this yourself. The correct procedure is explained in **The Smart Homeowner's Escrow Savings Guide** *(see the Product Information sheets at the end of this book for details).*

If your mortgage contract specifies an escrow reserve factor or fraction of one-twentieth (that's $5 for every $100 expected to be paid out), then the smallest end-of-month escrow balance in any year should not be more than ***1/20th*** *of the total annual payment for insurance and taxes on your property.*

For example, with a 1/20th escrow reserve requirement, if your property taxes and insurance for the year add up to $6,000, then the smallest end-of-month balance in your escrow account should be no more than $300.

Even if your mortgage contract does NOT call for an escrow cushion, the U.S. Department of Housing and Urban Development (HUD) still allows lenders that insist on it to maintain up to a *two-month cushion (1/6th or 16.6%)*. First, request from your bank a printout of the *Escrow Analysis* for the year you're monitoring. Examine the monthly mortgage statements for the year. *Focus on the end-of-month escrow balances.* Locate the smallest balance. *Compare that balance to the allowed cushion amount* (the total annual disbursements *times* either your mortgage contract's reserve fraction or HUD's **1/6th**). If that balance is more than the cushion, then you may have a complaint.

When you find more cushion money than required, ***don't rush and take out the surplus*** (the difference between smallest end-of-month balance and the allowed cushion)**.** Find out if there are any ***expected shortages*** because of forthcoming tax increases. When taxes or insurance premiums rise, the required reserve ***amount*** (not the percentage) also goes up. *So, use the* **surplus** *for mortgage prepayment ONLY if you get the assurance that your projected real estate taxes or insurance premium won't be much higher than the past year.* But, the surplus could be *so large that you can still use a portion of it, no matter what.* Find out from your bank whether the larger balance was needed to help service an increase in taxes. *If not, then discuss the possibility of a reduction in the escrow amount taken from your monthly payment.* If you get absolutely no cooperation, let them know about your awareness that you can choose to bring the matter to the attention of your state's trade and banking authorities. But, you probably won't ever have to resort to threats. The mortgage administration people at most banks are usually willing to help their clients fine tune things. When your equity is greater than 20%, some banks may even allow you to discontinue the escrow account and pay your own property taxes and insurance.

Banks normally adjust the escrow bill once a year. ***But, there are still many types of errors that could occur in the account and cost you.*** So, you should learn to monitor your escrow account. ***It could be a source of extra dollars.***

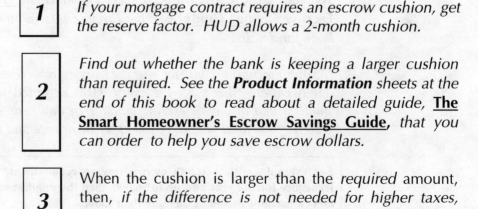

	MORTGAGE ESCROW ACCOUNT REDUCTION *ACTION STEPS*
1	*If your mortgage contract requires an escrow cushion, get the reserve factor. HUD allows a 2-month cushion.*
2	*Find out whether the bank is keeping a larger cushion than required. See the* **Product Information** *sheets at the end of this book to read about a detailed guide,* **The Smart Homeowner's Escrow Savings Guide,** *that you can order to help you save escrow dollars.*
3	When the cushion is larger than the *required* amount, then, *if the difference is not needed for higher taxes,* request a reduction in your monthly escrow deposits.

"SPONGE" # 6   RELATIVELY HIGH MORTGAGE INTEREST RATE

When the current mortgage interest rate drops below your mortgage rate by 2 points or more, it may be a good idea to refinance your mortgage to the lower rate. It makes sense to do that *only if you plan to stay in the house for a long time.*

When you refinance to a lower interest rate for the same remaining term, your monthly payment decreases. However, refinancing involves closing costs. You usually need up front cash to close. That can set you back a bit, even if you can finance the closing cost as part of the new balance *(you also pay interest on the cost).* It takes time to recuperate the cost and start benefiting from the lower payments. It's like a cost of going into business. You sort of function "in the red" until the accumulated savings from the lower payment equal the closing cost at the break-even point. Thereafter, it's pure savings. In fact, it is practical to refinance *when you intend to live in house **longer** than it takes for you to break even.*

So, before you refinance, you should:

• Get a good estimate of the *total closing cost*
• Get from the bank a statement of the *new monthly payment* amount.

With that information, you can estimate the number of years it'll take for you to recuperate the cost. *Base your decision on whether you'll be in the house longer than the break-even years.*

It's easy to determine the number of years required to break even. Just follow these steps:

 Subtract the new monthly payment from the old monthly payment. That gives you a ***difference.***

 Divide the closing cost by the difference you got in Step 1. That gives you the *number of months* to break-even.

 Divide the *number of months* **by 12** to get the answer in *years.*

 Multiply any fractional part of the *years* **by 12** to convert the fraction to months. Your final answer should be in years and months.

Example

For example, using the old $80,000-mortgage at 10% for 30 years, let's say you have a balance of $79,064.03 after two years. The current monthly payment is $702.06. The *current* interest rate is 7.5%. They tell you that, if you refinance, the closing cost would be $3,000 and the *new* monthly payment would be $563.62. **What is the break-even period?**

Subtract the new monthly payment from the old monthly payment. That gives you a ***difference:*** $702.06 - $563.62 = ***$138.44***

Divide the closing cost by the difference you got in Step 1. That gives *break-even* in months: $3,000 / $138.44 = 21.67003756 or over ***21.5 months***

Divide the *number of months **by 12*** to get the answers in years:
21.67003756 / 12 = **1.805836463** or over ***1.5 years***

Multiply any fractional part of the years by 12 to convert the fraction to months. Round the answer ***up*** to a whole month:
.805836463 x 12 = 9.67 or about ***10 months***

The break-even period is ***1 year and 10 months.*** After that time, you'll be saving ***$138.44*** each month. *You can use this extra money to reduce principal.*

After you refinance, if you just pay the new lower monthly payment, you save a lot of interest. But, *the term duration stays the same as it would have been before you refinanced.*

Make no mistake about it, the lower payment starts saving interest right away. But, to keep things in balance, the *difference* between the old and new monthly payments works during the break-even years to replace the money you shelled out in closing cost. Still, during the same time frame *and afterwards*, **this monthly savings can also work wonders to reduce your principal more quickly and shrink the term duration.**

Key Point

Use the monthly savings as new found money that you can prepay the mortgage with. The idea is to keep paying the old monthly amount. That does TWO wonderful things for you. The difference between the old monthly payment and the new one is a PREPAYMENT that not only saves you a LOT MORE interest money, but also shortens the term tremendously.

You should have no problem keeping up the old payment level, since you could do it before the refinancing. **You can achieve even more savings** *by using the pseudo bi-weekly technique in combination with this built-in extra monthly principal prepayment* (see the *Extra Annual Payment* method).

MORTGAGE INTEREST RATE REDUCTION
OR
HOW TO REFINANCE YOUR MORTGAGE CREATIVELY

ACTION STEPS

Consider this option ONLY IF your mortgage interest rate is at least 2 points above current rates.

---

1   Determine your break-even years.

2   Decide whether you plan to move soon or stay in the house longer than **the break-even years.**

Proceed with steps 3 and 4 ONLY if you plan to stay in the house longer than the break-even years.

3   Refinance your mortgage at the current lower rate to get the lower monthly payment and save on total interest.

4   **Keep making the monthly payment at the old higher rate.**

      Use the Extra Annual Payment method for even greater savings.

Notes

Chapter Seventeen

The POWER TECHNIQUE For DEBT ELIMINATION

⇒ *How to blast away ALL your short and long-term debts in no time flat*

If you add up the money you shell out every month on all your bills, you may find that you pile up quite a bit of dough. A lot of the money goes to paying short-term debts, such as retail card accounts, car loans, and personal loans.

Where does the money go?

Have you ever wondered what happens to your **buying power** when you finish paying one of those debts?

It seems like you get an infusion of new money. But, *the surge of buying power usually evaporates fast,* **as the money gets quickly consumed by new expenses.** That often happens automatically, *just out of habit.*

Ever wondered what it would be like *if all the money you pay on short-term debts, even what you pay on your mortgage, went into your savings account instead?* You can in fact *take control of your added money power. In a few short years,* you might be able to take the money that was available *every month* to pay off all your now defunct debts and deposit it all in a savings account. You can roll the money into other investments from there.

> *You just need a plan and the determination to stick to it.*

The overall objective is to get rid of your short-term debts, *so you can use the payments that used to go into those debts* **to prepay your mortgage.** The plan eliminates short-term debts *by prepaying each loan in turn, using payments that used to go into previous debts.* Here's a summary of the basic tactic.

The Basic Tactic

First, commit a small amount of *extra booster* money to monthly bill prepayment. Then, identify all your *short-term* debts, and pick the one to eliminate first.

When it comes to your mortgage, time is of the essence. *Small monthly prepayments at the very beginning of the term **save a lot more*** than the same prepayments much later in the life of the mortgage. So, *don't wait until you finish paying <u>all</u> your short-term debts before you start prepaying your mortgage. Right from the start, apply part of the dedicated money to prepaying your mortgage.* **Add** the rest to the <u>regular monthly payment</u> for **<u>ONE</u> short-term debt.** Do this every month until you pay off the short-term debt.

Each time you finish off one short-term debt, *the <u>regular</u> money you used to pay on that short-term debt becomes available* **as additional power money to speed the retirement of BOTH your mortgage and the NEXT short-term debt.** *Apply* a portion of the *now larger money pot to your mortgage prepayment.* Add the other portion to the regular monthly payment due on the NEXT short-term debt. *Repeat this process until you've eliminated all your short-term debts.*

With no more short-term debts, *concentrate the now tremendous extra cash amount mostly on mortgage prepayment.* Now, apply a small portion of the extra money every month to your regular savings. Repeat this new pattern until you've paid off the mortgage. When you've retired the mortgage, keep making the same power monthly payments, *but to yourself.*

Applying The Basic Tactic Step by Step

Let's go over the **basic tactic for controlling your money power** step by step.

*Dedicate a small amount of spare money every month as **booster cash** for debt elimination.*

Shoot to have a minimum of $100 each month for that purpose. But, any amount you can consistently muster will do. *If you have an automatic payroll savings plan at work,* **you can reduce the savings allotments so as to quickly free up some regular booster cash.**

Identify all your short-term debts.
Short-term debts include credit card balances, car loans, personal loans, and the like. We're **not** referring to monthly utility bills, like gas, electricity, telephone, and other such ongoing living expenses.

Suppose you've identified the following debts:

Description	Interest Rate	Initial Balance	Initial Monthly Payment
Personal loan	9%	$9,000	$210
Line of credit	16%	$4,500	$82
Car loan	14%	$16,000	$367
Credit card 1	18%	$2,300	$19
Credit card 2	18%	$3,500	$26

Pick the next short-term debt to eliminate first.

The general idea is to put the debts in sequence, going from the shortest term to the longest. But, you want to *rank* the debts *so you terminate the ones with the proportionally larger monthly payments first*. That gives you more money power sooner.

Here's how to accomplish the ranking:

Once you've got those debts listed, **put them in order by EXPECTED duration in months, going from the shortest to the longest.**

To get the expected duration in months, just divide the *initial* balance by the *initial* monthly payment (*"initial"* means *"as of the time you do the ranking"*). Round the answer *up* to a whole month.

Some financial consultants advocate putting the debts in sequence by *interest rate and balance*, taking the largest rate first and, for the same rate, the smallest balance first. With that approach, the list would look like this:

Description	Interest Rate	Initial Balance	Initial Monthly Payment
Credit card 1	18%	$2,300	$19
Credit card 2	18%	$3,500	$26
Line of credit	16%	$4,500	$82
Car loan	14%	$16,000	$367
Personal loan	9%	$9,000	$210

However, your primary objective is not so much to cut *short-term* high interest payments, but to *eliminate* a short-term debt so as to *free up* the monthly payment amount it used to absorb. The newly available money helps to quickly eliminate the *next* short-term debt. *It also contributes to mortgage principal prepayment, which results in much greater savings.*

Consequently, other people advise ignoring the interest rates and just listing the debts in sequence from the smallest to the largest initial balance, as follows:

Description	Interest Rate	Initial Balance	Initial Monthly Payment
Credit card 1	18%	*$2,300*	$19
Credit card 2	18%	*$3,500*	$26
Line of credit	16%	*$4,500*	$82
Personal loan	9%	*$9,000*	$210
Car loan	14%	*$16,000*	$367

But, even that second approach may not necessarily eliminate all the debts in the shortest time frame.

Free up more money sooner

You need to adopt a method that considers *both* the current balance *and* the monthly payment. You see, *the debts should be sequenced in order **going from the shortest to the longest expected duration.***

Naturally, that sequence would also put the ones with the *relatively* larger monthly payments (as compared to the balances) *first* in the list. When you eliminate a debt with a large monthly payment before one with a *relatively* smaller monthly payment, *you tend to free up more monthly money sooner.*

For instance, given a debt of $3,450 with a monthly payment of **$98** and another debt of $8,500 with a monthly payment of **$210**, *which one would you rank for pay-off first?*

Don't be too quick to jump on the larger monthly payment of $210! You see, the debt of $3,450 has a *relatively larger* monthly payment than the debt of $8,500. To determine that, just compare the *monthly payment amount* with the *balance due.* We'll compare the two amounts by dividing the *payment* by the *balance* to get a *ratio*.

So, let's look at the *payment-to-balance* ratio. In the first case, we have a ratio of $98 / $3,450 or **0.028**. But in the second case, the ratio is $210 / $8,500 or **0.025**. The larger ratio means that it would take *less* time to pay off the balance *(and make the money available)*. To determine that, just divide the *balance due* by the *monthly payment* to get *an expected duration in months*.

Rank from shortest to longest expected duration

The *expected* duration in the first case is $3,450 / $98 or **36 months** *(rounded up)*, compared to $8,500 / $210 or **41 months** in the second case. So, *the balance of $3,450 should be targeted before the balance of $8,500. However, we based that conclusion **not** on the smaller balance but on the expected duration.*

When you rank the debts by expected duration, *you get to eliminate all of them in the shortest time frame.* This technique focuses only on the number of months obtained by dividing the initial balance by the initial monthly payment. So, *items in the listing must go from the shortest to the longest expected duration,* as follows.

Description	Initial Balance	Initial Monthly Payment	Expected Duration (Months)	Expected Duration (Rounded)
Personal loan	$9,000	$210	*42.86*	*43.00*
Car loan	$16,000	$367	*43.60*	*44.00*
Line of credit	$4,500	$82	*54.88*	*55.00*
Credit card 1	$2,300	$19	*121.05*	*122.00*
Credit card 2	$3,500	$26	*134.62*	*135.00*

 Repeat actions I and II EVERY MONTH until you pay off the FIRST debt on the list.

> **I.   Add part of your booster cash to the usual monthly payment for the first debt.** Stick with the new monthly amount **or more** all the way.
>
> **II. Add the rest to the monthly mortgage payment to prepay mortgage principal.**

First Debt

Suppose you decide to put up a monthly booster amount of $100 to start with. Let's say you add 75% of this extra cash, or $75, to the regular payment for the first debt on the list. *That would leave $25 for monthly mortgage prepayment.*

You now have a *boosted* monthly payment of $285 that will terminate the first debt within 32 months. As you accelerate the payoff of the first debt, continue to make the initial monthly payment on the remaining debts.

Description	Initial Balance	Initial Monthly Payment	Initial Expected Duration (Months)	Current Balance	Boosted Monthly Payment	Boosted Expected Duration (Months)	Extra Mortgage Principal Payment
Personal loan	$9,000	$210	*43.00*	*$9,000.00*	$285.00	*32.00*	*$25.00*

Repeat Step 5 until you've paid off ALL your short-term debts

Do the following UNTIL you've paid off ALL your short-term debts:

- *Add the monthly payment from the debt you just paid off to booster cash*
- *Repeat actions 1 and 2 EVERY MONTH until you pay off the NEXT debt on the list:*

> *1. Add some of the **newly available** money to the monthly payment for this next debt. Stick with the new monthly amount **or more** all the way.*
>
> *2. **Add the rest to the monthly mortgage payment to prepay mortgage principal.***

Second Debt

After 32 months, when you finish off the first debt, you have a *new* total booster payment of $310. *Cross the first entry off your list.* At this point, you've also completed 32 payments at the initial amount on the *second* debt. That's a rough total of $11,744 (32 times $367), leaving a balance of $4,256 ($16,000 minus $11,744).

Continuing with the plan, you add *$232.59* (75% of that new booster amount) to the initial monthly payment of the *second* debt on the list. That gives a boosted monthly payment of $599.50. The expected duration of the current balance of $4,256 is only 8 months. The *extra* mortgage principal payment amount is now *$77.50* (25% of the *new* booster cash). Continue to make the initial monthly payments on the remaining debts.

Description	Initial Balance	Initial Monthly Payment	Initial Expected Duration (Months)	Current Balance	Boosted Monthly Payment	Boosted Expected Duration (Months)	Extra Mortgage Principal Payment
~~Personal loan~~	~~$9,000~~	~~$210~~	~~*43.00*~~	~~*$9,000.00*~~	~~$285.00~~	~~*32.00*~~	~~*$25.00*~~
Car loan	$16,000	$367	*44.00*	*$4,256.00*	$599.50	*8.00*	*$77.50*

Third Debt

When you finish off the second debt after the eight months, cross off the second entry. You've also completed 40 payments at the initial amount on the *third* debt. That's a rough total of $3,280 (40 times $82). So, you would have a current balance of $1,220 ($4,500 minus $3,280) remaining on the third debt. But, now there's a *new* total booster fund of $677.

Add *$507.75* (75% of $677) to the initial monthly payment of the *third* debt on the list. That gives a boosted monthly payment of $589.75. The expected duration of the current balance of $1,220 is only 3 months. The *extra* mortgage principal payment amount is now *$169.25* (25% of the *new* booster cash).

Description	Initial Balance	Initial Monthly Payment	Initial Expected Duration (Months)	Current Balance	Boosted Monthly Payment	Boosted Expected Duration (Months)	Extra Mortgage Principal Payment
~~Personal loan~~	~~$9,000~~	~~$210~~	*43.00*	*$9,000.00*	~~$285.00~~	*32.00*	*$25.00*
~~Car loan~~	~~$16,000~~	~~$367~~	*44.00*	*$4,256.00*	~~$599.50~~	*8.00*	*$77.50*
Line of credit	$4,500	$82	*55.00*	*$1,220.00*	$589.75	*3.00*	*$169.25*

Fourth Debt

When you finish off the third debt in three months, cross off the third entry. By that time, you've also completed 43 payments at the initial amount on the *fourth* debt. That's about $817 (43 times $19). So, you would have a current balance of $1,483 left on the *fourth* debt. But, now there's a *new* total booster payment of $759.

Add *$569.25* (75% of $759) to the initial monthly payment of the *fourth* debt on the list. That gives a boosted monthly payment of $588.25. The expected duration of the current balance of $1,483 is only 3 months. The *extra* mortgage principal payment amount is now *$189.75* (25% of the *new* booster cash).

Description	Initial Balance	Initial Monthly Payment	Initial Expected Duration (Months)	Current Balance	Boosted Monthly Payment	Boosted Expected Duration (Months)	Extra Mortgage Principal Payment
~~Personal loan~~	~~$9,000~~	~~$210~~	*43.00*	*$9,000.00*	~~$285.00~~	*32.00*	*$25.00*
~~Car loan~~	~~$16,000~~	~~$367~~	*44.00*	*$4,256.00*	~~$599.50~~	*8.00*	*$77.50*
~~Line of credit~~	~~$4,500~~	~~$82~~	*55.00*	*$1,220.00*	~~$589.75~~	*3.00*	*$169.25*
Credit card 1	$2,300	$19	*122.00*	*$1,483.00*	$588.25	*3.00*	*$189.75*

Fifth
Debt

When you finish off the fourth debt over the next three months, cross off the fourth entry. You've also completed 46 payments at the initial amount on the *fifth* debt. That's about $1196 (46 times $26). So, you would have a current balance of $2,304 left on the *fifth* debt. But, now there's a *new* total booster payment of $778.

Add *$583.50* (75% of $778) to the initial monthly payment of the *fifth* debt on the list. That gives a boosted monthly payment of $609.50. The expected duration of the current balance of $2,304 is only 4 months. The *extra* mortgage principal payment amount is now *$194.50* (25% of the *new* booster cash).

Description	Initial Balance	Initial Monthly Payment	Initial Expected Duration (Months)	Current Balance	Boosted Monthly Payment	Boosted Expected Duration (Months)	Extra Mortgage Principal Payment
Personal loan	$9,000	$210	*43.00*	*$9,000.00*	$285.00	*32.00*	*$25.00*
Car loan	$16,000	$367	*44.00*	*$4,256.00*	$599.50	*8.00*	*$77.50*
Line of credit	$4,500	$82	*55.00*	*$1,220.00*	$589.75	*3.00*	*$169.25*
Credit card 1	$2,300	$19	*122.00*	*$1,483.00*	$588.25	*3.00*	*$189.75*
Credit card 2	$3,500	$26	*135.00*	*$2,304.00*	$609.50	*4.00*	*$194.50*

Final
Results

Four months down the road, you eliminate the last short-term debt. Cross it off the list. Normally, the time to pay all those debts would stretch to *11 years and 4 months*. Using this technique, it would only take *4 years and 3 months* to get rid of all the listed debts. Then, you'd have a *new* total booster amount of *$804*.

Description	Initial Balance	Initial Monthly Payment	Initial Expected Duration (Months)	Current Balance	Boosted Monthly Payment	Boosted Expected Duration (Months)	Extra Mortgage Principal Payment
Personal loan	$9,000	$210	*43.00*	*$9,000.00*	$285.00	*32.00*	*$25.00*
Car loan	$16,000	$367	*44.00*	*$4,256.00*	$599.50	*8.00*	*$77.50*
Line of credit	$4,500	$82	*55.00*	*$1,220.00*	$589.75	*3.00*	*$169.25*
Credit card 1	$2,300	$19	*122.00*	*$1,483.00*	$588.25	*3.00*	*$189.75*
Credit card 2	$3,500	$26	*135.00*	*$2,304.00*	$609.50	*4.00*	*$194.50*
Totals			*135.00*			*50.00*	*$804.00*
Total Years			*11.25*			*4.17*	

Every month after you've eliminated the last short-term debt,

> - *Concentrate **most of the extra** money power on mortgage prepayment*
> - **Deposit the rest of the money into your savings account as you go.**

Repeat this step until you've retired your mortgage.

At this juncture, you could apply the whole booster amount of $804 to mortgage prepayment. That money would pay off the mortgage at lightning speed! *But, it is worthwhile to save a small portion of the cash.* You'll see why in a moment.

Keeping 25% of the last booster amount for monthly savings, the remaining 75% would now cover the mortgage. *You would now be able to deposit $201 a month in your savings account,* and there would be a monthly sum of $603 available for *extra* principal payment. That smaller sum would still pay off the mortgage at lightning speed! *Plus, it would allow you to build up additional cash to boot.*

Taking it from the first period, let's observe what would happen to the old 30-year mortgage of $80,000 at 10% with this *special* method. Let's also combine the prepayments with the *pseudo bi-weekly* method.

Prepaying with the full booster

If you apply the full $804 after the short-term debts are gone, the mortgage term would then last just another *five years for a total of **nine years**.* Of course, the larger the booster amount, the shorter the term and the greater the savings.

Results when you deposit part of the booster money into a savings account

In contrast, when you repay with the $603 booster money made available as planned above, *and save the difference of $201 for the duration,* the mortgage lasts a year longer and you pay a little more mortgage interest, but you reap some big benefits from saving the difference.

To be precise, the mortgage term would last another *six years, instead of five, for a total of **ten years**.* Also, you wind up paying $3,885.18 more in mortgage interest. But, if you invested the $201 at only 5% compounding monthly for the five years (4 years and 9 months to be exact), *you would accumulate **$12,901.76**.* The deposits would grow to **$16,029.89** by the time the mortgage ends on that sixth year. *That's cash on hand to do with as you please!*

Here's a comparative picture (see Figure 17.1 below).

Booster Prepayment Results
Two Semi-annual Prepayments Combined With Planned Monthly Prepayments

Mortgage Amount: $80,000   Term: *30 Years*   Interest Rate: *10%*

Accelerated Term	*Accelerated Term*
Semi-Annual Prepayments $351.03 **Combined with planned prepayments** **and 75% of final booster amount**	**Semi-Annual Prepayments $351.03** **Combined with planned prepayments** **and 100% of final booster amount**
Interest Savings: **$118,537.72** Duration: 10 Years Time Savings: **20 Years**	Interest Savings: **$122,422.90** Duration: 9 Years Time Savings: **21 Years**

Year	Payment	Interest	Principal	Balance	Payment	Interest	Principal	Balance
1	$9,426.78	$7,947.92	$1,478.86	$78,521.14	$9,426.78	$7,947.92	$1,478.86	$78,521.14
2	$9,426.78	$7,793.07	$1,633.71	$76,887.43	$9,426.78	$7,793.07	$1,633.71	$76,887.43
3	$9,636.78	$7,619.36	$2,017.42	$74,870.01	$9,636.78	$7,619.36	$2,017.42	$74,870.01
4	$10,903.53	$7,357.48	$3,546.05	$71,323.96	$10,903.53	$7,357.48	$3,546.05	$71,323.96
5	$15,555.78	$6,786.54	$8,769.24	$62,554.72	$17,555.78	$6,709.87	$10,845.91	$60,478.05
6	$16,374.78	$5,793.72	$10,581.06	$51,973.66	$18,774.78	$5,463.12	$13,311.66	$47,166.39
7	$16,374.78	$4,685.73	$11,689.05	$40,284.61	$18,774.78	$4,069.25	$14,705.53	$32,460.86
8	$16,374.78	$3,461.75	$12,913.03	$27,371.58	$18,774.78	$2,529.37	$16,245.41	$16,215.45
9	$16,374.78	$2,109.58	$14,265.20	$13,106.38	$17,043.72	$828.27	$16,215.45	$0.00
10	$13,730.42	$624.04	$13,106.38	$0.00				
Totals	$134,202.89	$54,202.89	$80,000.00		$130,317.71	$50,317.71	$80,000.00	

Figure 17.1

  From this point on, *make the boosted payments to yourself.*

When you have no more mortgage payments, *keep making the same monthly payments,* **but right into your savings account.** From there, **you can roll the money into investment accounts.**

Ideally, you should also get rid of your credit cards as you go. But, let's face it, certain credit cards are useful for various purposes, such as backing up a payment by check, and completing hotel or airline ticket reservations. So, you really won't cut up all of your cards. *However, use the ones you do keep very judiciously so you don't pile up short-term debt all over again.*

You can run through the whole process right up front and create a payoff table that schedules the elimination of your short-term debts and produces prepayment cash for your mortgage.

As an exercise, go through the steps and try to reproduce the following table on your own, using the debts given in this illustration.

Description	Initial Balance	Initial Monthly Payment	Initial Expected Duration (Months)	Current Balance	Boosted Monthly Payment	Boosted Expected Duration (Months)	Extra Mortgage Principal Payment
Personal loan	$9,000	$210	**43.00**	**$9,000.00**	$285.00	**32.00**	**$25.00**
Car loan	$16,000	$367	**44.00**	**$4,256.00**	$599.50	**8.00**	**$77.50**
Line of credit	$4,500	$82	**55.00**	**$1,220.00**	$589.75	**3.00**	**$169.25**
Credit card 1	$2,300	$19	**122.00**	**$1,483.00**	$588.25	**3.00**	**$189.75**
Credit card 2	$3,500	$26	**135.00**	**$2,304.00**	$609.50	**4.00**	**$194.50**
Totals			**135.00**			**50.00**	**$804.00**
Total Years			**11.25**			**4.17**	

Here's a working form for the exercise.

Short-Term Debt Elimination Schedule

Total Initial Booster Cash	$			Initial Booster Cash Percentage to Short-term Debt	%		

Description	Initial Balance	Initial Monthly Payment	Initial Expected Duration (Months)	Current Balance	Boosted Monthly Payment	Boosted Expected Duration (Months)	Extra Mortgage Principal Payment

Now, try working out your own personal schedule, using the blank worksheet on the next page. You'll also find a full-size master worksheet in *Appendix L* that you may make additional copies from.

Short-Term Debt Elimination Schedule

Total Initial Booster Cash $ [   ]

Initial Booster Cash Percentage to Short-term Debt   [   ] %

Description	Initial Balance	Initial Monthly Payment	Initial Expected Duration (Months)	Current Balance	Boosted Monthly Payment	Boosted Expected Duration (Months)	Extra Mortgage Principal Payment

© Copyright 1993 Capital Search Systems

Feel free to make copies of this page for your personal use.

HOW TO USE THE POWER TECHNIQUE
FOR DEBT ELIMINATION

ACTION STEPS

1 *Dedicate some money as **booster cash for debt elimination.***

2 *Identify and list all your short-term debts.*

3 *Rank the debts from shortest to longest expected duration.*

4 *Every month, add some of the **booster cash** to your mortgage payment; add the rest to the regular payment of the first debt on the list until you to pay off that first debt.*

5 *Repeat this step until you eliminate ALL short-term debts.*

ADD THE REGULAR PAYMENT AMOUNT YOU PAID ON THE LAST CLOSED DEBT TO BOOSTER CASH.

Every month, use the TOTAL available booster money as follows for your mortgage and the short-term debt currently being prepaid, until you eliminate the short-term debt:

- *Apply a portion of the **booster** money to mortgage prepayment*

- *Add the remaining portion of the **booster** money to the payment for the short-term balance you're prepaying.*

6 *Every month, use the TOTAL available booster money as follows until you eliminate the mortgage:*

- *Apply a portion of the **booster** money to mortgage prepayment*

- *Deposit the remaining portion of the **booster** money into your **savings account.***

7 *After you've retired the mortgage, **continue to deposit the same TOTAL monthly payments into your savings account**. If you just stopped prepaying, because you're really close to ending the mortgage, then continue to deposit the total booster payments into the savings account.*

Notes

Chapter Eighteen

ABOUT EFFECTS OF PREPAYMENTS ON YOUR TAXES

⇒ *Why you come out ahead by prepaying*

A Double-Edged Sword

Since mortgage interest is tax-deductible, why should you bother to reduce the interest payment? Doesn't a bigger interest payment give a bigger deduction?

Actually, the interest savings that you produce by prepaying during one year don't lower your tax deduction by much. In fact, the amount of additional tax you would pay in any given year because of the slightly lower deduction is ridiculously trivial.

If you're in the 31% tax bracket, every dollar of deductible interest you pay "saves" 31 cents of tax. *But, if you could have avoided the interest payment and did not, then the dollar that you unnecessarily pay in interest **actually LOSES 69 cents** for you.*

It's a double-edged sword that goes like this. You pay $1 of mortgage interest to the bank. Then, Uncle Sam refunds you 31 cents from the taxes you paid. So, you now have only 31 cents in your hand. You're also 69-cents short. ***Those 31 cents cost you 69 cents. That's a loss!*** For you to get back 31 cents to keep, you have to first pay out $1 and eventually lose 69 cents.

Put another way, *you have to pay $3 in unnecessary interests to get back a $1 refund **and lose $2**.* If you manage to cut out the $3 interest payment, you get no tax refund. *But, who cares. You still have $3 in your pocket.* Wouldn't you rather pay your taxes and save $3 in interests? Why pay more to the bank to avoid paying less to Uncle Sam? Consider this example:

Example

At the end of the first year, total payments on a ***$100,000*** fixed rate mortgage at 10% for 30 years will include total interest of $9,974.98 without prepayments. In a 31%-bracket, that gives a tax "savings" of $3,092.24 and a net interest cost of $6,882.74

But, with prepayments of $100 per month during the year, the total interest paid for the year would be $9,918.43. Here the tax refund would be $3,074.71, and the net interest cost would be $6,843.72.

In the following table, examine the *difference that a prepayment of $100-a-month makes in* **one** *year (also see the amortization table on the next page).*

	[A] Without Prepayment	[B] With $100 Prepayment	Difference [B] - [A]
Interest Paid	$9,974.98	$9,918.43	($56.55)
Tax Refund	$3,092.24	$3,074.71	($17.53)
Net Interest Paid	$6,882.74	$6,843.72	**($39.02)**
Total Interest **Saved**	$0.00	*$19,329.64*	**$19,329.64**
Remaining Term	29 Years	*27 Years*	**(2 Years)**

The Difference a Prepayment Makes

Here's what happens with the $100 prepayment each month of **the first year only** (Figure 18.1 below shows comparative amortization schedules)**:**

√   The additional tax would only be **$17.53** (you get refunded *$17.53 less*).

√   You pay *$39.02* **less** in scheduled interest for the year.   *That's money left in your pocket that year!*

√   The $1,200 total prepayment for the year would *save* **$19,329.64** from the total interest payment. *That's* **real** *money that would* **LEAVE** *your pocket over the next two years! You won't have to pay it anymore.*

√   You cut **1 year and 11 months, make that 2 years,** from the term of 30 years, leaving *only* **27 years** to go as of this point (*instead of 29*).

When you pay $3 to get back $1, *you're just giving away $2.*

When you pay $56.55 *more* to the bank to get back $17.53 *more* from Uncle Sam that one year, *you're just giving away* **$39.02**. But, here it's *much worse* than that. You're also **losing $19,329.64 to the bank over the longer pull!**

Isn't it much better to prepay $100 a month, let Uncle Sam keep $17.53 more in tax, pay **$39.02 less in interest** that year, eliminate **$19,329.64** from the total interest payment, *and cut the mortgage term by 2 years*? (See *Explanatory Notes for the Curious Only* in *Appendix M* for more information **about mortgage interest and your taxes**.)

When you prepay, the interest you save <u>does not</u> reduce your tax deduction appreciably. But, your prepayment **keeps a whole lot more** dollars in your pockets than you could ever get in tax refunds. The prepayment does something MORE: **it shortens your mortgage term.**

Fixed Prepayment Results
With $100-a-month prepayment during the first year only

Mortgage Amount: **$100,000** Term: *30 Years* Interest Rate: *10%*

Normal Term
No prepayments

Interest Savings: **$0**
Duration: 30 Years
Time Savings: **None**
Monthly Payment: **$877.57**

Accelerated Term
Fixed Prepayment $100/month

Interest Savings: **$19,329.64**
Duration: *28 Years 1 Month*
Time Savings: **1 Year 11 Months**
Monthly Payment: **$977.57** *(First Year)*

Year	Payment	Interest	Principal	Balance	Payment	Interest	Principal	Balance
1	$10,530.84	$9,974.98	$555.86	$99,444.14	$11,730.84	$9,918.43	$1,812.41	$98,187.59
2	$10,530.84	$9,916.77	$614.07	$98,830.07	$10,530.84	$9,785.22	$745.62	$97,441.97
3	$10,530.84	$9,852.46	$678.38	$98,151.69	$10,530.84	$9,707.12	$823.72	$96,618.25
4	$10,530.84	$9,781.44	$749.40	$97,402.29	$10,530.84	$9,620.87	$909.97	$95,708.28
5	$10,530.84	$9,702.96	$827.88	$96,574.41	$10,530.84	$9,525.57	$1,005.27	$94,703.01
6	$10,530.84	$9,616.27	$914.57	$95,659.84	$10,530.84	$9,420.32	$1,110.52	$93,592.49
7	$10,530.84	$9,520.53	$1,010.31	$94,649.53	$10,530.84	$9,304.04	$1,226.80	$92,365.69
8	$10,530.84	$9,414.73	$1,116.11	$93,533.42	$10,530.84	$9,175.56	$1,355.28	$91,010.41
9	$10,530.84	$9,297.86	$1,232.98	$92,300.44	$10,530.84	$9,033.66	$1,497.18	$89,513.23
10	$10,530.84	$9,168.75	$1,362.09	$90,938.35	$10,530.84	$8,876.88	$1,653.96	$87,859.27
11	$10,530.84	$9,026.12	$1,504.72	$89,433.63	$10,530.84	$8,703.69	$1,827.15	$86,032.12
12	$10,530.84	$8,868.57	$1,662.27	$87,771.36	$10,530.84	$8,512.36	$2,018.48	$84,013.64
13	$10,530.84	$8,694.49	$1,836.35	$85,935.01	$10,530.84	$8,300.98	$2,229.86	$81,783.78
14	$10,530.84	$8,502.21	$2,028.63	$83,906.38	$10,530.84	$8,067.50	$2,463.34	$79,320.44
15	$10,530.84	$8,289.75	$2,241.09	$81,665.29	$10,530.84	$7,809.55	$2,721.29	$76,599.15
16	$10,530.84	$8,055.10	$2,475.74	$79,189.55	$10,530.84	$7,524.60	$3,006.24	$73,592.91
17	$10,530.84	$7,795.85	$2,734.99	$76,454.56	$10,530.84	$7,209.81	$3,321.03	$70,271.88
18	$10,530.84	$7,509.48	$3,021.36	$73,433.20	$10,530.84	$6,862.07	$3,668.77	$66,603.11
19	$10,530.84	$7,193.09	$3,337.75	$70,095.45	$10,530.84	$6,477.91	$4,052.93	$62,550.18
20	$10,530.84	$6,843.59	$3,687.25	$66,408.20	$10,530.84	$6,053.49	$4,477.35	$58,072.83
21	$10,530.84	$6,457.48	$4,073.36	$62,334.84	$10,530.84	$5,584.65	$4,946.19	$53,126.64
22	$10,530.84	$6,030.94	$4,499.90	$57,834.94	$10,530.84	$5,066.72	$5,464.12	$47,662.52
23	$10,530.84	$5,559.76	$4,971.08	$52,863.86	$10,530.84	$4,494.56	$6,036.28	$41,626.24
24	$10,530.84	$5,039.21	$5,491.63	$47,372.23	$10,530.84	$3,862.48	$6,668.36	$34,957.88
25	$10,530.84	$4,464.17	$6,066.67	$41,305.56	$10,530.84	$3,164.23	$7,366.61	$27,591.27
26	$10,530.84	$3,828.90	$6,701.94	$34,603.62	$10,530.84	$2,392.84	$8,138.00	$19,453.27
27	$10,530.84	$3,127.12	$7,403.72	$27,199.90	$10,530.84	$1,540.68	$8,990.16	$10,463.11
28	$10,530.84	$2,351.87	$8,178.97	$19,020.93	$10,530.84	$599.31	$9,931.53	$531.58
29	$10,530.84	$1,495.43	$9,035.41	$9,985.52	$536.01	$4.43	$531.58	$0.00
30	$10,534.81	$549.29	$9,985.52	$0.00	**$0.00**	**$0.00**	**$0.00**	**$0.00**
Totals	$315,929.17	$215,929.17	$100,000.00		$296,599.53	$196,599.53	$100,000.00	

Figure 18.1

Notes

Chapter Nineteen

CONCERNS ABOUT BANK PREPAYMENT PENALTY

⇒ *Reasons why prepayment penalty should **not** bother you*

Banks try to collect a certain amount of interest money. So, they sometimes charge a prepayment penalty fee to discourage people from paying off their mortgages too early. *However, very few mortgage types come with prepayment penalties.*

In fact, the very existence of prepayment penalty clauses in mortgage contracts may be illegal in certain jurisdictions.

They Apply Only To Certain Situations

When prepayment penalties are in effect, they don't impact small regular or periodic prepayments on top of the scheduled monthly payments. Penalties are usually payable at the end of the term. They apply only to certain situations. Depending on the lender, the conditions may vary.

A penalty may be in effect for situations where the whole balance is being paid off. When a borrower pays off the whole balance, either within the first three to five years of the mortgage or at any time, the typical penalty amount can be a small percentage of the balance being paid off.

A prepayment penalty may also be stated *for situations where only a certain portion of the original balance is being paid off within a twelve-month period.* Mortgage contracts with this type of clause call for a penalty when the borrower prepays more than 20 percent of the original principal during any year. Then, the typical penalty may rise to a maximum of 180-day's interest payment on the ***excess*** prepayment being made.

For instance, let's say you have a mortgage of $80,000 at 10% for 30 years with a monthly payment of $702.06 that carries such a prepayment penalty clause. Before you get hit with a penalty, *you would have to prepay $16,000 (20% of $80,000) in one year **ON TOP** of your regular **total** scheduled payments of $8,424.72.* **That would be an average prepayment of $1,333.33 per month for the whole year.** *What's the likelihood for you to do that?*

Key Point

Don't let the idea of a prepayment penalty put a damper on your plans to prepay your mortgage. If you have to pay a penalty, *it will be an* **insignificant** *price to pay for all the interest you will save.*

A prepayment penalty clause may not exist in your mortgage at all. To be sure of this, check your mortgage contract. If you find a prepayment penalty clause, write to your lender. Explain your plans to prepay, and request a waiver or a suggestion on how to proceed.

Surprisingly, your lender may even encourage your prepayment plans. You see, your prepayment money does two good things for a bank:

- *It reduces the lender's risk or anxiety about getting back the money*

- *It becomes automatically available for new loans, often at HIGHER rates.*

Chapter Twenty

WHEN YOU DON'T NEED TO PREPAY

⇒ *How to determine whether you **don't** need to prepay*
⇒ *How to calculate **before-tax** and **after-tax** rates, and how to use the information*

If your house is *investment* property and you're getting rental income from it, your primary purpose is to generate cash flow. Because your tenants pay the mortgage for you, you don't need to prepay. But, you can still prepay to build up your equity and eventually increase your cash flow.

Three Situations

However, for your own residence, it's just the opposite. You usually have a strong incentive to prepay your mortgage. But, even when you have some extra money available, **there are three situations in which it makes more sense to invest the money rather than pay down the mortgage with it:**

1 **Home prices are going *down* tremendously fast in your neighborhood with no end in sight.**

There's a good chance you might want to bail out early to avoid paying more than the house is worth.

2 **You are very near the end of your mortgage term.**

Compared to the amounts that go to pay principal, interest payments become really small near the end of your mortgage term. *When you have less than five years to go on your mortgage, small routine prepayments have no effect on time. But, they still save some interest dollars.* This is a good time to compare the dollars savings with the yields of other investments.

3 **You can earn MUCH more with some other LOW-RISK investments.**

We'll explore this area in more detail in the rest of the chapter.

When you find low-risk investment opportunities that can earn more **after tax** than you can save on your mortgage interest, ***look harder.*** If one of those special opportunities ***allows you to apply small installments on a monthly basis,*** consider investing your extra cash in it.

*If your mortgage has a **very low** fixed rate compared to current interest rates,* it's even more likely to find good investment opportunities. For instance, with a mortgage rate of 5 percent, you will more easily find a low-risk investment vehicle that pays 8 percent or higher. If you do, then it makes sense to put your extra money in that investment instead of paying down the mortgage.

Key Point

When comparing interest rates of investments to your mortgage rate, first convert **all** the rates *(including the mortgage rate)* to **after-tax rates**. *This is important in order to get a true idea of the differences between the rates.* You want to compare *apples to apples*.

In general, no matter how high your mortgage rate, instead of prepaying, you would do better by investing your extra money in *a **low-risk** instrument with an **after-tax** rate that is SUBSTANTIALLY higher than your **after-tax** mortgage rate.*

*But, you must first **find** such a sure-fire investment. Then, you have to be able to invest **small** extra money amounts in that instrument EVERY MONTH during the balance of the mortgage term.*

Suppose your mortgage rate is 10 percent. *If you're in the 31 percent tax bracket, then your AFTER-TAX mortgage interest rate is **6.9** percent.*

A Passing Remark: If you care for more technical details **about mortgage interest and your taxes**, see the <u>Explanatory Notes for the Curious Only</u> in *Appendix M.*

Calculating after-tax rates

How do you calculate **ANY** AFTER-TAX interest rate in general?

The general formula is:

```
AFTER-TAX RATE = BEFORE-TAX RATE X (100 - TAX BRACKET) / 100
```

It applies to taxable investment interest rates as well as to mortgages.

To get your after-tax mortgage rate, apply the general formula using these three steps:

1 | Get the difference between 100 percent and your *tax bracket percentage.*

2 | Divide the *difference* by 100 to convert it to a decimal fraction.

3 | Multiply the *mortgage rate* by the resulting fraction.

Example

Suppose your mortgage rate is 12 percent. If you're in the 31 percent tax bracket, then your AFTER-TAX mortgage interest rate is <u>8.28 percent.</u>

1	(100 - 31) = 69
2	69 / 100 = .69
3	12 X .69 = 8.28

Using after-tax rates

*So, how do you **use** this information?*

One reason to convert a mortgage interest rate to an after-tax rate occurs when you want to compare your mortgage rate to several *tax-free* investments. Mortgage rates are normally *before-tax* rates. But, tax-free rates are practically *after-tax* rates.

Another reason has to do with getting a true picture. The difference in percentage points between two *before-tax* rates is <u>not the same</u> as the difference between the two equivalent *after-tax* rates.

Here is a situation to drive home the point.

Still using the 31 percent tax bracket, let's compare your 12-percent mortgage with a taxable mutual fund that yields 15 percent. Right off the bat, it would appear that the fund gives a solid 3 percent margin over prepaying the mortgage. ***Actually, the difference is only 2.07 percent after tax.***

How do we know that?

Since Uncle Sam gives you a 31 percent "subsidy" here (see the *Explanatory Note* in *Appendix M* for details), you wind up **paying a net of 69 percent** of your total annual mortgage interest to the bank. So, to get your after-tax mortgage rate, *multiply the 12 percent rate by **.69** to get **8.28***.

Also, since you may pay a tax of 31 percent on the interest you receive from the taxable mutual fund, you wind up **keeping 69 percent** of the interest income. So, to get the after-tax yield, *multiply the 15 percent rate by **.69** to get **10.35***. Compare the two **after-tax** rates of 10.35 and 8.28 to see the difference of <u>***2.07***</u>.

*What about **TAX-FREE** investments?*

Compared to an effective after-tax mortgage interest rate of 7.37 percent, a TAX-FREE municipal bond mutual fund investment at **9 percent** would be a good one. **This 9-percent tax-free investment is equivalent to a taxable instrument with a BEFORE-TAX rate of 13.43 percent.** Obviously, the 13.43 percent rate is also better than your 11-percent BEFORE-TAX mortgage rate.

When dealing with a particular tax-free investment, it is sometimes useful to compare it to several taxable alternatives.

Using before-tax rates

Since the rates you find in the financial news for taxable investments are BEFORE-TAX rates, you should convert the known tax-free rate to its equivalent BEFORE-TAX rate, so you can do rapid "ballpark" comparisons. It's just quicker to convert the *one* tax-free rate, instead of converting a whole bunch of before-tax rates to their after-tax equivalents.

Calculating before-tax rates

How do you calculate an equivalent BEFORE-TAX interest rate going from a TAX-FREE rate in general?   Well, just think of the tax-free rate as an after-tax rate (*which it is, because there's no tax on it*), and work the after-tax formula sort of in reverse.

Here is the "reverse" formula:

> BEFORE-TAX RATE = TAX-FREE RATE / (100 - TAX BRACKET) / 100

To get AN EQUIVALENT BEFORE-TAX interest rate, apply the "reverse" formula using these three steps:

1   Get the difference between 100 and your tax bracket

2   Divide the difference by 100

3   Divide the TAX-FREE rate by the result.

Example

Suppose that your mortgage rate is 11 percent and you're in the 31 percent tax bracket. You're trying to decide whether to go with a 12 percent taxable diversified stock mutual fund or with a 9-percent tax-free municipal bond mutual fund.

*What is the equivalent **before-tax** rate for the 9% tax-free municipal fund?*

1 | (100 - 31) = 69

2 | 69 / 100 = .69

3 | 9 / .69 = 13.03

The tax-free municipal fund rate of 9 percent is equivalent to a before-tax rate of ***13.03*** percent. *If you're allowed to make the **same small deposits** into the fund every month,* it would be a better investment for your extra cash than prepaying.

Chapter Twenty-one

WHEN YOU DEFINITELY SHOULD CONSIDER PREPAYING

⇒ *Another dramatic way to look at the astounding result of prepaying*

I f your mortgage interest rate is not unusually low in comparison to current rates or to the rate of return of some special low-risk investment, the longer you plan to stay in your house, the more it makes sense to prepay your mortgage. In fact, regardless how long you plan to stay in your house, it makes great sense to increase your equity in the house quickly, and eliminate giant interest payments you don't need to shell out. That's especially true at the beginning of the mortgage term.

Take Care Of The Basics First

However, you should start a vigorous paydown strategy on your mortgage only when you can afford it. *Take care of the basics first.* You should take precautions to cover yourself and your family against crises that call for large immediate cash expenditures. In addition to adequate life and health insurance, and a good retirement plan, you should build **an emergency fund** equal to **at least three-month's salary.** *Keep that emergency money in a liquid interest-bearing account, such as a money market fund, in reserve for rainy days.* With those preliminary measures in place, you should be ready for a long-term investment in your mortgage equity.

Investment opportunities that offer very high rates of return might come along. But, they may also bring significantly high risks. *When you are **not willing** to accept investments with **higher risk** than your mortgage, you should strongly consider investing your extra money in a good mortgage paydown plan.* Even if you're a speculator at heart, it would definitely be a good idea to **give first priority** to a great investment like your mortgage paydown.

In previous chapters, you have seen illustrations of the kind of return you get with a consistent paydown strategy. But, suppose we go one step further. Take a $100,000 mortgage with a term of 30 years at 10 percent. Let's say you prepay $100 each month right from the beginning. The mortgage would be paid off in 19 years. You would save $126,507.85 in interest costs.

A Different Way To Look At The Results

Now, consider the astounding results in a slightly different way. Over the 19 years, you would prepay a total of $23,000. Think of this amount as money that you could have aggressively invested somewhere else. But, you did choose to invest it in your mortgage. In this light, the $23,000 investment would come back to you as a total of $126,507.85.

So, the net return on your investment would be $103,507.85. ***That amazing sum represents a total yield of 450 percent! That's an average rate of 23.68 percent per year, TAX-FREE!*** What low-risk investment can you think of that gives a return anywhere near this?

If you're at the beginning of your mortgage term, you should vigorously consider prepaying. In fact, if you're about to close on a new mortgage, you should plan to include a prepayment right up front. Bring the check with you to the closing and just drop it in the pot. That's where a dollar of prepayment gets you the most savings.

You Owe It To Yourself

Regardless how many years you've had your mortgage, as long as there are still some years ahead of you, *you owe it to yourself to put at least the **Pseudo Bi-weekly** method to work for you. If you can afford it, **combine the Term-Based method with the Pseudo Bi-weekly for maximum results.***

Even if you only have a couple of years or so left to go on your mortgage, you still stand to save a few bucks by prepaying. *Why give away the money if you don't have to? Isn't it better in your pockets?* You can always keep your pockets in some high paying money fund at the bank.

Part Four

APPENDICES, GLOSSARY, AND INDEX

Part Four Contents

Appendix A	MONTHLY MORTGAGE CONSTANTS

Monthly Mortgage Constants

The monthly mortgage constant tables in this appendix can serve several purposes. We'll focus on two key functions and one minor function. The first function produces a monthly payment, given an interest rate and a desired term. The procedure is covered in detail in *Chapter Ten*. The second function **is *presented exclusively in this book.*** *Given an interest rate, a balance, and a monthly payment*, which may include a regular payment and a *base prepayment*, ***it produces the resulting term duration.*** See ***Appendix E*** for the procedure details of the second function.

The third function is summarized below in this appendix. It answers the question: *given a monthly payment that you can afford, a term of years, and an interest rate, **how much money can you borrow?*** This procedure gives the answer in a simple way, using the mortgage constant table.

Calculating Amount That Can Be Borrowed

Use this procedure to calculate the **amount that can be borrowed,**
given a monthly payment, a desired term, and an interest rate.

Procedure:
1. Select term of years under the **Terms** column
2. Go down the column to locate the *constant amount* in the same row as the interest **Rate**
3. Divide the given monthly payment by the *constant* to get the **amount to borrow**

Example: To find the ***amount to borrow,*** when you can keep up a monthly payment of ***$900*** for amortizing the loan within ***20 years*** at ***9.5%***

1. Pick the **20** years column
2. Go down to locate the constant ***0.009321*** in the same row as the rate 9.5
3. Divide $900 by 0.009321 to get the ***amount to borrow*** of ***$96,556.16.***

Monthly Mortgage Constants

Terms (years)	1	2	3	4	5	6	7
Rates (%)							
6	0.086066	0.044321	0.030422	0.023485	0.019333	0.016573	0.014609
6.25	0.086181	0.044433	0.030535	0.0236	0.019449	0.016691	0.014729
6.5	0.086296	0.044546	0.030649	0.023715	0.019566	0.01681	0.014849
6.75	0.086412	0.044659	0.030763	0.02383	0.019683	0.016929	0.014971
7	0.086527	0.044773	0.030877	0.023946	0.019801	0.017049	0.015093
7.25	0.086642	0.044886	0.030992	0.024062	0.019919	0.017169	0.015215
7.5	0.086757	0.045	0.031106	0.024179	0.020038	0.01729	0.015338
7.75	0.086873	0.045113	0.031221	0.024296	0.020157	0.017411	0.015462
8	0.086988	0.045227	0.031336	0.024413	0.020276	0.017533	0.015586
8.25	0.087104	0.045341	0.031452	0.02453	0.020396	0.017656	0.015711
8.5	0.08722	0.045456	0.031568	0.024648	0.020517	0.017778	0.015836
8.75	0.087336	0.04557	0.031684	0.024767	0.020637	0.017902	0.015962
9	0.087451	0.045685	0.0318	0.024885	0.020758	0.018026	0.016089
9.25	0.087567	0.0458	0.031916	0.025004	0.02088	0.01815	0.016216
9.5	0.087684	0.045914	0.032033	0.025123	0.021002	0.018275	0.016344
9.75	0.0878	0.04603	0.03215	0.025243	0.021124	0.0184	0.016472
10	0.087916	0.046145	0.032267	0.025363	0.021247	0.018526	0.016601
10.25	0.088032	0.04626	0.032385	0.025483	0.02137	0.018652	0.016731
10.5	0.088149	0.046376	0.032502	0.025603	0.021494	0.018779	0.016861
10.75	0.088265	0.046492	0.03262	0.025724	0.021618	0.018906	0.016991
11	0.088382	0.046608	0.032739	0.025846	0.021742	0.019034	0.017122
11.25	0.088498	0.046724	0.032857	0.025967	0.021867	0.019162	0.017254
11.5	0.088615	0.04684	0.032976	0.026089	0.021993	0.019291	0.017386
11.75	0.088732	0.046957	0.033095	0.026211	0.022118	0.01942	0.017519
12	0.088849	0.047073	0.033214	0.026334	0.022244	0.01955	0.017653
12.25	0.088966	0.04719	0.033334	0.026457	0.022371	0.01968	0.017787
12.5	0.089083	0.047307	0.033454	0.02658	0.022498	0.019811	0.017921
12.75	0.0892	0.047424	0.033574	0.026704	0.022625	0.019942	0.018056
13	0.089317	0.047542	0.033694	0.026827	0.022753	0.020074	0.018192
13.25	0.089435	0.047659	0.033814	0.026952	0.022881	0.020206	0.018328
13.5	0.089552	0.047777	0.033935	0.027076	0.02301	0.020339	0.018465
13.75	0.08967	0.047895	0.034056	0.027201	0.023139	0.020472	0.018602
14	0.089787	0.048013	0.034178	0.027326	0.023268	0.020606	0.01874
14.25	0.089905	0.048131	0.034299	0.027452	0.023398	0.02074	0.018878
14.5	0.090023	0.048249	0.034421	0.027578	0.023528	0.020874	0.019017
14.75	0.09014	0.048368	0.034543	0.027704	0.023659	0.021009	0.019157
15	0.090258	0.048487	0.034665	0.027831	0.02379	0.021145	0.019297
15.25	0.090376	0.048606	0.034788	0.027958	0.023921	0.021281	0.019437
15.5	0.090494	0.048725	0.034911	0.028085	0.024053	0.021417	0.019578
15.75	0.090613	0.048844	0.035034	0.028212	0.024185	0.021554	0.01972
16	0.090731	0.048963	0.035157	0.02834	0.024318	0.021692	0.019862

(Continued)   *Monthly Mortgage Constants*

Terms (years)	8	9	10	11	12	13	14
Rates (%)							
6	0.013141	0.012006	0.011102	0.010367	0.009759	0.009247	0.008812
6.25	0.013263	0.01213	0.011228	0.010495	0.009888	0.009379	0.008946
6.5	0.013386	0.012255	0.011355	0.010624	0.010019	0.009512	0.009081
6.75	0.01351	0.01238	0.011482	0.010753	0.010151	0.009646	0.009217
7	0.013634	0.012506	0.011611	0.010884	0.010284	0.009781	0.009354
7.25	0.013758	0.012633	0.01174	0.011016	0.010418	0.009917	0.009492
7.5	0.013884	0.012761	0.01187	0.011148	0.010552	0.010054	0.009631
7.75	0.01401	0.012889	0.012001	0.011281	0.010688	0.010192	0.009772
8	0.014137	0.013019	0.012133	0.011415	0.010825	0.010331	0.009913
8.25	0.014264	0.013149	0.012265	0.01155	0.010962	0.010471	0.010056
8.5	0.014392	0.013279	0.012399	0.011686	0.011101	0.010612	0.010199
8.75	0.014521	0.013411	0.012533	0.011823	0.01124	0.010754	0.010344
9	0.01465	0.013543	0.012668	0.011961	0.01138	0.010897	0.010489
9.25	0.01478	0.013676	0.012803	0.012099	0.011522	0.011041	0.010636
9.5	0.014911	0.013809	0.01294	0.012239	0.011664	0.011186	0.010784
9.75	0.015042	0.013944	0.013077	0.012379	0.011807	0.011332	0.010932
10	0.015174	0.014079	0.013215	0.01252	0.011951	0.011478	0.011082
10.25	0.015307	0.014214	0.013354	0.012662	0.012096	0.011626	0.011233
10.5	0.01544	0.014351	0.013493	0.012804	0.012241	0.011775	0.011384
10.75	0.015574	0.014488	0.013634	0.012948	0.012388	0.011925	0.011537
11	0.015708	0.014626	0.013775	0.013092	0.012536	0.012075	0.011691
11.25	0.015844	0.014764	0.013917	0.013238	0.012684	0.012227	0.011845
11.5	0.015979	0.014904	0.01406	0.013384	0.012833	0.012379	0.012001
11.75	0.016116	0.015044	0.014203	0.01353	0.012983	0.012532	0.012157
12	0.016253	0.015184	0.014347	0.013678	0.013134	0.012687	0.012314
12.25	0.016391	0.015326	0.014492	0.013826	0.013286	0.012842	0.012473
12.5	0.016529	0.015468	0.014638	0.013975	0.013439	0.012998	0.012632
12.75	0.016668	0.01561	0.014784	0.014125	0.013592	0.013154	0.012792
13	0.016807	0.015754	0.014931	0.014276	0.013746	0.013312	0.012953
13.25	0.016947	0.015898	0.015079	0.014428	0.013901	0.013471	0.013114
13.5	0.017088	0.016042	0.015227	0.01458	0.014057	0.01363	0.013277
13.75	0.01723	0.016188	0.015377	0.014733	0.014214	0.01379	0.013441
14	0.017372	0.016334	0.015527	0.014887	0.014371	0.013951	0.013605
14.25	0.017514	0.01648	0.015677	0.015041	0.014529	0.014113	0.01377
14.5	0.017657	0.016628	0.015829	0.015196	0.014688	0.014275	0.013936
14.75	0.017801	0.016776	0.015981	0.015352	0.014848	0.014439	0.014103
15	0.017945	0.016924	0.016133	0.015509	0.015009	0.014603	0.01427
15.25	0.01809	0.017074	0.016287	0.015667	0.01517	0.014768	0.014439
15.5	0.018236	0.017224	0.016441	0.015825	0.015332	0.014933	0.014608
15.75	0.018382	0.017374	0.016596	0.015984	0.015495	0.0151	0.014778
16	0.018529	0.017525	0.016751	0.016143	0.015658	0.015267	0.014948

Put Money in Your Pockets

(Continued) *Monthly Mortgage Constants*

Terms (years)	15	16	17	18	19	20	21
Rates (%)							
6	0.008439	0.008114	0.007831	0.007582	0.007361	0.007164	0.006989
6.25	0.008574	0.008252	0.00797	0.007723	0.007504	0.007309	0.007135
6.5	0.008711	0.008391	0.008111	0.007866	0.007649	0.007456	0.007284
6.75	0.008849	0.008531	0.008253	0.00801	0.007795	0.007604	0.007433
7	0.008988	0.008672	0.008397	0.008155	0.007942	0.007753	0.007585
7.25	0.009129	0.008815	0.008541	0.008302	0.008091	0.007904	0.007737
7.5	0.00927	0.008958	0.008687	0.00845	0.008241	0.008056	0.007892
7.75	0.009413	0.009103	0.008834	0.008599	0.008392	0.008209	0.008047
8	0.009557	0.009249	0.008983	0.00875	0.008545	0.008364	0.008204
8.25	0.009701	0.009397	0.009132	0.008901	0.008699	0.008521	0.008363
8.5	0.009847	0.009545	0.009283	0.009055	0.008854	0.008678	0.008522
8.75	0.009994	0.009694	0.009435	0.009209	0.009011	0.008837	0.008683
9	0.010143	0.009845	0.009588	0.009364	0.009169	0.008997	0.008846
9.25	0.010292	0.009997	0.009742	0.009521	0.009328	0.009159	0.009009
9.5	0.010442	0.01015	0.009898	0.009679	0.009488	0.009321	0.009174
9.75	0.010594	0.010304	0.010054	0.009838	0.00965	0.009485	0.00934
10	0.010746	0.010459	0.010212	0.009998	0.009813	0.00965	0.009508
10.25	0.0109	0.010615	0.010371	0.01016	0.009976	0.009816	0.009676
10.5	0.011054	0.010772	0.010531	0.010322	0.010141	0.009984	0.009846
10.75	0.011209	0.010931	0.010692	0.010486	0.010307	0.010152	0.010017
11	0.011366	0.01109	0.010854	0.01065	0.010475	0.010322	0.010189
11.25	0.011523	0.01125	0.011017	0.010816	0.010643	0.010493	0.010362
11.5	0.011682	0.011412	0.011181	0.010983	0.010812	0.010664	0.010536
11.75	0.011841	0.011574	0.011346	0.011151	0.010983	0.010837	0.010711
12	0.012002	0.011737	0.011512	0.01132	0.011154	0.011011	0.010887
12.25	0.012163	0.011902	0.011679	0.011489	0.011326	0.011186	0.011064
12.5	0.012325	0.012067	0.011847	0.01166	0.0115	0.011361	0.011242
12.75	0.012488	0.012233	0.012016	0.011832	0.011674	0.011538	0.011421
13	0.012652	0.0124	0.012186	0.012004	0.011849	0.011716	0.011601
13.25	0.012817	0.012568	0.012357	0.012178	0.012025	0.011894	0.011782
13.5	0.012983	0.012737	0.012529	0.012352	0.012202	0.012074	0.011964
13.75	0.01315	0.012906	0.012701	0.012528	0.01238	0.012254	0.012146
14	0.013317	0.013077	0.012875	0.012704	0.012559	0.012435	0.01233
14.25	0.013486	0.013248	0.013049	0.012881	0.012738	0.012617	0.012514
14.5	0.013655	0.013421	0.013224	0.013059	0.012919	0.0128	0.012699
14.75	0.013825	0.013594	0.0134	0.013237	0.0131	0.012984	0.012885
15	0.013996	0.013768	0.013577	0.013417	0.013282	0.013168	0.013071
15.25	0.014167	0.013942	0.013755	0.013597	0.013465	0.013353	0.013258
15.5	0.01434	0.014118	0.013933	0.013778	0.013648	0.013539	0.013446
15.75	0.014513	0.014294	0.014112	0.01396	0.013833	0.013725	0.013635
16	0.014687	0.014471	0.014292	0.014142	0.014017	0.013913	0.013824

(Continued)   *Monthly Mortgage Constants*

Terms (years)	22	23	24	25	26	27	28
Rates (%)							
6	0.008439	0.008114	0.007831	0.007582	0.007361	0.007164	0.006989
6.25	0.008574	0.008252	0.00797	0.007723	0.007504	0.007309	0.007135
6.5	0.008711	0.008391	0.008111	0.007866	0.007649	0.007456	0.007284
6.75	0.008849	0.008531	0.008253	0.00801	0.007795	0.007604	0.007433
7	0.008988	0.008672	0.008397	0.008155	0.007942	0.007753	0.007585
7.25	0.009129	0.008815	0.008541	0.008302	0.008091	0.007904	0.007737
7.5	0.00927	0.008958	0.008687	0.00845	0.008241	0.008056	0.007892
7.75	0.009413	0.009103	0.008834	0.008599	0.008392	0.008209	0.008047
8	0.009557	0.009249	0.008983	0.00875	0.008545	0.008364	0.008204
8.25	0.009701	0.009397	0.009132	0.008901	0.008699	0.008521	0.008363
8.5	0.009847	0.009545	0.009283	0.009055	0.008854	0.008678	0.008522
8.75	0.009994	0.009694	0.009435	0.009209	0.009011	0.008837	0.008683
9	0.010143	0.009845	0.009588	0.009364	0.009169	0.008997	0.008846
9.25	0.010292	0.009997	0.009742	0.009521	0.009328	0.009159	0.009009
9.5	0.010442	0.01015	0.009898	0.009679	0.009488	0.009321	0.009174
9.75	0.010594	0.010304	0.010054	0.009838	0.00965	0.009485	0.00934
10	0.010746	0.010459	0.010212	0.009998	0.009813	0.00965	0.009508
10.25	0.0109	0.010615	0.010371	0.01016	0.009976	0.009816	0.009676
10.5	0.011054	0.010772	0.010531	0.010322	0.010141	0.009984	0.009846
10.75	0.011209	0.010931	0.010692	0.010486	0.010307	0.010152	0.010017
11	0.011366	0.01109	0.010854	0.01065	0.010475	0.010322	0.010189
11.25	0.011523	0.01125	0.011017	0.010816	0.010643	0.010493	0.010362
11.5	0.011682	0.011412	0.011181	0.010983	0.010812	0.010664	0.010536
11.75	0.011841	0.011574	0.011346	0.011151	0.010983	0.010837	0.010711
12	0.012002	0.011737	0.011512	0.01132	0.011154	0.011011	0.010887
12.25	0.012163	0.011902	0.011679	0.011489	0.011326	0.011186	0.011064
12.5	0.012325	0.012067	0.011847	0.01166	0.0115	0.011361	0.011242
12.75	0.012488	0.012233	0.012016	0.011832	0.011674	0.011538	0.011421
13	0.012652	0.0124	0.012186	0.012004	0.011849	0.011716	0.011601
13.25	0.012817	0.012568	0.012357	0.012178	0.012025	0.011894	0.011782
13.5	0.012983	0.012737	0.012529	0.012352	0.012202	0.012074	0.011964
13.75	0.01315	0.012906	0.012701	0.012528	0.01238	0.012254	0.012146
14	0.013317	0.013077	0.012875	0.012704	0.012559	0.012435	0.01233
14.25	0.013486	0.013248	0.013049	0.012881	0.012738	0.012617	0.012514
14.5	0.013655	0.013421	0.013224	0.013059	0.012919	0.0128	0.012699
14.75	0.013825	0.013594	0.0134	0.013237	0.0131	0.012984	0.012885
15	0.013996	0.013768	0.013577	0.013417	0.013282	0.013168	0.013071
15.25	0.014167	0.013942	0.013755	0.013597	0.013465	0.013353	0.013258
15.5	0.01434	0.014118	0.013933	0.013778	0.013648	0.013539	0.013446
15.75	0.014513	0.014294	0.014112	0.01396	0.013833	0.013725	0.013635
16	0.014687	0.014471	0.014292	0.014142	0.014017	0.013913	0.013824

(Continued)   *Monthly Mortgage Constants*

Terms (years)	29	30	31	32	33	34	35
Rates (%)							
6	0.00607	0.005996	0.005927	0.005864	0.005806	0.005752	0.005702
6.25	0.00623	0.006157	0.00609	0.006028	0.005972	0.005919	0.005871
6.5	0.006392	0.006321	0.006255	0.006195	0.00614	0.006089	0.006042
6.75	0.006556	0.006486	0.006422	0.006363	0.006309	0.00626	0.006214
7	0.006721	0.006653	0.006591	0.006533	0.006481	0.006433	0.006389
7.25	0.006888	0.006822	0.006761	0.006705	0.006654	0.006608	0.006565
7.5	0.007057	0.006992	0.006933	0.006879	0.006829	0.006784	0.006742
7.75	0.007228	0.007164	0.007106	0.007054	0.007006	0.006962	0.006922
8	0.007399	0.007338	0.007281	0.00723	0.007184	0.007141	0.007103
8.25	0.007573	0.007513	0.007458	0.007408	0.007363	0.007322	0.007285
8.5	0.007748	0.007689	0.007636	0.007588	0.007544	0.007505	0.007469
8.75	0.007924	0.007867	0.007816	0.007769	0.007727	0.007688	0.007654
9	0.008102	0.008046	0.007996	0.007951	0.00791	0.007873	0.00784
9.25	0.008281	0.008227	0.008178	0.008135	0.008095	0.00806	0.008027
9.5	0.008461	0.008409	0.008362	0.008319	0.008281	0.008247	0.008216
9.75	0.008642	0.008592	0.008546	0.008505	0.008469	0.008436	0.008406
10	0.008825	0.008776	0.008732	0.008692	0.008657	0.008625	0.008597
10.25	0.009009	0.008961	0.008919	0.008881	0.008846	0.008816	0.008789
10.5	0.009193	0.009147	0.009106	0.00907	0.009037	0.009008	0.008981
10.75	0.009379	0.009335	0.009295	0.00926	0.009228	0.0092	0.009175
11	0.009566	0.009523	0.009485	0.009451	0.009421	0.009394	0.00937
11.25	0.009754	0.009713	0.009676	0.009643	0.009614	0.009588	0.009565
11.5	0.009943	0.009903	0.009867	0.009836	0.009808	0.009783	0.009761
11.75	0.010133	0.010094	0.01006	0.01003	0.010003	0.009979	0.009958
12	0.010324	0.010286	0.010253	0.010224	0.010198	0.010176	0.010155
12.25	0.010515	0.010479	0.010447	0.010419	0.010395	0.010373	0.010354
12.5	0.010707	0.010673	0.010642	0.010615	0.010592	0.010571	0.010553
12.75	0.0109	0.010867	0.010838	0.010812	0.010789	0.010769	0.010752
13	0.011094	0.011062	0.011034	0.011009	0.010987	0.010969	0.010952
13.25	0.011289	0.011258	0.011231	0.011207	0.011186	0.011168	0.011152
13.5	0.011484	0.011454	0.011428	0.011405	0.011386	0.011368	0.011353
13.75	0.01168	0.011651	0.011626	0.011604	0.011586	0.011569	0.011555
14	0.011876	0.011849	0.011825	0.011804	0.011786	0.01177	0.011757
14.25	0.012073	0.012047	0.012024	0.012004	0.011987	0.011972	0.011959
14.5	0.012271	0.012246	0.012224	0.012205	0.012188	0.012174	0.012162
14.75	0.012469	0.012445	0.012424	0.012405	0.01239	0.012376	0.012365
15	0.012668	0.012644	0.012624	0.012607	0.012592	0.012579	0.012568
15.25	0.012867	0.012845	0.012825	0.012809	0.012794	0.012782	0.012772
15.5	0.013067	0.013045	0.013027	0.013011	0.012997	0.012986	0.012976
15.75	0.013267	0.013246	0.013228	0.013213	0.013201	0.01319	0.01318
16	0.013467	0.013448	0.013431	0.013416	0.013404	0.013394	0.013385

Appendix B	*CALCULATING MONTHLY PAYMENT USING PUBLISHED AMORTIZATION BOOKLETS*

DETERMINING THE NECESSARY MONTHLY PAYMENT

Using Published Mortgage Amortization Booklets

It's a cinch. Just go to your nearest public library and get a copy of **The Consumers Amortization Guide**, a publication by Dugan Publishers. That little book has monthly mortgage payment tables, with interest rates ranging from 5% to 25% and covering mortgage amounts from $500 to $500,000 for term up to 40 years.

You probably could use other publications that provide the same information in a similar format. But, for our purposes, **The Consumers Amortization Guide** will do fine.

Go to *Section One*, the monthly payment schedule.

Find the monthly payment as follows:

 Locate the page that covers your interest rate

*Notice that the very first vertical column on every page contains amounts in **bold**.* ***Those are balance amounts to be amortized.***

Also notice that the first row (horizontal line) contains terms from 1 to 40 years.

 In the top horizontal line, find the term (number of years) you decided on.

 Go down the leftmost column under the balance AMOUNT in **bold,** locate your balance. Then, go down the column under the **term** you found in step *2*, locate the payment amount in the *same row* as the balance that matches your remaining balance. That's all there's to it.

 If you can't find the exact amount of your balance at the beginning of any row, just *find all the amounts that add up to your balance* (rounded to the nearest dollar) and *add the corresponding payment amounts under your term.* The sum will be your total monthly payment. Using interpolation, you can get a precise payment, even if you can't find a match for the smallest partial balance after you break up the balance into parts.

Problem

You've had your 30-year mortgage for 10 years. The interest rate is 10%. Your scheduled monthly payment is $702.06. The bank confirmed that your remaining balance is $72,750.42. There are 20 years to go. But, you decide to terminate the mortgage in 12 years. *What monthly payment will amortize the loan within 12 years?*

Solution

After turning to the **10%** section in the table, you locate the **12 years** term in the top horizontal line.

But, as you go down the *balance amount* column, you can NOT find the exact amount of $72,750.42. So, what do you do?

Just break up the balance into portions that you CAN find in the **amount** column. In this case, you can use 70,000 and 2,000. But, since 750.42 is not listed, round *up* to *800,* the next higher amount.

The amounts 70,000, 2,000, and 800 add up to 72,800, which is obviously a bit more than $72,750.42. Consequently, the payments corresponding to those sums will add up to *just a little bit* more than the total payment required precisely for $72,750.42. But, that's OK. The payment you get this way will only end the loan a few months earlier than you wanted.

Solution
(Continued)

Looking down the 12-year column, you'll find:

- a payment of **$836.55** for the $70,000 balance

- a payment of **$23.90** for the $2,000 balance

- a payment of **$9.56** for the $800 balance.

Those little payments add up to a monthly payment of ***$870.01*** to amortize the total balance of $72,800 within 12 years

Since the original balance of $72,750.42 is less than the $72,800 you could get from the table, the payment of $870.01 will actually end the mortgage in *less* than 12 years. To be exact, the remaining term will last *11 years and 4 months*.

NOTE: If the remaining balance is ***not*** a clean multiple of $100 (that is, ***not*** terminating exactly in *00.00*), you get an approximate payment amount from the tables. When you *round up* to get a payment, the answer will amortize the mortgage within the time frame you want all right, but a few months earlier than you planned.

You can get an **exact** answer by *interpolating* rather than rounding up.

How do you interpolate?

Just find the difference between the partial amount that was not in the table and the *next lower* amount in the table. In our problem, the partial amount that doesn't fit is *$750.42*, and the *next lower* amount in the table is *$700*. So, the *difference* is **$50.42**.

Find the *increment* from the *lower amount* and the next higher amount (the one you rounded to). Now, get the ratio between the *difference* and the *increment*. In the given problem, the increment between $700 and the *next higher amount* $800 is 100.

So, the ratio is $\frac{50.42}{100}$ or ***0.5042***.

Next, find the difference between the **payment** for the *higher* amount you rounded up to and the **payment** for the *lower* amount. In the example, the *payment* for the higher amount is $9.56, and the *payment* for the lower amount is $8.37. The difference between the two is ***$1.19.***

Solution
(Continued)

Then, multiply this difference by the ratio you just calculated earlier, and add the result to the lower payment to get the actual payment. Continuing with the example, *$1.19* times *0.5042* is 0.5999 or *.60*. Adding 0.60 to $8.37 gives *$8.97*.

Refining the figures, we now have:

- a payment of $836.55 for the $70,000 balance

- a payment of $23.90 for the $2,000 balance

- a payment of *$8.97* for the *$750.42* balance.

The partial payments now add up to a monthly payment of *$869.42* to amortize the total balance of $72,750.42 *exactly* within 12 years.

<table>
<tr><td>

Appendix C

</td><td>

CALCULATING THE MONTHLY PAYMENT WITH JUST A CALCULATOR

</td></tr>
</table>

If you can't find your *interest rate* or your *loan term* in the tables, your only recourse is to calculate the payment yourself. You don't have to be too mathematically inclined to do this. With a good calculator you can apply the procedure below to get an exact answer quickly.

Your calculator MUST have an exponentiation function. That's the key with the symbol X^y, which lets you calculate powers, such as 18^3 (an easy way to calculate 18 x 18 x 18). If you've never used the X^y function before, don't be alarmed. It's quite easy. For example, to calculate 18^3, do the following:

Step	*Action*
1	Key in **18**
2	Press X^y
3	Key in **3**
4	Press = Now, read the answer, **5832**, on the display.

You could just as easily calculate 18^{120}, 1.8^{360}, or *any* power in that range.

It would be useful, but not necessary, for your machine to also have the *reciprocal* key, with the symbol $1/X$, to quickly divide the digit **1** by any number without having to do the division operation yourself. To use the $1/X$ key, just key in or recall from memory the number you want to divide into 1, then press the $1/X$ key. For example, to calculate **1 / 20**, do these steps:

1	Key in **20** (or recall it from memory, if it was there)
2	Press $1/X$ Now, read the answer, **.05**, on the display.

Your calculator should also have the Memory In (**M in**) and Memory Recall (**MR**) functions to help save you some keystrokes.

The following procedure illustrates a payment calculation with data from our example problem in *Appendix B*. Practice a little. Go through the eight steps using the sample data, then calculate your own monthly payment.

PROCEDURE FOR CALCULATING AMORTIZATION PAYMENT

Directions: Put *underlined* items into corresponding *blank* boxes, **before** you perform the indicated **OPERATION**.   Put all answers in the **RESULT** column.   **NOTE:**   *The result from the operation in* **Step 1** *is referred to as* **Result 1**, *and so on for all steps.*

STEP	ACTION	OPERATION	RESULT
1	Multiply the *current remaining years* by **12**	┌12 years┐ x **12**	144
2	Divide your *annual interest percentage* by *1200*	┌10┐ / **1200**	.0083333 *(Short cut hint: Store* **Result 2** *in memory)*
3	Multiply **Result 2** by the *loan balance*	┌0.0083333┐ **x** ┌72750.42┐	606.25
4	*(Short cut hint: Recall* **Result 2** *from memory)* Add the digit **1** to **Result 2**	┌.0083333┐ + **1**	1.0083333
5	Using the X^y key, take **Result 4** and raise it to the power **Result 1**	┌1.00833333┐ ┌144┐	3.30464895 *(Short cut hint: Store* **Result 5** *in memory)*
6	Press the $^1/X$ key to divide **1** by **Result 5** (If you don't have the $^1/X$ key, just divide the digit **1** by **Result 5** yourself)	**1** / ┌3.30464895┐	0.30269559 *(Short cut hint: Store* **Result 6** *in memory)*
7	Subtract **Result 6** from the dig **1**	**1** - ┌0.30269559┐	0.6973044 *(Short cut hint: Store* **Result 7** *in memory)*
8	Divide **Result 3** by **Result 7**	┌606.25┐ / ┌0.6973044┐	**869.42**

In case you're wondering, the above procedure applies the following formula for calculating the payment:

$$Payment = \frac{\text{Loan Balance} \times \textit{Periodic interest}}{1 - V^n}$$

Where:

$$\textit{Periodic interest} = \frac{Annual\ interest\ percentage}{(12 \times 100)}$$

$$V^n = \frac{1}{(1 + \text{Periodic interest})^{\text{Term in months}}}$$

The final result, **Result 8** from Step 8, is the **required monthly payment $869.42**.

Determining the required PREPAYMENT

The required prepayment is just the difference between this new payment and what you pay now.

The new required monthly payment: $869.42

What you pay now: *$702.06*

STEP	ACTION	OPERATION	RESULT
1	Subtract your current monthly payment from the *new* required monthly payment	$869.42 - $702.06	*$167.36*

The required monthly **prepayment**:   **$167.36**

Use the following blank procedure sheet for your own calculation.

PROCEDURE FOR CALCULATING AMORTIZATION PAYMENT

Directions: Put **_underlined_** items into corresponding *blank* boxes, **before** you perform the indicated **OPERATION.** Put all answers in the **RESULT** column. **NOTE:** *The result from the operation in* **Step 1** *is referred to as* **Result 1,** *and so on for all steps.*

STEP	ACTION	OPERATION	RESULT
1	Multiply the **_current remaining years_** by **12**	[____] x **12**	
2	Divide your **_annual interest percentage_** by **1200**	[____] / **1200**	*(Short cut hint: Store* **Result 2** *in memory)*
3	Multiply **Result 2** by the **_loan balance_**	[_____] x [_____]	
4	*(Short cut hint: Recall* **Result 2** *from memory)* Add the digit **1** to **Result 2**	[_____] + **1**	
5	Using the X^y key, take **Result 4** and raise it to the power **Result 1**	[_____][____]	*(Short cut hint: Store* **Result 5** *in memory)*
6	*Press the* $^1/X$ *key to divide* **1** *by* **Result 5** *(If you don't have the* $^1/X$ *key, just divide the digit* **1** *by* **Result 5** *yourself)*	**1** / [_____]	*(Short cut hint: Store* **Result 6** *in memory)*
7	Subtract **Result 6** from the digit **1**	**1** - [_____]	*(Short cut hint: Store* **Result 7** *in memory)*
8	Divide **Result 3** by **Result 7**	[_____] / [_____]	

Appendix D	**FINDING INTEREST AND TIME SAVINGS** **From ONE Prepayment**

Using a current partial or complete normal amortization schedule, you can determine the savings from just *one* **prepayment** you make. Starting with the <u>current</u> balance *before the prepayment,* the amortization **must be based** on the *original* monthly payment *(one that does **not** include a prepayment).*

Take the first 30 scheduled payments in the amortization schedule for the $80,000-mortgage for 30 years at 10% (see Figure D.1). Examples from these entries will illustrate the procedure for finding the *savings from **one** prepayment.* The shaded periods are going to disappear after the prepayment.

PERIOD	PAYMENT	INTEREST	PRINCIPAL	BALANCE
1	$702.06	$666.67	$35.39	$79,964.61
2	$702.06	$666.37	$35.69	$79,928.92
3	$702.06	$666.07	$35.98	$79,892.94
4	$702.06	$665.77	$36.28	$79,856.66
5	$702.06	$665.47	$36.59	$79,820.07
6	$702.06	$665.17	$36.89	$79,783.18
7	$702.06	$664.86	$37.20	$79,745.99
8	$702.06	$664.55	$37.51	$79,708.48
9	$702.06	$664.24	$37.82	$79,670.66
10	$702.06	$663.92	$38.14	$79,632.52
11	$702.06	$663.60	$38.45	$79,594.07
12	$702.06	$663.28	$38.77	$79,555.30
13	$702.06	$662.96	$39.10	$79,516.20
14	$702.06	$662.64	$39.42	$79,476.78
15	$702.06	$662.31	$39.75	$79,437.03
16	$702.06	$661.98	$40.08	$79,396.95
17	$702.06	$661.64	$40.42	$79,356.53
18	$702.06	$661.30	$40.75	$79,315.78
19	$702.06	$660.96	$41.09	$79,274.68
20	$702.06	$660.62	$41.43	$79,233.25
21	$702.06	$660.28	$41.78	$79,191.47
22	$702.06	$659.93	$42.13	$79,149.34
23	$702.06	$659.58	$42.48	$79,106.86
24	$702.06	$659.22	$42.83	$79,064.03
25	$702.06	$658.87	$43.19	$79,020.84
26	$702.06	$658.51	$43.55	$78,977.29
27	$702.06	$658.14	$43.91	$78,933.37
28	$702.06	$657.78	$44.28	$78,889.10
29	$702.06	$657.41	$44.65	$78,844.45
30	$702.06	$657.04	$45.02	$78,799.43

Figure D.1

Use the following step-by-step procedure to get *interest* and *time* savings amounts from a single prepayment.

PROCEDURE FOR FINDING *INTEREST* AND *TIME* SAVINGS **From ONE Prepayment**	

STEP	ACTION
1	***Get the new balance*** Current Balance - Prepayment = **New Balance** [_____] - [_____] = [_____]
2	***Find the* FIRST PERIOD *in the range of periods covered by the prepayment* [____]** *It's the very next one after the current period.*
3	***Find the* LAST PERIOD *in the range of periods covered by the prepayment* [____]** *It's the **first** period with a balance that's NOT **GREATER** than the **NEW** balance.*
4	***Find the RATIO by which the* LAST PERIOD *in the range is covered:*** (Balance in *next to last period* - New Balance) / Principal portion in *last period* = ***Ratio*** ([_____] - [_____]) / [_____] = [_____]
5	***Find the* INTEREST *and the* DAYS *saved in the* LAST PERIOD** *Ratio* x *Interest portion in last period* = *Partial Interest saved* [_____] x [_____] = [_____] *Ratio* x *Number of days in month* = *Days saved* [_____] x [_____] = [_____]
6	***Find the* INTEREST *and the* TIME *saved in all* COVERED PERIODS** *Partial Interest saved* + *Total fully saved interest portions* = *Interest saved* [_____] + [_____] = [_____] *Days saved* + *Total fully saved months* = *Months and days saved* [_____] + [_____] = [_____]

Use this procedure table as a working document. Fill out one of these every time you prepay, once or twice a year. Record the final results from Step 6, *Interest and time saved*, in your worksheet. Keep all documents in the same folder. You'll find a master copy of this procedure sheet at the end of this *Appendix*.

Here is an expanded version of the procedure, complete with detailed explanations and examples. The illustration uses the amortization table entries from Figure D.1 above.

Illustration of the
PROCEDURE FOR FINDING *INTEREST* AND *TIME* SAVINGS
From ONE Prepayment

STEP	ACTION
1	**Get the new balance** Using the current amortization schedule, which does not reflect the prepayment, **subtract the prepayment amount from the current balance** *Example: The current period is number 12. The current balance is $79,555.30.* But, with a prepayment of $702.06, the new balance is $78,853.24
2	**Find the** FIRST PERIOD **in the range of periods covered by the prepayment** The first period in the range is the very next one after the current period. *Example: The first period covered by the prepayment is number 13.*
3	**Find the** LAST PERIOD **in the range of periods covered by the prepayment** Scan the balance column starting with the first period covered. The last period in the range either has a balance that equals the new balance exactly or has the one balance that would rank *immediately after* the new balance in a *descending* numeric sequence. ***NOTE:*** A balance that exactly matches marks a last period that is **covered in full.** That can occur only for a prepayment *in synch*. The last period in the range will most likely be covered in part. It has the *first* balance that's less than the new balance. When a prepayment covers one period only, that period is both the first and last one in the range. *Example: The last period covered is number 29. The balance in period 29 is $78,844.45.* Notice that $78,844.45 ranks *immediately after* the *new* balance of $78,853.24. In this example, the range of periods covered by the prepayment includes periods 13 through 29. Periods 13 through 28 are covered *in full.* Period 29 is covered *partly.*

(Continued on next page)

(Continued from preceding page)

4 — Find the RATIO by which the LAST PERIOD in the range is covered

Get the **difference** between the balance in *the NEXT TO LAST PERIOD* and the *new* balance, then divide that *difference* by the PRINCIPAL portion in the *last* period covered.

Example: The next to last period is number 28, and the balance in that period is $78,889.10.   The difference is $78,889.10 - $78,853.24 or $35.86.   The RATIO is $35.86 / $45.02 or 0.796534873.

5 — Find the INTEREST and the TIME saved in the LAST PERIOD

To get the partial interest savings, multiply the interest portion in the last period by the RATIO.

To get the number of days saved in the last period, multiply the number of days in the month corresponding to the last period by the RATIO.

Example: The interest portion in the last period is $657.41, so the partial interest saving is $657.41 X 0.796534873 or $523.65.   The number of days saved, assuming a 30-day month, is 30 X 0.796534873 or 24

6 — Find the INTEREST and the TIME saved in all COVERED PERIODS

To get the interest savings in all period covered, add the partial interest savings to the sum of the interest portions in all periods fully covered.

To get the number of months and days saved in all periods covered, add the number of days saved in the last period to the number of months covered fully.

The number of months covered fully is the difference between the next to last period number and the current period number. In the example, it's the difference between 28 and 12, which is 16 months.

Example: The interest saved in the last period is $523.65, and the interest portions in periods 13 through 28 add to $10,566.71. So, the amount of interest saved by the prepayment is approximately $11,090.36.   The actual savings is $11,094.69 (taking rounding errors into consideration).

The number of days saved in the last period is 24. The number of months covered fully is 16 months (period 28 minus period 12). So, the amount of time saved by the ONE prepayment is 16 months and 24 days.

When you get an updated amortization schedule AFTER the prepayment, the result will be astounding. Including the prepayment of $702.06, the actual payment associated with period 12 was $1,404.12. Notice the effect as *sixteen full periods and part of one period got eliminated.* Period 13 starts with the new balance of $78,853.24.

Figure **D.2** below shows the first 24 periods in the <u>updated</u> amortization schedule *after* the prepayment.

Sixteen FULL periods and *$11,090.36* just disappear because of the prepayment of $702.06 in Period 12!

The *new* Period 13 moved forward in time to a point in the *old* Period 29.

PERIOD	PAYMENT	INTEREST	PRINCIPAL	BALANCE
1	$702.06	$666.67	$35.39	$79,964.61
2	$702.06	$666.37	$35.69	$79,928.92
3	$702.06	$666.07	$35.98	$79,892.94
4	$702.06	$665.77	$36.28	$79,856.66
5	$702.06	$665.47	$36.59	$79,820.07
6	$702.06	$665.17	$36.89	$79,783.18
7	$702.06	$664.86	$37.20	$79,745.99
8	$702.06	$664.55	$37.51	$79,708.48
9	$702.06	$664.24	$37.82	$79,670.66
10	$702.06	$663.92	$38.14	$79,632.52
11	$702.06	$663.60	$38.45	$79,594.07
12	*$1,404.12*	$663.28	*$740.83*	*$78,853.24*
13	$702.06	$657.11	$44.95	$78,808.29
14	$702.06	$656.74	$45.32	$78,762.97
15	$702.06	$656.36	$45.70	$78,717.27
16	$702.06	$655.98	$46.08	$78,671.19
17	$702.06	$655.59	$46.46	$78,624.73
18	$702.06	$655.21	$46.85	$78,577.87
19	$702.06	$654.82	$47.24	$78,530.63
20	$702.06	$654.42	$47.64	$78,483.00
21	$702.06	$654.02	$48.03	$78,434.97
22	$702.06	$653.62	$48.43	$78,386.53
23	$702.06	$653.22	$48.84	$78,337.70
24	$702.06	$652.81	$49.24	$78,288.45

Figure D.2

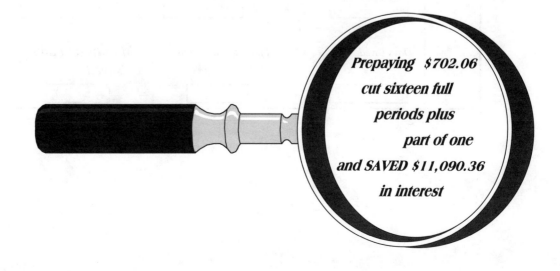

Prepaying $702.06 cut sixteen full periods plus part of one and SAVED $11,090.36 in interest

PROCEDURE FOR FINDING *INTEREST* AND *TIME* SAVINGS
From ONE Prepayment

STEP	ACTION
1	**Get the new balance** Current Balance　　-　　Prepayment　　=　　**New Balance** [ ]　-　[ ]　=　[ ]
2	**Find the** FIRST PERIOD **in the range of periods covered by the prepayment**　[ ] *It's the very next one after the current period.*
3	**Find the** LAST PERIOD **in the range of periods covered by the prepayment**　[ ] *It's the **first** period with a balance that's NOT **GREATER** than the **NEW** balance.*
4	**Find the RATIO by which the** LAST PERIOD **in the range is covered:** (Balance in *next to last period* - New Balance) / Principal portion in *last period* = **Ratio** ([ ] - [ ]) / [ ] = [ ]
5	**Find the** INTEREST **and the** DAYS **saved in the** LAST PERIOD *Ratio*　　　x　　*Interest portion in last period*　　=　　*Partial Interest saved* [ ]　x　[ ]　　=　[ ] *Ratio*　　　　x　　*Number of days in month*　= *Days saved* [ ]　x　[ ]　　=　[ ]
6	**Find the** INTEREST **and the** TIME **saved in all** COVERED PERIODS *Partial Interest saved*　+　*Total fully saved interest portions*　=　*Interest saved* [ ]　+　[ ]　=　[ ] *Days saved*　+　*Total fully saved months*　=　*Months and days saved* [ ]　+　[ ]　=　[ ]

Appendix E	**Determining the New Loan Term and Expected TOTAL Savings for the Fixed Prepayment Method**

This *Appendix* contains **"long-hand"** instructions for finding the **total** results from a *new* monthly payment obtained by adding a given *base* prepayment to a regular monthly payment. The results include the *new loan term,* and the expected TOTAL savings in *time* and *interest.* These "long-hand" instructions guide you to get precise results in two steps as follows:

 Determine the new loan term and your expected TOTAL savings in time

 Determine your expected TOTAL savings in interest

Apply these steps when you've decided on a *base* prepayment amount. The *new* monthly payment is the sum of the *regular* monthly payment and the base *prepayment* that you decided on. You also need an amortization schedule that features the new monthly payment, starting with the current loan balance.

Illustration

Let's use the mortgage of $80,000 at 10% for 30 years. The regular monthly payment is $702.06. Suppose you want to prepay $35 permanently. The new *base* monthly payment is **$737.06** (*$702.06 plus $35*). Figure **E.1** below shows the first seven and last five periods of new amortization schedule based on the new regular monthly payment of **$737.06**.

Period	Payment	Interest	Principal	Balance
1	$737.06	$666.67	$70.39	$79,929.61
2	$737.06	$666.08	$70.98	$79,858.63
3	$737.06	$665.49	$71.57	$79,787.05
4	$737.06	$664.89	$72.17	$79,714.88
5	$737.06	$664.29	$72.77	$79,642.11
6	$737.06	$663.68	$73.38	$79,568.74
7	$737.06	$663.07	$73.99	$79,494.75

•
•

279	$737.06	$29.96	$707.10	$2,887.83
280	$737.06	$24.07	$713.00	$2,174.83
281	$737.06	$18.12	$718.94	$1,455.90
282	$737.06	$12.13	$724.93	$730.97
283	$737.06	$6.09	$730.97	$0.00

Figure E.1

Step 1

Determine the new loan term and your expected TOTAL savings in time

You can find the new duration or term and the total savings in time that the new monthly payment can achieve, if you stick with it the whole time. To do that, you can either use the new amortization schedule or the *mortgage constant* tables in *Appendix A*.

Using Amortization Schedule

The time remaining, or *new term,* is the number of periods remaining to be paid from this point to the end of the schedule. This is true regardless of whether you're at the very beginning or a few years into your mortgage.

Example

Let's say here that the next period is 1.

The mortgage contract or previous amortization schedule indicates the last period in the term. On the original schedule, that would be 360. So, the remaining time is 360 periods *or 30 years.*

The **period number** in the last line of the new schedule will indicate the new term. Using the new schedule depicted in Figure **E.1** above, the last period, in which the balance becomes $0, is number 283.

Period	Payment	Interest	Principal	Balance
283	$737.06	$6.09	$730.97	$0.00

The last period is 283. In effect *283 months remain ahead.* That translates to a new *shorter* loan term of **23 years and 7 months**.

Time Savings

> **The savings in time is the *difference* between the remaining time on the *previous* amortization schedule and the remaining time on the new schedule.**

The savings in time is 77 periods or months (*the difference 360 - 283*). That's a *savings* of **6 years and 5 months.**

*Using
Mortgage
Constant
Tables*

You can find the new term quickly with the mortgage constant tables. Just divide the **new monthly payment** by your **initial** remaining balance (the balance *before* you make any payments at the new level). The division gives a factor which you can compare to the *mortgage constants* associated with your interest rate. The *closest* mortgage constants pinpoint the new term.

Refer to the partial table below, Figure E.2, for the discussion in this section. But, see Appendix A for the complete table of monthly mortgage constants.

Use this procedure with the Monthly Mortgage Constant table to find the remaining time for a *new* payment and a given balance.

HOW TO FIND REMAINING TERM USING MORTGAGE CONSTANT TABLES

STEP	ACTION
1	*Divide your **new monthly payment** by the **remaining balance** to get the comparison **factor**.*
2	*Look down the leftmost column and find your interest rate.*
3	*Go across the row with your interest rate to locate EITHER a constant that's EQUAL to your **factor** (Case One) OR the **first** monthly mortgage constant that's SMALLER than your **factor** (Case Two).*
4	**Case One:** *If you find a constant that **equals** your factor, go UP the column with that constant. The number at the top of the column is the **exact** TERM. You're done.* **Case Two:** *Otherwise, the first monthly mortgage constant that is SMALLER than your **factor** marks the **right** column boundary for your term. Step back to the LARGER constant to the immediate left. It marks the **left** column boundary. Go to the top of the left column to find the number of **years**.* If you're only looking for the number of years for a quick idea, then that's it. You've got the number. But, in this second case, there is a number of months remaining.

Terms (years)	22	23	24	25	26	27	28
Rates (%)							
6	0.006831	0.006688	0.00656	0.006443	0.006337	0.00624	0.006151
6.5	0.007129	0.006991	0.006865	0.006752	0.006649	0.006556	0.00647
7	0.007434	0.007299	0.007178	0.007068	0.006968	0.006878	0.006796
⋮							
9.5	0.009045	0.00893	0.008828	0.008737	0.008656	0.008584	0.008519
10	0.009382	0.009272	0.009174	0.009087	0.00901	0.008941	0.00888
10.5	0.009725	0.009619	0.009525	0.009442	0.009368	0.009303	0.009245

Figure E.2

In a Case Two, to find the exact number of months, you need to do a little *interpolation.* That's a lot easier than the name sounds. See the additional instructions below for four easy steps to find the number of months.

HERE'S HOW TO FIND THE REMAINING NUMBER OF MONTHS BY INTERPOLATION

STEP	ACTION
1	*Using your calculator,* SUBTRACT *the **smaller constant** on the right from the **larger constant**. Store the result in memory.*
2	SUBTRACT *the **smaller constant** from your **comparison factor**.*
3	DIVIDE *this second result by the result from Step 1 (recall it from memory).*
4	MULTIPLY *the result of the division by* **12**. *The whole number portion of the product is the <u>number of months</u> you want (drop the digits to the right of the decimal point).*

Practice Problem

Referring to the example above (we're still in **Step 1**), let's find the *term* when you repay the $80,000 balance at the rate of $737.06 a month, using *mortgage constants.*

Solution

Go through the next four steps to find the number of years. Then, find the remaining number of months, if any, by following the additional four instruction steps.

HOW TO FIND REMAINING TERM USING MORTGAGE CONSTANT TABLES

STEP	ACTION
1	*Divide your **new monthly payment** by the **remaining balance** to get the comparison **factor**.* *Example: $737.06 divided by $80,000 gives a factor of **0.00921325**.*
2	***Look down the leftmost column and find your interest rate.*** *Example: The interest rate is **10**.*
3	*Go across the row with your interest rate to locate EITHER a constant that's EQUAL to your **factor** OR the **first** monthly mortgage constant that's SMALLER than your **factor**.* *Example: The first constant smaller than the factor is **0.009174** (no constant is equal to the factor, **so it's a Case Two**)*

(Continued on next page)

(Continued from previous page)

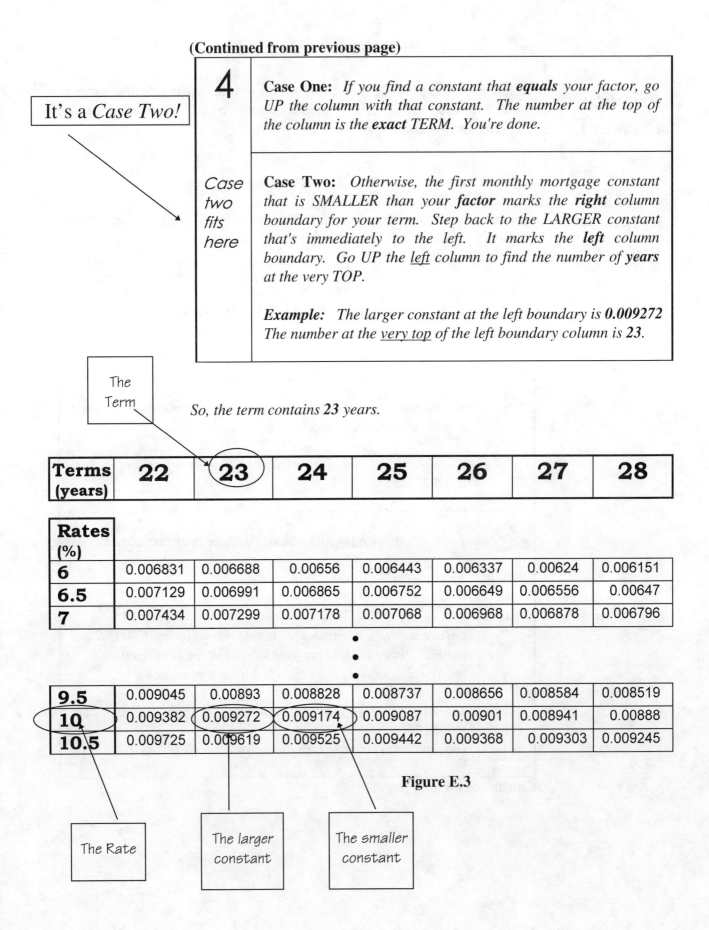

4	**Case One:** *If you find a constant that **equals** your factor, go UP the column with that constant. The number at the top of the column is the **exact** TERM. You're done.*
Case two fits here	**Case Two:** *Otherwise, the first monthly mortgage constant that is SMALLER than your **factor** marks the **right** column boundary for your term. Step back to the LARGER constant that's immediately to the left. It marks the **left** column boundary. Go UP the left column to find the number of **years** at the very TOP.* **Example:** *The larger constant at the left boundary is **0.009272** The number at the very top of the left boundary column is **23**.*

It's a *Case Two!*

The Term

*So, the term contains **23** years.*

Terms (years)	22	23	24	25	26	27	28

Rates (%)							
6	0.006831	0.006688	0.00656	0.006443	0.006337	0.00624	0.006151
6.5	0.007129	0.006991	0.006865	0.006752	0.006649	0.006556	0.00647
7	0.007434	0.007299	0.007178	0.007068	0.006968	0.006878	0.006796

⋮

9.5	0.009045	0.00893	0.008828	0.008737	0.008656	0.008584	0.008519
10	0.009382	0.009272	0.009174	0.009087	0.00901	0.008941	0.00888
10.5	0.009725	0.009619	0.009525	0.009442	0.009368	0.009303	0.009245

Figure E.3

The Rate

The larger constant

The smaller constant

Let's go on to find the remaining number of months.

HERE'S HOW TO FIND THE REMAINING NUMBER OF MONTHS BY INTERPOLATION

STEP	ACTION
1	*Using your calculator,* **Subtract** *the **smaller constant** on the right from the **larger constant**. Store the result in memory.* *Example: 0.009272 - 0.009174 = **0.000098***
2	**Subtract** *the **smaller constant** from your **comparison factor**.* *Example: 0.009272 - 0.00921325 = **0.00005875***
3	**Divide** *this second result by the result from Step 1 (recall it from memory).* *Example: 0.00005875 / 0.000098 = **0.599489795***
4	**Multiply** *the result of the division by **12**. The whole number portion of the answer is the <u>number of months</u> you want.* *Example: **0.599489795** X 12 = **7**.193877551* *The number of months is 7.*

The answer is *23 years and 7 months.*

The savings in time is the difference between **30** years and the *23* years *7* months. That comes to a savings of *6 years and 5 months.*

Step 2

Determine your expected TOTAL savings in interest

Interest Savings

The *total interest savings* is the difference between the ***original total interest*** and the ***expected total interest.*** Find the *interest savings* in *two* phases.

In ***phase one,*** you calculate the ***original total interest,*** which you would wind up paying *if you don't make any prepayments.*

In ***phase two,*** you calculate the *EXPECTED total interest* amount that you'll actually pay *when you make the NEW monthly payment.* -- ***PHASE TWO*** *considers TWO* SITUATIONS to calculate the ***expected total interest*** amount. Take *Situation 1* if you're *starting* a new mortgage. Take *Situation 2* if you've being paying off an old mortgage. Either way, you'll next calculate the interest *SAVINGS* by finding the *difference* between the *ORIGINAL total interest* amount and the *EXPECTED total interest* amount.

PHASE ONE

Getting the *original total interest* is easy. First, calculate the *original total payment* by multiplying the original monthly payment by the number of periods in the original term *YOU got with the mortgage.* Then, calculate the *original total interest* by subtracting the mortgage amount from the total payment.

Calculating Original Total Interest
(*for both old and new mortgages*)

STEP	ACTION
1	Calculate ***Total Payments*** **=** *Monthly Payment* **X** *Number of Periods in original term* *Example: $702.06* **X** *360 = $254,741.60*
2	Calculate ***Original Total Interest*** **=** *Total payments -* *Mortgage Amount* *Example: $254,741.60 - $80,000 = $172,741.60*

PHASE TWO
Situation 1

*If You
Have
a NEW
Mortgage*

If you're at the very beginning of the mortgage, you should calculate the **Total Interest Savings** as follows:

First, get the *new total payment* by multiplying the new monthly payment by the number of periods in the new term. Then, calculate the *expected total interest* just by subtracting the mortgage amount from the *new total payment*. To get the **Total Interest Savings**, just subtract the **expected** total interest from the **original** total interest.

Calculating Expected Total Interest *(for a new mortgage)*

STEP	ACTION
1	Calculate *New Total Payments* = *NEW Monthly Payment* **X** *Number of Periods in NEW term* *Example: $737.06* **X** *283 = $208,587.98*
2	Calculate *New Total Interest* = *New Total payment - Mortgage Amount* *Example: $208,587.98 - $80,000 = $128,587.98*

Calculating Total Interest Savings *(for a new mortgage)*

STEP	ACTION
3	Calculate *Total Interest Savings =* *Original Total Interest - Expected Total Interest* *Example: $172,741.60 - $128,587.98 = $44,153.62*

PHASE TWO
Situation 2

*If You
Have
an OLD
Mortgage*

If you're a few months or years into the mortgage, you can calculate a good approximation of the *new total **interest*** as follows. First, you need to get the *total interest paid **so far***. Next, calculate the *remaining total interest*. Then, add interest paid so far to the remaining total interest to get your estimated *new total interest*. This second situation has eight easy steps.

Calculating Expected Total Interest (for an OLD mortgage)

*Let's assume, for example, that you've had the mortgage for **eight** months at the time you decide to start prepaying. The balance due after eight months would be $79,708.48, as shown in the amortization schedule (Figure E.4).*

Period	Payment	Interest	Principal	Balance
1	$702.06	$666.67	$35.39	$79,964.61
2	$702.06	$666.37	$35.69	$79,928.92
3	$702.06	$666.07	$35.98	$79,892.94
4	$702.06	$665.77	$36.28	$79,856.66
5	$702.06	$665.47	$36.59	$79,820.07
6	$702.06	$665.17	$36.89	$79,783.18
7	$702.06	$664.86	$37.20	$79,745.99
8	$702.06	$664.55	$37.51	***$79,708.48***

Figure E.4

Use these three steps to get the ***total interest paid so far***, *after the **8** months*:

STEP	ACTION
1	Calculate ***Total Payments so far*** = *Old Monthly Payment* **X** *Current Period Number* *Example: $702.06* **X** *8 = **$5,616.48***
2	Calculate *Principal Paid so far* = *Mortgage Amount - Current Balance* *Example: $80,000 - $79,708.48 = **$291.52***
3	Calculate ***Total Interest Paid so far*** = *Total Payments so far - Principal Paid so far* *Example: $5,616.48 - $291.52 = **$5,324.96***

Your **new** amortization schedule would start from the balance at the point where you decide to prepay a constant minimum amount. It would reflect the remainder of the term, starting with the **ninth** month or Period **9**.

As Figure E.5 shows, with *eight* months into the mortgage, the new amortization schedule is based on a remaining balance of *$79,708.48 and the new monthly payment of $737.06.*

Period	Payment	Interest	Principal	Balance
9	$737.06	$664.24	$72.82	$79,635.66
10	$737.06	$663.63	$73.43	$79,562.23
11	$737.06	$663.02	$74.04	$79,488.19
12	$737.06	$662.40	$74.66	$79,413.54
13	$737.06	$661.78	$75.28	$79,338.26
14	$737.06	$661.15	$75.91	$79,262.35

•
•

282	$737.06	$35.32	$701.74	$3,536.33
283	$737.06	$29.47	$707.59	$2,828.75
284	$737.06	$23.57	$713.48	$2,115.26
285	$737.06	$17.63	$719.43	$1,395.83
286	$737.06	$11.63	$725.43	$670.41
287	**$675.99**	$5.59	$0.00	$0.00

Figure E.5

Again, the VERY LAST period number in the new schedule indicates the duration of the term. In this case, the *last* period number would be *287*.

Notice that the payment in the last period *is less than the usual monthly payment.* **Since that last payment** *only needs to be as large as required to pay the final principal balance and the interest in the last period, the bank credits you with the difference. So, you get to keep a few dollars in your pockets.*

In the example, the credit is for $61.07 (the difference between $737.06 and $675.99). See step 2 in the following procedure.

Now, proceed to get your **remaining total interest.** These next steps show you how.

To get the REMAINING total interest *(with the NEW monthly payment),* *follow these three steps:*

STEP	ACTION
4	Calculate *Periods Remaining =* *Last Period Number in **New Term** - Current Period Number* *Example: 287 - 8 = **279***
5	Calculate *Total Payments Remaining =* *(**New Monthly Payment X** Periods Remaining)* **- CREDIT in Last Payment** *Example:* *($737.06 **X** 279) - $61.07 **credit** = **$205,578.67***
6	Calculate ***Remaining Total Interest** =* *Total Payments Remaining - Current Balance* *Example: $205,578.67 - $79,708.48 = **$125,870.19***

So, *if you're a few months or years into the mortgage,* your *New total interest* is the sum of *total interest paid so far* and *remaining total interest.* Calculate it like this:

| 7 | Calculate ***Expected Total Interest*** *=*
 Total Interest Paid so far + Remaining Total Interest

 *Example: **$5,324.96 + $125,931.26 = $131,195.15*** |

Calculating Total Interest Savings (for an **old** mortgage)

To get the **Total Interest Savings,** subtract the ***expected*** *total interest* from the ***original*** *total interest.*

STEP	ACTION
8	Calculate ***Total Interest Savings*** = *Original Total Interest* ▪ *Expected Total Interest* *Example:* *$172,741.60* ▪ *$131,195.15* = ***$41,546.45***

The general idea:

Original total interest

Minus

Expected total interest

Equal

Total interest savings

Use copies of the blank forms provided below to do your own calculations.

PHASE ONE | **Calculating Original Total Interest**
(for both old and new mortgages)

STEP	ACTION
1	Calculate ***Total Payments*** = *Monthly Payment* **X** *Number of Periods in original term* [＿＿＿＿] **X** [＿＿＿＿] = [＿＿＿＿]
2	Calculate ***Original Total Interest*** = *Total payments -* *Mortgage Amount* [＿＿＿＿] **-** [＿＿＿＿] = [＿＿＿＿]

PHASE TWO
Option 1

Calculating Total Interest Savings (for a new mortgage)

STEP	ACTION
1	Calculate *New Total Payments* = *NEW Monthly Payment* **X** *Number of Periods in NEW term* ☐ **X** ☐ = ☐
2	Calculate *New Total Interest* = *New Total payment* - *Mortgage Amount* ☐ - ☐ = ☐
3	Calculate *Total Interest Savings* = *Original Total Interest* - *Expected Total Interest* ☐ - ☐ = ☐

PHASE TWO
Option 2

Calculating Total Interest Savings *(for an old mortgage)*

STEP	ACTION
1	Calculate ***Total Payments so far =*** *Old Monthly Payment* **X** *Current Period Number* ☐ **X** ☐ = ☐
2	Calculate *Principal Paid so far* = *Mortgage Amount -* *Current Balance* ☐ **-** ☐ = ☐
3	Calculate ***Total Interest Paid so far =*** *Total Payments so far* **-** *Principal Paid so far* ☐ **-** ☐ = ☐
4	Calculate *Periods Remaining =* *Last Period Number in* **New Term** **-** *Current Period Number* ☐ **-** ☐ = ☐

PHASE TWO
Option 2

Calculating Total Interest Savings *(for an old mortgage)*
(Continued)

STEP	ACTION
5	Calculate *Total Payments Remaining =* *(New Monthly Payment* **X** *Periods Remaining)* **- CREDIT in Last Payment** *Example:* ([＿＿＿] **X** [＿＿＿]) **-** [＿＿＿＿] *credit* = [＿＿＿＿]
6	Calculate **Remaining Total Interest =** *Total Payments Remaining* **-** *Current* *Balance* [＿＿＿＿] **-** [＿＿＿＿] **=** [＿＿＿＿]
7	Calculate <u>**New Total Interest**</u> **=** **Total Interest Paid so far + Remaining Total Interest** [＿＿＿＿] **+** [＿＿＿＿] **=** [＿＿＿＿]
8	Calculate **Total Interest Savings =** *Original Total Interest* **-** *Expected Total Interest* [＿＿＿＿] **-** [＿＿＿＿] **=** [＿＿＿＿]

Appendix F

Special Interest and Time Savings Tables
For The
Increasing Prepayment Method

You'll find special tables in this appendix that will give you a quick idea of what savings to expect when you use the *increasing prepayment method.*

The tables cover interest rates ranging from **5.25%** to **16%** by increments of 0.25%. If your particular interest rate is not in there, just use the closest *lower* rate to get a good ballpark estimate. For instance, if your annual interest rate happens to be 8.8%, work with 8.75% in the table.

The first set of tables focuses on **30-year** fixed-rate mortgages, and the second set deals with **15-year** fixed-rate mortgages. The factors in the *30-year* tables give *exact* answers for mortgage ages ranging from 0 to 25 years old by 5 year increments. The factors in the *15-year* tables give *exact* answers for mortgage ages ranging from 0 to 10 years old by 5 year increments.

Don't worry if you don't find the exact *current* age of your mortgage. You can use the factor for the *next higher* age as an *approximate* factor. So, for example, if your mortgage is 7 years old now, work with the **10 years Old** column. You then get a conservative answer. It tells you *exactly* what savings you would get *if you were to wait to start the method when your mortgage is 10 years old.* But, if you start now, your savings will climb even higher and the mortgage term will terminate *sooner* still than the table indicates.

Look up the action steps on the next page. Examine the examples too.

Take these easy steps to find your expected total interest and time savings in the following tables.

STEP	ACTION
1	Locate the table that covers your mortgage age range, then find the row starting with your interest rate.
2	In that row, go over to the column with your exact mortgage **AGE,** to locate an exact interest savings factor. If you don't find your exact mortgage age, go over to the **first** column that shows **a higher** mortgage **AGE than yours,** to locate an *approximate* factor.
3	To get your total interest savings in dollars, multiply the interest savings factor you find at that location by your **original** mortgage balance. If you're using an *approximate* factor, your *actual* savings will be **MORE** than the approximate interest savings amount you calculate.
4	At the top of the same column, read off how long your term will last. If you're using an *approximate* factor, your *actual* remaining term will be **SHORTER** than the term duration shown in the column.

Example

Suppose your *brand new* mortgage balance is $80,000 for 30 years at 10% with a monthly payment of $702.06. Use the table on the following page for answers.

First, look down the *rate* column to find the row starting with interest rate **10**. Next, go over to the column with the exact age of your mortgage. Multiply interest savings factor **1.078956** by $80,000 to get your total interest savings of **$86,316.48**. The term would last **15** years.

Second Example

It's the same mortgage of $80,000 for 30 years at 10%. You've had the mortgage for **eleven years.**

First, go over to the column with the **next higher age** of your mortgage. In this case, it's the **15 Years Old** column. Next, find the row starting with interest rate **10**. Multiply *approximate* interest savings factor **0.379797** by $80,000 to get your *approximate* total interest savings of **$30,383.76**. Your actual savings would be MORE than that amount. The term would last LESS THAN **22** years and **6** months.

INCREASING PREPAYMENT METHOD
30-YEAR FIXED-RATE MORTGAGE INTEREST SAVINGS TABLE

Refer to this table to quickly figure out your interest savings
when you use the *Increasing Prepayment* method

For mortgages up to *10* years old

If your Mortgage is	Brand New	5 Years old	10 Years old
The term will last	15 Years	17 Years 7 Months	20 Years
At this Interest rate (%)	Your interest savings factor is	Your interest savings factor is	Your interest savings factor is
5.25	0.493181	0.366549	0.252009
5.5	0.521218	0.388319	0.267699
5.75	0.549615	0.410435	0.283694
6	0.578362	0.432889	0.299989
6.25	0.607453	0.455672	0.316579
6.5	0.636877	0.478777	0.333457
6.75	0.666626	0.502195	0.350618
7	0.696692	0.525919	0.368055
7.25	0.727065	0.549941	0.385762
7.5	0.757737	0.574252	0.403732
7.75	0.788698	0.598843	0.42196
8	0.819941	0.623708	0.440439
8.25	0.851455	0.648836	0.459162
8.5	0.883233	0.674221	0.478122
8.75	0.915266	0.699855	0.497314
9	0.947545	0.725728	0.516731
9.25	0.980062	0.751833	0.536365
9.5	1.012808	0.778163	0.556211
9.75	1.045775	0.804709	0.576263
10	1.078956	0.831463	0.596513
10.25	1.112343	0.858419	0.616955
10.5	1.145926	0.885569	0.637584

If your Mortgage is	Brand New	5 Years old	10 Years old
The term will last	15 Years	17 Years 7 Months	20 Years
At this Interest rate (%)	Your interest savings factor is	Your interest savings factor is	Your interest savings factor is
10.75	1.179701	0.912905	0.658393
11	1.213657	0.940421	0.679375
11.25	1.24779	0.96811	0.700526
11.5	1.28209	0.995964	0.721839
11.75	1.316553	1.023977	0.743308
12	1.35117	1.052143	0.764927
12.25	1.385936	1.080456	0.786692
12.5	1.420844	1.108908	0.808597
12.75	1.455888	1.137496	0.830636
13	1.491062	1.166212	0.852804
13.25	1.526361	1.195051	0.875097
13.5	1.561779	1.224008	0.89751
13.75	1.597311	1.253077	0.920037
14	1.632951	1.282254	0.942674
14.25	1.668695	1.311534	0.965417
14.5	1.704538	1.340912	0.988262
14.75	1.740475	1.370383	1.011203
15	1.776502	1.399943	1.034238
15.25	1.812614	1.429588	1.057362
15.5	1.848808	1.459315	1.080572
15.75	1.88508	1.489118	1.103863
16	1.921426	1.518995	1.127233

NOTE: Locate the table that covers your mortgage age range. Find the row starting with your interest rate. In that row, go over to the column with your exact *or next higher* mortgage age. To get your total interest savings in dollars, multiply the interest savings factor you find at that location by your *original* mortgage balance. Read off your term duration at the top of the same column.

INCREASING PREPAYMENT METHOD
30-YEAR FIXED-RATE MORTGAGE INTEREST SAVINGS TABLE

Refer to this table to quickly figure out your interest savings
when you use the *Increasing Prepayment* method

For mortgages between *11* and *25* years old

If your Mortgage is	15 Years old	20 Years old	25 Years old
The term will last	22 Years 6 Months	25 Years	27 Years 7 Months
At this Interest rate (%)	Your interest savings factor is	Your interest savings factor is	Your interest savings factor is
5.25	0.152771	0.073423	0.019834
5.5	0.162767	0.078485	0.021274
5.75	0.172999	0.08369	0.022762
6	0.183465	0.089039	0.024299
6.25	0.194162	0.09453	0.025884
6.5	0.205086	0.100163	0.027518
6.75	0.216233	0.105936	0.0292
7	0.227602	0.111848	0.030931
7.25	0.239187	0.117898	0.032711
7.5	0.250985	0.124085	0.034539
7.75	0.262992	0.130408	0.036416
8	0.440439	0.136864	0.038341
8.25	0.287619	0.143453	0.040314
8.5	0.30023	0.150172	0.042336
8.75	0.313034	0.15702	0.044405
9	0.326026	0.163996	0.046522
9.25	0.339203	0.171096	0.048686
9.5	0.35256	0.17832	0.050897
9.75	0.366093	0.185666	0.053155
10	0.379797	0.193131	0.05546
10.25	0.393669	0.200713	0.05781
10.5	0.407703	0.208412	0.060207

If your Mortgage is	15 Years old	20 Years old	25 Years old
The term will last	22 Years 6 Months	25 Years	27 Years 7 Months
At this Interest rate (%)	Your interest savings factor is	Your interest savings factor is	Your interest savings factor is
10.75	0.421896	0.216223	0.062648
11	0.436243	0.224146	0.065135
11.25	0.450741	0.232178	0.067666
11.5	0.465384	0.240318	0.070241
11.75	0.480168	0.248562	0.07286
12	0.495091	0.25691	0.075522
12.25	0.510147	0.265358	0.078227
12.5	0.525332	0.273906	0.080975
12.75	0.830636	0.28255	0.083764
13	0.556075	0.291289	0.086595
13.25	0.571625	0.30012	0.089466
13.5	0.58729	0.309042	0.092378
13.75	0.603065	0.318052	0.09533
14	0.618947	0.327149	0.098322
14.25	0.634932	0.336331	0.101353
14.5	0.651017	0.345595	0.104422
14.75	0.667199	0.35494	0.107529
15	0.683474	0.364363	0.110673
15.25	0.699839	0.373864	0.113855
15.5	0.716291	0.383439	0.117073
15.75	0.732827	0.393087	0.120328
16	0.749445	0.402807	0.123618

NOTE: Locate the table that covers your mortgage age range. Find the row starting with your interest rate. In that row, go over to the column with your exact *or next higher* mortgage age. To get your total interest savings in dollars, multiply the interest savings factor you find at that location by your *original* mortgage balance. Read off your term duration at the top of the same column.

INCREASING PREPAYMENT METHOD
15-YEAR FIXED-RATE MORTGAGE INTEREST SAVINGS TABLE

Refer to this table to quickly figure out your interest savings
when you use the *Increasing Prepayment* method

For mortgages up to *10* years old

If your Mortgage is	Brand New	5 Years old	10 Years old
The term will last	7 Years 6 Months	10 Years	12 Years 6 Months
At this Interest rate (%)	Your interest savings factor is	Your interest savings factor is	Your interest savings factor is
5.25	0.222399	0.106886	0.028998
5.5	0.234232	0.112944	0.030753
5.75	0.246174	0.119089	0.032543
6	0.258224	0.125321	0.034368
6.25	0.270382	0.131639	0.036229
6.5	0.282646	0.138043	0.038125
6.75	0.295016	0.144532	0.040057
7	0.307491	0.151107	0.042025
7.25	0.320071	0.157767	0.044029
7.5	0.332753	0.164511	0.046069
7.75	0.345539	0.17134	0.048145
8	0.358426	0.178252	0.050256
8.25	0.371413	0.185246	0.052404
8.5	0.384501	0.192324	0.054588
8.75	0.397687	0.199484	0.056808
9	0.410972	0.206725	0.059064
9.25	0.424353	0.214047	0.061356
9.5	0.437831	0.221449	0.063684
9.75	0.451403	0.228931	0.066049
10	0.46507	0.236493	0.068449
10.25	0.478829	0.244133	0.070885
10.5	0.492681	0.251851	0.073357

If your Mortgage is	Brand New	5 Years old	10 Years old
The term will last	7 Years 6 Months	10 Years	12 Years 6 Months
At this Interest rate (%)	Your interest savings factor is	Your interest savings factor is	Your interest savings factor is
10.75	0.506624	0.259646	0.075865
11	0.520656	0.267518	0.078409
11.25	0.534777	0.275466	0.080988
11.5	0.548986	0.283489	0.083603
11.75	0.563282	0.291587	0.086254
12	0.577664	0.299758	0.08894
12.25	0.59213	0.308003	0.091662
12.5	0.606679	0.31632	0.094418
12.75	0.621311	0.324709	0.09721
13	0.636024	0.333168	0.100037
13.25	0.650818	0.341698	0.102899
13.5	0.66569	0.350297	0.105795
13.75	0.68064	0.358965	0.108726
14	0.695667	0.367701	0.111691
14.25	0.71077	0.376504	0.114691
14.5	0.725948	0.385373	0.117725
14.75	0.741199	0.394307	0.120792
15	0.756523	0.403306	0.123894
15.25	0.771918	0.412369	0.127029
15.5	0.787383	0.421495	0.130197
15.75	0.802917	0.430684	0.133398
16	0.818519	0.439933	0.136633

NOTE: Locate the table that covers your mortgage age range. Find the row starting with your interest rate. In that row, go over to the column with your exact *or next higher* mortgage age. To get your total interest savings in dollars, multiply the interest savings factor you find at that location by your *original* mortgage balance. Read off your term duration at the top of the same column.

Appendix G

Special Interest and Time Savings Tables
For The
Fixed Prepayment Method

This appendix contains special tables that will give you a quick idea of what savings to expect in interest dollars and time when you use the *fixed prepayment method.*

To give you the highest level of flexibility, prepayments are expressed in the tables as *percentages* of the *original* mortgage balance. The tables give factors for certain prepayment percentages selected between 1 and up to 60 percent.

So, it doesn't matter what your particular loan amount was. To get answers, just decide how much you want to prepay every month. Divide the prepayment amount by your *original* mortgage balance. Multiply the result by 100 to get a percentage. Then, work with the table percentage that's nearest to yours. Look up the action steps and examples on the next page.

The tables include interest rates ranging from **5.25%** to **16%** by increments of 0.25%. If your particular interest rate does not appear, just use the closest *lower* rate to get a good ballpark estimate. For instance, if you have an annual interest rate of 8.8%, take 8.75% in the table.

You'll find tables for **30-year** fixed-rate mortgages and for **15-year** fixed-rate mortgages. The factors in the *30-year* tables give *exact* answers for mortgage ages ranging from 0 to 25 years old by 5 year increments. The factors in the *15-year* tables give *exact* answers for mortgage ages ranging from 0 to 10 years old by 5 year increments.

If you don't find the *current* age of your mortgage, use the factor for the *next higher* age as an *approximate* factor. For example, if your mortgage is 14 years old now, work with the **15 years Old** column. The answer tells you *exactly* what savings you would get *if you were to wait to start the method when your mortgage is 15 years old.* But, if you start now, you will accumulate greater savings and end the mortgage term earlier still than the table indicates.

Follow these easy steps to find your expected total interest savings.

STEP	ACTION
1	Find the column with your exact mortgage **AGE** and the *percentage* you want to prepay each month. If you don't find your exact mortgage age, go over to the **first** column that shows **a higher** mortgage **AGE than yours,** to locate an *approximate* factor.
2	Under that column, find the row starting with your interest rate, to locate an interest savings factor.
3	To get your total interest savings in dollars, multiply the interest savings factor you find at that location by your **original** mortgage balance. If you're using an *approximate* factor, your *actual* savings will be **MORE** than the approximate interest savings amount you calculate.
4	In the same row, read off how long your term will last. If you're using an *approximate* factor, you'll *actually* save **MORE** than the number of years and months shown in the row.

First Example

Say your *brand new* mortgage balance is $80,000 for 30 years at 10% and you want to prepay 5% of the monthly payment. Use following tables. First, go over to the column with the exact age of your mortgage that shows 5% prepayment. Next, look down the *rate* column to find the row starting with **10**. Find the interest savings factor in that row. Multiply interest savings factor **0.55297** by $80,000 to get your total interest savings of **$44,237.60**. You would also **SAVE 6** years and **5** months.

Second Example

It's the same mortgage of $80,000 for 30 years at 10%. You've had the mortgage for **three years** and you want to prepay 5% of the monthly payment. First, go over to the column with the **next higher age** of your mortgage. In this case, it's the **5 Years Old** column. Next, find the row starting with **10**. Multiply *approximate* interest savings factor **0.338029** by $80,000 to get your *approximate* total interest savings of **$27,042.32**. Your actual savings would be **MORE** than that amount. You'd **save MORE than 4** years and **2** months from the point the mortgage is 5 years old.

FIXED PREPAYMENT METHOD
30-YEAR FIXED-RATE MORTGAGE SAVINGS TABLE

Refer to this table to quickly figure out your *total* interest and time savings
when you use the *Fixed Prepayment* method

If your Mortgage is	Brand New		
and you *prepay* each month	1% of the *regular monthly payment*		
At this Interest rate (%)	Your interest savings factor is	You'll *save* this many years	and this many months
5.25	0.027479	0	8
5.5	0.030503	0	8
5.75	0.033784	0	9
6	0.037339	0	9
6.25	0.041188	0	10
6.5	0.045352	0	10
6.75	0.049852	0	11
7	0.054711	0	11
7.25	0.059953	1	0
7.5	0.065604	1	0
7.75	0.07169	1	1
8	0.078239	1	2
8.25	0.08528	1	2
8.5	0.092844	1	3
8.75	0.100962	1	4
9	0.109668	1	5
9.25	0.118995	1	5
9.5	0.128978	1	6
9.75	0.139653	1	7
10	0.151059	1	8
10.25	0.163232	1	9
10.5	0.176212	1	10

If your Mortgage is	Brand New		
and you *prepay* each month	1% of the *regular monthly payment*		
At this Interest rate (%)	Your interest savings factor is	You'll *save* this many years	and this many months
10.75	0.190037	1	11
11	0.204747	2	0
11.25	0.220383	2	2
11.5	0.236983	2	3
11.75	0.254587	2	4
12	0.273234	2	5
12.25	0.292963	2	7
12.5	0.313811	2	8
12.75	0.335813	2	10
13	0.359004	2	11
13.25	0.383417	3	1
13.5	0.409081	3	2
13.75	0.436025	3	4
14	0.464274	3	6
14.25	0.49385	3	8
14.5	0.524771	3	9
14.75	0.557055	3	11
15	0.590712	4	1
15.25	0.625752	4	3
15.5	0.662179	4	5
15.75	0.699994	4	7
16	0.739195	4	9

NOTE: Find the row starting with your interest rate. To get your total interest savings
in dollars, just multiply the interest savings factor you find in that row by your *original*
mortgage balance. Read off your time savings in the same row.

FIXED PREPAYMENT METHOD
30-YEAR FIXED-RATE MORTGAGE SAVINGS TABLE

Refer to this table to quickly figure out your **total** interest and time savings
when you use the *Fixed Prepayment* method

If your Mortgage is	Brand New		
and you *prepay* each month	2% of the *regular monthly payment*		
At this Interest rate (%)	Your interest savings factor is	You'll *save* this many years	and this many months
5.25	0.053297	1	4
5.5	0.059056	1	5
5.75	0.065281	1	6
6	0.072002	1	6
6.25	0.079252	1	7
6.5	0.087062	1	8
6.75	0.095466	1	9
7	0.1045	1	10
7.25	0.114198	1	11
7.5	0.124599	2	0
7.75	0.135741	2	1
8	0.147661	2	2
8.25	0.1604	2	3
8.5	0.173998	2	5
8.75	0.188495	2	6
9	0.203931	2	7
9.25	0.220347	2	9
9.5	0.237783	2	10
9.75	0.256278	3	0
10	0.275872	3	1
10.25	0.296601	3	3
10.5	0.318501	3	5

If your Mortgage is	Brand New		
and you *prepay* each month	2% of the *regular monthly payment*		
At this Interest rate (%)	Your interest savings factor is	You'll *save* this many years	and this many months
10.75	0.341608	3	6
11	0.365953	3	8
11.25	0.391566	3	10
11.5	0.418476	4	0
11.75	0.446707	4	2
12	0.476281	4	4
12.25	0.507216	4	6
12.5	0.539527	4	8
12.75	0.573226	4	10
13	0.60832	5	0
13.25	0.644813	5	3
13.5	0.682706	5	5
13.75	0.721994	5	7
14	0.76267	5	10
14.25	0.804723	6	0
14.5	0.848138	6	2
14.75	0.892896	6	5
15	0.938976	6	7
15.25	0.986354	6	10
15.5	1.035002	7	0
15.75	1.08489	7	3
16	1.135988	7	5

NOTE: Find the row starting with your interest rate. To get your total interest savings
in dollars, just multiply the interest savings factor you find in that row by your **original**
mortgage balance. Read off your time savings in the same row.

FIXED PREPAYMENT METHOD
30-YEAR FIXED-RATE MORTGAGE SAVINGS TABLE

Refer to this table to quickly figure out your *total* interest and time savings when you use the *Fixed Prepayment* method

If your Mortgage is	Brand New			If your Mortgage is	Brand New		
and you *prepay* each month	3% of the *regular monthly payment*			and you *prepay* each month	3% of the *regular monthly payment*		
At this Interest rate (%)	Your interest savings factor is	You'll *save* this many years	and this many months	At this Interest rate (%)	Your interest savings factor is	You'll *save* this many years	and this many months
5.25	0.077613	2	0	10.75	0.466835	4	11
5.5	0.085854	2	1	11	0.497965	5	1
5.75	0.094735	2	2	11.25	0.530484	5	3
6	0.104294	2	3	11.5	0.564402	5	5
6.25	0.114568	2	4	11.75	0.599726	5	8
6.5	0.125596	2	5	12	0.636459	5	10
6.75	0.137417	2	7	12.25	0.674598	6	0
7	0.150073	2	8	12.5	0.71414	6	3
7.25	0.163604	2	9	12.75	0.755074	6	5
7.5	0.178051	2	11	13	0.797388	6	8
7.75	0.193455	3	0	13.25	0.841067	6	11
8	0.209856	3	2	13.5	0.886089	7	1
8.25	0.227296	3	3	13.75	0.932434	7	4
8.5	0.245813	3	5	14	0.980074	7	6
8.75	0.265448	3	7	14.25	1.028982	7	9
9	0.286237	3	9	14.5	1.079126	8	0
9.25	0.308216	3	10	14.75	1.130475	8	2
9.5	0.331419	4	0	15	1.182993	8	5
9.75	0.355879	4	2	15.25	1.236644	8	7
10	0.381625	4	4	15.5	1.291391	8	10
10.25	0.408685	4	6	15.75	1.347195	9	1
10.5	0.437081	4	8	16	1.404017	9	3

NOTE: Find the row starting with your interest rate. To get your total interest savings in dollars, just multiply the interest savings factor you find in that row by your *original* mortgage balance. Read off your time savings in the same row.

FIXED PREPAYMENT METHOD
30-YEAR FIXED-RATE MORTGAGE SAVINGS TABLE

Refer to this table to quickly figure out your *total* interest and time savings
when you use the *Fixed Prepayment* method

If your Mortgage is	Brand New		
and you *prepay* each month	4% of the *regular monthly payment*		
At this Interest rate (%)	Your interest savings factor is	You'll *save* this many years	and this many months
5.25	0.100563	2	7
5.5	0.111067	2	8
5.75	0.122356	2	10
6	0.13447	2	11
6.25	0.14745	3	0
6.5	0.161337	3	2
6.75	0.176174	3	3
7	0.192001	3	5
7.25	0.20886	3	7
7.5	0.226792	3	9
7.75	0.245835	3	10
8	0.266028	4	0
8.25	0.287408	4	2
8.5	0.31001	4	4
8.75	0.333867	4	6
9	0.359009	4	8
9.25	0.385464	4	10
9.5	0.413258	5	1
9.75	0.442411	5	3
10	0.472943	5	5
10.25	0.504868	5	8
10.5	0.538198	5	10

If your Mortgage is	Brand New		
and you *prepay* each month	4% of the *regular monthly payment*		
At this Interest rate (%)	Your interest savings factor is	You'll *save* this many years	and this many months
10.75	0.57294	6	0
11	0.609096	6	3
11.25	0.646668	6	5
11.5	0.68565	6	8
11.75	0.726035	6	11
12	0.76781	7	1
12.25	0.81096	7	4
12.5	0.855467	7	6
12.75	0.901307	7	9
13	0.948455	8	0
13.25	0.996885	8	2
13.5	1.046566	8	5
13.75	1.097464	8	8
14	1.149546	8	11
14.25	1.202776	9	1
14.5	1.257116	9	4
14.75	1.312527	9	7
15	1.368972	9	9
15.25	1.42641	10	0
15.5	1.484801	10	3
15.75	1.544106	10	5
16	1.604284	10	8

NOTE: Find the row starting with your interest rate. To get your total interest savings
in dollars, just multiply the interest savings factor you find in that row by your *original*
mortgage balance. Read off your time savings in the same row.

FIXED PREPAYMENT METHOD
30-YEAR FIXED-RATE MORTGAGE SAVINGS TABLE

Refer to this table to quickly figure out your **total** interest and time savings
when you use the *Fixed Prepayment* method

If your Mortgage is	Brand New		
and you *prepay* each month	5% of the regular monthly payment		
At this Interest rate *(%)*	Your interest savings factor is	You'll *save* this many years	and this many months
5.25	0.122268	3	2
5.5	0.134844	3	3
5.75	0.148324	3	5
6	0.16275	3	6
6.25	0.178164	3	8
6.5	0.194608	3	10
6.75	0.212123	4	0
7	0.230748	4	2
7.25	0.250523	4	4
7.5	0.271485	4	6
7.75	0.29367	4	8
8	0.317111	4	10
8.25	0.341839	5	0
8.5	0.367883	5	2
8.75	0.395268	5	4
9	0.424016	5	7
9.25	0.454147	5	9
9.5	0.485676	6	0
9.75	0.518615	6	2
10	0.55297	6	5
10.25	0.588748	6	7
10.5	0.625946	6	10

If your Mortgage is	Brand New		
and you *prepay* each month	5% of the regular monthly payment		
At this Interest rate *(%)*	Your interest savings factor is	You'll *save* this many years	and this many months
10.75	0.664562	7	0
11	0.704587	7	3
11.25	0.74601	7	6
11.5	0.788817	7	9
11.75	0.832987	7	11
12	0.878499	8	2
12.25	0.925329	8	5
12.5	0.973448	8	8
12.75	1.022827	8	10
13	1.073432	9	1
13.25	1.12523	9	4
13.5	1.178185	9	7
13.75	1.232259	9	9
14	1.287414	10	0
14.25	1.343611	10	3
14.5	1.40081	10	6
14.75	1.458971	10	8
15	1.518055	10	11
15.25	1.578021	11	2
15.5	1.63883	11	4
15.75	1.700443	11	7
16	1.762821	11	9

NOTE: Find the row starting with your interest rate. To get your total interest savings
in dollars, just multiply the interest savings factor you find in that row by your **original**
mortgage balance. Read off your time savings in the same row.

FIXED PREPAYMENT METHOD
30-YEAR FIXED-RATE MORTGAGE SAVINGS TABLE

Refer to this table to quickly figure out your **total** interest and time savings
when you use the *Fixed Prepayment* method

If your Mortgage is	Brand New			If your Mortgage is	Brand New		
and you *prepay* each month	10% of the *regular monthly payment*			and you *prepay* each month	10% of the *regular monthly payment*		
At this Interest rate (%)	Your interest savings factor is	You'll *save* this many years	and this many months	*At this* Interest rate (%)	Your interest savings factor is	You'll *save* this many years	and this many months
5.25	0.215421	5	8	10.75	0.989821	10	9
5.5	0.236167	5	10	11	1.040642	11	0
5.75	0.258177	6	0	11.25	1.092648	11	2
6	0.281486	6	3	11.5	1.145799	11	5
6.25	0.306122	6	5	11.75	1.200059	11	8
6.5	0.332114	6	8	12	1.255387	11	11
6.75	0.359485	6	11	12.25	1.311744	12	2
7	0.388255	7	1	12.5	1.369089	12	5
7.25	0.418441	7	4	12.75	1.427384	12	8
7.5	0.450057	7	7	13	1.486587	12	10
7.75	0.483111	7	10	13.25	1.546659	13	1
8	0.517607	8	0	13.5	1.607561	13	4
8.25	0.553547	8	3	13.75	1.669254	13	6
8.5	0.590928	8	6	14	1.731701	13	9
8.75	0.629743	8	9	14.25	1.794864	14	0
9	0.66998	9	0	14.5	1.858708	14	2
9.25	0.711624	9	3	14.75	1.923198	14	5
9.5	0.754659	9	6	15	1.988301	14	7
9.75	0.799062	9	9	15.25	2.053983	14	10
10	0.844808	10	0	15.5	2.120214	15	0
10.25	0.89187	10	3	15.75	2.186963	15	2
10.5	0.940219	10	6	16	2.254202	15	5

NOTE: Find the row starting with your interest rate. To get your total interest savings in dollars, just multiply the interest savings factor you find in that row by your **original** mortgage balance. Read off your time savings in the same row.

FIXED PREPAYMENT METHOD
30-YEAR FIXED-RATE MORTGAGE SAVINGS TABLE

Refer to this table to quickly figure out your *total* interest and time savings when you use the *Fixed Prepayment* method

If your Mortgage is	Brand New		
and you *prepay* each month	15% of the *regular monthly payment*		
At this Interest rate (%)	Your interest savings factor is	You'll *save* this many years	and this many months
5.25	0.289206	7	8
5.5	0.315654	7	11
5.75	0.343513	8	2
6	0.372802	8	5
6.25	0.403532	8	7
6.5	0.435714	8	10
6.75	0.469353	9	1
7	0.504449	9	4
7.25	0.541001	9	7
7.5	0.579001	9	10
7.75	0.618438	10	2
8	0.659297	10	5
8.25	0.701561	10	8
8.5	0.745207	10	11
8.75	0.790212	11	2
9	0.836548	11	5
9.25	0.884184	11	8
9.5	0.933089	11	11
9.75	0.983229	12	2
10	1.034566	12	5
10.25	1.087065	12	8
10.5	1.140687	12	11

If your Mortgage is	Brand New		
and you *prepay* each month	15% of the *regular monthly payment*		
At this Interest rate (%)	Your interest savings factor is	You'll *save* this many years	and this many months
10.75	1.195393	13	2
11	1.251142	13	5
11.25	1.307895	13	8
11.5	1.365613	13	10
11.75	1.424254	14	1
12	1.483779	14	4
12.25	1.54415	14	7
12.5	1.605327	14	9
12.75	1.667272	15	0
13	1.72995	15	2
13.25	1.793324	15	5
13.5	1.85736	15	7
13.75	1.922022	15	10
14	1.98728	16	0
14.25	2.053101	16	3
14.5	2.119456	16	5
14.75	2.186314	16	7
15	2.25365	16	9
15.25	2.321435	17	0
15.5	2.389646	17	2
15.75	2.458257	17	4
16	2.527245	17	6

NOTE: Find the row starting with your interest rate. To get your total interest savings in dollars, just multiply the interest savings factor you find in that row by your *original* mortgage balance. Read off your time savings in the same row.

FIXED PREPAYMENT METHOD
30-YEAR FIXED-RATE MORTGAGE SAVINGS TABLE

Refer to this table to quickly figure out your **total** interest and time savings
when you use the *Fixed Prepayment* method

If your Mortgage is	Brand New			If your Mortgage is	Brand New		
and you **prepay** each month	20% of the **regular monthly payment**			and you **prepay** each month	20% of the **regular monthly payment**		
At this Interest rate (%)	Your interest savings factor is	You'll **save** this many years	and this many months	**At this Interest rate (%)**	Your interest savings factor is	You'll **save** this many years	and this many months
5.25	0.349337	9	4	10.75	1.340771	14	11
5.5	0.379973	9	7	11	1.39931	15	2
5.75	0.412074	9	10	11.25	1.458729	15	5
6	0.445641	10	1	11.5	1.518988	15	7
6.25	0.480676	10	5	11.75	1.58005	15	10
6.5	0.517173	10	8	12	1.641876	16	1
6.75	0.555124	10	11	12.25	1.704432	16	3
7	0.594516	11	2	12.5	1.767681	16	6
7.25	0.635334	11	5	12.75	1.831588	16	8
7.5	0.677557	11	8	13	1.896122	16	10
7.75	0.721162	11	11	13.25	1.96125	17	1
8	0.766125	12	3	13.5	2.02694	17	3
8.25	0.812416	12	6	13.75	2.093164	17	5
8.5	0.860005	12	9	14	2.159892	17	7
8.75	0.908858	13	0	14.25	2.227097	17	10
9	0.958941	13	3	14.5	2.294753	18	0
9.25	1.010217	13	6	14.75	2.362836	18	2
9.5	1.062648	13	9	15	2.431321	18	4
9.75	1.116197	14	0	15.25	2.500186	18	6
10	1.170823	14	3	15.5	2.569408	18	8
10.25	1.226488	14	6	15.75	2.638968	18	10
10.5	1.28315	14	8	16	2.708847	18	11

NOTE: Find the row starting with your interest rate. To get your total interest savings
in dollars, just multiply the interest savings factor you find in that row by your **original**
mortgage balance. Read off your time savings in the same row.

FIXED PREPAYMENT METHOD
30-YEAR FIXED-RATE MORTGAGE SAVINGS TABLE

Refer to this table to quickly figure out your **total** interest and time savings
when you use the *Fixed Prepayment* method

If your Mortgage is	5 Years Old		
and you prepay each month	1% of the regular monthly payment		
At this Interest rate (%)	Your interest savings factor is	You'll **save** this many years	and this many months
5.25	0.017198	0	6
5.5	0.018982	0	6
5.75	0.020902	0	6
6	0.022967	0	6
6.25	0.025187	0	7
6.5	0.027569	0	7
6.75	0.030126	0	7
7	0.032866	0	7
7.25	0.035801	0	8
7.5	0.038942	0	8
7.75	0.042302	0	8
8	0.045893	0	9
8.25	0.049727	0	9
8.5	0.05382	0	9
8.75	0.058184	0	10
9	0.062835	0	10
9.25	0.067789	0	11
9.5	0.073061	0	11
9.75	0.078668	1	0
10	0.084628	1	0
10.25	0.090959	1	1
10.5	0.097678	1	1

If your Mortgage is	5 Years Old		
and you prepay each month	1% of the regular monthly payment		
At this Interest rate (%)	Your interest savings factor is	You'll **save** this many years	and this many months
10.75	0.104805	1	2
11	0.112361	1	2
11.25	0.120364	1	3
11.5	0.128835	1	3
11.75	0.137797	1	4
12	0.14727	1	5
12.25	0.157276	1	5
12.5	0.167837	1	6
12.75	0.178977	1	7
13	0.190718	1	8
13.25	0.203083	1	8
13.5	0.216095	1	9
13.75	0.229777	1	10
14	0.244151	1	11
14.25	0.259241	2	0
14.5	0.275068	2	1
14.75	0.291654	2	2
15	0.309022	2	3
15.25	0.327191	2	4
15.5	0.346181	2	5
15.75	0.366012	2	6
16	0.386701	2	7

NOTE: Find the row starting with your interest rate. To get your total interest savings
in dollars, just multiply the interest savings factor you find in that row by your **original**
mortgage balance. Read off your time savings in the same row.

FIXED PREPAYMENT METHOD
30-YEAR FIXED-RATE MORTGAGE SAVINGS TABLE

Refer to this table to quickly figure out your *total* interest and time savings when you use the *Fixed Prepayment* method

If your Mortgage is	5 Years Old		
and you prepay each month	2% of the regular monthly payment		
At this Interest rate (%)	Your interest savings factor is	You'll *save* this many years	and this many months
5.25	0.033544	0	11
5.5	0.036978	1	0
5.75	0.040666	1	0
6	0.044624	1	1
6.25	0.048866	1	1
6.5	0.053409	1	2
6.75	0.05827	1	2
7	0.063466	1	3
7.25	0.069014	1	3
7.5	0.074933	1	4
7.75	0.081242	1	5
8	0.087961	1	5
8.25	0.09511	1	6
8.5	0.10271	1	6
8.75	0.110782	1	7
9	0.119347	1	8
9.25	0.128429	1	9
9.5	0.13805	1	9
9.75	0.148232	1	10
10	0.158999	1	11
10.25	0.170374	2	0
10.5	0.182381	2	1

If your Mortgage is	5 Years Old		
and you prepay each month	2% of the regular monthly payment		
At this Interest rate (%)	Your interest savings factor is	You'll *save* this many years	and this many months
10.75	0.195043	2	2
11	0.208384	2	3
11.25	0.222426	2	4
11.5	0.237194	2	5
11.75	0.25271	2	6
12	0.268995	2	7
12.25	0.286073	2	8
12.5	0.303964	2	9
12.75	0.322687	2	10
13	0.342264	3	0
13.25	0.362711	3	1
13.5	0.384045	3	2
13.75	0.406284	3	4
14	0.429441	3	5
14.25	0.453529	3	6
14.5	0.47856	3	8
14.75	0.504544	3	9
15	0.531488	3	11
15.25	0.5594	4	0
15.5	0.588284	4	2
15.75	0.618142	4	3
16	0.648976	4	5

NOTE: Find the row starting with your interest rate. To get your total interest savings in dollars, just multiply the interest savings factor you find in that row by your *original* mortgage balance. Read off your time savings in the same row.

FIXED PREPAYMENT METHOD
30-YEAR FIXED-RATE MORTGAGE SAVINGS TABLE

Refer to this table to quickly figure out your *total* interest and time savings
when you use the *Fixed Prepayment* method

If your Mortgage is	5 Years Old		
and you *prepay* each month	**3% of the regular monthly payment**		
At this Interest rate (%)	Your interest savings factor is	You'll *save* this many years	and this many months
5.25	0.049102	1	5
5.5	0.054067	1	5
5.75	0.059388	1	6
6	0.065086	1	7
6.25	0.07118	1	7
6.5	0.077691	1	8
6.75	0.084639	1	9
7	0.092046	1	10
7.25	0.099935	1	10
7.5	0.108326	1	11
7.75	0.117244	2	0
8	0.126712	2	1
8.25	0.136753	2	2
8.5	0.147391	2	3
8.75	0.15865	2	4
9	0.170555	2	5
9.25	0.183128	2	6
9.5	0.196394	2	7
9.75	0.210377	2	8
10	0.2251	2	9
10.25	0.240587	2	10
10.5	0.25686	3	0

If your Mortgage is	5 Years Old		
and you *prepay* each month	**3% of the regular monthly payment**		
At this Interest rate (%)	Your interest savings factor is	You'll *save* this many years	and this many months
10.75	0.27394	3	1
11	0.291849	3	2
11.25	0.310606	3	3
11.5	0.330233	3	5
11.75	0.350745	3	6
12	0.372161	3	7
12.25	0.394496	3	9
12.5	0.417764	3	10
12.75	0.441977	4	0
13	0.467147	4	1
13.25	0.493283	4	3
13.5	0.520392	4	4
13.75	0.54848	4	6
14	0.577551	4	8
14.25	0.607607	4	9
14.5	0.638648	4	11
14.75	0.670672	5	1
15	0.703676	5	2
15.25	0.737653	5	4
15.5	0.772597	5	6
15.75	0.808499	5	7
16	0.845348	5	9

NOTE: Find the row starting with your interest rate. To get your total interest savings in dollars, just multiply the interest savings factor you find in that row by your *original* mortgage balance. Read off your time savings in the same row.

FIXED PREPAYMENT METHOD
30-YEAR FIXED-RATE MORTGAGE SAVINGS TABLE

Refer to this table to quickly figure out your **total** interest and time savings
when you use the *Fixed Prepayment* method

If your Mortgage is	5 Years Old		
and you prepay each month	**4% of the regular monthly payment**		
At this Interest rate (%)	Your interest savings factor is	You'll **save** this many years	and this many months
5.25	0.063933	*1*	*10*
5.5	0.070321	*1*	*11*
5.75	0.077155	*2*	*0*
6	0.084458	*2*	*1*
6.25	0.092253	*2*	*1*
6.5	0.100562	*2*	*2*
6.75	0.109409	*2*	*3*
7	0.118819	*2*	*4*
7.25	0.128814	*2*	*5*
7.5	0.139421	*2*	*6*
7.75	0.150662	*2*	*7*
8	0.162563	*2*	*8*
8.25	0.175149	*2*	*9*
8.5	0.188443	*2*	*11*
8.75	0.20247	*3*	*0*
9	0.217253	*3*	*1*
9.25	0.232815	*3*	*2*
9.5	0.24918	*3*	*4*
9.75	0.266369	*3*	*5*
10	0.284404	*3*	*6*
10.25	0.303303	*3*	*8*
10.5	0.323087	*3*	*9*

If your Mortgage is	5 Years Old		
and you prepay each month	**4% of the regular monthly payment**		
At this Interest rate (%)	Your interest savings factor is	You'll **save** this many years	and this many months
10.75	0.343774	*3*	*10*
11	0.365378	*4*	*0*
11.25	0.387917	*4*	*1*
11.5	0.411403	*4*	*3*
11.75	0.435848	*4*	*5*
12	0.461262	*4*	*6*
12.25	0.487655	*4*	*8*
12.5	0.515033	*4*	*9*
12.75	0.543399	*4*	*11*
13	0.572759	*5*	*1*
13.25	0.603112	*5*	*3*
13.5	0.634457	*5*	*4*
13.75	0.666792	*5*	*6*
14	0.700112	*5*	*8*
14.25	0.734411	*5*	*10*
14.5	0.76968	*5*	*11*
14.75	0.805909	*6*	*1*
15	0.843086	*6*	*3*
15.25	0.881198	*6*	*5*
15.5	0.920231	*6*	*7*
15.75	0.960168	*6*	*9*
16	1.000992	*6*	*11*

NOTE: Find the row starting with your interest rate. To get your total interest savings
in dollars, just multiply the interest savings factor you find in that row by your ***original***
mortgage balance. Read off your time savings in the same row.

FIXED PREPAYMENT METHOD
30-YEAR FIXED-RATE MORTGAGE SAVINGS TABLE

Refer to this table to quickly figure out your *total* interest and time savings
when you use the *Fixed Prepayment* method

If your Mortgage is	5 Years Old		
and you *prepay* each month	5% of the *regular monthly payment*		
At this *Interest rate* (%)	Your interest savings factor is	You'll *save* this many years	and this many months
5.25	0.078088	2	3
5.5	0.085803	2	4
5.75	0.094042	2	5
6	0.102831	2	6
6.25	0.112192	2	7
6.5	0.122151	2	8
6.75	0.132733	2	9
7	0.143963	2	10
7.25	0.155866	3	0
7.5	0.168466	3	1
7.75	0.181789	3	2
8	0.195859	3	3
8.25	0.2107	3	4
8.5	0.226334	3	6
8.75	0.242786	3	7
9	0.260076	3	9
9.25	0.278226	3	10
9.5	0.297256	3	11
9.75	0.317185	4	1
10	0.338029	4	2
10.25	0.359806	4	4
10.5	0.382529	4	6

If your Mortgage is	5 Years Old		
and you *prepay* each month	5% of the *regular monthly payment*		
At this *Interest rate* (%)	Your interest savings factor is	You'll *save* this many years	and this many months
10.75	0.406212	4	7
11	0.430866	4	9
11.25	0.456502	4	11
11.5	0.483125	5	0
11.75	0.510743	5	2
12	0.53936	5	4
12.25	0.568977	5	5
12.5	0.599595	5	7
12.75	0.631212	5	9
13	0.663823	5	11
13.25	0.697424	6	1
13.5	0.732008	6	3
13.75	0.767563	6	5
14	0.804081	6	6
14.25	0.841548	6	8
14.5	0.87995	6	10
14.75	0.919271	7	0
15	0.959496	7	2
15.25	1.000604	7	4
15.5	1.042579	7	6
15.75	1.085398	7	8
16	1.129043	7	10

NOTE: Find the row starting with your interest rate. To get your total interest savings
in dollars, just multiply the interest savings factor you find in that row by your ***original***
mortgage balance. Read off your time savings in the same row.

FIXED PREPAYMENT METHOD
30-YEAR FIXED-RATE MORTGAGE SAVINGS TABLE

Refer to this table to quickly figure out your **total** interest and time savings
when you use the *Fixed Prepayment* method

If your Mortgage is	5 Years Old		
and you *prepay* each month	10% of the *regular monthly payment*		
At this Interest rate (%)	Your interest savings factor is	You'll **save** this many years	and this many months
5.25	0.14025	4	2
5.5	0.153441	4	3
5.75	0.167426	4	5
6	0.182228	4	6
6.25	0.197871	4	8
6.5	0.21438	4	10
6.75	0.231775	4	11
7	0.250078	5	1
7.25	0.269308	5	3
7.5	0.289484	5	4
7.75	0.310622	5	6
8	0.332738	5	8
8.25	0.355843	5	10
8.5	0.37995	6	0
8.75	0.405068	6	2
9	0.431205	6	3
9.25	0.458365	6	5
9.5	0.486553	6	7
9.75	0.51577	6	9
10	0.546014	6	11
10.25	0.577284	7	1
10.5	0.609575	7	3

If your Mortgage is	5 Years Old		
and you *prepay* each month	10% of the *regular monthly payment*		
At this Interest rate (%)	Your interest savings factor is	You'll **save** this many years	and this many months
10.75	0.642879	7	5
11	0.677189	7	7
11.25	0.712493	7	9
11.5	0.74878	8	0
11.75	0.786037	8	2
12	0.824247	8	4
12.25	0.863393	8	6
12.5	0.903459	8	8
12.75	0.944425	8	10
13	0.98627	9	0
13.25	1.028974	9	2
13.5	1.072514	9	4
13.75	1.116867	9	6
14	1.162011	9	8
14.25	1.207922	9	10
14.5	1.254576	10	0
14.75	1.301949	10	2
15	1.350015	10	4
15.25	1.398752	10	6
15.5	1.448135	10	8
15.75	1.49814	10	10
16	1.548743	10	11

NOTE: Find the row starting with your interest rate. To get your total interest savings
in dollars, just multiply the interest savings factor you find in that row by your **original**
mortgage balance. Read off your time savings in the same row.

FIXED PREPAYMENT METHOD
30-YEAR FIXED-RATE MORTGAGE SAVINGS TABLE

Refer to this table to quickly figure out your *total* interest and time savings
when you use the *Fixed Prepayment* method

If your Mortgage is	5 Years Old		
and you *prepay* **each month**	**15%** **of the** *regular monthly payment*		
At this Interest rate (%)	Your interest savings factor is	You'll *save* this many years	and this many months
5.25	0.191083	5	9
5.5	0.208351	5	11
5.75	0.226556	6	0
6	0.245716	6	2
6.25	0.26585	6	4
6.5	0.286974	6	6
6.75	0.309102	6	8
7	0.332246	6	10
7.25	0.356417	7	0
7.5	0.381623	7	2
7.75	0.407871	7	4
8	0.435164	7	6
8.25	0.463505	7	8
8.5	0.492892	7	10
8.75	0.523325	8	0
9	0.554799	8	3
9.25	0.587306	8	5
9.5	0.62084	8	7
9.75	0.655389	8	9
10	0.690942	8	11
10.25	0.727485	9	1
10.5	0.765002	9	3

If your Mortgage is	5 Years Old		
and you *prepay* **each month**	**15%** **of the** *regular monthly payment*		
At this Interest rate (%)	Your interest savings factor is	You'll *save* this many years	and this many months
10.75	0.803477	9	5
11	0.842892	9	8
11.25	0.883227	9	10
11.5	0.924462	10	0
11.75	0.966576	10	2
12	1.009546	10	4
12.25	1.053349	10	6
12.5	1.097962	10	8
12.75	1.143361	10	10
13	1.189522	11	0
13.25	1.23642	11	2
13.5	1.28403	11	4
13.75	1.332328	11	6
14	1.38129	11	8
14.25	1.430889	11	10
14.5	1.481104	12	0
14.75	1.531909	12	2
15	1.58328	12	4
15.25	1.635196	12	5
15.5	1.687633	12	7
15.75	1.740568	12	9
16	1.793981	12	11

NOTE: Find the row starting with your interest rate. To get your total interest savings
in dollars, just multiply the interest savings factor you find in that row by your *original*
mortgage balance. Read off your time savings in the same row.

FIXED PREPAYMENT METHOD
30-YEAR FIXED-RATE MORTGAGE SAVINGS TABLE

Refer to this table to quickly figure out your ***total*** interest and time savings when you use the *Fixed Prepayment* method

If your Mortgage is	5 Years Old		
and you *prepay* each month	20% of the *regular monthly payment*		
At this Interest rate (%)	Your interest savings factor is	You'll *save* this many years	and this many months
5.25	0.233526	7	1
5.5	0.25394	7	3
5.75	0.275368	7	5
6	0.297823	7	7
6.25	0.321317	7	9
6.5	0.345859	7	11
6.75	0.371454	8	1
7	0.398109	8	3
7.25	0.425824	8	6
7.5	0.4546	8	8
7.75	0.484435	8	10
8	0.515325	9	0
8.25	0.547264	9	2
8.5	0.580242	9	4
8.75	0.614251	9	7
9	0.649278	9	9
9.25	0.685309	9	11
9.5	0.722328	10	1
9.75	0.76032	10	3
10	0.799265	10	5
10.25	0.839145	10	8
10.5	0.879938	10	10

If your Mortgage is	5 Years Old		
and you *prepay* each month	20% of the *regular monthly payment*		
At this Interest rate (%)	Your interest savings factor is	You'll *save* this many years	and this many months
10.75	0.921623	11	0
11	0.964178	11	2
11.25	1.00758	11	4
11.5	1.051804	11	6
11.75	1.096827	11	8
12	1.142624	11	10
12.25	1.189171	12	0
12.5	1.236442	12	2
12.75	1.284413	12	4
13	1.333059	12	6
13.25	1.382355	12	8
13.5	1.432277	12	10
13.75	1.4828	13	0
14	1.533901	13	1
14.25	1.585556	13	3
14.5	1.637742	13	5
14.75	1.690438	13	7
15	1.74362	13	8
15.25	1.797268	13	10
15.5	1.851362	14	0
15.75	1.90588	14	1
16	1.960803	14	3

NOTE: Find the row starting with your interest rate. To get your total interest savings in dollars, just multiply the interest savings factor you find in that row by your ***original*** mortgage balance. Read off your time savings in the same row.

FIXED PREPAYMENT METHOD
30-YEAR FIXED-RATE MORTGAGE SAVINGS TABLE

Refer to this table to quickly figure out your ***total*** interest and time savings when you use the *Fixed Prepayment* method

If your Mortgage is	10 Years Old		
and you *prepay* each month	1% of the *regular monthly payment*		
At this Interest rate (%)	Your interest savings factor is	You'll *save* this many years	and this many months
5.25	0.009951	0	4
5.5	0.010922	0	4
5.75	0.011961	0	4
6	0.013069	0	4
6.25	0.014251	0	4
6.5	0.01551	0	4
6.75	0.016852	0	4
7	0.018278	0	5
7.25	0.019795	0	5
7.5	0.021407	0	5
7.75	0.023117	0	5
8	0.024932	0	5
8.25	0.026856	0	5
8.5	0.028894	0	6
8.75	0.031052	0	6
9	0.033335	0	6
9.25	0.03575	0	6
9.5	0.038302	0	6
9.75	0.040997	0	7
10	0.043843	0	7
10.25	0.046846	0	7
10.5	0.050012	0	7

If your Mortgage is	10 Years Old		
and you *prepay* each month	1% of the *regular monthly payment*		
At this Interest rate (%)	Your interest savings factor is	You'll *save* this many years	and this many months
10.75	0.05335	0	8
11	0.056866	0	8
11.25	0.060569	0	8
11.5	0.064465	0	8
11.75	0.068564	0	9
12	0.072874	0	9
12.25	0.077403	0	9
12.5	0.082161	0	9
12.75	0.087155	0	10
13	0.092397	0	10
13.25	0.097896	0	10
13.5	0.10366	0	11
13.75	0.109701	0	11
14	0.116029	1	0
14.25	0.122654	1	0
14.5	0.129586	1	0
14.75	0.136837	1	1
15	0.144418	1	1
15.25	0.15234	1	2
15.5	0.160613	1	2
15.75	0.169251	1	3
16	0.178263	1	3

NOTE: Find the row starting with your interest rate. To get your total interest savings in dollars, just multiply the interest savings factor you find in that row by your ***original*** mortgage balance. Read off your time savings in the same row.

FIXED PREPAYMENT METHOD
30-YEAR FIXED-RATE MORTGAGE SAVINGS TABLE

Refer to this table to quickly figure out your *total* interest and time savings when you use the *Fixed Prepayment* method

If your Mortgage is	10 Years Old		
and you prepay each month	2% of the regular monthly payment		
At this Interest rate (%)	Your interest savings factor is	You'll save this many years	and this many months
5.25	0.019495	0	8
5.5	0.021382	0	8
5.75	0.023396	0	8
6	0.025542	0	8
6.25	0.027828	0	9
6.5	0.03026	0	9
6.75	0.032844	0	9
7	0.03559	0	9
7.25	0.038503	0	10
7.5	0.041593	0	10
7.75	0.044866	0	10
8	0.048331	0	11
8.25	0.051996	0	11
8.5	0.055871	0	11
8.75	0.059964	1	0
9	0.064285	1	0
9.25	0.068843	1	0
9.5	0.073648	1	1
9.75	0.078709	1	1
10	0.084037	1	2
10.25	0.089642	1	2
10.5	0.095535	1	2

If your Mortgage is	10 Years Old		
and you prepay each month	2% of the regular monthly payment		
At this Interest rate (%)	Your interest savings factor is	You'll save this many years	and this many months
10.75	0.101728	1	3
11	0.108229	1	3
11.25	0.115052	1	4
11.5	0.122207	1	4
11.75	0.129706	1	5
12	0.13756	1	5
12.25	0.145782	1	6
12.5	0.154382	1	6
12.75	0.163373	1	7
13	0.172768	1	8
13.25	0.182577	1	8
13.5	0.192813	1	9
13.75	0.203487	1	9
14	0.214613	1	10
14.25	0.2262	1	11
14.5	0.238262	1	11
14.75	0.250808	2	0
15	0.263852	2	1
15.25	0.277402	2	1
15.5	0.291471	2	2
15.75	0.306069	2	3
16	0.321205	2	4

NOTE: Find the row starting with your interest rate. To get your total interest savings in dollars, just multiply the interest savings factor you find in that row by your *original* mortgage balance. Read off your time savings in the same row.

FIXED PREPAYMENT METHOD
30-YEAR FIXED-RATE MORTGAGE SAVINGS TABLE

Refer to this table to quickly figure out your **total** interest and time savings
when you use the *Fixed Prepayment* method

If your Mortgage is	10 Years Old		
and you prepay each month	**3% of the regular monthly payment**		
At this Interest rate (%)	Your interest savings factor is	You'll **save** this many years	and this many months
5.25	0.028659	*1*	*0*
5.5	0.03141	*1*	*0*
5.75	0.034341	*1*	*0*
6	0.037462	*1*	*1*
6.25	0.04078	*1*	*1*
6.5	0.044305	*1*	*1*
6.75	0.048047	*1*	*2*
7	0.052014	*1*	*2*
7.25	0.056217	*1*	*2*
7.5	0.060667	*1*	*3*
7.75	0.065372	*1*	*3*
8	0.070345	*1*	*4*
8.25	0.075594	*1*	*4*
8.5	0.081133	*1*	*5*
8.75	0.086971	*1*	*5*
9	0.093121	*1*	*6*
9.25	0.099593	*1*	*6*
9.5	0.1064	*1*	*7*
9.75	0.113554	*1*	*7*
10	0.121065	*1*	*8*
10.25	0.128948	*1*	*8*
10.5	0.137213	*1*	*9*

If your Mortgage is	10 Years Old		
and you prepay each month	**3% of the regular monthly payment**		
At this Interest rate (%)	Your interest savings factor is	You'll **save** this many years	and this many months
10.75	0.145873	*1*	*10*
11	0.154941	*1*	*10*
11.25	0.164428	*1*	*11*
11.5	0.174347	*2*	*0*
11.75	0.184711	*2*	*0*
12	0.19553	*2*	*1*
12.25	0.206818	*2*	*2*
12.5	0.218586	*2*	*2*
12.75	0.230847	*2*	*3*
13	0.24361	*2*	*4*
13.25	0.256889	*2*	*5*
13.5	0.270692	*2*	*5*
13.75	0.285032	*2*	*6*
14	0.299918	*2*	*7*
14.25	0.315361	*2*	*8*
14.5	0.331368	*2*	*9*
14.75	0.34795	*2*	*10*
15	0.365115	*2*	*11*
15.25	0.38287	*2*	*11*
15.5	0.401222	*3*	*0*
15.75	0.420179	*3*	*1*
16	0.439745	*3*	*2*

NOTE: Find the row starting with your interest rate. To get your total interest savings
in dollars, just multiply the interest savings factor you find in that row by your ***original***
mortgage balance. Read off your time savings in the same row.

FIXED PREPAYMENT METHOD
30-YEAR FIXED-RATE MORTGAGE SAVINGS TABLE

Refer to this table to quickly figure out your *total* interest and time savings
when you use the *Fixed Prepayment* method

If your Mortgage is	10 Years Old		
and you *prepay* each month	4% of the *regular monthly payment*		
At this Interest rate (%)	Your interest savings factor is	You'll *save* this many years	and this many months
5.25	0.037466	1	3
5.5	0.041033	1	4
5.75	0.04483	1	4
6	0.048866	1	5
6.25	0.053152	1	5
6.5	0.057699	1	6
6.75	0.062519	1	6
7	0.067622	1	7
7.25	0.07302	1	7
7.5	0.078725	1	8
7.75	0.084748	1	8
8	0.091102	1	9
8.25	0.097799	1	9
8.5	0.104851	1	10
8.75	0.112271	1	10
9	0.120071	1	11
9.25	0.128263	2	0
9.5	0.136862	2	0
9.75	0.145878	2	1
10	0.155326	2	2
10.25	0.165216	2	2
10.5	0.175563	2	3

If your Mortgage is	10 Years Old		
and you *prepay* each month	4% of the *regular monthly payment*		
At this Interest rate (%)	Your interest savings factor is	You'll *save* this many years	and this many months
10.75	0.186378	2	4
11	0.197674	2	5
11.25	0.209462	2	5
11.5	0.221755	2	6
11.75	0.234564	2	7
12	0.2479	2	8
12.25	0.261775	2	9
12.5	0.276198	2	10
12.75	0.291181	2	10
13	0.306732	2	11
13.25	0.322862	3	0
13.5	0.339577	3	1
13.75	0.356888	3	2
14	0.3748	3	3
14.25	0.393322	3	4
14.5	0.412459	3	5
14.75	0.432217	3	6
15	0.4526	3	7
15.25	0.473613	3	8
15.5	0.495258	3	9
15.75	0.51754	3	10
16	0.540459	3	11

NOTE: Find the row starting with your interest rate. To get your total interest savings
in dollars, just multiply the interest savings factor you find in that row by your *original*
mortgage balance. Read off your time savings in the same row.

FIXED PREPAYMENT METHOD
30-YEAR FIXED-RATE MORTGAGE SAVINGS TABLE

Refer to this table to quickly figure out your *total* interest and time savings
when you use the *Fixed Prepayment* method

If your Mortgage is	10 Years Old		
and you *prepay* each month	5% of the *regular monthly payment*		
At this Interest rate (%)	Your interest savings factor is	You'll *save* this many years	and this many months
5.25	0.045937	1	7
5.5	0.050277	1	7
5.75	0.05489	1	8
6	0.059788	1	8
6.25	0.064984	1	9
6.5	0.070489	1	10
6.75	0.076316	1	10
7	0.082476	1	11
7.25	0.088984	1	11
7.5	0.095851	2	0
7.75	0.103091	2	1
8	0.110716	2	1
8.25	0.118739	2	2
8.5	0.127174	2	3
8.75	0.136033	2	3
9	0.145329	2	4
9.25	0.155076	2	5
9.5	0.165286	2	6
9.75	0.175972	2	6
10	0.187146	2	7
10.25	0.198821	2	8
10.5	0.211009	2	9

If your Mortgage is	10 Years Old		
and you *prepay* each month	5% of the *regular monthly payment*		
At this Interest rate (%)	Your interest savings factor is	You'll *save* this many years	and this many months
10.75	0.223721	2	10
11	0.236969	2	11
11.25	0.250764	3	0
11.5	0.265117	3	0
11.75	0.280038	3	1
12	0.295536	3	2
12.25	0.311622	3	3
12.5	0.328302	3	4
12.75	0.345586	3	5
13	0.363482	3	6
13.25	0.381995	3	7
13.5	0.401131	3	8
13.75	0.420897	3	9
14	0.441297	3	10
14.25	0.462334	3	11
14.5	0.484012	4	1
14.75	0.506334	4	2
15	0.529299	4	3
15.25	0.55291	4	4
15.5	0.577166	4	5
15.75	0.602067	4	6
16	0.62761	4	7

NOTE: Find the row starting with your interest rate. To get your total interest savings in dollars, just multiply the interest savings factor you find in that row by your *original* mortgage balance. Read off your time savings in the same row.

FIXED PREPAYMENT METHOD
30-YEAR FIXED-RATE MORTGAGE SAVINGS TABLE

Refer to this table to quickly figure out your **total** interest and time savings
when you use the *Fixed Prepayment* method

If your Mortgage is	10 Years Old		
and you *prepay* each month	10% of the *regular monthly payment*		
At this Interest rate (%)	Your interest savings factor is	You'll **save** this many years	and this many months
5.25	0.083888	2	11
5.5	0.091541	3	0
5.75	0.099636	3	1
6	0.108187	3	2
6.25	0.117208	3	3
6.5	0.126715	3	4
6.75	0.136721	3	4
7	0.147241	3	5
7.25	0.158286	3	6
7.5	0.169872	3	7
7.75	0.18201	3	8
8	0.194713	3	9
8.25	0.207993	3	10
8.5	0.221861	4	0
8.75	0.236328	4	1
9	0.251405	4	2
9.25	0.2671	4	3
9.5	0.283423	4	4
9.75	0.300383	4	5
10	0.317985	4	6
10.25	0.336238	4	7
10.5	0.355147	4	9

If your Mortgage is	10 Years Old		
and you *prepay* each month	10% of the *regular monthly payment*		
At this Interest rate (%)	Your interest savings factor is	You'll **save** this many years	and this many months
10.75	0.374716	4	10
11	0.394951	4	11
11.25	0.415854	5	0
11.5	0.437428	5	1
11.75	0.459674	5	3
12	0.482594	5	4
12.25	0.506186	5	5
12.5	0.53045	5	7
12.75	0.555384	5	8
13	0.580985	5	9
13.25	0.60725	5	10
13.5	0.634174	6	0
13.75	0.661751	6	1
14	0.689976	6	2
14.25	0.718843	6	4
14.5	0.748343	6	5
14.75	0.778469	6	6
15	0.809212	6	7
15.25	0.840564	6	9
15.5	0.872513	6	10
15.75	0.90505	6	11
16	0.938164	7	1

NOTE: Find the row starting with your interest rate. To get your total interest savings
in dollars, just multiply the interest savings factor you find in that row by your **original**
mortgage balance. Read off your time savings in the same row.

FIXED PREPAYMENT METHOD
30-YEAR FIXED-RATE MORTGAGE SAVINGS TABLE

Refer to this table to quickly figure out your *total* interest and time savings
when you use the *Fixed Prepayment* method

If your Mortgage is	10 Years Old		
and you **prepay** each month	15% of the regular monthly payment		
At this Interest rate (%)	Your interest savings factor is	You'll **save** this many years	and this many months
5.25	0.115824	4	1
5.5	0.126086	4	2
5.75	0.136897	4	3
6	0.148272	4	4
6.25	0.160223	4	5
6.5	0.172764	4	7
6.75	0.185908	4	8
7	0.199666	4	9
7.25	0.214049	4	10
7.5	0.229067	4	11
7.75	0.244731	5	1
8	0.261049	5	2
8.25	0.278029	5	3
8.5	0.295678	5	4
8.75	0.314003	5	6
9	0.333009	5	7
9.25	0.3527	5	8
9.5	0.37308	5	9
9.75	0.394151	5	11
10	0.415915	6	0
10.25	0.438374	6	1
10.5	0.461525	6	3

If your Mortgage is	10 Years Old		
and you **prepay** each month	15% of the regular monthly payment		
At this Interest rate (%)	Your interest savings factor is	You'll **save** this many years	and this many months
10.75	0.485369	6	4
11	0.509902	6	5
11.25	0.535123	6	7
11.5	0.561026	6	8
11.75	0.587608	6	9
12	0.614862	6	11
12.25	0.642783	7	0
12.5	0.671362	7	2
12.75	0.700593	7	3
13	0.730466	7	4
13.25	0.760973	7	6
13.5	0.792103	7	7
13.75	0.823846	7	8
14	0.856191	7	10
14.25	0.889128	7	11
14.5	0.922644	8	0
14.75	0.956727	8	2
15	0.991366	8	3
15.25	1.026546	8	4
15.5	1.062256	8	6
15.75	1.098483	8	7
16	1.135212	8	8

NOTE: Find the row starting with your interest rate. To get your total interest savings in dollars, just multiply the interest savings factor you find in that row by your *original* mortgage balance. Read off your time savings in the same row.

FIXED PREPAYMENT METHOD
30-YEAR FIXED-RATE MORTGAGE SAVINGS TABLE

Refer to this table to quickly figure out your **total** interest and time savings
when you use the *Fixed Prepayment* method

If your Mortgage is	10 Years Old		
and you *prepay* each month	20% of the *regular monthly payment*		
At this Interest rate (%)	Your interest savings factor is	You'll *save* this many years	and this many months
5.25	0.143107	5	1
5.5	0.155473	5	2
5.75	0.16846	5	4
6	0.182079	5	5
6.25	0.196342	5	6
6.5	0.211259	5	7
6.75	0.226841	5	9
7	0.243096	5	10
7.25	0.260032	5	11
7.5	0.277655	6	1
7.75	0.295973	6	2
8	0.31499	6	3
8.25	0.33471	6	5
8.5	0.355137	6	6
8.75	0.376271	6	7
9	0.398115	6	9
9.25	0.420669	6	10
9.5	0.44393	6	11
9.75	0.467898	7	1
10	0.492569	7	2
10.25	0.517941	7	4
10.5	0.544006	7	5

If your Mortgage is	10 Years Old		
and you *prepay* each month	20% of the *regular monthly payment*		
At this Interest rate (%)	Your interest savings factor is	You'll *save* this many years	and this many months
10.75	0.570762	7	6
11	0.5982	7	8
11.25	0.626313	7	9
11.5	0.655094	7	11
11.75	0.684534	8	0
12	0.714623	8	1
12.25	0.745351	8	3
12.5	0.776708	8	4
12.75	0.808683	8	6
13	0.841264	8	7
13.25	0.874439	8	8
13.5	0.908195	8	10
13.75	0.942521	8	11
14	0.977402	9	0
14.25	1.012826	9	2
14.5	1.04878	9	3
14.75	1.085249	9	4
15	1.12222	9	5
15.25	1.159679	9	7
15.5	1.197613	9	8
15.75	1.236008	9	9
16	1.27485	9	11

NOTE: Find the row starting with your interest rate. To get your total interest savings
in dollars, just multiply the interest savings factor you find in that row by your **original**
mortgage balance. Read off your time savings in the same row.

FIXED PREPAYMENT METHOD
30-YEAR FIXED-RATE MORTGAGE SAVINGS TABLE

Refer to this table to quickly figure out your ***total*** interest and time savings
when you use the *Fixed Prepayment* method

If your Mortgage is	15 Years Old		
and you *prepay* each month	1% of the *regular monthly payment*		
At this Interest rate (%)	Your interest savings factor is	You'll ***save*** this many years	and this many months
5.25	0.005077	*0*	*2*
5.5	0.005543	*0*	*2*
5.75	0.006038	*0*	*2*
6	0.006563	*0*	*2*
6.25	0.007118	*0*	*2*
6.5	0.007706	*0*	*2*
6.75	0.008327	*0*	*3*
7	0.008982	*0*	*3*
7.25	0.009674	*0*	*3*
7.5	0.010404	*0*	*3*
7.75	0.011172	*0*	*3*
8	0.011981	*0*	*3*
8.25	0.012833	*0*	*3*
8.5	0.013728	*0*	*3*
8.75	0.014669	*0*	*3*
9	0.015657	*0*	*3*
9.25	0.016694	*0*	*3*
9.5	0.017782	*0*	*3*
9.75	0.018922	*0*	*3*
10	0.020117	*0*	*4*
10.25	0.021369	*0*	*4*
10.5	0.022679	*0*	*4*

If your Mortgage is	15 Years Old		
and you *prepay* each month	1% of the *regular monthly payment*		
At this Interest rate (%)	Your interest savings factor is	You'll ***save*** this many years	and this many months
10.75	0.02405	*0*	*4*
11	0.025484	*0*	*4*
11.25	0.026983	*0*	*4*
11.5	0.028549	*0*	*4*
11.75	0.030185	*0*	*4*
12	0.031892	*0*	*4*
12.25	0.033674	*0*	*4*
12.5	0.035534	*0*	*5*
12.75	0.037472	*0*	*5*
13	0.039493	*0*	*5*
13.25	0.041599	*0*	*5*
13.5	0.043793	*0*	*5*
13.75	0.046077	*0*	*5*
14	0.048454	*0*	*5*
14.25	0.050928	*0*	*5*
14.5	0.053502	*0*	*6*
14.75	0.056178	*0*	*6*
15	0.05896	*0*	*6*
15.25	0.061852	*0*	*6*
15.5	0.064856	*0*	*6*
15.75	0.067976	*0*	*6*
16	0.071216	*0*	*7*

NOTE: Find the row starting with your interest rate. To get your total interest savings
in dollars, just multiply the interest savings factor you find in that row by your ***original***
mortgage balance. Read off your time savings in the same row.

FIXED PREPAYMENT METHOD
30-YEAR FIXED-RATE MORTGAGE SAVINGS TABLE

Refer to this table to quickly figure out your **total** interest and time savings when you use the *Fixed Prepayment* method

If your Mortgage is	15 Years Old		
and you *prepay* **each month**	**2%** of the *regular* monthly payment		
At this **Interest rate** *(%)*	Your interest savings factor is	You'll *save* this many years	and this many months
5.25	0.009982	0	5
5.5	0.010895	0	5
5.75	0.011862	0	5
6	0.012886	0	5
6.25	0.01397	0	5
6.5	0.015114	0	5
6.75	0.016323	0	5
7	0.017598	0	6
7.25	0.018943	0	6
7.5	0.020359	0	6
7.75	0.021849	0	6
8	0.023417	0	6
8.25	0.025065	0	6
8.5	0.026795	0	6
8.75	0.028611	0	7
9	0.030516	0	7
9.25	0.032513	0	7
9.5	0.034606	0	7
9.75	0.036796	0	7
10	0.039088	0	7
10.25	0.041486	0	8
10.5	0.043991	0	8

If your Mortgage is	15 Years Old		
and you *prepay* **each month**	**2%** of the *regular* monthly payment		
At this **Interest rate** *(%)*	Your interest savings factor is	You'll *save* this many years	and this many months
10.75	0.046609	0	8
11	0.049343	0	8
11.25	0.052195	0	8
11.5	0.055171	0	8
11.75	0.058274	0	9
12	0.061507	0	9
12.25	0.064875	0	9
12.5	0.068382	0	9
12.75	0.072031	0	10
13	0.075828	0	10
13.25	0.079775	0	10
13.5	0.083879	0	10
13.75	0.088142	0	10
14	0.092569	0	11
14.25	0.097165	0	11
14.5	0.101935	0	11
14.75	0.106883	0	11
15	0.112013	1	0
15.25	0.11733	1	0
15.5	0.12284	1	0
15.75	0.128546	1	1
16	0.134454	1	1

NOTE: Find the row starting with your interest rate. To get your total interest savings in dollars, just multiply the interest savings factor you find in that row by your ***original*** mortgage balance. Read off your time savings in the same row.

FIXED PREPAYMENT METHOD
30-YEAR FIXED-RATE MORTGAGE SAVINGS TABLE

Refer to this table to quickly figure out your ***total*** interest and time savings when you use the *Fixed Prepayment* method

If your Mortgage is	15 Years Old		
and you *prepay* each month	3% of the regular monthly payment		
At this Interest rate (%)	Your interest savings factor is	You'll *save* this many years	and this many months
5.25	0.014726	0	7
5.5	0.016065	0	7
5.75	0.017483	0	8
6	0.018983	0	8
6.25	0.020569	0	8
6.5	0.022243	0	8
6.75	0.024009	0	8
7	0.025871	0	9
7.25	0.027832	0	9
7.5	0.029896	0	9
7.75	0.032066	0	9
8	0.034345	0	9
8.25	0.036739	0	9
8.5	0.03925	0	10
8.75	0.041883	0	10
9	0.044642	0	10
9.25	0.04753	0	10
9.5	0.050553	0	11
9.75	0.053713	0	11
10	0.057016	0	11
10.25	0.060465	0	11
10.5	0.064066	1	0

If your Mortgage is	15 Years Old		
and you *prepay* each month	3% of the regular monthly payment		
At this Interest rate (%)	Your interest savings factor is	You'll *save* this many years	and this many months
10.75	0.067823	1	0
11	0.071739	1	0
11.25	0.075821	1	0
11.5	0.080072	1	1
11.75	0.084497	1	1
12	0.089101	1	1
12.25	0.093889	1	1
12.5	0.098866	1	2
12.75	0.104036	1	2
13	0.109405	1	2
13.25	0.114978	1	3
13.5	0.120758	1	3
13.75	0.126753	1	3
14	0.132965	1	4
14.25	0.139402	1	4
14.5	0.146067	1	4
14.75	0.152966	1	5
15	0.160104	1	5
15.25	0.167485	1	5
15.5	0.175116	1	6
15.75	0.183	1	6
16	0.191144	1	7

NOTE: Find the row starting with your interest rate. To get your total interest savings in dollars, just multiply the interest savings factor you find in that row by your ***original*** mortgage balance. Read off your time savings in the same row.

FIXED PREPAYMENT METHOD
30-YEAR FIXED-RATE MORTGAGE SAVINGS TABLE

Refer to this table to quickly figure out your *total* interest and time savings
when you use the *Fixed Prepayment* method

If your Mortgage is	15 Years Old		
and you prepay each month	**4% of the regular monthly payment**		
At this Interest rate (%)	Your interest savings factor is	You'll *save* this many years	and this many months
5.25	0.019315	0	10
5.5	0.021062	0	10
5.75	0.022911	0	10
6	0.024866	0	10
6.25	0.02693	0	11
6.5	0.029108	0	11
6.75	0.031404	0	11
7	0.033822	0	11
7.25	0.036366	1	0
7.5	0.039041	1	0
7.75	0.041851	1	0
8	0.044801	1	0
8.25	0.047896	1	1
8.5	0.051139	1	1
8.75	0.054535	1	1
9	0.05809	1	1
9.25	0.061808	1	2
9.5	0.065694	1	2
9.75	0.069753	1	2
10	0.073989	1	3
10.25	0.078409	1	3
10.5	0.083016	1	3

If your Mortgage is	15 Years Old		
and you prepay each month	**4% of the regular monthly payment**		
At this Interest rate (%)	Your interest savings factor is	You'll *save* this many years	and this many months
10.75	0.087817	1	3
11	0.092815	1	4
11.25	0.098017	1	4
11.5	0.103427	1	4
11.75	0.109051	1	5
12	0.114894	1	5
12.25	0.120961	1	6
12.5	0.127257	1	6
12.75	0.133788	1	6
13	0.140558	1	7
13.25	0.147574	1	7
13.5	0.15484	1	7
13.75	0.162361	1	8
14	0.170143	1	8
14.25	0.17819	1	9
14.5	0.186508	1	9
14.75	0.195101	1	9
15	0.203975	1	10
15.25	0.213134	1	10
15.5	0.222584	1	11
15.75	0.232327	1	11
16	0.242371	2	0

NOTE: Find the row starting with your interest rate. To get your total interest savings
in dollars, just multiply the interest savings factor you find in that row by your *original*
mortgage balance. Read off your time savings in the same row.

FIXED PREPAYMENT METHOD
30-YEAR FIXED-RATE MORTGAGE SAVINGS TABLE

Refer to this table to quickly figure out your **total** interest and time savings when you use the *Fixed Prepayment* method

If your Mortgage is	15 Years Old		
and you *prepay* each month	5% of the *regular monthly payment*		
At this Interest rate (%)	Your interest savings factor is	You'll *save* this many years	and this many months
5.25	0.023757	1	0
5.5	0.025895	1	0
5.75	0.028157	1	1
6	0.030545	1	1
6.25	0.033066	1	1
6.5	0.035724	1	1
6.75	0.038523	1	2
7	0.041469	1	2
7.25	0.044566	1	2
7.5	0.04782	1	3
7.75	0.051235	1	3
8	0.054816	1	3
8.25	0.058569	1	3
8.5	0.062499	1	4
8.75	0.066611	1	4
9	0.070911	1	4
9.25	0.075403	1	5
9.5	0.080093	1	5
9.75	0.084986	1	5
10	0.090088	1	6
10.25	0.095404	1	6
10.5	0.10094	1	7

If your Mortgage is	15 Years Old		
and you *prepay* each month	5% of the *regular monthly payment*		
At this Interest rate (%)	Your interest savings factor is	You'll *save* this many years	and this many months
10.75	0.106701	1	7
11	0.112692	1	7
11.25	0.11892	1	8
11.5	0.125388	1	8
11.75	0.132103	1	9
12	0.13907	1	9
12.25	0.146295	1	9
12.5	0.153782	1	10
12.75	0.161537	1	10
13	0.169565	1	11
13.25	0.177872	1	11
13.5	0.186461	2	0
13.75	0.195339	2	0
14	0.20451	2	1
14.25	0.213979	2	1
14.5	0.22375	2	1
14.75	0.233829	2	2
15	0.244219	2	2
15.25	0.254925	2	3
15.5	0.26595	2	3
15.75	0.2773	2	4
16	0.288977	2	5

NOTE: Find the row starting with your interest rate. To get your total interest savings in dollars, just multiply the interest savings factor you find in that row by your **original** mortgage balance. Read off your time savings in the same row.

FIXED PREPAYMENT METHOD
30-YEAR FIXED-RATE MORTGAGE SAVINGS TABLE

Refer to this table to quickly figure out your **total** interest and time savings
when you use the *Fixed Prepayment* method

If your Mortgage is	15 Years Old		
and you *prepay* **each month**	**10% of the** *regular* **monthly payment**		
At this Interest rate (%)	Your interest savings factor is	You'll **save** this many years	and this many months
5.25	0.044003	*1*	*11*
5.5	0.047873	*2*	*0*
5.75	0.051954	*2*	*0*
6	0.056251	*2*	*0*
6.25	0.06077	*2*	*1*
6.5	0.065519	*2*	*1*
6.75	0.070504	*2*	*2*
7	0.075732	*2*	*2*
7.25	0.081208	*2*	*3*
7.5	0.08694	*2*	*3*
7.75	0.092934	*2*	*4*
8	0.099196	*2*	*4*
8.25	0.105732	*2*	*5*
8.5	0.112549	*2*	*5*
8.75	0.119653	*2*	*6*
9	0.127049	*2*	*6*
9.25	0.134744	*2*	*7*
9.5	0.142743	*2*	*7*
9.75	0.151052	*2*	*8*
10	0.159676	*2*	*8*
10.25	0.168621	*2*	*9*
10.5	0.177892	*2*	*10*

If your Mortgage is	15 Years Old		
and you *prepay* **each month**	**10% of the** *regular* **monthly payment**		
At this Interest rate (%)	Your interest savings factor is	You'll **save** this many years	and this many months
10.75	0.187494	*2*	*10*
11	0.197431	*2*	*11*
11.25	0.207708	*2*	*11*
11.5	0.21833	*3*	*0*
11.75	0.2293	*3*	*1*
12	0.240623	*3*	*1*
12.25	0.252303	*3*	*2*
12.5	0.264343	*3*	*2*
12.75	0.276746	*3*	*3*
13	0.289516	*3*	*4*
13.25	0.302655	*3*	*4*
13.5	0.316165	*3*	*5*
13.75	0.33005	*3*	*6*
14	0.34431	*3*	*6*
14.25	0.358948	*3*	*7*
14.5	0.373965	*3*	*8*
14.75	0.389363	*3*	*8*
15	0.405142	*3*	*9*
15.25	0.421303	*3*	*10*
15.5	0.437846	*3*	*10*
15.75	0.454772	*3*	*11*
16	0.47208	*4*	*0*

NOTE: Find the row starting with your interest rate. To get your total interest savings
in dollars, just multiply the interest savings factor you find in that row by your **original**
mortgage balance. Read off your time savings in the same row.

FIXED PREPAYMENT METHOD
30-YEAR FIXED-RATE MORTGAGE SAVINGS TABLE

Refer to this table to quickly figure out your *total* interest and time savings
when you use the *Fixed Prepayment* method

If your Mortgage is	15 Years Old		
and you *prepay* each month	15% of the regular monthly payment		
At this Interest rate (%)	Your interest savings factor is	You'll *save* this many years	and this many months
5.25	0.061476	2	9
5.5	0.066777	2	9
5.75	0.072352	2	10
6	0.078206	2	10
6.25	0.084348	2	11
6.5	0.090784	2	11
6.75	0.097522	3	0
7	0.104567	3	1
7.25	0.111927	3	1
7.5	0.119608	3	2
7.75	0.127616	3	2
8	0.135957	3	3
8.25	0.144637	3	4
8.5	0.153662	3	4
8.75	0.163038	3	5
9	0.172768	3	6
9.25	0.182859	3	6
9.5	0.193315	3	7
9.75	0.20414	3	8
10	0.215338	3	8
10.25	0.226914	3	9
10.5	0.238871	3	10

If your Mortgage is	15 Years Old		
and you *prepay* each month	15% of the regular monthly payment		
At this Interest rate (%)	Your interest savings factor is	You'll *save* this many years	and this many months
10.75	0.251212	3	10
11	0.26394	3	11
11.25	0.277058	4	0
11.5	0.290568	4	0
11.75	0.304472	4	1
12	0.318772	4	2
12.25	0.33347	4	3
12.5	0.348566	4	3
12.75	0.364061	4	4
13	0.379956	4	5
13.25	0.39625	4	6
13.5	0.412945	4	6
13.75	0.430039	4	7
14	0.447531	4	8
14.25	0.46542	4	9
14.5	0.483706	4	9
14.75	0.502386	4	10
15	0.521459	4	11
15.25	0.540922	5	0
15.5	0.560772	5	0
15.75	0.581008	5	1
16	0.601626	5	2

NOTE: Find the row starting with your interest rate. To get your total interest savings in dollars, just multiply the interest savings factor you find in that row by your *original* mortgage balance. Read off your time savings in the same row.

FIXED PREPAYMENT METHOD
30-YEAR FIXED-RATE MORTGAGE SAVINGS TABLE

Refer to this table to quickly figure out your **total** interest and time savings when you use the *Fixed Prepayment* method

If your Mortgage is	15 Years Old		
and you **prepay** each month	20% of the **regular monthly payment**		
At this Interest rate (%)	Your interest savings factor is	You'll **save** this many years	and this many months
5.25	0.076718	3	5
5.5	0.083221	3	6
5.75	0.090043	3	6
6	0.097193	3	7
6.25	0.104677	3	8
6.5	0.112502	3	8
6.75	0.120675	3	9
7	0.129201	3	10
7.25	0.138088	3	10
7.5	0.14734	3	11
7.75	0.156963	4	0
8	0.166963	4	0
8.25	0.177344	4	1
8.5	0.188111	4	2
8.75	0.199268	4	3
9	0.21082	4	3
9.25	0.222769	4	4
9.5	0.235119	4	5
9.75	0.247872	4	6
10	0.261033	4	6
10.25	0.274602	4	7
10.5	0.288581	4	8

If your Mortgage is	15 Years Old		
and you **prepay** each month	20% of the **regular monthly payment**		
At this Interest rate (%)	Your interest savings factor is	You'll **save** this many years	and this many months
10.75	0.302972	4	9
11	0.317777	4	9
11.25	0.332995	4	10
11.5	0.348628	4	11
11.75	0.364674	5	0
12	0.381135	5	0
12.25	0.39801	5	1
12.5	0.415297	5	2
12.75	0.432995	5	3
13	0.451103	5	3
13.25	0.469618	5	4
13.5	0.488539	5	5
13.75	0.507863	5	6
14	0.527587	5	7
14.25	0.547709	5	7
14.5	0.568224	5	8
14.75	0.589129	5	9
15	0.610421	5	10
15.25	0.632095	5	11
15.5	0.654147	5	11
15.75	0.676573	6	0
16	0.699367	6	1

NOTE: Find the row starting with your interest rate. To get your total interest savings in dollars, just multiply the interest savings factor you find in that row by your **original** mortgage balance. Read off your time savings in the same row.

FIXED PREPAYMENT METHOD
30-YEAR FIXED-RATE MORTGAGE SAVINGS TABLE

Refer to this table to quickly figure out your *total* interest and time savings
when you use the *Fixed Prepayment* method

If your Mortgage is	20 Years Old		
and you *prepay* each month	1% of the *regular monthly payment*		
At this Interest rate (%)	Your interest savings factor is	You'll *save* this many years	and this many months
5.25	0.002053	0	1
5.5	0.002231	0	1
5.75	0.002419	0	1
6	0.002616	0	1
6.25	0.002823	0	1
6.5	0.00304	0	1
6.75	0.003269	0	1
7	0.003508	0	1
7.25	0.003759	0	1
7.5	0.004021	0	1
7.75	0.004296	0	1
8	0.004583	0	1
8.25	0.004883	0	1
8.5	0.005195	0	1
8.75	0.005522	0	1
9	0.005862	0	1
9.25	0.006217	0	1
9.5	0.006586	0	1
9.75	0.00697	0	1
10	0.00737	0	2
10.25	0.007785	0	2
10.5	0.008217	0	2

If your Mortgage is	20 Years Old		
and you *prepay* each month	1% of the *regular monthly payment*		
At this Interest rate (%)	Your interest savings factor is	You'll *save* this many years	and this many months
10.75	0.008665	0	2
11	0.00913	0	2
11.25	0.009613	0	2
11.5	0.010113	0	2
11.75	0.010632	0	2
12	0.01117	0	2
12.25	0.011727	0	2
12.5	0.012304	0	2
12.75	0.0129	0	2
13	0.013518	0	2
13.25	0.014156	0	2
13.5	0.014816	0	2
13.75	0.015499	0	2
14	0.016204	0	2
14.25	0.016932	0	2
14.5	0.017683	0	2
14.75	0.018459	0	2
15	0.01926	0	2
15.25	0.020086	0	2
15.5	0.020938	0	2
15.75	0.021817	0	2
16	0.022723	0	2

NOTE: Find the row starting with your interest rate. To get your total interest savings
in dollars, just multiply the interest savings factor you find in that row by your *original*
mortgage balance. Read off your time savings in the same row.

FIXED PREPAYMENT METHOD
30-YEAR FIXED-RATE MORTGAGE SAVINGS TABLE

Refer to this table to quickly figure out your *total* interest and time savings when you use the *Fixed Prepayment* method

If your Mortgage is	20 Years Old		
and you prepay each month	2% of the regular monthly payment		
At this Interest rate (%)	Your interest savings factor is	You'll *save* this many years	and this many months
5.25	0.004049	0	3
5.5	0.004399	0	3
5.75	0.004767	0	3
6	0.005154	0	3
6.25	0.005561	0	3
6.5	0.005988	0	3
6.75	0.006436	0	3
7	0.006905	0	3
7.25	0.007396	0	3
7.5	0.007911	0	3
7.75	0.008448	0	3
8	0.00901	0	3
8.25	0.009596	0	3
8.5	0.010208	0	3
8.75	0.010846	0	3
9	0.01151	0	3
9.25	0.012202	0	3
9.5	0.012923	0	3
9.75	0.013672	0	3
10	0.01445	0	3
10.25	0.015259	0	4
10.5	0.016099	0	4

If your Mortgage is	20 Years Old		
and you prepay each month	2% of the regular monthly payment		
At this Interest rate (%)	Your interest savings factor is	You'll *save* this many years	and this many months
10.75	0.01697	0	4
11	0.017875	0	4
11.25	0.018812	0	4
11.5	0.019784	0	4
11.75	0.02079	0	4
12	0.021832	0	4
12.25	0.022911	0	4
12.5	0.024027	0	4
12.75	0.025181	0	4
13	0.026374	0	4
13.25	0.027607	0	4
13.5	0.02888	0	4
13.75	0.030195	0	4
14	0.031553	0	4
14.25	0.032954	0	5
14.5	0.034399	0	5
14.75	0.035889	0	5
15	0.037426	0	5
15.25	0.03901	0	5
15.5	0.040641	0	5
15.75	0.042322	0	5
16	0.044053	0	5

NOTE: Find the row starting with your interest rate. To get your total interest savings in dollars, just multiply the interest savings factor you find in that row by your *original* mortgage balance. Read off your time savings in the same row.

FIXED PREPAYMENT METHOD
30-YEAR FIXED-RATE MORTGAGE SAVINGS TABLE

Refer to this table to quickly figure out your *total* interest and time savings
when you use the *Fixed Prepayment* method

If your Mortgage is	20 Years Old		
and you *prepay* each month	3% of the regular monthly payment		
At this Interest rate (%)	Your interest savings factor is	You'll *save* this many years	and this many months
5.25	0.00599	*0*	*4*
5.5	0.006506	*0*	*4*
5.75	0.007048	*0*	*4*
6	0.007619	*0*	*4*
6.25	0.008218	*0*	*4*
6.5	0.008847	*0*	*4*
6.75	0.009506	*0*	*4*
7	0.010196	*0*	*4*
7.25	0.010919	*0*	*5*
7.5	0.011675	*0*	*5*
7.75	0.012464	*0*	*5*
8	0.013289	*0*	*5*
8.25	0.01415	*0*	*5*
8.5	0.015047	*0*	*5*
8.75	0.015982	*0*	*5*
9	0.016956	*0*	*5*
9.25	0.01797	*0*	*5*
9.5	0.019024	*0*	*5*
9.75	0.02012	*0*	*5*
10	0.021258	*0*	*5*
10.25	0.02244	*0*	*5*
10.5	0.023667	*0*	*6*

If your Mortgage is	20 Years Old		
and you *prepay* each month	3% of the regular monthly payment		
At this Interest rate (%)	Your interest savings factor is	You'll *save* this many years	and this many months
10.75	0.024939	*0*	*6*
11	0.026258	*0*	*6*
11.25	0.027625	*0*	*6*
11.5	0.029041	*0*	*6*
11.75	0.030506	*0*	*6*
12	0.032022	*0*	*6*
12.25	0.03359	*0*	*6*
12.5	0.035212	*0*	*6*
12.75	0.036887	*0*	*6*
13	0.038618	*0*	*6*
13.25	0.040405	*0*	*6*
13.5	0.04225	*0*	*7*
13.75	0.044154	*0*	*7*
14	0.046117	*0*	*7*
14.25	0.048142	*0*	*7*
14.5	0.050229	*0*	*7*
14.75	0.052379	*0*	*7*
15	0.054594	*0*	*7*
15.25	0.056875	*0*	*7*
15.5	0.059223	*0*	*7*
15.75	0.06164	*0*	*8*
16	0.064126	*0*	*8*

NOTE: Find the row starting with your interest rate. To get your total interest savings
in dollars, just multiply the interest savings factor you find in that row by your *original*
mortgage balance. Read off your time savings in the same row.

FIXED PREPAYMENT METHOD
30-YEAR FIXED-RATE MORTGAGE SAVINGS TABLE

Refer to this table to quickly figure out your **total** interest and time savings when you use the *Fixed Prepayment* method

If your Mortgage is	20 Years Old		
and you prepay each month	4% of the regular monthly payment		
At this Interest rate (%)	Your interest savings factor is	You'll **save** this many years	and this many months
5.25	0.007879	0	5
5.5	0.008555	0	6
5.75	0.009266	0	6
6	0.010013	0	6
6.25	0.010798	0	6
6.5	0.011621	0	6
6.75	0.012484	0	6
7	0.013387	0	6
7.25	0.014332	0	6
7.5	0.01532	0	6
7.75	0.016351	0	6
8	0.017428	0	6
8.25	0.018552	0	6
8.5	0.019722	0	7
8.75	0.020942	0	7
9	0.022211	0	7
9.25	0.023532	0	7
9.5	0.024904	0	7
9.75	0.02633	0	7
10	0.027811	0	7
10.25	0.029347	0	7
10.5	0.030941	0	7

If your Mortgage is	20 Years Old		
and you prepay each month	4% of the regular monthly payment		
At this Interest rate (%)	Your interest savings factor is	You'll **save** this many years	and this many months
10.75	0.032593	0	7
11	0.034304	0	8
11.25	0.036077	0	8
11.5	0.037912	0	8
11.75	0.039809	0	8
12	0.041772	0	8
12.25	0.043801	0	8
12.5	0.045897	0	8
12.75	0.048061	0	8
13	0.050296	0	8
13.25	0.052602	0	9
13.5	0.05498	0	9
13.75	0.057432	0	9
14	0.05996	0	9
14.25	0.062564	0	9
14.5	0.065247	0	9
14.75	0.068008	0	9
15	0.070851	0	10
15.25	0.073776	0	10
15.5	0.076784	0	10
15.75	0.079878	0	10
16	0.083058	0	10

NOTE: Find the row starting with your interest rate. To get your total interest savings in dollars, just multiply the interest savings factor you find in that row by your **original** mortgage balance. Read off your time savings in the same row.

FIXED PREPAYMENT METHOD
30-YEAR FIXED-RATE MORTGAGE SAVINGS TABLE

Refer to this table to quickly figure out your *total* interest and time savings
when you use the *Fixed Prepayment* method

If your Mortgage is	20 Years Old		
and you prepay each month	5% of the regular monthly payment		
At this Interest rate (%)	Your interest savings factor is	You'll save this many years	and this many months
5.25	0.009716	0	7
5.5	0.010548	0	7
5.75	0.011422	0	7
6	0.01234	0	7
6.25	0.013304	0	7
6.5	0.014315	0	7
6.75	0.015373	0	7
7	0.016481	0	8
7.25	0.01764	0	8
7.5	0.018851	0	8
7.75	0.020115	0	8
8	0.021434	0	8
8.25	0.022809	0	8
8.5	0.024242	0	8
8.75	0.025733	0	8
9	0.027285	0	8
9.25	0.028898	0	9
9.5	0.030575	0	9
9.75	0.032315	0	9
10	0.034122	0	9
10.25	0.035995	0	9
10.5	0.037938	0	9

If your Mortgage is	20 Years Old		
and you prepay each month	5% of the regular monthly payment		
At this Interest rate (%)	Your interest savings factor is	You'll save this many years	and this many months
10.75	0.03995	0	9
11	0.042034	0	9
11.25	0.04419	0	10
11.5	0.046421	0	10
11.75	0.048728	0	10
12	0.051111	0	10
12.25	0.053574	0	10
12.5	0.056117	0	10
12.75	0.058741	0	10
13	0.061448	0	11
13.25	0.064239	0	11
13.5	0.067117	0	11
13.75	0.070082	0	11
14	0.073136	0	11
14.25	0.076281	0	11
14.5	0.079517	0	11
14.75	0.082847	1	0
15	0.086272	1	0
15.25	0.089793	1	0
15.5	0.093412	1	0
15.75	0.097131	1	0
16	0.10095	1	0

NOTE: Find the row starting with your interest rate. To get your total interest savings
in dollars, just multiply the interest savings factor you find in that row by your ***original***
mortgage balance. Read off your time savings in the same row.

FIXED PREPAYMENT METHOD
30-YEAR FIXED-RATE MORTGAGE SAVINGS TABLE

Refer to this table to quickly figure out your **total** interest and time savings when you use the *Fixed Prepayment* method

If your Mortgage is	20 Years Old		
and you **prepay** each month	10% of the regular monthly payment		
At this Interest rate (%)	Your interest savings factor is	You'll **save** this many years	and this many months
5.25	0.018213	1	1
5.5	0.01975	1	2
5.75	0.021364	1	2
6	0.023057	1	2
6.25	0.024831	1	2
6.5	0.026687	1	2
6.75	0.028628	1	2
7	0.030656	1	3
7.25	0.032773	1	3
7.5	0.034981	1	3
7.75	0.037282	1	3
8	0.039678	1	3
8.25	0.04217	1	4
8.5	0.044762	1	4
8.75	0.047454	1	4
9	0.05025	1	4
9.25	0.05315	1	4
9.5	0.056157	1	4
9.75	0.059272	1	5
10	0.062498	1	5
10.25	0.065836	1	5
10.5	0.069289	1	5

If your Mortgage is	20 Years Old		
and you **prepay** each month	10% of the regular monthly payment		
At this Interest rate (%)	Your interest savings factor is	You'll **save** this many years	and this many months
10.75	0.072857	1	6
11	0.076544	1	6
11.25	0.08035	1	6
11.5	0.084277	1	6
11.75	0.088328	1	6
12	0.092503	1	7
12.25	0.096806	1	7
12.5	0.101236	1	7
12.75	0.105797	1	7
13	0.110488	1	7
13.25	0.115314	1	8
13.5	0.120274	1	8
13.75	0.12537	1	8
14	0.130604	1	8
14.25	0.135977	1	9
14.5	0.141491	1	9
14.75	0.147148	1	9
15	0.152948	1	9
15.25	0.158893	1	10
15.5	0.164984	1	10
15.75	0.171224	1	10
16	0.177612	1	10

NOTE: Find the row starting with your interest rate. To get your total interest savings in dollars, just multiply the interest savings factor you find in that row by your **original** mortgage balance. Read off your time savings in the same row.

FIXED PREPAYMENT METHOD
30-YEAR FIXED-RATE MORTGAGE SAVINGS TABLE

Refer to this table to quickly figure out your *total* interest and time savings
when you use the *Fixed Prepayment* method

If your Mortgage is	20 Years Old		
and you prepay each month	15% of the regular monthly payment		
At this Interest rate (%)	Your interest savings factor is	You'll save this many years	and this many months
5.25	0.025707	1	7
5.5	0.027852	1	7
5.75	0.030101	1	8
6	0.032455	1	8
6.25	0.034919	1	8
6.5	0.037493	1	8
6.75	0.040181	1	9
7	0.042984	1	9
7.25	0.045906	1	9
7.5	0.048949	1	9
7.75	0.052115	1	9
8	0.055406	1	10
8.25	0.058824	1	10
8.5	0.062372	1	10
8.75	0.066052	1	10
9	0.069867	1	11
9.25	0.073817	1	11
9.5	0.077905	1	11
9.75	0.082133	1	11
10	0.086503	2	0
10.25	0.091018	2	0
10.5	0.095678	2	0

If your Mortgage is	20 Years Old		
and you prepay each month	15% of the regular monthly payment		
At this Interest rate (%)	Your interest savings factor is	You'll save this many years	and this many months
10.75	0.100485	2	1
11	0.105442	2	1
11.25	0.11055	2	1
11.5	0.115811	2	1
11.75	0.121226	2	2
12	0.126797	2	2
12.25	0.132525	2	2
12.5	0.138412	2	2
12.75	0.14446	2	3
13	0.150669	2	3
13.25	0.15704	2	3
13.5	0.163576	2	4
13.75	0.170277	2	4
14	0.177145	2	4
14.25	0.18418	2	4
14.5	0.191384	2	5
14.75	0.198757	2	5
15	0.206301	2	5
15.25	0.214016	2	6
15.5	0.221903	2	6
15.75	0.229962	2	6
16	0.238196	2	7

NOTE: Find the row starting with your interest rate. To get your total interest savings in dollars, just multiply the interest savings factor you find in that row by your *original* mortgage balance. Read off your time savings in the same row.

FIXED PREPAYMENT METHOD
30-YEAR FIXED-RATE MORTGAGE SAVINGS TABLE

Refer to this table to quickly figure out your **total** interest and time savings
when you use the *Fixed Prepayment* method

If your Mortgage is	20 Years Old		
and you **prepay each** month	20% of the *regular monthly payment*		
At this Interest rate (%)	Your interest savings factor is	You'll **save** this many years	and this many months
5.25	0.032369	2	0
5.5	0.035042	2	1
5.75	0.03784	2	1
6	0.040767	2	1
6.25	0.043824	2	1
6.5	0.047015	2	2
6.75	0.050343	2	2
7	0.053809	2	2
7.25	0.057417	2	3
7.5	0.061169	2	3
7.75	0.065067	2	3
8	0.069114	2	3
8.25	0.073312	2	4
8.5	0.077663	2	4
8.75	0.082169	2	4
9	0.086832	2	4
9.25	0.091655	2	5
9.5	0.096639	2	5
9.75	0.101787	2	5
10	0.107099	2	6
10.25	0.112578	2	6
10.5	0.118225	2	6

If your Mortgage is	20 Years Old		
and you **prepay each** month	20% of the *regular monthly payment*		
At this Interest rate (%)	Your interest savings factor is	You'll **save** this many years	and this many months
10.75	0.124042	2	7
11	0.130031	2	7
11.25	0.136192	2	7
11.5	0.142528	2	7
11.75	0.149039	2	8
12	0.155727	2	8
12.25	0.162593	2	8
12.5	0.169638	2	9
12.75	0.176862	2	9
13	0.184268	2	9
13.25	0.191855	2	10
13.5	0.199625	2	10
13.75	0.207578	2	10
14	0.215715	2	11
14.25	0.224036	2	11
14.5	0.232543	2	11
14.75	0.241235	3	0
15	0.250112	3	0
15.25	0.259176	3	0
15.5	0.268426	3	1
15.75	0.277862	3	1
16	0.287485	3	1

NOTE: Find the row starting with your interest rate. To get your total interest savings
in dollars, just multiply the interest savings factor you find in that row by your **original**
mortgage balance. Read off your time savings in the same row.

FIXED PREPAYMENT METHOD
30-YEAR FIXED-RATE MORTGAGE SAVINGS TABLE

Refer to this table to quickly figure out your *total* interest and time savings
when you use the *Fixed Prepayment* method

If your Mortgage is	25 Years Old				If your Mortgage is	25 Years Old		
and you prepay each month	**5% of the regular monthly payment**				**and you prepay each month**	**5% of the regular monthly payment**		
At this Interest rate (%)	Your interest savings factor is	You'll **save** this many years	and this many months		**At this Interest rate (%)**	Your interest savings factor is	You'll **save** this many years	and this many months
5.25	0.002238	*0*	*3*		10.75	0.008419	*0*	*3*
5.5	0.00242	*0*	*3*		11	0.008822	*0*	*3*
5.75	0.00261	*0*	*3*		11.25	0.009237	*0*	*3*
6	0.002809	*0*	*3*		11.5	0.009664	*0*	*3*
6.25	0.003016	*0*	*3*		11.75	0.010103	*0*	*3*
6.5	0.003232	*0*	*3*		12	0.010554	*0*	*3*
6.75	0.003457	*0*	*3*		12.25	0.011018	*0*	*3*
7	0.003691	*0*	*3*		12.5	0.011495	*0*	*3*
7.25	0.003935	*0*	*3*		12.75	0.011984	*0*	*3*
7.5	0.004188	*0*	*3*		13	0.012486	*0*	*3*
7.75	0.004451	*0*	*3*		13.25	0.013	*0*	*3*
8	0.004724	*0*	*3*		13.5	0.013528	*0*	*3*
8.25	0.005006	*0*	*3*		13.75	0.01407	*0*	*4*
8.5	0.005299	*0*	*3*		14	0.014624	*0*	*4*
8.75	0.005602	*0*	*3*		14.25	0.015193	*0*	*4*
9	0.005916	*0*	*3*		14.5	0.015774	*0*	*4*
9.25	0.00624	*0*	*3*		14.75	0.01637	*0*	*4*
9.5	0.006575	*0*	*3*		15	0.01698	*0*	*4*
9.75	0.006922	*0*	*3*		15.25	0.017603	*0*	*4*
10	0.007279	*0*	*3*		15.5	0.018241	*0*	*4*
10.25	0.007647	*0*	*3*		15.75	0.018893	*0*	*4*
10.5	0.008027	*0*	*3*		16	0.01956	*0*	*4*

NOTE: Find the row starting with your interest rate. To get your total interest savings
in dollars, just multiply the interest savings factor you find in that row by your *original*
mortgage balance. Read off your time savings in the same row.

FIXED PREPAYMENT METHOD
30-YEAR FIXED-RATE MORTGAGE SAVINGS TABLE

Refer to this table to quickly figure out your **total** interest and time savings
when you use the *Fixed Prepayment* method

If your Mortgage is	25 Years Old		
and you prepay each month	**10% of the regular monthly payment**		
At this Interest rate (%)	Your interest savings factor is	You'll **save** this many years	and this many months
5.25	0.004238	*0*	6
5.5	0.00458	*0*	6
5.75	0.004938	*0*	6
6	0.005311	*0*	6
6.25	0.0057	*0*	6
6.5	0.006106	*0*	6
6.75	0.006528	*0*	6
7	0.006967	*0*	6
7.25	0.007423	*0*	6
7.5	0.007897	*0*	6
7.75	0.008389	*0*	6
8	0.008899	*0*	6
8.25	0.009427	*0*	6
8.5	0.009973	*0*	6
8.75	0.010539	*0*	6
9	0.011123	*0*	6
9.25	0.011727	*0*	6
9.5	0.012351	*0*	6
9.75	0.012995	*0*	6
10	0.013658	*0*	6
10.25	0.014343	*0*	6
10.5	0.015047	*0*	6

If your Mortgage is	25 Years Old		
and you prepay each month	**10% of the regular monthly payment**		
At this Interest rate (%)	Your interest savings factor is	You'll **save** this many years	and this many months
10.75	0.015773	*0*	6
11	0.01652	*0*	7
11.25	0.017288	*0*	7
11.5	0.018077	*0*	7
11.75	0.018889	*0*	7
12	0.019722	*0*	7
12.25	0.020577	*0*	7
12.5	0.021455	*0*	7
12.75	0.022356	*0*	7
13	0.023279	*0*	7
13.25	0.024226	*0*	7
13.5	0.025195	*0*	7
13.75	0.026188	*0*	7
14	0.027205	*0*	7
14.25	0.028245	*0*	7
14.5	0.02931	*0*	7
14.75	0.030399	*0*	7
15	0.031512	*0*	7
15.25	0.03265	*0*	7
15.5	0.033812	*0*	7
15.75	0.035	*0*	7
16	0.036212	*0*	7

NOTE: Find the row starting with your interest rate. To get your total interest savings
in dollars, just multiply the interest savings factor you find in that row by your **original**
mortgage balance. Read off your time savings in the same row.

FIXED PREPAYMENT METHOD
30-YEAR FIXED-RATE MORTGAGE SAVINGS TABLE

Refer to this table to quickly figure out your *total* interest and time savings
when you use the *Fixed Prepayment* method

If your Mortgage is	25 Years Old		
and you prepay each month	15% of the regular monthly payment		
At this Interest rate (%)	Your interest savings factor is	You'll save this many years	and this many months
5.25	0.006035	0	8
5.5	0.00652	0	8
5.75	0.007026	0	8
6	0.007554	0	8
6.25	0.008105	0	8
6.5	0.008678	0	9
6.75	0.009274	0	9
7	0.009894	0	9
7.25	0.010538	0	9
7.5	0.011206	0	9
7.75	0.011898	0	9
8	0.012616	0	9
8.25	0.013359	0	9
8.5	0.014127	0	9
8.75	0.014922	0	9
9	0.015743	0	9
9.25	0.016591	0	9
9.5	0.017466	0	9
9.75	0.018368	0	9
10	0.019297	0	9
10.25	0.020255	0	9
10.5	0.02124	0	9

If your Mortgage is	25 Years Old		
and you prepay each month	15% of the regular monthly payment		
At this Interest rate (%)	Your interest savings factor is	You'll save this many years	and this many months
10.75	0.022255	0	9
11	0.023298	0	9
11.25	0.02437	0	10
11.5	0.025471	0	10
11.75	0.026602	0	10
12	0.027762	0	10
12.25	0.028953	0	10
12.5	0.030174	0	10
12.75	0.031425	0	10
13	0.032707	0	10
13.25	0.03402	0	10
13.5	0.035365	0	10
13.75	0.036741	0	10
14	0.038148	0	10
14.25	0.039587	0	10
14.5	0.041059	0	10
14.75	0.042563	0	10
15	0.044099	0	10
15.25	0.045668	0	10
15.5	0.04727	0	10
15.75	0.048905	0	11
16	0.050573	0	11

NOTE: Find the row starting with your interest rate. To get your total interest savings
in dollars, just multiply the interest savings factor you find in that row by your *original*
mortgage balance. Read off your time savings in the same row.

FIXED PREPAYMENT METHOD
30-YEAR FIXED-RATE MORTGAGE SAVINGS TABLE

Refer to this table to quickly figure out your **total** interest and time savings
when you use the *Fixed Prepayment* method

If your Mortgage is	25 Years Old				If your Mortgage is	25 Years Old		
and you *prepay* each month	20% of the *regular monthly payment*				and you *prepay* each month	20% of the *regular monthly payment*		
At this Interest rate (%)	Your interest savings factor is	You'll *save* this many years	and this many months		At this Interest rate (%)	Your interest savings factor is	You'll *save* this many years	and this many months
5.25	0.007659	0	11		10.75	0.028012	1	0
5.5	0.008271	0	11		11	0.029313	1	0
5.75	0.00891	0	11		11.25	0.030649	1	0
6	0.009577	0	11		11.5	0.032021	1	0
6.25	0.010271	0	11		11.75	0.033429	1	0
6.5	0.010993	0	11		12	0.034873	1	0
6.75	0.011744	0	11		12.25	0.036354	1	0
7	0.012525	0	11		12.5	0.037871	1	0
7.25	0.013335	0	11		12.75	0.039425	1	1
7.5	0.014175	0	11		13	0.041017	1	1
7.75	0.015045	0	11		13.25	0.042645	1	1
8	0.015947	0	11		13.5	0.044312	1	1
8.25	0.01688	0	11		13.75	0.046016	1	1
8.5	0.017844	0	11		14	0.047758	1	1
8.75	0.018841	0	11		14.25	0.049539	1	1
9	0.01987	1	0		14.5	0.051358	1	1
9.25	0.020932	1	0		14.75	0.053216	1	1
9.5	0.022027	1	0		15	0.055113	1	1
9.75	0.023156	1	0		15.25	0.057048	1	1
10	0.024318	1	0		15.5	0.059023	1	1
10.25	0.025515	1	0		15.75	0.061037	1	1
10.5	0.026746	1	0		16	0.063091	1	1

NOTE: Find the row starting with your interest rate. To get your total interest savings
in dollars, just multiply the interest savings factor you find in that row by your **original**
mortgage balance. Read off your time savings in the same row.

FIXED PREPAYMENT METHOD
30-YEAR FIXED-RATE MORTGAGE SAVINGS TABLE

Refer to this table to quickly figure out your *total* interest and time savings
when you use the *Fixed Prepayment* method

If your Mortgage is	25 Years Old		
and you prepay each month	25% of the regular monthly payment		
At this Interest rate (%)	Your interest savings factor is	You'll *save* this many years	and this many months
5.25	0.009133	1	1
5.5	0.00986	1	1
5.75	0.010619	1	1
6	0.01141	1	1
6.25	0.012233	1	1
6.5	0.013089	1	1
6.75	0.013979	1	1
7	0.014903	1	1
7.25	0.015861	1	1
7.5	0.016855	1	1
7.75	0.017884	1	1
8	0.01895	1	2
8.25	0.020051	1	2
8.5	0.02119	1	2
8.75	0.022366	1	2
9	0.023579	1	2
9.25	0.024831	1	2
9.5	0.026121	1	2
9.75	0.02745	1	2
10	0.028818	1	2
10.25	0.030225	1	2
10.5	0.031673	1	2

If your Mortgage is	25 Years Old		
and you prepay each month	25% of the regular monthly payment		
At this Interest rate (%)	Your interest savings factor is	You'll *save* this many years	and this many months
10.75	0.03316	1	2
11	0.034688	1	2
11.25	0.036256	1	2
11.5	0.037866	1	3
11.75	0.039516	1	3
12	0.041209	1	3
12.25	0.042943	1	3
12.5	0.044718	1	3
12.75	0.046537	1	3
13	0.048397	1	3
13.25	0.050301	1	3
13.5	0.052247	1	3
13.75	0.054236	1	3
14	0.056268	1	3
14.25	0.058344	1	3
14.5	0.060464	1	3
14.75	0.062627	1	4
15	0.064834	1	4
15.25	0.067086	1	4
15.5	0.069382	1	4
15.75	0.071722	1	4
16	0.074106	1	4

NOTE: Find the row starting with your interest rate. To get your total interest savings in dollars, just multiply the interest savings factor you find in that row by your *original* mortgage balance. Read off your time savings in the same row.

FIXED PREPAYMENT METHOD
30-YEAR FIXED-RATE MORTGAGE SAVINGS TABLE

Refer to this table to quickly figure out your **total** interest and time savings
when you use the *Fixed Prepayment* method

If your Mortgage is	25 Years Old		
and you *prepay* **each month**	**30% of the** *regular* **monthly payment**		
At this Interest rate (%)	Your interest savings factor is	You'll *save* this many years	and this many months
5.25	0.010478	1	3
5.5	0.01131	1	3
5.75	0.012176	1	3
6	0.013079	1	3
6.25	0.014018	1	3
6.5	0.014995	1	3
6.75	0.01601	1	3
7	0.017063	1	3
7.25	0.018155	1	3
7.5	0.019287	1	3
7.75	0.020458	1	4
8	0.02167	1	4
8.25	0.022923	1	4
8.5	0.024217	1	4
8.75	0.025553	1	4
9	0.026932	1	4
9.25	0.028353	1	4
9.5	0.029816	1	4
9.75	0.031323	1	4
10	0.032874	1	4
10.25	0.034469	1	4
10.5	0.036108	1	4

If your Mortgage is	25 Years Old		
and you *prepay* **each month**	**30% of the** *regular* **monthly payment**		
At this Interest rate (%)	Your interest savings factor is	You'll *save* this many years	and this many months
10.75	0.037792	1	4
11	0.039521	1	5
11.25	0.041294	1	5
11.5	0.043114	1	5
11.75	0.044979	1	5
12	0.04689	1	5
12.25	0.048847	1	5
12.5	0.050851	1	5
12.75	0.052901	1	5
13	0.054998	1	5
13.25	0.057142	1	5
13.5	0.059334	1	5
13.75	0.061572	1	5
14	0.063859	1	5
14.25	0.066192	1	6
14.5	0.068574	1	6
14.75	0.071004	1	6
15	0.073482	1	6
15.25	0.076008	1	6
15.5	0.078583	1	6
15.75	0.081206	1	6
16	0.083877	1	6

NOTE: Find the row starting with your interest rate. To get your total interest savings
in dollars, just multiply the interest savings factor you find in that row by your **original**
mortgage balance. Read off your time savings in the same row.

FIXED PREPAYMENT METHOD
15-YEAR FIXED-RATE MORTGAGE SAVINGS TABLE

Refer to this table to quickly figure out your *total* interest and time savings when you use the *Fixed Prepayment* method

If your Mortgage is	Brand New		
and you prepay each month	**5% of the regular monthly payment**		
At this Interest rate (%)	Your interest savings factor is	You'll *save* this many years	and this many months
5.25	0.034585	1	0
5.5	0.037265	1	0
5.75	0.040066	1	1
6	0.042992	1	1
6.25	0.046047	1	1
6.5	0.049234	1	1
6.75	0.052559	1	2
7	0.056025	1	2
7.25	0.059637	1	2
7.5	0.063399	1	3
7.75	0.067316	1	3
8	0.071393	1	3
8.25	0.075633	1	3
8.5	0.080042	1	4
8.75	0.084625	1	4
9	0.089386	1	4
9.25	0.094331	1	5
9.5	0.099464	1	5
9.75	0.10479	1	5
10	0.110315	1	6
10.25	0.116043	1	6
10.5	0.121979	1	7

If your Mortgage is	Brand New		
and you prepay each month	**5% of the regular monthly payment**		
At this Interest rate (%)	Your interest savings factor is	You'll *save* this many years	and this many months
10.75	0.128129	1	7
11	0.134498	1	7
11.25	0.141091	1	8
11.5	0.147913	1	8
11.75	0.154969	1	9
12	0.162265	1	9
12.25	0.169805	1	9
12.5	0.177595	1	10
12.75	0.18564	1	10
13	0.193944	1	11
13.25	0.202514	1	11
13.5	0.211353	2	0
13.75	0.220467	2	0
14	0.22986	2	1
14.25	0.239538	2	1
14.5	0.249504	2	1
14.75	0.259763	2	2
15	0.270321	2	2
15.25	0.28118	2	3
15.5	0.292346	2	3
15.75	0.303822	2	4
16	0.315612	2	5

NOTE: Find the row starting with your interest rate. To get your total interest savings in dollars, just multiply the interest savings factor you find in that row by your *original* mortgage balance. Read off your time savings in the same row.

FIXED PREPAYMENT METHOD
15-YEAR FIXED-RATE MORTGAGE SAVINGS TABLE

Refer to this table to quickly figure out your **total** interest and time savings
when you use the *Fixed Prepayment* method

If your Mortgage is	Brand New		
and you *prepay* each month	**10% of the *regular monthly payment***		
At this Interest rate (%)	Your interest savings factor is	You'll **save** this many years	and this many months
5.25	0.064058	*1*	*11*
5.5	0.068893	*2*	*0*
5.75	0.073929	*2*	*0*
6	0.079172	*2*	*0*
6.25	0.084626	*2*	*1*
6.5	0.090298	*2*	*1*
6.75	0.096192	*2*	*2*
7	0.102314	*2*	*2*
7.25	0.10867	*2*	*3*
7.5	0.115265	*2*	*3*
7.75	0.122104	*2*	*4*
8	0.129193	*2*	*4*
8.25	0.136537	*2*	*5*
8.5	0.144141	*2*	*5*
8.75	0.152011	*2*	*6*
9	0.160152	*2*	*6*
9.25	0.168569	*2*	*7*
9.5	0.177267	*2*	*7*
9.75	0.186252	*2*	*8*
10	0.195527	*2*	*8*
10.25	0.205099	*2*	*9*
10.5	0.21497	*2*	*10*

If your Mortgage is	Brand New		
and you *prepay* each month	**10% of the *regular monthly payment***		
At this Interest rate (%)	Your interest savings factor is	You'll **save** this many years	and this many months
10.75	0.225147	*2*	*10*
11	0.235633	*2*	*11*
11.25	0.246433	*2*	*11*
11.5	0.257551	*3*	*0*
11.75	0.26899	*3*	*1*
12	0.280755	*3*	*1*
12.25	0.29285	*3*	*2*
12.5	0.305277	*3*	*2*
12.75	0.318039	*3*	*3*
13	0.331141	*3*	*4*
13.25	0.344584	*3*	*4*
13.5	0.358371	*3*	*5*
13.75	0.372506	*3*	*6*
14	0.386989	*3*	*6*
14.25	0.401822	*3*	*7*
14.5	0.417008	*3*	*8*
14.75	0.432548	*3*	*8*
15	0.448443	*3*	*9*
15.25	0.464695	*3*	*10*
15.5	0.481303	*3*	*10*
15.75	0.498268	*3*	*11*
16	0.515591	*4*	*0*

NOTE: Find the row starting with your interest rate. To get your total interest savings
in dollars, just multiply the interest savings factor you find in that row by your **original**
mortgage balance. Read off your time savings in the same row.

FIXED PREPAYMENT METHOD
15-YEAR FIXED-RATE MORTGAGE SAVINGS TABLE

Refer to this table to quickly figure out your *total* interest and time savings when you use the *Fixed Prepayment* method

If your Mortgage is	Brand New		
and you prepay each month	**15% of the regular monthly payment**		
At this Interest rate (%)	Your interest savings factor is	You'll **save** this many years	and this many months
5.25	0.089494	2	9
5.5	0.096097	2	9
5.75	0.102955	2	10
6	0.110074	2	10
6.25	0.11746	2	11
6.5	0.125118	2	11
6.75	0.133053	3	0
7	0.141271	3	1
7.25	0.149776	3	1
7.5	0.158575	3	2
7.75	0.167671	3	2
8	0.17707	3	3
8.25	0.186776	3	4
8.5	0.196794	3	4
8.75	0.207128	3	5
9	0.217783	3	6
9.25	0.228762	3	6
9.5	0.24007	3	7
9.75	0.25171	3	8
10	0.263686	3	8
10.25	0.276001	3	9
10.5	0.288659	3	10

If your Mortgage is	Brand New		
and you prepay each month	**15% of the regular monthly payment**		
At this Interest rate (%)	Your interest savings factor is	You'll **save** this many years	and this many months
10.75	0.301662	3	10
11	0.315012	3	11
11.25	0.328713	4	0
11.5	0.342766	4	0
11.75	0.357174	4	1
12	0.371938	4	2
12.25	0.38706	4	3
12.5	0.402541	4	3
12.75	0.418382	4	4
13	0.434583	4	5
13.25	0.451146	4	6
13.5	0.468071	4	6
13.75	0.485357	4	7
14	0.503004	4	8
14.25	0.521012	4	9
14.5	0.53938	4	9
14.75	0.558107	4	10
15	0.577192	4	11
15.25	0.596633	5	0
15.5	0.616429	5	0
15.75	0.636577	5	1
16	0.657076	5	2

NOTE: Find the row starting with your interest rate. To get your total interest savings in dollars, just multiply the interest savings factor you find in that row by your *original* mortgage balance. Read off your time savings in the same row.

FIXED PREPAYMENT METHOD
15-YEAR FIXED-RATE MORTGAGE SAVINGS TABLE

Refer to this table to quickly figure out your **total** interest and time savings
when you use the *Fixed Prepayment* method

If your Mortgage is	Brand New			If your Mortgage is	Brand New		
and you *prepay* each month	20% of the *regular monthly payment*			and you *prepay* each month	20% of the *regular monthly payment*		
At this Interest rate (%)	Your interest savings factor is	You'll **save** this many years	and this many months	At this Interest rate (%)	Your interest savings factor is	You'll **save** this many years	and this many months
5.25	0.111683	3	5	10.75	0.363817	4	9
5.5	0.11976	3	6	11	0.379266	4	9
5.75	0.12813	3	6	11.25	0.395079	4	10
6	0.136798	3	7	11.5	0.411256	4	11
6.25	0.145769	3	8	11.75	0.427797	5	0
6.5	0.155049	3	8	12	0.444702	5	0
6.75	0.164642	3	9	12.25	0.461972	5	1
7	0.174552	3	10	12.5	0.479605	5	2
7.25	0.184784	3	10	12.75	0.497601	5	3
7.5	0.195342	3	11	13	0.515959	5	3
7.75	0.20623	4	0	13.25	0.534678	5	4
8	0.217452	4	0	13.5	0.553756	5	5
8.25	0.229012	4	1	13.75	0.573192	5	6
8.5	0.240912	4	2	14	0.592984	5	7
8.75	0.253157	4	3	14.25	0.613129	5	7
9	0.265749	4	3	14.5	0.633626	5	8
9.25	0.27869	4	4	14.75	0.654471	5	9
9.5	0.291985	4	5	15	0.675662	5	10
9.75	0.305634	4	6	15.25	0.697197	5	11
10	0.31964	4	6	15.5	0.719071	5	11
10.25	0.334005	4	7	15.75	0.741282	6	0
10.5	0.34873	4	8	16	0.763827	6	1

NOTE: Find the row starting with your interest rate. To get your total interest savings
in dollars, just multiply the interest savings factor you find in that row by your **original**
mortgage balance. Read off your time savings in the same row.

FIXED PREPAYMENT METHOD
15-YEAR FIXED-RATE MORTGAGE SAVINGS TABLE

Refer to this table to quickly figure out your **total** interest and time savings when you use the *Fixed Prepayment* method

If your Mortgage is	Brand New			If your Mortgage is	Brand New		
and you prepay each month	25% of the regular monthly payment			and you prepay each month	25% of the regular monthly payment		
At this Interest rate (%)	Your interest savings factor is	You'll save this many years	and this many months	At this Interest rate (%)	Your interest savings factor is	You'll save this many years	and this many months
5.25	0.131218	4	1	10.75	0.415459	5	5
5.5	0.140542	4	1	11	0.432508	5	6
5.75	0.150185	4	2	11.25	0.449922	5	7
6	0.160152	4	3	11.5	0.467701	5	8
6.25	0.170447	4	3	11.75	0.485843	5	8
6.5	0.181075	4	4	12	0.504348	5	9
6.75	0.192038	4	5	12.25	0.523215	5	10
7	0.203342	4	6	12.5	0.54244	5	11
7.25	0.214988	4	6	12.75	0.562023	6	0
7.5	0.226981	4	7	13	0.581961	6	0
7.75	0.239324	4	8	13.25	0.602253	6	1
8	0.252019	4	9	13.5	0.622894	6	2
8.25	0.265068	4	9	13.75	0.643883	6	3
8.5	0.278475	4	10	14	0.665217	6	3
8.75	0.292241	4	11	14.25	0.686892	6	4
9	0.306368	5	0	14.5	0.708905	6	5
9.25	0.320857	5	0	14.75	0.731252	6	6
9.5	0.33571	5	1	15	0.753931	6	7
9.75	0.350928	5	2	15.25	0.776937	6	7
10	0.366512	5	3	15.5	0.800266	6	8
10.25	0.382461	5	4	15.75	0.823915	6	9
10.5	0.398777	5	4	16	0.847879	6	10

NOTE: Find the row starting with your interest rate. To get your total interest savings in dollars, just multiply the interest savings factor you find in that row by your **original** mortgage balance. Read off your time savings in the same row.

FIXED PREPAYMENT METHOD
15-YEAR FIXED-RATE MORTGAGE SAVINGS TABLE

Refer to this table to quickly figure out your *total* interest and time savings
when you use the *Fixed Prepayment* method

If your Mortgage is	5 Years Old		
and you *prepay* each month	**10% of the regular monthly payment**		
At this Interest rate (%)	Your interest savings factor is	You'll *save* this many years	and this many months
5.25	0.026513	*1*	*1*
5.5	0.028422	*1*	*2*
5.75	0.030401	*1*	*2*
6	0.032453	*1*	*2*
6.25	0.034578	*1*	*2*
6.5	0.03678	*1*	*2*
6.75	0.039059	*1*	*2*
7	0.041417	*1*	*3*
7.25	0.043856	*1*	*3*
7.5	0.046378	*1*	*3*
7.75	0.048984	*1*	*3*
8	0.051676	*1*	*3*
8.25	0.054456	*1*	*4*
8.5	0.057326	*1*	*4*
8.75	0.060287	*1*	*4*
9	0.063342	*1*	*4*
9.25	0.066492	*1*	*4*
9.5	0.069739	*1*	*4*
9.75	0.073084	*1*	*5*
10	0.07653	*1*	*5*
10.25	0.080078	*1*	*5*
10.5	0.083731	*1*	*5*

If your Mortgage is	5 Years Old		
and you *prepay* each month	**10% of the regular monthly payment**		
At this Interest rate (%)	Your interest savings factor is	You'll *save* this many years	and this many months
10.75	0.087489	*1*	*6*
11	0.091355	*1*	*6*
11.25	0.09533	*1*	*6*
11.5	0.099417	*1*	*6*
11.75	0.103617	*1*	*6*
12	0.107932	*1*	*7*
12.25	0.112363	*1*	*7*
12.5	0.116912	*1*	*7*
12.75	0.121582	*1*	*7*
13	0.126374	*1*	*7*
13.25	0.131289	*1*	*8*
13.5	0.136329	*1*	*8*
13.75	0.141497	*1*	*8*
14	0.146793	*1*	*8*
14.25	0.152219	*1*	*9*
14.5	0.157777	*1*	*9*
14.75	0.163468	*1*	*9*
15	0.169295	*1*	*9*
15.25	0.175258	*1*	*10*
15.5	0.181359	*1*	*10*
15.75	0.1876	*1*	*10*
16	0.193982	*1*	*10*

NOTE: Find the row starting with your interest rate. To get your total interest savings
in dollars, just multiply the interest savings factor you find in that row by your ***original***
mortgage balance. Read off your time savings in the same row.

FIXED PREPAYMENT METHOD
15-YEAR FIXED-RATE MORTGAGE SAVINGS TABLE

Refer to this table to quickly figure out your ***total*** interest and time savings when you use the *Fixed Prepayment* method

If your Mortgage is	5 Years Old		
and you *prepay* each month	15% of the regular monthly payment		
At this Interest rate (%)	Your interest savings factor is	You'll *save* this many years	and this many months
5.25	0.037424	1	7
5.5	0.040081	1	7
5.75	0.042833	1	8
6	0.04568	1	8
6.25	0.048626	1	8
6.5	0.051672	1	8
6.75	0.05482	1	9
7	0.058072	1	9
7.25	0.06143	1	9
7.5	0.064896	1	9
7.75	0.068472	1	9
8	0.07216	1	10
8.25	0.075962	1	10
8.5	0.07988	1	10
8.75	0.083915	1	10
9	0.08807	1	11
9.25	0.092347	1	11
9.5	0.096747	1	11
9.75	0.101273	1	11
10	0.105925	2	0
10.25	0.110707	2	0
10.5	0.11562	2	0

If your Mortgage is	5 Years Old		
and you *prepay* each month	15% of the regular monthly payment		
At this Interest rate (%)	Your interest savings factor is	You'll *save* this many years	and this many months
10.75	0.120665	2	1
11	0.125845	2	1
11.25	0.131161	2	1
11.5	0.136616	2	1
11.75	0.142209	2	2
12	0.147945	2	2
12.25	0.153823	2	2
12.5	0.159845	2	2
12.75	0.166014	2	3
13	0.172331	2	3
13.25	0.178796	2	3
13.5	0.185413	2	4
13.75	0.192181	2	4
14	0.199103	2	4
14.25	0.206179	2	4
14.5	0.213412	2	5
14.75	0.220802	2	5
15	0.22835	2	5
15.25	0.236058	2	6
15.5	0.243926	2	6
15.75	0.251957	2	6
16	0.26015	2	7

NOTE: Find the row starting with your interest rate. To get your total interest savings in dollars, just multiply the interest savings factor you find in that row by your ***original*** mortgage balance. Read off your time savings in the same row.

FIXED PREPAYMENT METHOD
15-YEAR FIXED-RATE MORTGAGE SAVINGS TABLE

Refer to this table to quickly figure out your **total** interest and time savings
when you use the *Fixed Prepayment* method

If your Mortgage is	5 Years Old		
and you *prepay* each month	20% of the *regular monthly payment*		
At this Interest rate (%)	Your interest savings factor is	You'll *save* this many years	and this many months
5.25	0.047122	2	0
5.5	0.050427	2	1
5.75	0.053845	2	1
6	0.057378	2	1
6.25	0.061028	2	1
6.5	0.064796	2	2
6.75	0.068685	2	2
7	0.072697	2	2
7.25	0.076834	2	3
7.5	0.081098	2	3
7.75	0.08549	2	3
8	0.090014	2	3
8.25	0.094671	2	4
8.5	0.099462	2	4
8.75	0.10439	2	4
9	0.109457	2	4
9.25	0.114664	2	5
9.5	0.120013	2	5
9.75	0.125506	2	5
10	0.131145	2	6
10.25	0.136931	2	6
10.5	0.142867	2	6

If your Mortgage is	5 Years Old		
and you *prepay* each month	20% of the *regular monthly payment*		
At this Interest rate (%)	Your interest savings factor is	You'll *save* this many years	and this many months
10.75	0.148953	2	7
11	0.155192	2	7
11.25	0.161584	2	7
11.5	0.168132	2	7
11.75	0.174837	2	8
12	0.1817	2	8
12.25	0.188722	2	8
12.5	0.195906	2	9
12.75	0.203252	2	9
13	0.210761	2	9
13.25	0.218434	2	10
13.5	0.226274	2	10
13.75	0.23428	2	10
14	0.242454	2	11
14.25	0.250796	2	11
14.5	0.259308	2	11
14.75	0.267991	3	0
15	0.276844	3	0
15.25	0.285869	3	0
15.5	0.295067	3	1
15.75	0.304437	3	1
16	0.313982	3	1

NOTE: Find the row starting with your interest rate. To get your total interest savings
in dollars, just multiply the interest savings factor you find in that row by your **original**
mortgage balance. Read off your time savings in the same row.

FIXED PREPAYMENT METHOD
15-YEAR FIXED-RATE MORTGAGE SAVINGS TABLE

Refer to this table to quickly figure out your *total* interest and time savings
when you use the *Fixed Prepayment* method

If your Mortgage is	5 Years Old		
and you prepay each month	**25% of the regular monthly payment**		
At this Interest rate (%)	Your interest savings factor is	You'll **save** this many years	and this many months
5.25	0.0558	2	5
5.5	0.059672	2	5
5.75	0.063671	2	6
6	0.067799	2	6
6.25	0.072059	2	6
6.5	0.076451	2	7
6.75	0.080979	2	7
7	0.085645	2	7
7.25	0.09045	2	7
7.5	0.095396	2	8
7.75	0.100486	2	8
8	0.105721	2	8
8.25	0.111102	2	9
8.5	0.116633	2	9
8.75	0.122314	2	9
9	0.128148	2	10
9.25	0.134135	2	10
9.5	0.140278	2	10
9.75	0.146579	2	11
10	0.153038	2	11
10.25	0.159658	2	11
10.5	0.166439	3	0

If your Mortgage is	5 Years Old		
and you prepay each month	**25% of the regular monthly payment**		
At this Interest rate (%)	Your interest savings factor is	You'll **save** this many years	and this many months
10.75	0.173383	3	0
11	0.180492	3	0
11.25	0.187767	3	1
11.5	0.195209	3	1
11.75	0.202818	3	1
12	0.210598	3	2
12.25	0.218547	3	2
12.5	0.226668	3	2
12.75	0.234961	3	3
13	0.243428	3	3
13.25	0.252068	3	3
13.5	0.260883	3	4
13.75	0.269873	3	4
14	0.27904	3	4
14.25	0.288383	3	5
14.5	0.297903	3	5
14.75	0.3076	3	5
15	0.317476	3	6
15.25	0.327529	3	6
15.5	0.337761	3	6
15.75	0.348171	3	7
16	0.358761	3	7

NOTE: Find the row starting with your interest rate. To get your total interest savings
in dollars, just multiply the interest savings factor you find in that row by your *original*
mortgage balance. Read off your time savings in the same row.

FIXED PREPAYMENT METHOD
15-YEAR FIXED-RATE MORTGAGE SAVINGS TABLE

Refer to this table to quickly figure out your *total* interest and time savings
when you use the *Fixed Prepayment* method

If your Mortgage is	10 Years Old		
and you *prepay* each month	20% of the regular monthly payment		
At this Interest rate (%)	Your interest savings factor is	You'll *save* this many years	and this many months
5.25	0.011149	0	11
5.5	0.011903	0	11
5.75	0.012679	0	11
6	0.013479	0	11
6.25	0.014303	0	11
6.5	0.015151	0	11
6.75	0.016023	0	11
7	0.016921	0	11
7.25	0.017844	0	11
7.5	0.018793	0	11
7.75	0.019768	0	11
8	0.020769	0	11
8.25	0.021798	0	11
8.5	0.022853	0	11
8.75	0.023936	0	11
9	0.025047	1	0
9.25	0.026186	1	0
9.5	0.027354	1	0
9.75	0.028551	1	0
10	0.029778	1	0
10.25	0.031034	1	0
10.5	0.03232	1	0

If your Mortgage is	10 Years Old		
and you *prepay* each month	20% of the regular monthly payment		
At this Interest rate (%)	Your interest savings factor is	You'll *save* this many years	and this many months
10.75	0.033637	1	0
11	0.034985	1	0
11.25	0.036363	1	0
11.5	0.037773	1	0
11.75	0.039215	1	0
12	0.040689	1	0
12.25	0.042196	1	0
12.5	0.043735	1	0
12.75	0.045308	1	1
13	0.046914	1	1
13.25	0.048553	1	1
13.5	0.050227	1	1
13.75	0.051935	1	1
14	0.053678	1	1
14.25	0.055456	1	1
14.5	0.057269	1	1
14.75	0.059118	1	1
15	0.061003	1	1
15.25	0.062924	1	1
15.5	0.064881	1	1
15.75	0.066875	1	1
16	0.068906	1	1

NOTE: Find the row starting with your interest rate. To get your total interest savings
in dollars, just multiply the interest savings factor you find in that row by your *original*
mortgage balance. Read off your time savings in the same row.

FIXED PREPAYMENT METHOD
15-YEAR FIXED-RATE MORTGAGE SAVINGS TABLE

Refer to this table to quickly figure out your *total* interest and time savings
when you use the *Fixed Prepayment* method

If your Mortgage is	10 Years Old			If your Mortgage is	10 Years Old		
and you *prepay* each month	25% of the *regular monthly payment*			and you *prepay* each month	25% of the *regular monthly payment*		
At this Interest rate (%)	Your interest savings factor is	You'll *save* this many years	and this many months	*At this Interest rate (%)*	Your interest savings factor is	You'll *save* this many years	and this many months
5.25	0.013296	1	1	10.75	0.039819	1	2
5.5	0.01419	1	1	11	0.0414	1	2
5.75	0.015111	1	1	11.25	0.043016	1	2
6	0.016059	1	1	11.5	0.044668	1	3
6.25	0.017035	1	1	11.75	0.046356	1	3
6.5	0.018039	1	1	12	0.048081	1	3
6.75	0.019072	1	1	12.25	0.049844	1	3
7	0.020134	1	1	12.5	0.051643	1	3
7.25	0.021225	1	1	12.75	0.05348	1	3
7.5	0.022346	1	1	13	0.055355	1	3
7.75	0.023498	1	1	13.25	0.057269	1	3
8	0.02468	1	2	13.5	0.059221	1	3
8.25	0.025893	1	2	13.75	0.061212	1	3
8.5	0.027138	1	2	14	0.063243	1	3
8.75	0.028414	1	2	14.25	0.065313	1	3
9	0.029723	1	2	14.5	0.067423	1	3
9.25	0.031064	1	2	14.75	0.069573	1	4
9.5	0.032439	1	2	15	0.071764	1	4
9.75	0.033846	1	2	15.25	0.073995	1	4
10	0.035288	1	2	15.5	0.076268	1	4
10.25	0.036764	1	2	15.75	0.078581	1	4
10.5	0.038274	1	2	16	0.080937	1	4

NOTE: Find the row starting with your interest rate. To get your total interest savings
in dollars, just multiply the interest savings factor you find in that row by your ***original***
mortgage balance. Read off your time savings in the same row.

FIXED PREPAYMENT METHOD
15-YEAR FIXED-RATE MORTGAGE SAVINGS TABLE

Refer to this table to quickly figure out your *total* interest and time savings
when you use the *Fixed Prepayment* method

If your Mortgage is	10 Years Old		
and you *prepay* each month	30% of the *regular monthly payment*		
At this Interest rate (%)	Your interest savings factor is	You'll *save* this many years	and this many months
5.25	0.015254	1	3
5.5	0.016275	1	3
5.75	0.017326	1	3
6	0.018408	1	3
6.25	0.019521	1	3
6.5	0.020666	1	3
6.75	0.021843	1	3
7	0.023052	1	3
7.25	0.024294	1	3
7.5	0.02557	1	3
7.75	0.02688	1	4
8	0.028223	1	4
8.25	0.029602	1	4
8.5	0.031015	1	4
8.75	0.032464	1	4
9	0.033949	1	4
9.25	0.03547	1	4
9.5	0.037028	1	4
9.75	0.038623	1	4
10	0.040255	1	4
10.25	0.041926	1	4
10.5	0.043634	1	4

If your Mortgage is	10 Years Old		
and you *prepay* each month	30% of the *regular monthly payment*		
At this Interest rate (%)	Your interest savings factor is	You'll *save* this many years	and this many months
10.75	0.045382	1	4
11	0.047168	1	5
11.25	0.048993	1	5
11.5	0.050859	1	5
11.75	0.052764	1	5
12	0.05471	1	5
12.25	0.056697	1	5
12.5	0.058725	1	5
12.75	0.060794	1	5
13	0.062905	1	5
13.25	0.065059	1	5
13.5	0.067254	1	5
13.75	0.069493	1	5
14	0.071774	1	5
14.25	0.074099	1	6
14.5	0.076467	1	6
14.75	0.078879	1	6
15	0.081336	1	6
15.25	0.083836	1	6
15.5	0.086382	1	6
15.75	0.088972	1	6
16	0.091608	1	6

NOTE: Find the row starting with your interest rate. To get your total interest savings
in dollars, just multiply the interest savings factor you find in that row by your *original*
mortgage balance. Read off your time savings in the same row.

FIXED PREPAYMENT METHOD
15-YEAR FIXED-RATE MORTGAGE SAVINGS TABLE

Refer to this table to quickly figure out your ***total*** interest and time savings
when you use the *Fixed Prepayment* method

If your Mortgage is	10 Years Old
and you **prepay** each month	60% of the **regular monthly payment**

At this Interest rate (%)	Your interest savings factor is	You'll **save** this many years	and this many months
5.25	0.024147	2	0
5.5	0.025729	2	0
5.75	0.027356	2	0
6	0.029026	2	0
6.25	0.030741	2	0
6.5	0.032501	2	0
6.75	0.034307	2	0
7	0.036159	2	1
7.25	0.038057	2	1
7.5	0.040003	2	1
7.75	0.041996	2	1
8	0.044036	2	1
8.25	0.046126	2	1
8.5	0.048264	2	1
8.75	0.050451	2	1
9	0.052688	2	1
9.25	0.054975	2	1
9.5	0.057312	2	1
9.75	0.0597	2	2
10	0.062139	2	2
10.25	0.06463	2	2
10.5	0.067173	2	2

If your Mortgage is	10 Years Old
and you **prepay** each month	60% of the **regular monthly payment**

At this Interest rate (%)	Your interest savings factor is	You'll **save** this many years	and this many months
10.75	0.069768	2	2
11	0.072415	2	2
11.25	0.075116	2	2
11.5	0.077869	2	2
11.75	0.080676	2	2
12	0.083537	2	2
12.25	0.086452	2	2
12.5	0.089421	2	3
12.75	0.092444	2	3
13	0.095522	2	3
13.25	0.098656	2	3
13.5	0.101844	2	3
13.75	0.105088	2	3
14	0.108388	2	3
14.25	0.111743	2	3
14.5	0.115155	2	3
14.75	0.118622	2	3
15	0.122146	2	3
15.25	0.125726	2	4
15.5	0.129363	2	4
15.75	0.133056	2	4
16	0.136806	2	4

NOTE: Find the row starting with your interest rate. To get your total interest savings in dollars, just multiply the interest savings factor you find in that row by your ***original*** mortgage balance. Read off your time savings in the same row.

Notes

Appendix H	*Special Interest Savings Tables* **For The** **Term-Based Prepayment Method**

This appendix offers special tables that will give you a quick idea of what dollar savings to expect when you use the *term-based prepayment method* to cut a specific number of years off your mortgage term. You also find factors that tell you exactly how much you need to prepay every month to get those results.

The tables give factors to reduce a 30-year fixed-rate mortgage term by 5, 10, 15, 20, or 25 years, depending on the age of the mortgage. They also contain factors to reduce a *15-year* fixed-rate mortgage term by 2, 3, 4, 5, 8, or 10 years, depending on the age of the mortgage.

So, it doesn't matter what your particular loan amount was. To get answers, just decide how many years you want to cut from your mortgage term. If that number of years is not featured in the tables, work with the table number that's nearest to your choice for a ballpark answer.

The tables carry interest rates ranging from **5.25%** to **16%** by increments of 0.25%. If your particular interest rate is not shown, just use the closest *lower* rate to get a good ballpark estimate. For example, if your annual interest rate is 8.8%, just pick 8.75% in the table.

Two sets of tables give answers for **30-year** and **15-year** fixed-rate mortgages. The factors in the *30-year* tables give *exact* answers for mortgage ages ranging from 0 to 25 years old by 5 year increments. The factors in the *15-year* tables give *exact* answers for mortgage ages ranging from 0 to 10 years old by 5 year increments.

You can use the tables productively even if you don't find the exact *current* age of your mortgage. Just use the factor for the *next higher* age as an *approximate* factor. For instance, if your mortgage is 3 years old now, work with the **5 years Old** column. You then find out *exactly* what you should prepay and what savings you would get *if you were to wait to start the method when your mortgage is 5 years old.* But, if you start now, you will save even MORE and end the term even SOONER than the table indicates.

Study the action steps and examples on the next page.

Follow these easy steps to find your expected total interest savings.

STEP	ACTION
1	Find the column with your exact mortgage **AGE** and the *number of years* by which you want to CUT the term. **If you don't find your exact mortgage age, use the *next higher* mortgage age. The factors you find will give you approximate results.**
2	Under that column, find the row starting with your interest rate, to locate a *prepayment* factor.
3	To get your *required monthly prepayment* in dollars, multiply the *prepayment* factor you find at that location by your **original** monthly payment.
4	Next in the same row, locate the interest savings factor.
5	To get your total interest savings in dollars, multiply the interest savings factor you find at that location by your **original** mortgage balance.

Example

Use the following tables. Say your *brand new* mortgage balance is $80,000 for 30 years at 10% with a monthly payment of $702.06. Say also that you want to CUT the term by *5* years.

First, go over to the column with the **exact** age of your mortgage that specifies a *5-year CUT*. Next, look down the *rate* column to find the row that starts with interest rate *10*.

Find the *prepayment* factor right next to the interest rate. Multiply *prepayment* factor *0.035472* by $702.06 to get your *necessary* prepayment of *$24.90*.

Move to the right to find the interest savings factor in that row. Multiply interest savings factor *0.433155* by $80,000 to get your total interest savings of *$34,652.40*.

Second Example

It's the same mortgage of $80,000 for 30 years at 10%. Suppose you've had the mortgage for **eight years**. Say also that you want to CUT the term by *15* years.

First, go over to the column with the **next higher age** of your mortgage that specifies a **15-year CUT**. In this case, it's a **10 Years Old** column. Next, find the row starting with interest rate **10**. Find the *prepayment* factor right next to the interest rate. Multiply *prepayment* factor *1.201717* by $702.06 to get your *necessary* **prepayment** of *$843.67*.

Move to the right to find the interest savings factor in that row. Multiply interest savings factor *0.946873* by $80,000 to get your total interest savings of *$75,749.84*. If you start prepaying now, you will save MORE than that amount and end the mortgage in LESS than *FIVE* years from the point the mortgage is 10 years old.

TERM-BASED PREPAYMENT METHOD
30-YEAR FIXED-RATE MORTGAGE SAVINGS TABLE

Refer to this table to quickly figure out your interest savings
when you use the *Term-based Prepayment* method

If your Mortgage is	Brand New	
and you want to CUT the term by	5 years	
Find your Interest rate below (%)	Then prepay by this factor each month	To get this interest savings factor
5.25	0.085193	0.19019
5.5	0.081542	0.201778
5.75	0.078025	0.213543
6	0.074641	0.225478
6.25	0.071384	0.237574
6.5	0.068251	0.249823
6.75	0.065238	0.262219
7	0.062343	0.274751
7.25	0.05956	0.287414
7.5	0.056888	0.300199
7.75	0.054321	0.313098
8	0.051858	0.326104
8.25	0.049494	0.339209
8.5	0.047227	0.352407
8.75	0.045053	0.365691
9	0.042969	0.379052
9.25	0.040972	0.392486
9.5	0.039058	0.405985
9.75	0.037226	0.419544
10	0.035472	0.433155
10.25	0.033793	0.446815
10.5	0.032187	0.460516

If your Mortgage is	Brand New	
and you want to CUT the term by	5 years	
Find your Interest rate below (%)	Then prepay by this factor each month	To get this interest savings factor
10.75	0.03065	0.474255
11	0.029181	0.488025
11.25	0.027776	0.501822
11.5	0.026434	0.515642
11.75	0.025152	0.52948
12	0.023927	0.543333
12.25	0.022757	0.557196
12.5	0.021641	0.571066
12.75	0.020575	0.584939
13	0.019559	0.598812
13.25	0.018589	0.612683
13.5	0.017664	0.626549
13.75	0.016782	0.640407
14	0.015942	0.654255
14.25	0.015141	0.668091
14.5	0.014378	0.681913
14.75	0.013652	0.695718
15	0.01296	0.709507
15.25	0.012301	0.723276
15.5	0.011674	0.737025
15.75	0.011077	0.750753
16	0.010509	0.764459

NOTE: Find the row starting with your interest rate. To get the *necessary* prepayment amount in dollars, just multiply the prepayment factor in that row by the *regular monthly payment*. To get your total interest savings in dollars, just multiply the interest savings factor by your **original** mortgage balance.

TERM-BASED PREPAYMENT METHOD
30-YEAR FIXED-RATE MORTGAGE SAVINGS TABLE

Refer to this table to quickly figure out your interest savings
when you use the *Term-based Prepayment* method

If your Mortgage is	Brand New	
and you want to CUT the term by	10 years	
Find your Interest rate below (%)	Then prepay by this factor each month	To get this interest savings factor
5.25	0.220282	0.370707
5.5	0.211519	0.393111
5.75	0.203078	0.415862
6	0.194947	0.438947
6.25	0.187117	0.462354
6.5	0.179577	0.486069
6.75	0.172319	0.51008
7	0.165333	0.534372
7.25	0.15861	0.558932
7.5	0.15214	0.583749
7.75	0.145916	0.608808
8	0.13993	0.634096
8.25	0.134172	0.659602
8.5	0.128636	0.685313
8.75	0.123313	0.711216
9	0.118196	0.737299
9.25	0.113278	0.763551
9.5	0.108553	0.78996
9.75	0.104012	0.816515
10	0.09965	0.843206
10.25	0.09546	0.870021
10.5	0.091437	0.89695

If your Mortgage is	Brand New	
and you want to CUT the term by	10 years	
Find your Interest rate below (%)	Then prepay by this factor each month	To get this interest savings factor
10.75	0.087573	0.923983
11	0.083863	0.951112
11.25	0.080302	0.978327
11.5	0.076885	1.005618
11.75	0.073605	1.032978
12	0.070458	1.060399
12.25	0.067438	1.087872
12.5	0.064542	1.115391
12.75	0.061764	1.142948
13	0.0591	1.170537
13.25	0.056545	1.198151
13.5	0.054096	1.225785
13.75	0.051749	1.253432
14	0.049498	1.281088
14.25	0.047342	1.308748
14.5	0.045275	1.336407
14.75	0.043295	1.36406
15	0.041398	1.391703
15.25	0.039581	1.419334
15.5	0.037841	1.446947
15.75	0.036174	1.474541
16	0.034578	1.502111

NOTE: Find the row starting with your interest rate. To get the *necessary* prepayment amount in dollars, just multiply the prepayment factor in that row by the *regular monthly payment*. To get your total interest savings in dollars, just multiply the interest savings factor by your ***original*** mortgage balance.

TERM-BASED PREPAYMENT METHOD
30-YEAR FIXED-RATE MORTGAGE SAVINGS TABLE

Refer to this table to quickly figure out your interest savings
when you use the *Term-based Prepayment* method

If your Mortgage is	Brand New	
and you want to CUT the term by	15 years	
Find your Interest rate below (%)	Then prepay by this factor each month	To get this interest savings factor
5.25	0.455763	0.540953
5.5	0.439062	0.57329
5.75	0.422976	0.606124
6	0.407482	0.63944
6.25	0.39256	0.673221
6.5	0.378186	0.707452
6.75	0.364342	0.742116
7	0.351007	0.777198
7.25	0.338163	0.812681
7.5	0.325791	0.84855
7.75	0.313874	0.884788
8	0.302396	0.921379
8.25	0.29134	0.958307
8.5	0.28069	0.995557
8.75	0.270431	1.033114
9	0.260549	1.070962
9.25	0.251031	1.109085
9.5	0.241862	1.147471
9.75	0.233029	1.186103
10	0.224521	1.224968
10.25	0.216326	1.264053
10.5	0.208431	1.303343

If your Mortgage is	Brand New	
and you want to CUT the term by	15 years	
Find your Interest rate below (%)	Then prepay by this factor each month	To get this interest savings factor
10.75	0.200825	1.342827
11	0.193499	1.38249
11.25	0.186441	1.422321
11.5	0.179642	1.462308
11.75	0.173093	1.502439
12	0.166783	1.542703
12.25	0.160705	1.583089
12.5	0.154849	1.623588
12.75	0.149208	1.664189
13	0.143774	1.704882
13.25	0.138538	1.745659
13.5	0.133495	1.78651
13.75	0.128635	1.827428
14	0.123954	1.868404
14.25	0.119444	1.90943
14.5	0.115099	1.9505
14.75	0.110913	1.991606
15	0.106879	2.032742
15.25	0.102994	2.073901
15.5	0.09925	2.115078
15.75	0.095643	2.156268
16	0.092168	2.197464

NOTE: Find the row starting with your interest rate. To get the *necessary* prepayment amount in dollars, just multiply the prepayment factor in that row by the *regular monthly payment*. To get your total interest savings in dollars, just multiply the interest savings factor by your **original** mortgage balance.

TERM-BASED PREPAYMENT METHOD
30-YEAR FIXED-RATE MORTGAGE SAVINGS TABLE

Refer to this table to quickly figure out your interest savings
when you use the *Term-based Prepayment* method

If your Mortgage is	Brand New	
and you want to CUT the term by	20 years	
Find your Interest rate below (%)	Then prepay by this factor each month	To get this interest savings factor
5.25	0.942973	0.700433
5.5	0.911384	0.741725
5.75	0.880986	0.783632
6	0.851729	0.826136
6.25	0.823566	0.869221
6.5	0.796452	0.912869
6.75	0.770343	0.957064
7	0.745198	1.001787
7.25	0.720978	1.047022
7.5	0.697645	1.092751
7.75	0.675162	1.138957
8	0.653495	1.185621
8.25	0.632611	1.232728
8.5	0.612479	1.28026
8.75	0.593068	1.3282
9	0.57435	1.376532
9.25	0.556297	1.425239
9.5	0.538882	1.474304
9.75	0.522081	1.523713
10	0.505868	1.573449
10.25	0.490222	1.623497
10.5	0.47512	1.673841

If your Mortgage is	Brand New	
and you want to CUT the term by	20 years	
Find your Interest rate below (%)	Then prepay by this factor each month	To get this interest savings factor
10.75	0.46054	1.724469
11	0.446463	1.775364
11.25	0.432868	1.826514
11.5	0.419738	1.877904
11.75	0.407055	1.929522
12	0.394801	1.981354
12.25	0.38296	2.033389
12.5	0.371517	2.085614
12.75	0.360456	2.138018
13	0.349763	2.190589
13.25	0.339425	2.243318
13.5	0.329428	2.296192
13.75	0.319759	2.349203
14	0.310407	2.402341
14.25	0.30136	2.455596
14.5	0.292606	2.50896
14.75	0.284135	2.562424
15	0.275936	2.615979
15.25	0.268	2.669618
15.5	0.260317	2.723334
15.75	0.252879	2.77712
16	0.245676	2.830968

NOTE: Find the row starting with your interest rate. To get the *necessary* prepayment amount in dollars, just multiply the prepayment factor in that row by the *regular monthly payment*. To get your total interest savings in dollars, just multiply the interest savings factor by your **original** mortgage balance.

TERM-BASED PREPAYMENT METHOD
30-YEAR FIXED-RATE MORTGAGE SAVINGS TABLE

Refer to this table to quickly figure out your interest savings
when you use the *Term-based Prepayment* method

If your Mortgage is	Brand New		If your Mortgage is	Brand New	
and you want to CUT the term by	25 years		and you want to CUT the term by	25 years	
Find your Interest rate below (%)	Then prepay by this factor each month	To get this interest savings factor	Find your Interest rate below (%)	Then prepay by this factor each month	To get this interest savings factor
5.25	2.438221	0.848774	10.75	1.315842	2.063456
5.5	2.36413	0.897971	11	1.283092	2.123819
5.75	2.292951	0.947856	11.25	1.251434	2.184503
6	2.224549	0.998414	11.5	1.220822	2.245493
6.25	2.158798	1.049626	11.75	1.191213	2.306776
6.5	2.095576	1.101476	12	1.162568	2.368338
6.75	2.03477	1.153946	12.25	1.134847	2.430168
7	1.97627	1.207017	12.5	1.108014	2.492252
7.25	1.919973	1.260673	12.75	1.082032	2.554578
7.5	1.86578	1.314895	13	1.056869	2.617134
7.75	1.813598	1.369666	13.25	1.032492	2.679909
8	1.763338	1.424969	13.5	1.00887	2.742893
8.25	1.714915	1.480785	13.75	0.985975	2.806074
8.5	1.66825	1.537097	14	0.963778	2.869443
8.75	1.623265	1.593887	14.25	0.942252	2.93299
9	1.579887	1.65114	14.5	0.921373	2.996704
9.25	1.538048	1.708838	14.75	0.901114	3.060578
9.5	1.497682	1.766963	15	0.881454	3.124603
9.75	1.458725	1.825501	15.25	0.862369	3.188769
10	1.421118	1.884435	15.5	0.843839	3.253069
10.25	1.384804	1.943749	15.75	0.825843	3.317496
10.5	1.34973	2.003427	16	0.808361	3.382042

NOTE: Find the row starting with your interest rate. To get the *necessary* prepayment amount in dollars, just multiply the prepayment factor in that row by the *regular monthly payment*. To get your total interest savings in dollars, just multiply the interest savings factor by your ***original*** mortgage balance.

TERM-BASED PREPAYMENT METHOD
30-YEAR FIXED-RATE MORTGAGE SAVINGS TABLE

Refer to this table to quickly figure out your interest savings
when you use the *Term-based Prepayment* method

If your Mortgage is	5 Years Old	
and you want to CUT the term by	**5 years**	
Find your Interest rate below (%)	Then prepay by this factor each month	To get this interest savings factor
5.25	0.124483	0.166346
5.5	0.120178	0.176908
5.75	0.116001	0.187675
6	0.11195	0.198643
6.25	0.108022	0.209804
6.5	0.104214	0.221152
6.75	0.100523	0.232681
7	0.096946	0.244385
7.25	0.093482	0.256256
7.5	0.090126	0.268288
7.75	0.086876	0.280474
8	0.08373	0.292808
8.25	0.080684	0.305283
8.5	0.077737	0.317892
8.75	0.074886	0.330629
9	0.072128	0.343488
9.25	0.069461	0.35646
9.5	0.066882	0.369541
9.75	0.064389	0.382724
10	0.06198	0.396003
10.25	0.059651	0.409372
10.5	0.057402	0.422824

If your Mortgage is	5 Years Old	
and you want to CUT the term by	**5 years**	
Find your Interest rate below (%)	Then prepay by this factor each month	To get this interest savings factor
10.75	0.05523	0.436354
11	0.053132	0.449957
11.25	0.051106	0.463626
11.5	0.049151	0.477357
11.75	0.047264	0.491144
12	0.045443	0.504983
12.25	0.043687	0.518868
12.5	0.041992	0.532795
12.75	0.040358	0.546759
13	0.038783	0.560757
13.25	0.037264	0.574783
13.5	0.0358	0.588834
13.75	0.034389	0.602907
14	0.03303	0.616997
14.25	0.03172	0.631101
14.5	0.030459	0.645217
14.75	0.029244	0.65934
15	0.028075	0.673469
15.25	0.026949	0.6876
15.5	0.025865	0.70173
15.75	0.024822	0.715858
16	0.023819	0.729981

NOTE: Find the row starting with your interest rate. To get the *necessary* prepayment amount in dollars, just multiply the prepayment factor in that row by the *regular monthly payment*. To get your total interest savings in dollars, just multiply the interest savings factor by your ***original*** mortgage balance.

TERM-BASED PREPAYMENT METHOD
30-YEAR FIXED-RATE MORTGAGE SAVINGS TABLE

Refer to this table to quickly figure out your interest savings
when you use the *Term-based Prepayment* method

If your Mortgage is	5 Years Old	
and you want to CUT the term by	10 years	
Find your Interest rate below (%)	Then prepay by this factor each month	To get this interest savings factor
5.25	0.341478	0.323227
5.5	0.330565	0.343502
5.75	0.319984	0.364167
6	0.309724	0.38521
6.25	0.299777	0.406621
6.5	0.290133	0.42839
6.75	0.280785	0.450507
7	0.271724	0.472961
7.25	0.262942	0.495741
7.5	0.25443	0.518836
7.75	0.24618	0.542235
8	0.238186	0.565927
8.25	0.23044	0.589901
8.5	0.222934	0.614146
8.75	0.215662	0.63865
9	0.208617	0.663404
9.25	0.201791	0.688395
9.5	0.19518	0.713613
9.75	0.188776	0.739048
10	0.182573	0.764688
10.25	0.176566	0.790524
10.5	0.170748	0.816545

If your Mortgage is	5 Years Old	
and you want to CUT the term by	10 years	
Find your Interest rate below (%)	Then prepay by this factor each month	To get this interest savings factor
10.75	0.165114	0.842742
11	0.159659	0.869104
11.25	0.154377	0.895621
11.5	0.149263	0.922285
11.75	0.144311	0.949087
12	0.139518	0.976017
12.25	0.134878	1.003067
12.5	0.130387	1.030228
12.75	0.12604	1.057492
13	0.121832	1.084852
13.25	0.11776	1.112299
13.5	0.11382	1.139827
13.75	0.110007	1.167429
14	0.106317	1.195096
14.25	0.102747	1.222824
14.5	0.099293	1.250606
14.75	0.095951	1.278435
15	0.092718	1.306306
15.25	0.089591	1.334213
15.5	0.086566	1.362152
15.75	0.08364	1.390117
16	0.08081	1.418103

NOTE: Find the row starting with your interest rate. To get the *necessary* prepayment amount in dollars, just multiply the prepayment factor in that row by the *regular monthly payment*. To get your total interest savings in dollars, just multiply the interest savings factor by your ***original*** mortgage balance.

TERM-BASED PREPAYMENT METHOD
30-YEAR FIXED-RATE MORTGAGE SAVINGS TABLE

Refer to this table to quickly figure out your interest savings
when you use the *Term-based Prepayment* method

If your Mortgage is	5 Years Old	
and you want to CUT the term by	15 years	
Find your Interest rate below (%)	Then prepay by this factor each month	To get this interest savings factor
5.25	0.79044	0.470186
5.5	0.767277	0.499238
5.75	0.744843	0.528827
6	0.723114	0.558939
6.25	0.702066	0.589562
6.5	0.681676	0.620684
6.75	0.661922	0.652291
7	0.642783	0.68437
7.25	0.624238	0.716909
7.5	0.606268	0.749893
7.75	0.588853	0.783308
8	0.571975	0.817142
8.25	0.555617	0.85138
8.5	0.539761	0.886009
8.75	0.52439	0.921015
9	0.509489	0.956385
9.25	0.495042	0.992105
9.5	0.481035	1.028161
9.75	0.467453	1.064541
10	0.454282	1.101231
10.25	0.441509	1.138218
10.5	0.429121	1.17549

If your Mortgage is	5 Years Old	
and you want to CUT the term by	15 years	
Find your Interest rate below (%)	Then prepay by this factor each month	To get this interest savings factor
10.75	0.417105	1.213034
11	0.40545	1.250838
11.25	0.394144	1.288891
11.5	0.383175	1.327179
11.75	0.372533	1.365691
12	0.362207	1.404418
12.25	0.352188	1.443346
12.5	0.342464	1.482467
12.75	0.333028	1.521768
13	0.32387	1.561241
13.25	0.314981	1.600876
13.5	0.306352	1.640662
13.75	0.297976	1.680592
14	0.289844	1.720655
14.25	0.281949	1.760844
14.5	0.274284	1.80115
14.75	0.26684	1.841565
15	0.259612	1.882081
15.25	0.252592	1.922692
15.5	0.245775	1.96339
15.75	0.239153	2.004167
16	0.232721	2.045018

NOTE: Find the row starting with your interest rate. To get the *necessary* prepayment amount in dollars, just multiply the prepayment factor in that row by the *regular monthly payment*. To get your total interest savings in dollars, just multiply the interest savings factor by your **original** mortgage balance.

TERM-BASED PREPAYMENT METHOD
30-YEAR FIXED-RATE MORTGAGE SAVINGS TABLE

Refer to this table to quickly figure out your interest savings
when you use the *Term-based Prepayment* method

If your Mortgage is	5 Years Old	
and you want to *CUT* the term by	20 years	
Find your Interest rate below (%)	Then prepay by this factor each month	To get this interest savings factor
5.25	2.168303	0.606882
5.5	2.110495	0.643704
5.75	2.054613	0.681165
6	2.000583	0.719251
6.25	1.948335	0.757947
6.5	1.897799	0.79724
6.75	1.848912	0.837115
7	1.80161	0.877557
7.25	1.755835	0.91855
7.5	1.711527	0.96008
7.75	1.668634	1.002132
8	1.627101	1.044689
8.25	1.586879	1.087738
8.5	1.547919	1.131263
8.75	1.510174	1.175248
9	1.473599	1.219679
9.25	1.438153	1.264541
9.5	1.403793	1.309819
9.75	1.370481	1.355498
10	1.338178	1.401563
10.25	1.306849	1.448002
10.5	1.276458	1.494799

If your Mortgage is	5 Years Old	
and you want to *CUT* the term by	20 years	
Find your Interest rate below (%)	Then prepay by this factor each month	To get this interest savings factor
10.75	1.246972	1.54194
11	1.218359	1.589413
11.25	1.190587	1.637204
11.5	1.163628	1.685301
11.75	1.137453	1.73369
12	1.112034	1.782359
12.25	1.087345	1.831297
12.5	1.063361	1.880491
12.75	1.040057	1.92993
13	1.017411	1.979603
13.25	0.9954	2.0295
13.5	0.974001	2.079609
13.75	0.953196	2.129922
14	0.932963	2.180428
14.25	0.913283	2.231117
14.5	0.894138	2.281981
14.75	0.875511	2.333011
15	0.857383	2.384198
15.25	0.839739	2.435534
15.5	0.822563	2.487012
15.75	0.80584	2.538623
16	0.789554	2.590361

NOTE: Find the row starting with your interest rate. To get the *necessary* prepayment amount in dollars, just multiply the prepayment factor in that row by the *regular monthly payment*. To get your total interest savings in dollars, just multiply the interest savings factor by your **original** mortgage balance.

TERM-BASED PREPAYMENT METHOD
30-YEAR FIXED-RATE MORTGAGE SAVINGS TABLE

Refer to this table to quickly figure out your interest savings
when you use the *Term-based Prepayment* method

If your Mortgage is	10 Years Old	
and you want to CUT the term by	5 years	
Find your Interest rate below (%)	Then prepay by this factor each month	To get this interest savings factor
5.25	0.192973	0.139514
5.5	0.187816	0.148722
5.75	0.18278	0.158146
6	0.177862	0.167783
6.25	0.17306	0.177629
6.5	0.168373	0.187679
6.75	0.163797	0.19793
7	0.159331	0.208375
7.25	0.154973	0.219012
7.5	0.15072	0.229834
7.75	0.146571	0.240838
8	0.142523	0.252018
8.25	0.138575	0.263368
8.5	0.134724	0.274885
8.75	0.130968	0.286561
9	0.127306	0.298393
9.25	0.123736	0.310375
9.5	0.120255	0.322502
9.75	0.116862	0.334768
10	0.113555	0.347167
10.25	0.110333	0.359696
10.5	0.107193	0.372348

If your Mortgage is	10 Years Old	
and you want to CUT the term by	5 years	
Find your Interest rate below (%)	Then prepay by this factor each month	To get this interest savings factor
10.75	0.104133	0.385117
11	0.101153	0.398
11.25	0.098249	0.410991
11.5	0.095421	0.424084
11.75	0.092667	0.437275
12	0.089986	0.450559
12.25	0.087374	0.463931
12.5	0.084832	0.477386
12.75	0.082358	0.49092
13	0.079949	0.504528
13.25	0.077605	0.518206
13.5	0.075324	0.531949
13.75	0.073104	0.545754
14	0.070944	0.559615
14.25	0.068843	0.57353
14.5	0.066799	0.587494
14.75	0.064812	0.601504
15	0.062878	0.615555
15.25	0.060998	0.629645
15.5	0.05917	0.64377
15.75	0.057393	0.657927
16	0.055665	0.672113

NOTE: Find the row starting with your interest rate. To get the *necessary* prepayment amount in dollars, just multiply the prepayment factor in that row by the *regular monthly payment*. To get your total interest savings in dollars, just multiply the interest savings factor by your ***original*** mortgage balance.

TERM-BASED PREPAYMENT METHOD
30-YEAR FIXED-RATE MORTGAGE SAVINGS TABLE

Refer to this table to quickly figure out your interest savings
when you use the *Term-based Prepayment* method

If your Mortgage is	10 Years Old	
and you want to CUT the term by	10 years	
Find your Interest rate below (%)	Then prepay by this factor each month	To get this interest savings factor
5.25	0.592233	0.270204
5.5	0.577675	0.28775
5.75	0.563478	0.305691
6	0.549633	0.324022
6.25	0.53613	0.342735
6.5	0.522962	0.361824
6.75	0.51012	0.381282
7	0.497596	0.401101
7.25	0.485382	0.421272
7.5	0.47347	0.441789
7.75	0.461853	0.462642
8	0.450523	0.483824
8.25	0.439474	0.505325
8.5	0.428698	0.527139
8.75	0.418188	0.549255
9	0.407937	0.571664
9.25	0.39794	0.59436
9.5	0.38819	0.617331
9.75	0.378681	0.64057
10	0.369407	0.664069
10.25	0.360362	0.687817
10.5	0.35154	0.711807

If your Mortgage is	10 Years Old	
and you want to CUT the term by	10 years	
Find your Interest rate below (%)	Then prepay by this factor each month	To get this interest savings factor
10.75	0.342935	0.736029
11	0.334543	0.760476
11.25	0.326358	0.785139
11.5	0.318375	0.810009
11.75	0.310589	0.835078
12	0.302995	0.860338
12.25	0.295588	0.885781
12.5	0.288363	0.9114
12.75	0.281317	0.937186
13	0.274444	0.963132
13.25	0.26774	0.98923
13.5	0.261202	1.015474
13.75	0.254824	1.041857
14	0.248603	1.06837
14.25	0.242536	1.095009
14.5	0.236618	1.121765
14.75	0.230845	1.148634
15	0.225214	1.175608
15.25	0.219722	1.202681
15.5	0.214365	1.229849
15.75	0.20914	1.257105
16	0.204042	1.284443

NOTE: Find the row starting with your interest rate. To get the *necessary* prepayment amount in dollars, just multiply the prepayment factor in that row by the *regular monthly payment*. To get your total interest savings in dollars, just multiply the interest savings factor by your ***original*** mortgage balance.

TERM-BASED PREPAYMENT METHOD
30-YEAR FIXED-RATE MORTGAGE SAVINGS TABLE

Refer to this table to quickly figure out your interest savings
when you use the *Term-based Prepayment* method

If your Mortgage is	10 Years Old	
and you want to CUT the term by	**15 years**	
Find your Interest rate below (%)	Then prepay by this factor each month	To get this interest savings factor
5.25	1.817563	0.391768
5.5	1.776787	0.416716
5.75	1.737106	0.442194
6	1.698487	0.468194
6.25	1.660899	0.494704
6.5	1.62431	0.521718
6.75	1.588689	0.549224
7	1.554008	0.577213
7.25	1.520239	0.605675
7.5	1.487353	0.634599
7.75	1.455326	0.663974
8	1.42413	0.693791
8.25	1.393742	0.724037
8.5	1.364137	0.754702
8.75	1.335293	0.785775
9	1.307186	0.817246
9.25	1.279796	0.849102
9.5	1.253101	0.881332
9.75	1.227082	0.913926
10	1.201717	0.946873
10.25	1.176989	0.980162
10.5	1.152878	1.013781

If your Mortgage is	10 Years Old	
and you want to CUT the term by	**15 years**	
Find your Interest rate below (%)	Then prepay by this factor each month	To get this interest savings factor
10.75	1.129367	1.04772
11	1.106439	1.081969
11.25	1.084077	1.116517
11.5	1.062265	1.151353
11.75	1.040987	1.186468
12	1.020228	1.221851
12.25	0.999973	1.257493
12.5	0.980207	1.293384
12.75	0.960918	1.329514
13	0.942092	1.365874
13.25	0.923715	1.402456
13.5	0.905775	1.43925
13.75	0.88826	1.476249
14	0.871159	1.513442
14.25	0.854459	1.550823
14.5	0.83815	1.588384
14.75	0.822221	1.626116
15	0.806661	1.664012
15.25	0.791461	1.702066
15.5	0.776611	1.740269
15.75	0.762101	1.778616
16	0.747921	1.817099

NOTE: Find the row starting with your interest rate. To get the *necessary* prepayment amount in dollars, just multiply the prepayment factor in that row by the *regular monthly payment*. To get your total interest savings in dollars, just multiply the interest savings factor by your **original** mortgage balance.

TERM-BASED PREPAYMENT METHOD
30-YEAR FIXED-RATE MORTGAGE SAVINGS TABLE

Refer to this table to quickly figure out your interest savings
when you use the *Term-based Prepayment* method

If your Mortgage is	15 Years Old
and you want to CUT the term by	5 years

Find your Interest rate below (%)	Then prepay by this factor each month	To get this interest savings factor
5.25	0.334677	0.10955
5.5	0.328215	0.117045
5.75	0.321868	0.124744
6	0.315632	0.132646
6.25	0.309507	0.140748
6.5	0.30349	0.149049
6.75	0.29758	0.157547
7	0.291776	0.166238
7.25	0.286075	0.175121
7.5	0.280477	0.184193
7.75	0.274978	0.19345
8	0.269579	0.20289
8.25	0.264277	0.212509
8.5	0.259071	0.222304
8.75	0.253959	0.232273
9	0.24894	0.242411
9.25	0.244012	0.252714
9.5	0.239174	0.26318
9.75	0.234424	0.273805
10	0.229761	0.284585
10.25	0.225184	0.295516
10.5	0.220691	0.306594

If your Mortgage is	15 Years Old
and you want to CUT the term by	5 years

Find your Interest rate below (%)	Then prepay by this factor each month	To get this interest savings factor
10.75	0.21628	0.317817
11	0.211951	0.329179
11.25	0.207703	0.340677
11.5	0.203533	0.352307
11.75	0.19944	0.364066
12	0.195424	0.375949
12.25	0.191483	0.387953
12.5	0.187615	0.400074
12.75	0.18382	0.412309
13	0.180096	0.424653
13.25	0.176442	0.437103
13.5	0.172858	0.449655
13.75	0.169341	0.462306
14	0.16589	0.475053
14.25	0.162505	0.487891
14.5	0.159185	0.500817
14.75	0.155928	0.513828
15	0.152733	0.52692
15.25	0.149599	0.540091
15.5	0.146525	0.553337
15.75	0.14351	0.566655
16	0.140553	0.580042

NOTE: Find the row starting with your interest rate. To get the *necessary* prepayment amount in dollars, just multiply the prepayment factor in that row by the *regular monthly payment*. To get your total interest savings in dollars, just multiply the interest savings factor by your **original** mortgage balance.

TERM-BASED PREPAYMENT METHOD
30-YEAR FIXED-RATE MORTGAGE SAVINGS TABLE

Refer to this table to quickly figure out your interest savings
when you use the *Term-based Prepayment* method

If your Mortgage is	15 Years Old	
and you want to *CUT* the term by	10 years	
Find your Interest rate below (%)	Then prepay by this factor each month	To get this interest savings factor
5.25	1.3618	0.21145
5.5	1.337725	0.22562
5.75	1.31413	0.240153
6	1.291005	0.255047
6.25	1.26834	0.270298
6.5	1.246124	0.285901
6.75	1.224347	0.301852
7	1.203001	0.318147
7.25	1.182076	0.334781
7.5	1.161562	0.351749
7.75	1.141451	0.369045
8	1.121734	0.386664
8.25	1.102402	0.404601
8.5	1.083447	0.42285
8.75	1.064862	0.441404
9	1.046637	0.460258
9.25	1.028766	0.479406
9.5	1.01124	0.498842
9.75	0.994052	0.518559
10	0.977196	0.53855
10.25	0.960663	0.558811
10.5	0.944447	0.579333

If your Mortgage is	15 Years Old	
and you want to *CUT* the term by	10 years	
Find your Interest rate below (%)	Then prepay by this factor each month	To get this interest savings factor
10.75	0.928542	0.600112
11	0.91294	0.621139
11.25	0.897636	0.64241
11.5	0.882623	0.663917
11.75	0.867894	0.685655
12	0.853444	0.707617
12.25	0.839268	0.729796
12.5	0.825358	0.752188
12.75	0.81171	0.774784
13	0.798318	0.79758
13.25	0.785176	0.82057
13.5	0.77228	0.843747
13.75	0.759625	0.867106
14	0.747205	0.890641
14.25	0.735015	0.914346
14.5	0.723051	0.938217
14.75	0.711308	0.962247
15	0.699782	0.986432
15.25	0.688468	1.010765
15.5	0.677361	1.035243
15.75	0.666457	1.05986
16	0.655753	1.084611

NOTE: Find the row starting with your interest rate. To get the *necessary* prepayment amount in dollars, just multiply the prepayment factor in that row by the *regular monthly payment*. To get your total interest savings in dollars, just multiply the interest savings factor by your **original** mortgage balance.

TERM-BASED PREPAYMENT METHOD
30-YEAR FIXED-RATE MORTGAGE SAVINGS TABLE

Refer to this table to quickly figure out your interest savings
when you use the *Term-based Prepayment* method

If your Mortgage is	20 Years Old	
and you want to CUT the term by	5 years	
Find your Interest rate below (%)	Then prepay by this factor each month	To get this interest savings factor
5.25	0.769567	0.076348
5.5	0.76005	0.081745
5.75	0.750652	0.087308
6	0.741372	0.093036
6.25	0.732209	0.09893
6.5	0.723161	0.104989
6.75	0.714227	0.111211
7	0.705405	0.117597
7.25	0.696694	0.124145
7.5	0.688092	0.130854
7.75	0.679598	0.137724
8	0.67121	0.144752
8.25	0.662928	0.151938
8.5	0.65475	0.15928
8.75	0.646674	0.166777
9	0.6387	0.174426
9.25	0.630825	0.182227
9.5	0.623049	0.190176
9.75	0.615371	0.198274
10	0.607789	0.206516
10.25	0.600301	0.214902
10.5	0.592908	0.22343

If your Mortgage is	20 Years Old	
and you want to CUT the term by	5 years	
Find your Interest rate below (%)	Then prepay by this factor each month	To get this interest savings factor
10.75	0.585607	0.232097
11	0.578397	0.240901
11.25	0.571278	0.249841
11.5	0.564248	0.258913
11.75	0.557305	0.268116
12	0.55045	0.277448
12.25	0.54368	0.286906
12.5	0.536995	0.296488
12.75	0.530393	0.306191
13	0.523874	0.316014
13.25	0.517436	0.325955
13.5	0.511079	0.33601
13.75	0.504801	0.346178
14	0.498601	0.356456
14.25	0.492479	0.366842
14.5	0.486434	0.377334
14.75	0.480463	0.38793
15	0.474568	0.398628
15.25	0.468745	0.409425
15.5	0.462996	0.420319
15.75	0.457318	0.431308
16	0.451711	0.44239

NOTE: Find the row starting with your interest rate. To get the *necessary* prepayment amount in dollars, just multiply the prepayment factor in that row by the *regular monthly payment*. To get your total interest savings in dollars, just multiply the interest savings factor by your ***original*** mortgage balance.

TERM-BASED PREPAYMENT METHOD
15-YEAR FIXED-RATE MORTGAGE SAVINGS TABLE

Refer to this table to quickly figure out your interest savings
when you use the *Term-based Prepayment* method

If your Mortgage is	Brand New	
and you want to CUT the term by	5 years	
Find your Interest rate below (%)	Then prepay by this factor each month	To get this interest savings factor
5.25	0.334677	0.159479
5.5	0.328215	0.168435
5.75	0.321868	0.177508
6	0.315632	0.186696
6.25	0.309507	0.196
6.5	0.30349	0.205418
6.75	0.29758	0.214948
7	0.291776	0.224589
7.25	0.286075	0.234341
7.5	0.280477	0.244201
7.75	0.274978	0.254169
8	0.269579	0.264243
8.25	0.264277	0.274421
8.5	0.259071	0.284703
8.75	0.253959	0.295087
9	0.24894	0.305571
9.25	0.244012	0.316153
9.5	0.239174	0.326834
9.75	0.234424	0.33761
10	0.229761	0.34848
10.25	0.225184	0.359444
10.5	0.220691	0.370498

If your Mortgage is	Brand New	
and you want to CUT the term by	5 years	
Find your Interest rate below (%)	Then prepay by this factor each month	To get this interest savings factor
10.75	0.21628	0.381642
11	0.211951	0.392874
11.25	0.207703	0.404193
11.5	0.203533	0.415596
11.75	0.19944	0.427083
12	0.195424	0.438651
12.25	0.191483	0.450299
12.5	0.187615	0.462026
12.75	0.18382	0.473829
13	0.180096	0.485707
13.25	0.176442	0.497659
13.5	0.172858	0.509682
13.75	0.169341	0.521775
14	0.16589	0.533937
14.25	0.162505	0.546166
14.5	0.159185	0.55846
14.75	0.155928	0.570818
15	0.152733	0.583237
15.25	0.149599	0.595717
15.5	0.146525	0.608256
15.75	0.14351	0.620852
16	0.140553	0.633504

NOTE: Find the row starting with your interest rate. To get the *necessary* prepayment amount in dollars, just multiply the prepayment factor in that row by the *regular monthly payment*. To get your total interest savings in dollars, just multiply the interest savings factor by your **original** mortgage balance.

TERM-BASED PREPAYMENT METHOD
15-YEAR FIXED-RATE MORTGAGE SAVINGS TABLE

Refer to this table to quickly figure out your interest savings
when you use the *Term-based Prepayment* method

If your Mortgage is	Brand New	
and you want to CUT the term by	**8 years**	
Find your Interest rate below (%)	Then prepay by this factor each month	To get this interest savings factor
5.25	0.772866	0.249839
5.5	0.7587	0.263667
5.75	0.744801	0.277662
6	0.731165	0.291824
6.25	0.717787	0.30615
6.5	0.704662	0.320641
6.75	0.691785	0.335293
7	0.679151	0.350106
7.25	0.666755	0.365078
7.5	0.654592	0.380207
7.75	0.642659	0.395492
8	0.630951	0.410932
8.25	0.619462	0.426524
8.5	0.60819	0.442266
8.75	0.59713	0.458158
9	0.586277	0.474197
9.25	0.575628	0.490382
9.5	0.565179	0.50671
9.75	0.554925	0.52318
10	0.544864	0.53979
10.25	0.534991	0.556538
10.5	0.525302	0.573422

If your Mortgage is	Brand New	
and you want to CUT the term by	**8 years**	
Find your Interest rate below (%)	Then prepay by this factor each month	To get this interest savings factor
10.75	0.515795	0.59044
11	0.506465	0.60759
11.25	0.49731	0.62487
11.5	0.488325	0.642279
11.75	0.479508	0.659814
12	0.470855	0.677473
12.25	0.462363	0.695254
12.5	0.45403	0.713156
12.75	0.445851	0.731175
13	0.437825	0.749311
13.25	0.429947	0.767561
13.5	0.422216	0.785922
13.75	0.414628	0.804394
14	0.407181	0.822974
14.25	0.399872	0.841659
14.5	0.392698	0.860448
14.75	0.385657	0.879339
15	0.378746	0.898329
15.25	0.371963	0.917418
15.5	0.365305	0.936601
15.75	0.35877	0.955879
16	0.352356	0.975248

NOTE: Find the row starting with your interest rate. To get the *necessary* prepayment amount in dollars, just multiply the prepayment factor in that row by the *regular monthly payment*. To get your total interest savings in dollars, just multiply the interest savings factor by your **original** mortgage balance.

TERM-BASED PREPAYMENT METHOD
15-YEAR FIXED-RATE MORTGAGE SAVINGS TABLE

Refer to this table to quickly figure out your interest savings
when you use the *Term-based Prepayment* method

If your Mortgage is	Brand New			If your Mortgage is	Brand New	
and you want to CUT the term by	10 years			and you want to CUT the term by	10 years	
Find your Interest rate below (%)	Then prepay by this factor each month	To get this interest savings factor		Find your Interest rate below (%)	Then prepay by this factor each month	To get this interest savings factor
5.25	1.3618	0.307821		10.75	0.928542	0.720629
5.5	1.337725	0.32468		11	0.91294	0.741329
5.75	1.31413	0.341732		11.25	0.897636	0.762182
6	1.291005	0.358974		11.5	0.882623	0.783185
6.25	1.26834	0.376405		11.75	0.867894	0.804337
6.5	1.246124	0.394024		12	0.853444	0.825636
6.75	1.224347	0.411829		12.25	0.839268	0.847078
7	1.203001	0.429819		12.5	0.825358	0.868663
7.25	1.182076	0.447992		12.75	0.81171	0.890389
7.5	1.161562	0.466345		13	0.798318	0.912252
7.75	1.141451	0.484879		13.25	0.785176	0.93425
8	1.121734	0.50359		13.5	0.77228	0.956383
8.25	1.102402	0.522478		13.75	0.759625	0.978646
8.5	1.083447	0.541539		14	0.747205	1.001039
8.75	1.064862	0.560774		14.25	0.735015	1.02356
9	1.046637	0.580179		14.5	0.723051	1.046205
9.25	1.028766	0.599752		14.75	0.711308	1.068973
9.5	1.01124	0.619493		15	0.699782	1.091861
9.75	0.994052	0.639398		15.25	0.688468	1.114868
10	0.977196	0.659467		15.5	0.677361	1.137991
10.25	0.960663	0.679696		15.75	0.666457	1.161229
10.5	0.944447	0.700084		16	0.655753	1.184578

NOTE: Find the row starting with your interest rate. To get the *necessary* prepayment amount in dollars, just multiply the prepayment factor in that row by the *regular monthly payment*. To get your total interest savings in dollars, just multiply the interest savings factor by your ***original*** mortgage balance.

TERM-BASED PREPAYMENT METHOD
15-YEAR FIXED-RATE MORTGAGE SAVINGS TABLE

Refer to this table to quickly figure out your interest savings
when you use the *Term-based Prepayment* method

If your Mortgage is	5 Years Old
and you want to CUT the term by	3 years

Find your Interest rate below (%)	Then prepay by this factor each month	To get this interest savings factor
5.25	0.328311	0.067701
5.5	0.324107	0.071699
5.75	0.319951	0.075767
6	0.315843	0.079906
6.25	0.311782	0.084116
6.5	0.307768	0.088396
6.75	0.3038	0.092746
7	0.299878	0.097166
7.25	0.296001	0.101656
7.5	0.292169	0.106215
7.75	0.288382	0.110844
8	0.284639	0.115542
8.25	0.280939	0.120308
8.5	0.277283	0.125143
8.75	0.27367	0.130045
9	0.270099	0.135016
9.25	0.26657	0.140054
9.5	0.263083	0.145158
9.75	0.259636	0.150329
10	0.256231	0.155566
10.25	0.252866	0.160869
10.5	0.24954	0.166237

If your Mortgage is	5 Years Old
and you want to CUT the term by	3 years

Find your Interest rate below (%)	Then prepay by this factor each month	To get this interest savings factor
10.75	0.246255	0.171669
11	0.243008	0.177165
11.25	0.2398	0.182725
11.5	0.23663	0.188348
11.75	0.233499	0.194033
12	0.230405	0.19978
12.25	0.227348	0.205588
12.5	0.224328	0.211457
12.75	0.221344	0.217386
13	0.218396	0.223375
13.25	0.215484	0.229422
13.5	0.212607	0.235528
13.75	0.209766	0.241691
14	0.206958	0.24791
14.25	0.204185	0.254186
14.5	0.201446	0.260517
14.75	0.19874	0.266904
15	0.196068	0.273344
15.25	0.193428	0.279837
15.5	0.190821	0.286383
15.75	0.188245	0.292981
16	0.185702	0.29963

NOTE: Find the row starting with your interest rate. To get the *necessary* prepayment amount in dollars, just multiply the prepayment factor in that row by the *regular monthly payment*. To get your total interest savings in dollars, just multiply the interest savings factor by your ***original*** mortgage balance.

TERM-BASED PREPAYMENT METHOD
15-YEAR FIXED-RATE MORTGAGE SAVINGS TABLE

Refer to this table to quickly figure out your interest savings
when you use the *Term-based Prepayment* method

If your Mortgage is	5 Years Old
and you want to CUT the term by	**5 years**

Find your Interest rate below (%)	Then prepay by this factor each month	To get this interest savings factor
5.25	0.769567	0.111144
5.5	0.76005	0.117636
5.75	0.750652	0.124237
6	0.741372	0.130947
6.25	0.732209	0.137766
6.5	0.723161	0.144694
6.75	0.714227	0.15173
7	0.705405	0.158874
7.25	0.696694	0.166126
7.5	0.688092	0.173486
7.75	0.679598	0.180952
8	0.67121	0.188525
8.25	0.662928	0.196204
8.5	0.65475	0.203989
8.75	0.646674	0.211879
9	0.6387	0.219873
9.25	0.630825	0.227971
9.5	0.623049	0.236173
9.75	0.615371	0.244477
10	0.607789	0.252883
10.25	0.600301	0.261391
10.5	0.592908	0.27

If your Mortgage is	5 Years Old
and you want to CUT the term by	**5 years**

Find your Interest rate below (%)	Then prepay by this factor each month	To get this interest savings factor
10.75	0.585607	0.278708
11	0.578397	0.287515
11.25	0.571278	0.296421
11.5	0.564248	0.305425
11.75	0.557305	0.314525
12	0.55045	0.323722
12.25	0.54368	0.333013
12.5	0.536995	0.342399
12.75	0.530393	0.351878
13	0.523874	0.361449
13.25	0.517436	0.371112
13.5	0.511079	0.380865
13.75	0.504801	0.390708
14	0.498601	0.40064
14.25	0.492479	0.410659
14.5	0.486434	0.420765
14.75	0.480463	0.430957
15	0.474568	0.441233
15.25	0.468745	0.451593
15.5	0.462996	0.462035
15.75	0.457318	0.472559
16	0.451711	0.483164

NOTE: Find the row starting with your interest rate. To get the *necessary* prepayment amount in dollars, just multiply the prepayment factor in that row by the *regular monthly payment*. To get your total interest savings in dollars, just multiply the interest savings factor by your ***original*** mortgage balance.

TERM-BASED PREPAYMENT METHOD
15-YEAR FIXED-RATE MORTGAGE SAVINGS TABLE

Refer to this table to quickly figure out your interest savings
when you use the *Term-based Prepayment* method

If your Mortgage is	5 Years Old	
and you want to *CUT* the term by	8 years	
Find your Interest rate below (%)	Then prepay by this factor each month	To get this interest savings factor
5.25	3.099426	0.173748
5.5	3.063132	0.18372
5.75	3.027363	0.193845
6	2.99211	0.204123
6.25	2.957366	0.214555
6.5	2.923122	0.225138
6.75	2.889369	0.235874
7	2.856099	0.246761
7.25	2.823305	0.257799
7.5	2.790979	0.268987
7.75	2.759113	0.280324
8	2.7277	0.29181
8.25	2.696733	0.303445
8.5	2.666203	0.315226
8.75	2.636105	0.327154
9	2.606431	0.339228
9.25	2.577174	0.351447
9.5	2.548328	0.363809
9.75	2.519885	0.376315
10	2.49184	0.388962
10.25	2.464186	0.401751
10.5	2.436917	0.414679

If your Mortgage is	5 Years Old	
and you want to *CUT* the term by	8 years	
Find your Interest rate below (%)	Then prepay by this factor each month	To get this interest savings factor
10.75	2.410027	0.427747
11	2.383509	0.440952
11.25	2.357358	0.454294
11.5	2.331567	0.467771
11.75	2.306132	0.481383
12	2.281046	0.495128
12.25	2.256303	0.509005
12.5	2.2319	0.523013
12.75	2.207829	0.537151
13	2.184086	0.551417
13.25	2.160666	0.56581
13.5	2.137563	0.580329
13.75	2.114773	0.594972
14	2.09229	0.609738
14.25	2.07011	0.624626
14.5	2.048228	0.639635
14.75	2.02664	0.654763
15	2.00534	0.670008
15.25	1.984325	0.68537
15.5	1.96359	0.700846
15.75	1.94313	0.716436
16	1.922942	0.732138

NOTE: Find the row starting with your interest rate. To get the *necessary* prepayment amount in dollars, just multiply the prepayment factor in that row by the *regular monthly payment*. To get your total interest savings in dollars, just multiply the interest savings factor by your **original** mortgage balance.

TERM-BASED PREPAYMENT METHOD
15-YEAR FIXED-RATE MORTGAGE SAVINGS TABLE

Refer to this table to quickly figure out your interest savings
when you use the *Term-based Prepayment* method

If your Mortgage is	10 Years Old	
and you want to CUT the term by	**2 years**	
Find your Interest rate below (%)	Then prepay by this factor each month	To get this interest savings factor
5.25	0.584499	0.023779
5.5	0.580841	0.025246
5.75	0.577205	0.026744
6	0.573592	0.028275
6.25	0.57	0.029838
6.5	0.56643	0.031434
6.75	0.562882	0.033062
7	0.559355	0.034724
7.25	0.55585	0.036418
7.5	0.552365	0.038145
7.75	0.548902	0.039906
8	0.54546	0.041699
8.25	0.542039	0.043526
8.5	0.538639	0.045387
8.75	0.535259	0.047281
9	0.5319	0.049208
9.25	0.528562	0.051169
9.5	0.525243	0.053164
9.75	0.521945	0.055193
10	0.518667	0.057255
10.25	0.515409	0.059351
10.5	0.512171	0.061481

If your Mortgage is	10 Years Old	
and you want to CUT the term by	**2 years**	
Find your Interest rate below (%)	Then prepay by this factor each month	To get this interest savings factor
10.75	0.508952	0.063644
11	0.505753	0.065842
11.25	0.502573	0.068073
11.5	0.499413	0.070338
11.75	0.496272	0.072637
12	0.493151	0.074969
12.25	0.490048	0.077336
12.5	0.486964	0.079735
12.75	0.483899	0.082169
13	0.480853	0.084636
13.25	0.477825	0.087136
13.5	0.474816	0.08967
13.75	0.471825	0.092237
14	0.468853	0.094837
14.25	0.465898	0.097471
14.5	0.462962	0.100137
14.75	0.460043	0.102837
15	0.457143	0.105569
15.25	0.45426	0.108334
15.5	0.451395	0.111131
15.75	0.448547	0.113961
16	0.445717	0.116823

NOTE: Find the row starting with your interest rate. To get the *necessary* prepayment amount in dollars, just multiply the prepayment factor in that row by the *regular monthly payment*. To get your total interest savings in dollars, just multiply the interest savings factor by your **original** mortgage balance.

TERM-BASED PREPAYMENT METHOD
15-YEAR FIXED-RATE MORTGAGE SAVINGS TABLE

Refer to this table to quickly figure out your interest savings
when you use the *Term-based Prepayment* method

If your Mortgage is	10 Years Old	
and you want to CUT the term by	**4 years**	
Find your Interest rate below (%)	Then prepay by this factor each month	To get this interest savings factor
5.25	3.51502	0.046784
5.5	3.493799	0.049633
5.75	3.472738	0.052541
6	3.451834	0.055509
6.25	3.431088	0.058536
6.5	3.410496	0.061623
6.75	3.390058	0.064769
7	3.369773	0.067976
7.25	3.349639	0.071243
7.5	3.329656	0.07457
7.75	3.309821	0.077958
8	3.290133	0.081406
8.25	3.270592	0.084915
8.5	3.251195	0.088485
8.75	3.231943	0.092116
9	3.212833	0.095808
9.25	3.193864	0.09956
9.5	3.175035	0.103374
9.75	3.156346	0.107248
10	3.137794	0.111184
10.25	3.119378	0.11518
10.5	3.101099	0.119237

If your Mortgage is	10 Years Old	
and you want to CUT the term by	**4 years**	
Find your Interest rate below (%)	Then prepay by this factor each month	To get this interest savings factor
10.75	3.082953	0.123355
11	3.064941	0.127534
11.25	3.04706	0.131774
11.5	3.029311	0.136074
11.75	3.011691	0.140434
12	2.994201	0.144855
12.25	2.976838	0.149337
12.5	2.959601	0.153878
12.75	2.94249	0.158479
13	2.925504	0.16314
13.25	2.908641	0.16786
13.5	2.8919	0.17264
13.75	2.875281	0.177479
14	2.858782	0.182377
14.25	2.842403	0.187333
14.5	2.826142	0.192348
14.75	2.809998	0.197422
15	2.793971	0.202553
15.25	2.77806	0.207742
15.5	2.762262	0.212988
15.75	2.746579	0.218292
16	2.731008	0.223652

NOTE: Find the row starting with your interest rate. To get the *necessary* prepayment amount in dollars, just multiply the prepayment factor in that row by the *regular monthly payment*. To get your total interest savings in dollars, just multiply the interest savings factor by your **original** mortgage balance.

| **Appendix I** | **Special Interest and Time Savings Tables For The Extra-Annual Payment Method** |

The special tables in this appendix will give you a quick idea of what dollar and time savings to expect when you use the *extra-annual payment method*. You'll find answers for BOTH the **one-prepayment** *(annual)* and the **two-prepayment** *(semi-annual)* approaches.

Due to the nature of the *pseudo* bi-weekly amortization process, the dollar savings answers are not deadly accurate to the dollar. But, they do come well inside of $10 from the actual figures for mortgage amounts under one million dollars, and within $100 of the actual savings for mortgage amounts above one million.

The time savings are accurate.

The tables contain interest rates ranging from **5.25%** to **16%** by increments of 0.25%. If you don't find your particular interest rate, just use the closest *lower* rate for a good approximation. For instance, if your annual interest rate equals 8.8%, use *8.75%* in the table.

This appendix provides tables for BOTH **30-year** and **15-year** fixed-rate mortgages. The factors in the *30-year* tables give answers for mortgage ages ranging from 0 to 25 years old by 5 year increments. The factors in the *15-year* tables give answers for mortgage ages ranging from 0 to 10 years old by 5 year increments.

If you don't find the exact *current* age of your mortgage, use the factor for the *next higher* age as an *approximate* factor. So, for example, if your mortgage is 7 years old now, work with the **10 years Old** column. You find out approximately what savings you would receive *if you were to wait to start the method when your mortgage is 10 years old.* Of course, if you start now, your savings will stack even higher and the term will end even SOONER than the table indicates.

Go on to the next page for the specific action steps and some examples.

Follow these easy steps to find your expected total interest savings.

STEP	ACTION
1	Find the column with your exact mortgage *AGE*. If you don't find your exact mortgage age, go over to the *first* column that shows **a higher** mortgage **AGE than yours,** to locate an *approximate* factor.
2	Under that column, find the row starting with your interest rate, to locate the *interest savings* factor.
3	To get your total interest savings in dollars, multiply the interest savings factor you find at that location by your **original** mortgage balance. If you're using an *approximate* factor, your *actual* savings will be **MORE** than the approximate interest savings amount you calculate.
4	In the same row, read off how many years and months you'll save. If you're using an *approximate* factor, you'll *actually* save **MORE** than the number of years and months shown in the row.

First Example

Use the following tables. Say your *brand new* mortgage balance is $80,000 for 30 years at 10% and you want to prepay ONCE *annually*.

First, go over to the column with the exact age of your mortgage. Next, look down the *rate* column to find the row starting with interest rate **10**. Find the interest savings factor in that row. Multiply interest savings factor **0.7341** by $80,000 to get your total interest savings of **$58,728**. You would also **SAVE 8** years and **8** months.

Second Example

It's the same mortgage of $80,000 for 30 years at 10%. Suppose you've had the mortgage for **three years**.

First, go over to the column with the **next higher age** of your mortgage. In this case, it's the **5 Years Old** column. Next, find the row starting with interest rate **10**. Multiply *approximate* interest savings factor **0.4633** by $80,000 to get your *approximate* total interest savings of *more than $37,064*. Your actual savings would be *MORE* than that amount. You would also **SAVE MORE THAN 6 years** from the point the mortgage is 5 years old**.**

EXTRA ANNUAL PAYMENT METHOD
Pseudo Bi-weekly with Annual Prepayments
30-YEAR FIXED-RATE MORTGAGE SAVINGS TABLE

Refer to this table to quickly figure out your interest savings
when you use the *Extra Annual Payment* method

If your Mortgage is	*Brand New*		
and you *prepay every 12th* month	**One FULL-Size *monthly* payment**		
At this Interest rate (%)	Your interest savings factor is	You'll *save* this many years	and this many months
5.25	0.18	*4*	*9*
5.5	0.1977	*5*	*0*
5.75	0.2164	*5*	*1*
6	0.2364	*5*	*3*
6.25	0.2575	*5*	*5*
6.5	0.2798	*5*	*8*
6.75	0.3036	*5*	*11*
7	0.3285	*6*	*0*
7.25	0.3549	*6*	*3*
7.5	0.3823	*6*	*5*
7.75	0.4113	*6*	*7*
8	0.4416	*6*	*11*
8.25	0.4732	*7*	*0*
8.5	0.5064	*7*	*3*
8.75	0.541	*7*	*7*
9	0.5767	*7*	*11*
9.25	0.6142	*8*	*0*
9.5	0.6528	*8*	*2*
9.75	0.6928	*8*	*5*
10	0.7341	*8*	*8*
10.25	0.7769	*8*	*11*
10.5	0.8211	*9*	*1*

If your Mortgage is	*Brand New*		
and you *prepay every 12th* month	**One FULL-Size *monthly* payment**		
At this Interest rate (%)	Your interest savings factor is	You'll *save* this many years	and this many months
10.75	0.8666	*9*	*4*
11	0.9129	*9*	*7*
11.25	0.9608	*9*	*11*
11.5	1.0078	*10*	*0*
11.75	1.0602	*10*	*3*
12	1.1116	*10*	*7*
12.25	1.1643	*10*	*11*
12.5	1.2176	*11*	*0*
12.75	1.2725	*11*	*3*
13	1.3281	*11*	*6*
13.25	1.3844	*11*	*8*
13.5	1.4419	*11*	*11*
13.75	1.5003	*12*	*1*
14	1.5596	*12*	*4*
14.25	1.6199	*12*	*7*
14.5	1.6805	*12*	*11*
14.75	1.742	*13*	*0*
15	1.8043	*13*	*2*
15.25	1.8671	*13*	*5*
15.5	1.9306	*13*	*8*
15.75	1.9946	*13*	*11*
16	2.0592	*14*	*0*

NOTE: Find the row starting with your interest rate. To get your total interest savings in dollars, just multiply the interest savings factor you find in that row by your ***original*** mortgage balance. Read off your time savings in the same row.

EXTRA ANNUAL PAYMENT METHOD
Pseudo Bi-weekly with Annual Prepayments
30-YEAR FIXED-RATE MORTGAGE SAVINGS TABLE

Refer to this table to quickly figure out your interest savings
when you use the *Extra Annual Payment* method

If your Mortgage is	5 Years Old			If your Mortgage is	5 Years Old		
and you *prepay* every *12th* month	One FULL-Size *monthly payment*			and you *prepay* every *12th* month	One FULL-Size *monthly payment*		
At this Interest rate (%)	Your interest savings factor is	You'll *save* this many years	and this many months	*At this Interest rate (%)*	Your interest savings factor is	You'll *save* this many years	and this many months
5.25	0.1158	3	5	10.75	0.5492	6	4
5.5	0.1269	3	7	11	0.5791	6	6
5.75	0.1384	3	9	11.25	0.6106	6	8
6	0.1509	3	11	11.5	0.6432	6	11
6.25	0.164	4	0	11.75	0.6762	7	0
6.5	0.1779	4	0	12	0.7106	7	2
6.75	0.1927	4	2	12.25	0.7461	7	4
7	0.2082	4	4	12.5	0.7821	7	5
7.25	0.2247	4	4	12.75	0.8194	7	8
7.5	0.2416	4	6	13	0.8573	7	11
7.75	0.2596	4	7	13.25	0.8957	8	0
8	0.2785	4	11	13.5	0.9357	8	1
8.25	0.2983	4	11	13.75	0.9764	8	3
8.5	0.319	5	0	14	1.0178	8	6
8.75	0.3408	5	2	14.25	1.0605	8	8
9	0.3633	5	4	14.5	1.1034	8	11
9.25	0.3873	5	6	14.75	1.1474	8	11
9.5	0.4116	5	8	15	1.1918	9	0
9.75	0.4371	5	9	15.25	1.237	9	2
10	0.4633	6	0	15.5	1.2829	9	6
10.25	0.491	6	0	15.75	1.3297	9	7
10.5	0.5196	6	3	16	1.3772	9	9

NOTE: Find the row starting with your interest rate. To get your total interest savings in dollars, just multiply the interest savings factor you find in that row by your **original** mortgage balance. Read off your time savings in the same row.

EXTRA ANNUAL PAYMENT METHOD
Pseudo Bi-weekly with Annual Prepayments
30-YEAR FIXED-RATE MORTGAGE SAVINGS TABLE

Refer to this table to quickly figure out your interest savings
when you use the *Extra Annual Payment* method

If your Mortgage is	10 Years Old		
and you prepay every 12th month	**One FULL-Size monthly payment**		
At this Interest rate (%)	Your interest savings factor is	You'll *save* this many years	and this many months
5.25	0.0682	2	5
5.5	0.0746	2	6
5.75	0.0811	2	7
6	0.0882	2	8
6.25	0.0955	2	8
6.5	0.1033	2	9
6.75	0.1117	2	11
7	0.1203	2	11
7.25	0.1296	2	11
7.5	0.1389	3	0
7.75	0.149	3	0
8	0.1596	3	2
8.25	0.1706	3	2
8.5	0.1823	3	3
8.75	0.1945	3	5
9	0.2069	3	6
9.25	0.2205	3	7
9.5	0.2339	3	8
9.75	0.2482	3	8
10	0.2629	3	11
10.25	0.2785	3	11
10.5	0.2947	4	0

If your Mortgage is	10 Years Old		
and you prepay every 12th month	**One FULL-Size monthly payment**		
At this Interest rate (%)	Your interest savings factor is	You'll *save* this many years	and this many months
10.75	0.3114	4	0
11	0.3281	4	0
11.25	0.3462	4	2
11.5	0.365	4	3
11.75	0.3838	4	4
12	0.4035	4	7
12.25	0.4241	4	7
12.5	0.4448	4	8
12.75	0.4667	4	11
13	0.4888	4	11
13.25	0.5111	5	0
13.5	0.5348	5	0
13.75	0.5591	5	1
14	0.5836	5	3
14.25	0.6099	5	5
14.5	0.6355	5	6
14.75	0.6629	5	6
15	0.6896	5	7
15.25	0.7172	5	8
15.5	0.7453	6	0
15.75	0.7742	6	0
16	0.8043	6	1

NOTE: Find the row starting with your interest rate. To get your total interest savings in dollars, just multiply the interest savings factor you find in that row by your **original** mortgage balance. Read off your time savings in the same row.

EXTRA ANNUAL PAYMENT METHOD
Pseudo Bi-weekly with Annual Prepayments
30-YEAR FIXED-RATE MORTGAGE SAVINGS TABLE

Refer to this table to quickly figure out your interest savings
when you use the *Extra Annual Payment* method

If your Mortgage is	15 Years Old				If your Mortgage is	15 Years Old		
and you prepay every 12th month	One FULL-Size monthly payment				and you prepay every 12th month	One FULL-Size monthly payment		
At this Interest rate (%)	Your interest savings factor is	You'll *save* this many years	and this many months		At this Interest rate (%)	Your interest savings factor is	You'll *save* this many years	and this many months
5.25	0.0351	1	7		10.75	0.1512	2	4
5.5	0.0382	1	7		11	0.1586	2	4
5.75	0.0413	1	8		11.25	0.1672	2	5
6	0.0449	1	8		11.5	0.1763	2	5
6.25	0.0484	1	8		11.75	0.1849	2	6
6.5	0.0522	1	9		12	0.1941	2	6
6.75	0.0563	1	9		12.25	0.204	2	7
7	0.0605	1	11		12.5	0.2137	2	8
7.25	0.0651	1	11		12.75	0.2243	2	8
7.5	0.0694	1	11		13	0.2346	2	9
7.75	0.0742	1	11		13.25	0.2447	2	9
8	0.0792	1	11		13.5	0.2563	2	11
8.25	0.0844	2	0		13.75	0.2677	2	11
8.5	0.0899	2	0		14	0.2791	2	11
8.75	0.0958	2	0		14.25	0.2924	3	0
9	0.1015	2	0		14.5	0.3043	3	0
9.25	0.1083	2	1		14.75	0.3182	3	0
9.5	0.1144	2	1		15	0.3308	3	1
9.75	0.1212	2	2		15.25	0.3438	3	1
10	0.1279	2	2		15.5	0.3572	3	2
10.25	0.1355	2	3		15.75	0.3715	3	3
10.5	0.1432	2	3		16	0.3867	3	3

NOTE: Find the row starting with your interest rate. To get your total interest savings in dollars, just multiply the interest savings factor you find in that row by your *original* mortgage balance. Read off your time savings in the same row.

EXTRA ANNUAL PAYMENT METHOD
Pseudo Bi-weekly with Annual Prepayments
30-YEAR FIXED-RATE MORTGAGE SAVINGS TABLE

Refer to this table to quickly figure out your interest savings
when you use the *Extra Annual Payment* method

If your Mortgage is	20 Years Old		
and you prepay every 12th month	**One FULL-Size monthly payment**		
At this Interest rate (%)	Your interest savings factor is	You'll *save* this many years	and this many months
5.25	0.014	*0*	*11*
5.5	0.0152	*0*	*11*
5.75	0.0163	*0*	*11*
6	0.0177	*0*	*11*
6.25	0.0189	*1*	*0*
6.5	0.0204	*1*	*0*
6.75	0.022	*1*	*0*
7	0.0235	*1*	*0*
7.25	0.0254	*1*	*0*
7.5	0.0267	*1*	*0*
7.75	0.0285	*1*	*0*
8	0.0303	*1*	*0*
8.25	0.0322	*1*	*0*
8.5	0.0342	*1*	*0*
8.75	0.0364	*1*	*0*
9	0.0383	*1*	*0*
9.25	0.0412	*1*	*1*
9.5	0.0431	*1*	*1*
9.75	0.0455	*1*	*1*
10	0.0477	*1*	*1*
10.25	0.0506	*1*	*1*
10.5	0.0535	*1*	*1*

If your Mortgage is	20 Years Old		
and you prepay every 12th month	**One FULL-Size monthly payment**		
At this Interest rate (%)	Your interest savings factor is	You'll *save* this many years	and this many months
10.75	0.0564	*1*	*2*
11	0.0584	*1*	*2*
11.25	0.0615	*1*	*2*
11.5	0.065	*1*	*2*
11.75	0.0678	*1*	*2*
12	0.0709	*1*	*2*
12.25	0.0747	*1*	*3*
12.5	0.0777	*1*	*3*
12.75	0.0818	*1*	*3*
13	0.0851	*1*	*3*
13.25	0.0881	*1*	*3*
13.5	0.0923	*1*	*4*
13.75	0.0962	*1*	*4*
14	0.0998	*1*	*4*
14.25	0.1055	*1*	*4*
14.5	0.109	*1*	*4*
14.75	0.1148	*1*	*5*
15	0.1184	*1*	*5*
15.25	0.1224	*1*	*5*
15.5	0.1265	*1*	*5*
15.75	0.1313	*1*	*5*
16	0.1371	*1*	*6*

NOTE: Find the row starting with your interest rate. To get your total interest savings in dollars, just multiply the interest savings factor you find in that row by your *original* mortgage balance. Read off your time savings in the same row.

EXTRA ANNUAL PAYMENT METHOD
Pseudo Bi-weekly with Annual Prepayments
30-YEAR FIXED-RATE MORTGAGE SAVINGS TABLE

Refer to this table to quickly figure out your interest savings
when you use the *Extra Annual Payment* method

If your Mortgage is	25 Years Old		
and you prepay every 12th month	One FULL-Size monthly payment		
At this Interest rate (%)	Your interest savings factor is	You'll *save* this many years	and this many months
5.25	0.0029	0	4
5.5	0.0032	0	4
5.75	0.0033	0	4
6	0.0037	0	4
6.25	0.0038	0	4
6.5	0.0041	0	4
6.75	0.0045	0	4
7	0.0048	0	4
7.25	0.0054	0	4
7.5	0.0053	0	4
7.75	0.0057	0	4
8	0.006	0	4
8.25	0.0063	0	4
8.5	0.0067	0	4
8.75	0.0073	0	4
9	0.0074	0	4
9.25	0.0085	0	5
9.5	0.0085	0	5
9.75	0.0089	0	5
10	0.009	0	5
10.25	0.0099	0	5
10.5	0.0106	0	5

If your Mortgage is	25 Years Old		
and you prepay every 12th month	One FULL-Size monthly payment		
At this Interest rate (%)	Your interest savings factor is	You'll *save* this many years	and this many months
10.75	0.0113	0	5
11	0.0109	0	5
11.25	0.0116	0	5
11.5	0.0127	0	5
11.75	0.0128	0	5
12	0.0132	0	5
12.25	0.0143	0	5
12.5	0.0145	0	5
12.75	0.0157	0	5
13	0.016	0	5
13.25	0.0157	0	5
13.5	0.0168	0	5
13.75	0.0174	0	5
14	0.0176	0	5
14.25	0.0201	0	5
14.5	0.0198	0	5
14.75	0.0222	0	5
15	0.0219	0	5
15.25	0.0219	0	5
15.5	0.022	0	5
15.75	0.0227	0	5
16	0.0245	0	5

NOTE: Find the row starting with your interest rate. To get your total interest savings in dollars, just multiply the interest savings factor you find in that row by your **original** mortgage balance. Read off your time savings in the same row.

EXTRA ANNUAL PAYMENT METHOD
Pseudo Bi-weekly with **Semi-annual** Prepayments
30-YEAR FIXED-RATE MORTGAGE SAVINGS TABLE

Refer to this table to quickly figure out your interest savings
when you use the *Extra Annual Payment* method

If your Mortgage is — and you *prepay* every **6th** month At this Interest rate (%)	Brand New — HALF of the regular monthly payment Your interest savings factor is	You'll *save* this many years	and this many months
5.25	0.1838	4	10
5.5	0.2018	5	0
5.75	0.221	5	2
6	0.2414	5	5
6.25	0.263	5	6
6.5	0.2859	5	9
6.75	0.31	5	11
7	0.3355	6	2
7.25	0.3624	6	5
7.5	0.3906	6	6
7.75	0.4202	6	9
8	0.4511	7	0
8.25	0.4836	7	2
8.5	0.5173	7	5
8.75	0.5526	7	8
9	0.5892	7	11
9.25	0.6273	8	1
9.5	0.6668	8	5
9.75	0.7076	8	7
10	0.7498	8	10
10.25	0.7934	9	1
10.5	0.8383	9	4

If your Mortgage is — and you *prepay* every **6th** month At this Interest rate (%)	Brand New — HALF of the regular monthly payment Your interest savings factor is	You'll *save* this many years	and this many months
10.75	0.8845	9	6
11	0.9321	9	9
11.25	0.9808	10	0
11.5	1.0308	10	3
11.75	1.0819	10	6
12	1.1343	10	9
12.25	1.1877	11	0
12.5	1.2423	11	2
12.75	1.2978	11	5
13	1.3543	11	8
13.25	1.4118	11	11
13.5	1.4702	12	1
13.75	1.5295	12	5
14	1.5896	12	7
14.25	1.6505	12	9
14.5	1.7121	13	0
14.75	1.7746	13	3
15	1.8376	13	5
15.25	1.9015	13	8
15.5	1.9658	13	11
15.75	2.0307	14	0
16	2.0963	14	3

NOTE: Find the row starting with your interest rate. To get your total interest savings in dollars, just multiply the interest savings factor you find in that row by your **original** mortgage balance. Read off your time savings in the same row.

EXTRA ANNUAL PAYMENT METHOD
Pseudo Bi-weekly with **Semi-annual** Prepayments
30-YEAR FIXED-RATE MORTGAGE SAVINGS TABLE

Refer to this table to quickly figure out your interest savings
when you use the *Extra Annual Payment* method

If your Mortgage is	5 Years Old		
and you *prepay* every **6th** month	**HALF** of the *regular monthly payment*		
At this Interest rate (%)	Your interest savings factor is	You'll *save* this many years	and this many months
5.25	0.1186	3	6
5.5	0.1299	3	7
5.75	0.1419	3	9
6	0.1547	3	11
6.25	0.1682	4	0
6.5	0.1825	4	1
6.75	0.1975	4	2
7	0.2135	4	5
7.25	0.2302	4	6
7.5	0.2478	4	7
7.75	0.2664	4	9
8	0.2858	4	11
8.25	0.3061	5	0
8.5	0.3274	5	2
8.75	0.3497	5	3
9	0.3729	5	5
9.25	0.3971	5	7
9.5	0.4223	5	9
9.75	0.4485	5	11
10	0.4756	6	0
10.25	0.5038	6	2
10.5	0.533	6	5

If your Mortgage is	5 Years Old		
and you *prepay* every **6th** month	**HALF** of the *regular monthly payment*		
At this Interest rate (%)	Your interest savings factor is	You'll *save* this many years	and this many months
10.75	0.5631	6	6
11	0.5943	6	8
11.25	0.6266	6	11
11.5	0.6597	7	0
11.75	0.6939	7	2
12	0.729	7	4
12.25	0.765	7	6
12.5	0.8021	7	8
12.75	0.8401	7	10
13	0.8789	8	0
13.25	0.9188	8	2
13.5	0.9594	8	4
13.75	1.0009	8	6
14	1.0433	8	8
14.25	1.0865	8	10
14.5	1.1305	9	0
14.75	1.1753	9	1
15	1.2208	9	4
15.25	1.267	9	6
15.5	1.3139	9	7
15.75	1.3616	9	9
16	1.4099	9	11

NOTE: Find the row starting with your interest rate. To get your total interest savings in dollars, just multiply the interest savings factor you find in that row by your **original** mortgage balance. Read off your time savings in the same row.

EXTRA ANNUAL PAYMENT METHOD
Pseudo Bi-weekly with **Semi-annual** Prepayments
30-YEAR FIXED-RATE MORTGAGE SAVINGS TABLE

Refer to this table to quickly figure out your interest savings
when you use the *Extra Annual Payment* method

If your Mortgage is	10 Years Old		
and you *prepay* every **6th** month	HALF of the regular monthly payment		
At this Interest rate (%)	Your interest savings factor is	You'll **save** this many years	and this many months
5.25	0.0703	2	6
5.5	0.0767	2	6
5.75	0.0836	2	7
6	0.0908	2	8
6.25	0.0985	2	9
6.5	0.1066	2	9
6.75	0.1151	2	11
7	0.1241	2	11
7.25	0.1335	3	0
7.5	0.1434	3	1
7.75	0.1539	3	1
8	0.1648	3	2
8.25	0.1762	3	3
8.5	0.1882	3	5
8.75	0.2007	3	5
9	0.2137	3	6
9.25	0.2273	3	7
9.5	0.2415	3	7
9.75	0.2563	3	9
10	0.2717	3	11
10.25	0.2876	4	0
10.5	0.3042	4	0

If your Mortgage is	10 Years Old		
and you *prepay* every **6th** month	HALF of the regular monthly payment		
At this Interest rate (%)	Your interest savings factor is	You'll **save** this many years	and this many months
10.75	0.3214	4	1
11	0.3392	4	3
11.25	0.3577	4	4
11.5	0.3768	4	5
11.75	0.3965	4	6
12	0.4169	4	7
12.25	0.4379	4	8
12.5	0.4596	4	10
12.75	0.4819	4	11
13	0.5048	5	0
13.25	0.5285	5	1
13.5	0.5527	5	2
13.75	0.5777	5	4
14	0.6032	5	5
14.25	0.6294	5	6
14.5	0.6563	5	7
14.75	0.6838	5	8
15	0.7118	5	10
15.25	0.7406	5	11
15.5	0.7699	6	0
15.75	0.7998	6	1
16	0.8305	6	3

NOTE: Find the row starting with your interest rate. To get your total interest savings in dollars, just multiply the interest savings factor you find in that row by your **original** mortgage balance. Read off your time savings in the same row.

EXTRA ANNUAL PAYMENT METHOD
Pseudo Bi-weekly with **Semi-annual** Prepayments
30-YEAR FIXED-RATE MORTGAGE SAVINGS TABLE

Refer to this table to quickly figure out your interest savings
when you use the *Extra Annual Payment* method

If your Mortgage is — and you prepay every **6th** month	15 Years Old — HALF of the regular monthly payment				If your Mortgage is — and you prepay every **6th** month	15 Years Old — HALF of the regular monthly payment		
At this Interest rate (%)	Your interest savings factor is	You'll *save* this many years	and this many months		At this Interest rate (%)	Your interest savings factor is	You'll *save* this many years	and this many months
5.25	0.0364	1	7		10.75	0.1573	2	5
5.5	0.0397	1	8		11	0.1658	2	5
5.75	0.0431	1	8		11.25	0.1745	2	6
6	0.0466	1	8		11.5	0.1836	2	6
6.25	0.0504	1	9		11.75	0.1931	2	7
6.5	0.0544	1	9		12	0.2027	2	7
6.75	0.0585	1	10		12.25	0.2128	2	8
7	0.0629	1	11		12.5	0.2232	2	8
7.25	0.0675	1	11		12.75	0.2338	2	9
7.5	0.0723	1	11		13	0.2448	2	10
7.75	0.0774	1	11		13.25	0.2562	2	11
8	0.0826	2	0		13.5	0.2679	2	11
8.25	0.0881	2	0		13.75	0.2799	3	0
8.5	0.0938	2	0		14	0.2922	3	0
8.75	0.0998	2	1		14.25	0.305	3	0
9	0.1061	2	1		14.5	0.3181	3	1
9.25	0.1126	2	2		14.75	0.3316	3	2
9.5	0.1193	2	2		15	0.3453	3	2
9.75	0.1264	2	3		15.25	0.3595	3	3
10	0.1337	2	3		15.5	0.374	3	4
10.25	0.1413	2	4		15.75	0.3889	3	5
10.5	0.1492	2	5		16	0.4042	3	5

NOTE: Find the row starting with your interest rate. To get your total interest savings in dollars, just multiply the interest savings factor you find in that row by your **original** mortgage balance. Read off your time savings in the same row.

```
┌─────────────────────────────────────────────────────────┐
│              EXTRA ANNUAL PAYMENT METHOD                 │
│     Pseudo Bi-weekly with Semi-annual Prepayments        │
│     30-YEAR FIXED-RATE MORTGAGE SAVINGS TABLE            │
└─────────────────────────────────────────────────────────┘
```

Refer to this table to quickly figure out your interest savings
when you use the *Extra Annual Payment* method

If your Mortgage is	20 Years Old		
and you *prepay* every **6th** month	HALF of the *regular monthly payment*		
At this Interest rate (%)	Your interest savings factor is	You'll *save* this many years	and this many months
5.25	0.0148	*0*	*11*
5.5	0.0161	*0*	*11*
5.75	0.0174	*0*	*11*
6	0.0188	*1*	*0*
6.25	0.0202	*1*	*0*
6.5	0.0217	*1*	*0*
6.75	0.0233	*1*	*0*
7	0.025	*1*	*0*
7.25	0.0267	*1*	*0*
7.5	0.0285	*1*	*0*
7.75	0.0304	*1*	*0*
8	0.0323	*1*	*0*
8.25	0.0344	*1*	*1*
8.5	0.0365	*1*	*1*
8.75	0.0387	*1*	*1*
9	0.041	*1*	*1*
9.25	0.0434	*1*	*1*
9.5	0.0458	*1*	*1*
9.75	0.0484	*1*	*2*
10	0.051	*1*	*2*
10.25	0.0538	*1*	*2*
10.5	0.0566	*1*	*2*

If your Mortgage is	20 Years Old		
and you *prepay* every **6th** month	HALF of the *regular monthly payment*		
At this Interest rate (%)	Your interest savings factor is	You'll *save* this many years	and this many months
10.75	0.0596	*1*	*2*
11	0.0626	*1*	*3*
11.25	0.0657	*1*	*3*
11.5	0.069	*1*	*3*
11.75	0.0724	*1*	*3*
12	0.0757	*1*	*3*
12.25	0.0793	*1*	*4*
12.5	0.083	*1*	*4*
12.75	0.0868	*1*	*4*
13	0.0906	*1*	*5*
13.25	0.0946	*1*	*5*
13.5	0.0987	*1*	*5*
13.75	0.1029	*1*	*5*
14	0.1072	*1*	*5*
14.25	0.1117	*1*	*5*
14.5	0.1163	*1*	*5*
14.75	0.121	*1*	*6*
15	0.1257	*1*	*6*
15.25	0.1308	*1*	*6*
15.5	0.1358	*1*	*6*
15.75	0.141	*1*	*6*
16	0.1465	*1*	*6*

NOTE: Find the row starting with your interest rate. To get your total interest savings in dollars, just multiply the interest savings factor you find in that row by your ***original*** mortgage balance. Read off your time savings in the same row.

EXTRA ANNUAL PAYMENT METHOD
Pseudo Bi-weekly with **Semi-annual** Prepayments
30-YEAR FIXED-RATE MORTGAGE SAVINGS TABLE

Refer to this table to quickly figure out your interest savings
when you use the *Extra Annual Payment* method

If your Mortgage is	25 Years Old			If your Mortgage is	25 Years Old		
and you *prepay* every **6th** month	HALF of the *regular monthly payment*			and you *prepay* every **6th** month	HALF of the *regular monthly payment*		
At this Interest rate (%)	Your interest savings factor is	You'll *save* this many years	and this many months	At this Interest rate (%)	Your interest savings factor is	You'll *save* this many years	and this many months
5.25	0.0033	0	5	10.75	0.0122	0	5
5.5	0.0035	0	5	11	0.0128	0	5
5.75	0.0038	0	5	11.25	0.0133	0	5
6	0.0041	0	5	11.5	0.014	0	5
6.25	0.0044	0	5	11.75	0.0147	0	5
6.5	0.0047	0	5	12	0.0153	0	6
6.75	0.005	0	5	12.25	0.0159	0	6
7	0.0054	0	5	12.5	0.0166	0	6
7.25	0.0057	0	5	12.75	0.0173	0	6
7.5	0.0061	0	5	13	0.018	0	6
7.75	0.0065	0	5	13.25	0.0188	0	6
8	0.0069	0	5	13.5	0.0195	0	6
8.25	0.0073	0	5	13.75	0.0202	0	6
8.5	0.0077	0	5	14	0.021	0	6
8.75	0.0082	0	5	14.25	0.0219	0	6
9	0.0086	0	5	14.5	0.0226	0	6
9.25	0.0091	0	5	14.75	0.0236	0	6
9.5	0.0096	0	5	15	0.0243	0	6
9.75	0.0101	0	5	15.25	0.0253	0	6
10	0.0106	0	5	15.5	0.0262	0	6
10.25	0.0111	0	5	15.75	0.027	0	6
10.5	0.0116	0	5	16	0.0282	0	6

NOTE: Find the row starting with your interest rate. To get your total interest savings in dollars, just multiply the interest savings factor you find in that row by your ***original*** mortgage balance. Read off your time savings in the same row.

EXTRA ANNUAL PAYMENT METHOD
Pseudo Bi-weekly with Annual Prepayments
15-YEAR FIXED-RATE MORTGAGE SAVINGS TABLE

Refer to this table to quickly figure out your interest savings
when you use the *Extra Annual Payment* method

If your Mortgage is and you prepay every 12th month	Brand New One FULL-Size monthly payment				If your Mortgage is and you prepay every 12th month	Brand New One FULL-Size monthly payment		
At this Interest rate (%)	Your interest savings factor is	You'll *save* this many years	and this many months		**At this Interest rate (%)**	Your interest savings factor is	You'll *save* this many years	and this many months
5.25	0.0511	1	7		10.75	0.1812	2	4
5.5	0.0549	1	7		11	0.1898	2	4
5.75	0.0589	1	8		11.25	0.1986	2	5
6	0.0631	1	8		11.5	0.2078	2	5
6.25	0.0675	1	8		11.75	0.2172	2	6
6.5	0.0721	1	9		12	0.2268	2	6
6.75	0.0768	1	9		12.25	0.2367	2	7
7	0.0818	1	11		12.5	0.2469	2	8
7.25	0.0868	1	11		12.75	0.2575	2	8
7.5	0.0921	1	11		13	0.2683	2	9
7.75	0.0976	1	11		13.25	0.2795	2	9
8	0.1033	1	11		13.5	0.2909	2	11
8.25	0.1092	2	0		13.75	0.3026	2	11
8.5	0.1153	2	0		14	0.3146	2	11
8.75	0.1217	2	0		14.25	0.327	3	0
9	0.1283	2	0		14.5	0.3395	3	0
9.25	0.1351	2	1		14.75	0.3525	3	0
9.5	0.1421	2	1		15	0.366	3	1
9.75	0.1495	2	2		15.25	0.3796	3	1
10	0.157	2	2		15.5	0.3936	3	2
10.25	0.1649	2	3		15.75	0.4079	3	3
10.5	0.1729	2	3		16	0.4226	3	3

NOTE: Find the row starting with your interest rate. To get your total interest savings in dollars, just multiply the interest savings factor you find in that row by your ***original*** mortgage balance. Read off your time savings in the same row.

EXTRA ANNUAL PAYMENT METHOD
Pseudo Bi-weekly with Annual Prepayments
15-YEAR FIXED-RATE MORTGAGE SAVINGS TABLE

Refer to this table to quickly figure out your interest savings
when you use the *Extra Annual Payment* method

If your Mortgage is	5 Years Old			If your Mortgage is	5 Years Old		
and you prepay every 12th month	One FULL-Size monthly payment			and you prepay every 12th month	One FULL-Size monthly payment		
At this Interest rate (%)	Your interest savings factor is	You'll *save* this many years	and this many months	**At this Interest rate (%)**	Your interest savings factor is	You'll *save* this many years	and this many months
5.25	0.0204	0	11	10.75	0.0673	1	2
5.5	0.0218	0	11	11	0.0703	1	2
5.75	0.0233	0	11	11.25	0.0734	1	2
6	0.0249	0	11	11.5	0.0765	1	2
6.25	0.0265	1	0	11.75	0.0798	1	2
6.5	0.0282	1	0	12	0.0831	1	2
6.75	0.03	1	0	12.25	0.0866	1	3
7	0.0318	1	0	12.5	0.09	1	3
7.25	0.0336	1	0	12.75	0.0937	1	3
7.5	0.0356	1	0	13	0.0974	1	3
7.75	0.0376	1	0	13.25	0.1013	1	3
8	0.0396	1	0	13.5	0.1051	1	4
8.25	0.0418	1	0	13.75	0.1092	1	4
8.5	0.044	1	0	14	0.1133	1	4
8.75	0.0463	1	0	14.25	0.1176	1	4
9	0.0486	1	0	14.5	0.1218	1	4
9.25	0.0511	1	0	14.75	0.1263	1	5
9.5	0.0535	1	1	15	0.1309	1	5
9.75	0.0561	1	1	15.25	0.1355	1	5
10	0.0588	1	1	15.5	0.1403	1	5
10.25	0.0616	1	1	15.75	0.1451	1	5
10.5	0.0644	1	1	16	0.1501	1	6

NOTE: Find the row starting with your interest rate. To get your total interest savings in dollars, just multiply the interest savings factor you find in that row by your *original* mortgage balance. Read off your time savings in the same row.

EXTRA ANNUAL PAYMENT METHOD
Pseudo Bi-weekly with Annual Prepayments
15-YEAR FIXED-RATE MORTGAGE SAVINGS TABLE

Refer to this table to quickly figure out your interest savings
when you use the *Extra Annual Payment* method

If your Mortgage is	**10 Years Old**				**If your Mortgage is**	**10 Years Old**		
and you prepay every 12th month	**One FULL-Size monthly payment**				**and you prepay every 12th month**	**One FULL-Size monthly payment**		
At this Interest rate (%)	Your interest savings factor is	You'll *save* this many years	and this many months		**At this Interest rate (%)**	Your interest savings factor is	You'll *save* this many years	and this many months
5.25	0.0043	0	4		10.75	0.0131	0	5
5.5	0.0046	0	4		11	0.0136	0	5
5.75	0.0049	0	4		11.25	0.0142	0	5
6	0.0052	0	4		11.5	0.0147	0	5
6.25	0.0055	0	4		11.75	0.0153	0	5
6.5	0.0058	0	4		12	0.0158	0	5
6.75	0.0062	0	4		12.25	0.0165	0	5
7	0.0065	0	4		12.5	0.017	0	5
7.25	0.0069	0	4		12.75	0.0177	0	5
7.5	0.0072	0	4		13	0.0184	0	5
7.75	0.0077	0	4		13.25	0.0191	0	5
8	0.008	0	4		13.5	0.0196	0	5
8.25	0.0084	0	4		13.75	0.0204	0	5
8.5	0.0089	0	4		14	0.0211	0	5
8.75	0.0093	0	4		14.25	0.0218	0	5
9	0.0097	0	4		14.5	0.0225	0	5
9.25	0.0102	0	4		14.75	0.0232	0	5
9.5	0.0106	0	5		15	0.0241	0	5
9.75	0.011	0	5		15.25	0.0248	0	5
10	0.0115	0	5		15.5	0.0256	0	5
10.25	0.0121	0	5		15.75	0.0263	0	5
10.5	0.0126	0	5		16	0.0272	0	5

NOTE: Find the row starting with your interest rate. To get your total interest savings in dollars, just multiply the interest savings factor you find in that row by your ***original*** mortgage balance. Read off your time savings in the same row.

EXTRA ANNUAL PAYMENT METHOD
Pseudo Bi-weekly with **Semi-annual** Prepayments
15-YEAR FIXED-RATE MORTGAGE SAVINGS TABLE

Refer to this table to quickly figure out your interest savings
when you use the *Extra Annual Payment* method

If your Mortgage is and you prepay every 6th month	Brand New HALF of the regular monthly payment		
At this Interest rate (%)	Your interest savings factor is	You'll *save* this many years	and this many months
5.25	0.053	1	7
5.5	0.0571	1	7
5.75	0.0613	1	8
6	0.0657	1	8
6.25	0.0702	1	9
6.5	0.075	1	9
6.75	0.0799	1	10
7	0.085	1	10
7.25	0.0904	1	11
7.5	0.0959	1	11
7.75	0.1016	1	11
8	0.1076	2	0
8.25	0.1137	2	0
8.5	0.1202	2	0
8.75	0.1268	2	1
9	0.1337	2	1
9.25	0.1408	2	2
9.5	0.1482	2	2
9.75	0.1558	2	3
10	0.1637	2	3
10.25	0.1719	2	4
10.5	0.1803	2	5

If your Mortgage is and you prepay every 6th month	Brand New HALF of the regular monthly payment		
At this Interest rate (%)	Your interest savings factor is	You'll *save* this many years	and this many months
10.75	0.1889	2	5
11	0.1979	2	5
11.25	0.2071	2	6
11.5	0.2166	2	6
11.75	0.2265	2	7
12	0.2366	2	7
12.25	0.247	2	8
12.5	0.2577	2	8
12.75	0.2687	2	9
13	0.2801	2	10
13.25	0.2917	2	11
13.5	0.3036	2	11
13.75	0.3159	3	0
14	0.3285	3	0
14.25	0.3415	3	0
14.5	0.3547	3	1
14.75	0.3683	3	1
15	0.3823	3	2
15.25	0.3965	3	3
15.5	0.4111	3	4
15.75	0.4261	3	5
16	0.4413	3	5

NOTE: Find the row starting with your interest rate. To get your total interest savings in dollars, just multiply the interest savings factor you find in that row by your **original** mortgage balance. Read off your time savings in the same row.

EXTRA ANNUAL PAYMENT METHOD
Pseudo Bi-weekly with **Semi-annual** *Prepayments*
15-YEAR FIXED-RATE MORTGAGE SAVINGS TABLE

Refer to this table to quickly figure out your interest savings
when you use the *Extra Annual Payment* method

If your Mortgage is	5 Years Old			If your Mortgage is	5 Years Old		
and you *prepay* every **6th** month	HALF of the *regular monthly payment*			and you *prepay* every **6th** month	HALF of the *regular monthly payment*		
At this *Interest rate* (%)	Your interest savings factor is	You'll *save* this many years	and this many months	At this *Interest rate* (%)	Your interest savings factor is	You'll *save* this many years	and this many months
5.25	0.0216	*0*	*11*	10.75	0.0715	*1*	*2*
5.5	0.0231	*0*	*11*	11	0.0747	*1*	*3*
5.75	0.0247	*0*	*11*	11.25	0.078	*1*	*3*
6	0.0264	*1*	*0*	11.5	0.0814	*1*	*3*
6.25	0.0281	*1*	*0*	11.75	0.0848	*1*	*3*
6.5	0.0299	*1*	*0*	12	0.0884	*1*	*3*
6.75	0.0318	*1*	*0*	12.25	0.0921	*1*	*4*
7	0.0337	*1*	*0*	12.5	0.0958	*1*	*4*
7.25	0.0357	*1*	*0*	12.75	0.0997	*1*	*5*
7.5	0.0378	*1*	*0*	13	0.1037	*1*	*5*
7.75	0.0399	*1*	*0*	13.25	0.1077	*1*	*5*
8	0.0421	*1*	*0*	13.5	0.1119	*1*	*5*
8.25	0.0444	*1*	*1*	13.75	0.1162	*1*	*5*
8.5	0.0467	*1*	*1*	14	0.1206	*1*	*5*
8.75	0.0492	*1*	*1*	14.25	0.1251	*1*	*5*
9	0.0517	*1*	*1*	14.5	0.1297	*1*	*5*
9.25	0.0543	*1*	*1*	14.75	0.1344	*1*	*6*
9.5	0.0569	*1*	*1*	15	0.1393	*1*	*6*
9.75	0.0597	*1*	*2*	15.25	0.1442	*1*	*6*
10	0.0625	*1*	*2*	15.5	0.1493	*1*	*6*
10.25	0.0654	*1*	*2*	15.75	0.1545	*1*	*6*
10.5	0.0684	*1*	*2*	16	0.1599	*1*	*6*

NOTE: Find the row starting with your interest rate. To get your total interest savings in dollars, just multiply the interest savings factor you find in that row by your **original** mortgage balance. Read off your time savings in the same row.

EXTRA ANNUAL PAYMENT METHOD
Pseudo Bi-weekly with **Semi-annual** Prepayments
15-YEAR FIXED-RATE MORTGAGE SAVINGS TABLE

Refer to this table to quickly figure out your interest savings
when you use the *Extra Annual Payment* method

If your Mortgage is	10 Years Old			If your Mortgage is	10 Years Old		
and you *prepay every* **6th** month	HALF of the *regular monthly payment*			and you *prepay every* **6th** month	HALF of the *regular monthly payment*		
At this Interest rate (%)	Your interest savings factor is	You'll *save* this many years	and this many months	*At this Interest rate (%)*	Your interest savings factor is	You'll *save* this many years	and this many months
5.25	0.0048	0	5	10.75	0.0147	0	5
5.5	0.0051	0	5	11	0.0153	0	5
5.75	0.0054	0	5	11.25	0.0159	0	5
6	0.0058	0	5	11.5	0.0165	0	5
6.25	0.0062	0	5	11.75	0.0172	0	5
6.5	0.0065	0	5	12	0.0178	0	5
6.75	0.0069	0	5	12.25	0.0185	0	6
7	0.0073	0	5	12.5	0.0192	0	6
7.25	0.0077	0	5	12.75	0.0199	0	6
7.5	0.0081	0	5	13	0.0206	0	6
7.75	0.0085	0	5	13.25	0.0214	0	6
8	0.009	0	5	13.5	0.0221	0	6
8.25	0.0094	0	5	13.75	0.0229	0	6
8.5	0.0099	0	5	14	0.0237	0	6
8.75	0.0104	0	5	14.25	0.0245	0	6
9	0.0109	0	5	14.5	0.0253	0	6
9.25	0.0114	0	5	14.75	0.0262	0	6
9.5	0.0119	0	5	15	0.027	0	6
9.75	0.0124	0	5	15.25	0.0279	0	6
10	0.013	0	5	15.5	0.0288	0	6
10.25	0.0135	0	5	15.75	0.0297	0	6
10.5	0.0141	0	5	16	0.0306	0	6

NOTE: Find the row starting with your interest rate. To get your total interest savings in dollars, just multiply the interest savings factor you find in that row by your *original* mortgage balance. Read off your time savings in the same row.

Appendix J

Cover the basics
Select a method
Get preliminary info
Make prepayments
Keep records

PREPAYMENT TRACKING WORKSHEET

MORTGAGE PREPAYMENT TRACKING WORKSHEET

Page ___ of ___

MORTGAGE TYPE	TERM OF YEARS	REMAINING YEARS	ORIGINAL BALANCE	REMAINING BALANCE	INTEREST RATE	EFFECTIVE DATE	MONTHLY PAYMENT

Period No.	Date Paid	Principal Payment Due	Amount Paid	Principal Pre-paid	Interest Saved	Cumulative Interest Saved	Principal Balance	Months Saved	Cumul. Months Saved

Feel free to make copies of this page for your personal use.

MORTGAGE PREPAYMENT TRACKING WORKSHEET

Page ___ of ___

Period No.	Date Paid	Principal Payment Due	Amount Paid	Principal Pre-paid	Interest Saved	Cumulative Interest Saved	Principal Balance	Months Saved	Cumul. Months Saved

MORTGAGE PREPAYMENT TRACKING WORKSHEET
Explanation of Header Entries

MORTGAGE TYPE
The type of your mortgage
example: Fixed rate, Adjustable rate

TERM OF YEARS
The original term of years
example: 30

REMAINING YEARS
Number of years remaining to pay off the mortgage
example: 30 (if you're at the very beginning of the term)

ORIGINAL BALANCE
The original amount of the mortgage loan
example: $80,000

REMAINING BALANCE
The balance due at the time you start using this worksheet
example: $80,000 (if you're at the very beginning of the term)

INTEREST RATE
The interest rate you're currently paying
example: 10%

NOTE: *If the interest rate changes for whatever reason, such as a new adjustable rate, a new buydown rate change, or refinancing, **just get a new amortization schedule and start a new worksheet.***

EFFECTIVE DATE
The effective date of the interest rate you're currently paying. If there were no rate changes, this date is the same as the mortgage origination date.

example: 1/1/93

MONTHLY PAYMENT
The scheduled monthly payment specified in the mortgage contract (*not including taxes and insurance*).

example: $702.06

MORTGAGE PREPAYMENT TRACKING WORKSHEET
Explanation of Detail Entries

PERIOD NO.

The period number corresponding to the payment due. This is extracted from the amortization schedule *or derived from the last worksheet entry.*
example: 2

DATE PAID

The date on the prepayment check
example: 3/1/93

PRINCIPAL PAYMENT DUE

Scheduled principal portion of the current payment due
example: $35.69

AMOUNT PAID

Total amount paid including prepayment.
This may be just the prepayment amount if you're sending a separate check.
example: $774.32

PRINCIPAL PRE-PAID

Amount of principal *prepayment*
example: $72.36

INTEREST SAVED

Amount of interest saved as a result of the prepayment
example: $1,331.84

CUMULATIVE INTEREST SAVED

Total interest saved to date. *This is the sum of the current interest saved and the cumulative interest saved in the **last** entry.*
example: $1,331.84

PRINCIPAL BALANCE

Balance due *after the current total payment*
example: $79,856.66

MONTHS SAVED

Months saved as a result of the prepayment
example: 2

CUMULATIVE MONTHS SAVED

Number of months saved to date. *This is the sum of the current months saved and the cumulative months saved in the **last** entry.*
example: 2

Appendix K	MORTGAGE PAYMENT And PREPAYMENT SLIP

MORTGAGE PAYMENT STUB

Mortgage No. _____

Date: _____

Check No. _____

Period No. _____

Amount Due $ _____

Amount To Principal Only $ _____

Total Amount Enclosed $ _____

Keep this stub with your records

Copyright 1993 Capital Search Systems

MORTGAGE PAYMENT SLIP   TO: _____

Mortgage No. _____

Date: _____

Name: _____

Address: _____

City: _____

State,ZIP: _____

Amount Due _____

This Amount To Principal Only $ [　　　]

Total Amount Enclosed $ _____

Check No. _____

Mail this slip with your check

Copyright 1993 Capital Search Systems

MORTGAGE PAYMENT STUB

Mortgage No. _____

Date: _____

Check No. _____

Period No. _____

Amount Due $ _____

Amount To Principal Only $ _____

Total Amount Enclosed $ _____

Keep this stub with your records

Copyright 1993 Capital Search Systems

MORTGAGE PAYMENT SLIP   TO: _____

Mortgage No. _____

Date: _____

Name: _____

Address: _____

City: _____

State,ZIP: _____

Amount Due _____

This Amount To Principal Only $ [　　　]

Total Amount Enclosed $ _____

Check No. _____

Mail this slip with your check

Copyright 1993 Capital Search Systems

MORTGAGE PAYMENT STUB

Mortgage No. _____

Date: _____

Check No. _____

Period No. _____

Amount Due $ _____

Amount To Principal Only $ _____

Total Amount Enclosed $ _____

Keep this stub with your records

Copyright 1993 Capital Search Systems

MORTGAGE PAYMENT SLIP   TO: _____

Mortgage No. _____

Date: _____

Name: _____

Address: _____

City: _____

State,ZIP: _____

Amount Due _____

This Amount To Principal Only $ [　　　]

Total Amount Enclosed $ _____

Check No. _____

Mail this slip with your check

Copyright 1993 Capital Search Systems

Appendix L	SHORT-TERM DEBT ELIMINATION SCHEDULE

Short-Term Debt Elimination Schedule

Total Initial Booster Cash $ [ ]   Initial Booster Cash Percentage to Short-term Debt   [%]

Description	Initial Balance	Initial Monthly Payment	Initial Expected Duration (Months)	Current Balance	Boosted Monthly Payment	Boosted Expected Duration (Months)	Extra Mortgage Principal Payment

Appendix M 	***EXPLANATORY NOTES ABOUT TAXES***

EXPLANATORY NOTES   *FOR THE CURIOUS ONLY*
About Mortgage Interest and Your Taxes

Everyone uses the general formula (INCOME - DEDUCTION) x TAX RATE to compute **tax amount**. Here, **Deduction** is the mortgage interest you paid. So, after you subtract the interest **amount** from your **Income** you get *taxable income.* Then you multiply the *taxable income* by the *Tax Rate* percentage to get the tax due.

Let's say you're in a 31 percent tax bracket. When you subtract the *mortgage interest deduction* from your income, *you are NOT subtracting the **TOTAL MORTGAGE INTEREST** amount you paid during the year from your **TAX BILL.*** But, as you multiply the difference between Income and Deduction by Tax Rate, what you are really doing is this:

> *You are subtracting **ONLY 31 PERCENT** of the total mortgage interest amount you paid during the year from the tax amount you would otherwise pay without the deduction.*

The truth of this has something to do with the ***Distributive Principle*** of mathematics. It's nothing fancy when you get right down to it.

The distributive principle states in general that:

$$(A - B) \times C$$

is the same as

$$(A \times C) - (B \times C)$$

For example, when **A=10**, **B=2**, and **C=5**, the equation now looks like:

$$(10 - 2) \times 5 \quad = \quad (10 \times 5) - (2 \times 5)$$

| **It becomes:** | (8) x 5 | = | (50) - (10) |
| **which is:** | 40 | = | 40 |

So then, the formula:

$$(\text{INCOME - DEDUCTION}) \times \text{TAX RATE} = \text{TAX AMOUNT}$$

is the same as:

$$(\text{INCOME} \times \text{TAX RATE}) - (\text{DEDUCTION} \times \text{TAX RATE}) = \text{TAX AMOUNT}$$

When you look at this arrangement of the formula,

$$\boxed{(\text{INCOME} \times \text{TAX RATE}) - (\text{DEDUCTION} \times \text{TAX RATE}) = \text{TAX AMOUNT}}$$

things should become clearer.

Income times **Tax Rate** gives **Unadjusted Tax**. **Deduction** is the mortgage interest that compounded at 10 percent throughout the year. **Deduction** times **Tax Rate** gives *net deduction*. Again, Tax Rate is 31 percent. Then, it should be clear that **ONLY 31% of the mortgage interest** (the *net deduction*) is subtracted from **Unadjusted Tax** to give **Tax Amount**.

So, practically speaking, the 10 percent *mortgage interest* rate (which is represented in the Deduction) gets reduced by 31 percent or 3.1 to the 6.9 percent mark.

You pay 10% to the bank. From your point of view, when you get back 3.1% from Uncle Sam, that's like paying 6.9% to the bank. But, don't get fooled, the bank keeps its full 10%.

Consider this example *(using only interest deduction for simplicity).*

	Without Mortgage	With Mortgage (30-Year at 10% no prepayments)	
Mortgage balance	$0.00	$80,000.00	*(At the **start** of the first year)*
Interest paid to bank	$0.00	*$7,979.98**	*(At the **end** of the first year)*
Income	$55,000.00	$55,000.00	
Tax rate	31%	31%	
Taxable income	$55,000.00	$47,020.02	*(Income - Interest Paid)*
Tax Amount	$17,050.00	$14,576.21	*(Income - Interest Paid) X Tax rate*
Net deduction	*$0.00*	*$2,473.79*	
[A] Income x tax rate	$17,050.00	$17,050.00	
[B] Interest x tax rate	$0.00	*$2,473.79*	
[A] - [B] Tax Amount	$17,050.00	$14,576.21	

*****Total interest taken on balance that got smaller with each payment during the year.*

Appendix N

PREPAYMENT METHOD COMBINATION CHART

Prepayment Method Combination Chart

Prepayment Method In Use	Prepayment Method to combine **On Top** of it	Prepayment Method to combine **On Top** of it	Prepayment Method to combine **On Top** of it	Prepayment Method to combine **On Top** of it
	Increasing	Fixed	Term-based	Extra Annual
Increasing		🚫	🚫	✓
Fixed	✓		🚫	✓
Term-based	✓	✓		✓
Extra Annual	✓	✓	✓	

✓ Means **OK** to combine

🚫 Means **NOT OK** to combine

Notes:

- The *Extra-annual payment* mehod combines with or on top of any of the other three.

- When using the *Increasing* prepayment method, you can **only** combine the *Extra Annual* payment method on top of it.

- When using the *Fixed* prepayment method, you can combine the *Increasing Prepayment* method on top of it just by making the increasing prepayments as additional prepayments *in synch* with the amortization schedule. You can also combine the *Extra Annual* payment method on top of it. But, it does not make sense to combine the *Term-based* prepayment method on top of the *Fixed* method, although the converse is possible. If you want to cut a specific number of years, you might as well change over to the *Term-based* as the primary method.

- When using the *Term-based* prepayment method as the primary method, you can combine the *Increasing Prepayment* method on top of it just by making increasing prepayments as additional prepayments *in synch* with the amortization schedule. You can even combine in the *Fixed* prepayment method by making additional prepayments as random prepayments *out of synch* with the amortization schedule. The *Extra Annual* payment method combines naturally on top of the *Term-based* method.

GLOSSARY

Acceleration Clause	Clause in a mortgage contract that allows the lender to ask for immediate payment of the full balance, when something specific happens, for instance the borrower does not make payments on time.
Accrued Interest	Interest due for payment at the end of a time frame called a period.
Accrual Period	Time period during which interest gets earned.
Adjustable-Rate Mortgage (ARM)	Mortgage that allows the lender to raise or lower the interest rate on the basis of some other rate considered as an index.
After-Tax Rate	The portion of a rate of interest that remains *tax-free*. It is the *difference* between a given rate of interest and the result you get by multiplying the same rate by the tax percentage rate of the person who receives the given rate.
Amortization	The repayment of a loan balance by regular deposits that also include accrued interest.
Amortization Schedule	The table that shows each scheduled payment over the duration of a mortgage loan. For each payment, the schedule indicates principal and interest components, and the remaining balance.
Annuity	A series of equal deposits or payments made at regular time intervals.
Appraised Value	The market value of a house as determined by a professional appraiser.
Assessment Ratio	A percentage, set by law or by practice, which is used to determine the proportion of the market value of a property that will be subject to taxation. Also called *Assessment Rate*.
Assessed Value	Value of a house for property taxation purpose, derived by multiplying the appraised value of the house by the assessment ratio.

Assets	Marketable possessions that a person owns free and clear.
Bank Bi-Weekly Mortgage	A type of mortgage where the bank *requires* payment *every two weeks.* Interest accrues every two weeks
Before-Tax Rate	A rate of interest that may be subject to taxation.
Break-even Years	The number of years that must elapse before the accumulated savings resulting from a lower monthly payment get to equal the closing cost of refinancing a mortgage loan. The calculation of break-even should take into account the effects of inflation and taxes.
Buydown	Monthly payment based on a reduced interest rate offered as an incentive to buy.
Closing	Meeting between buyer, lender, seller, their lawyers and other representatives to complete the sale and purchase of a house.
Closing Costs	Expenses and fees that a borrower pays at the closing of a mortgage loan to cover appraisal fees, discount points, downpayment, origination fee, credit report, title insurance, escrow deposits for homeowners' insurance and property taxes, and other such items.
Compound Interest	Interest taken on *both* principal and interest that accrued previously.
Deed of Trust	A loan taken for the purchase of real estate in which the property secures the loan and a third party holds the deed to the title, with the lender as the beneficiary, until the loan is paid off.
Equity	The *difference* between what a house is worth on the market and whatever mortgage balance the owner still owes on the house.
Escrow	Money deposit required by a lending bank to cover homeowners' liability and hazard insurance, and property taxes. The term also designates a process that starts when a buyer and seller go into a formal real estate purchase agreement, with the participation of an impartial third party as an arbiter, and ends at closing.
Fair Market Value	The highest price that a property is expected to sell for in an today's market.
Fixed-Rate Mortgage	Mortgage in which the rate of interest stays constant for the duration of the loan.
Interest	Amount of money due as payment for the use of a sum of money received as a loan over a certain time frame.
Interest Rate	Percentage at which interest is calculated over a given time frame.

Interpolation	The process of estimating a factor, amount, quantity, or ratio that lies between two other values.
Investment	The acquisition of an asset that appreciates in value over time. It is also the placement of money so that it produces a return over time.
Investment Property	Real estate property acquired for its potential to increase in value over time. It also refers to property that is rented to produced a return.
Liabilities	What a person *owes*.
Mortgage	A loan taken for the purchase of real estate in which the property secures the loan and the lender holds the deed to the title until the loan is paid off.
Mortgagee	The lender who loans out funds to purchase real estate used as security for the loan and who receives a mortgage as an IOU.
Mortgagor	The borrower who receives a loan to purchase property and engages to repay it by signing a mortgage agreement as an IOU.
Mortgage Banker	An institution that makes mortgage loans using its own money then turns around and sells the loans at a discount to other parties.
Negative Amortization	Occurs when payments are too small to cover interest due. The unpaid interest then becomes part of the principal balance due, causing the balance to grow larger and larger.
Net Worth	The difference between assets and liabilities.
Period	The regular time frame required for interest to be earned on the current loan balance. This repeating time frame is also known as *accrual period*.
Period Number	The sequence number assigned to an interest accrual period.
Points	The up-front charge imposed by a lender once only, usually as port of closing costs, to compensate for a lower rate of interest on a mortgage loan. One point is *one percent* of the total mortgage amount. Points are also called *discount points* or *origination fees*.
Prepayment	Amount of money paid in advance on the principal of a loan.
Prepayment Penalty	The amount of money allowed to be charged, as specified by a clause in the mortgage contract, when the whole principal balance or a major portion of it is paid off before the end of the mortgage term.
Principal	The initial amount of money borrowed.
Principal Balance	The amount of borrowed money remaining outstanding at a given point in time.

Pseudo Bi-Weekly Mortgage	A method of repaying a standard mortgage where one half of the monthly payment is *deposited* in a holding account *every two weeks*. The bank still expects a **monthly** payment. Interest accrues over a period of *one* month. So, a full payment is made every month from the holding account. This method allows an extra sum the size of one monthly payment amount to be accumulated at the end of every year. The extra money is normally used to prepay principal. You can manage this method yourself.
Refinance	The negotiation of a new loan, usually at a lower rate of interest, to pay off and replace an older loan.
Rental Income	Money received in payment from the rental of real estate property.
Short-Term	Time duration of a loan which is meant to exist for less than five years.
Term	The duration of a loan. A mortgage is usually a long-term loan that can last between five and thirty years.
Terms	The conditions, regulations, rules, and stipulations spelled out in a mortgage contract.
Title	A valid document that proves an owner has legal possession of a property.
Yield	The total amount of money earned or produced by an investment.

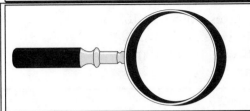

INDEX

Your Registration Form
for *Put Money In Your Pockets*

REGISTER NOW!

Register with this form for advance notification of updates, new books, and other products and services that will help put more money in your pockets. ***When you register you also qualify for special customer discounts on books and other products or services you order! So, act FAST!***

⇒ **To register:** *Fill out this form and mail it in as indicated at the bottom right of the other side.*

Rate the quality of *information* in this book:	☐ Excellent ☐ Very Good ☐ Good ☐ Satisfactory ☐ Fair ☐ Poor

Rate the quality of the *printed materials*:	☐ Excellent ☐ Very Good ☐ Good ☐ Satisfactory ☐ Fair ☐ Poor

Rate the *format* of this book:	☐ Excellent ☐ Very Good ☐ Good ☐ Satisfactory ☐ Fair ☐ Poor

Did the book provide the information you needed? ☐ Yes ☐ No

What topics or concepts did you like most in this book? _____
_____

What topics or concepts would you like to change, add, or remove in future editions of this book?
_____
_____

Other Comments: _____
_____
_____

The material in the book is: ☐ Clear and easy to follow ☐ Too complicated ☐ Too elementary

Are the worksheets easy to use? ☐ Yes ☐ No ☐ Not applicable to me

Indicate how you feel about the price: ☐ Lower than expected ☐ About right ☐ Too expensive

The type of your Mortgage is: ☐ Fixed rate ☐ Adjustable rate ☐ Other _____

What prepayment methods are you planning to use?
_____

Would you like us to help you maximize your mortgage interest savings? ☐ Yes ☐ No

If you liked the book, may we quote you in future promotional materials?
☐ Yes, by name ☐ Yes, by occupation: _____ ☐ No

Name (Please PRINT): _____

Address - Street: _____

City/State/Zipcode: _____

Please FOLD exactly along this line FIRST

BUSINESS REPLY MAIL
FIRST CLASS MAIL   PERMIT NO. 1316   HEMPSTEAD, NY

POSTAGE WILL BE PAID BY ADDRESSEE

CAPITAL SEARCH SYSTEMS
P.O. BOX 4518
HEMPSTEAD, NY 11551-9841

NO POSTAGE
NECESSARY
IF MAILED
IN THE
UNITED STATES

FOLD exactly along this line SECOND

1	Please CUT along this *vertical* line
2	FOLD twice
3	TAPE together **(NO STAPLES)**
4	and MAIL

Thanks

NOW you can order extra copies for relatives, friends, or clients!

- *Great birthday or holiday gift for people you care about!*
- *It's a unique and thoughtful wedding shower gift.*
- *Perfect for young people who're planning to buy a home!*

Look for **Put Money in Your Pockets** at your local bookstore or book distributor or use this order form to request additional copies from *Capital Search Systems.* If someone beat you to this form, you can order by mailing a check or money order to **Capital Search Systems**, P.O. Box 4518, Hempstead, NY 11550. Include the registration form to get the book buyer price of *$24.95* per book (New York residents add 8.5% sales tax), $4.50 per order plus $1.00 for each additional book for shipping and handling, and a note with your name and address.

Book Order Form

Item		Unit Price	Quantity	Amount
Put Money in Your Pockets	ISBN 0-9641964-2-5	$24.95		

Subtotal	
New York residents add 8.5% **Sales Tax**	
$4.50 first copy and $1.00 each additional copy **for Shipping and Handling**	
(Allow 4-6 weeks for delivery) **Total**	

Please send check or money order (no COD or cash).

Make checks payable to *Capital Search Systems.*

Prices and availability are subject to change without notice.

Guarantee
All Capital Search Systems publications and products come with a 30-day money-back guarantee.

☐ **Yes!** Send me _____ copies of **Put Money in Your Pockets,** I'm enclosing $_____

Ship To:

PLEASE PRINT!

Name _____

Address _____

(If possible, please write a street address, not a P.O. Box)

City/State/Zip _____

Daytime Phone _____

Please mail check or money order with this order form to:

Capital Search Systems, P.O. Box 4518, Hempstead, NY 11550

Thank You!

Product Information

USE YOUR REGISTRATION DISCOUNT TO GET THESE PRODUCTS!

Now you can take advantage of your *registration discount* to order these products, even if you're registering at the same time. Use the *product order form* to order from this list. When ordering amortization schedules and short-term debt elimination projections, please make certain you **fill out** and **attach** one of the information forms on the following pages.

Get these products from us to complete your tool kit and give you a convenient booster when you decide to start *putting money in your pockets.*

The Smart Homeowner's Escrow Savings Guide *by Josh Bruno*	Guide book gives detailed instructions on how to inspect your escrow account, identify excess money balances, and get refunds from your lender. Explains contents of lender's **escrow analysis** report. Shows how to look at both past records and future disbursements. Gives easy step-by-step instructions and examples. Regular Price: $21.95 / *Registered book buyers:* **$16.95**
Regular amortization schedule	Shows complete amortization schedule for current state of a mortgage. Use to see schedule of regular payments that remain ahead without the application of any prepayments. Required when working with *Increasing Prepayment* method. Useful for *Extra-Annual Payment* method after each semi-annual or annual prepayment. Useful for *Fixed Prepayment* method after making a prepayment **out of synch.** Regular Price: $16.95 / *Registered book buyers:* **$11.95**
Amortization schedule for the Increasing Prepayment method	Shows complete amortization schedule when *Increasing Prepayment* method is applied. Starts with current state of a mortgage. Shows total interest savings and new term duration. Good projection tool to have **before** starting *Increasing Prepayment* method. Regular Price: $17.95 / *Registered book buyers:* **$12.95**

Amortization schedule for the Fixed Prepayment method or Term-Based Prepayment method	Complete amortization schedule for *Fixed Prepayment* method. Shows the effects of a given *base* prepayment. Starts with current state of a mortgage. Shows total interest savings and new term duration or total savings for *selected* new term. Good projection tool to have **before** starting *Fixed Prepayment or Term-Based Prepayment* method. Regular Price: $17.95 / *Registered book buyers:* ***$12.95***
Amortization schedule for the Extra-Annual Payment method	Shows complete **Pseudo** *Bi-weekly* amortization schedule from the current state of a mortgage. *Not the same* as *bank* bi-weekly amortization. Great projection tool to have **before** starting the *Extra-Annual Payment* method. It provides a guiding frame of reference throughout the term. Regular Price: $19.95 / *Registered book buyers:* ***$14.95***
Personalized Comparative Amortization Report	Shows amortization schedule for a prepayment method in comparison with ***(a)*** the original regular amortization schedule, ***(b)*** the same method using different selected parameters or ***(c)*** with another method. Regular Price: $21.95 / *Registered book buyers:* ***$16.95***
Prepayment Tracking Book	Perfect companion workbook for ***Put Money In Your Pockets.*** Contains complete supply of prepayment tracking worksheets, a block of mortgage prepayment stubs and slips to last for the duration, and a supply of short-term debt elimination worksheets. Gives a current snapshot of your mortgage payments. Makes tracking prepayments a breeze. Keeps records together. Comes with binder for convenient storage. ***Deluxe version*** *comes personalized with your name, address, mortgage number, and lender name on the prepayment slips.* Regular version: $21.95 *Registered book buyers:* ***$16.95*** **Deluxe version:** $27.95 *Registered book buyers:* ***$22.95***
Short-term Debt Elimination Projection	Shows estimated schedule for the elimination of short-term debts. You get a report that ranks your short-term debt in the order you need to prepay them so you get rid of them the fastest. The report indicates your savings in time. It saves you the burden of doing the calculations yourself, or provides a double-check if you do it yourself. Regular Price: $19.95 / *Registered book buyers:* ***$14.95***

Use this form to order products and services associated with *Put Money in Your Pockets.*

1 Write in prices from the *Product Information* sheet, specify quantities, and calculate the total.

2 *Fill out* and *attach* information forms for amortization schedules or short-term debt projections you're ordering.

3 Write out and attach a check or money order for the total and mail the complete order to the address below.

Capital Search Systems

Product Order Form

Item	Unit Price	Quantity	Amount
The Smart Homeowner's Escrow Savings Guide			
Regular amortization schedule			
Amortization schedule for the Increasing Prepayment method			
Amortization schedule for the Fixed or Term-Based Prepayment method			
Amortization schedule for the Extra-Annual Payment method			
Personalized Comparative Amortization Report			
Prepayment Tracking Book θ **Deluxe version** (See other side)			
Short-term Debt Elimination Projection			

Subtotal

New York residents add 8.5% **Sales Tax**

$4.50 first product and $1.00 each additional product **for Shipping and Handling**

(Allow 3-5 weeks for delivery) **Total**

Please send check or money order (no COD or cash).

Make checks payable to *Capital Search Systems.*

Prices and availability are subject to change without notice.

Guarantee
All Capital Search Systems publications and products come with a 30-day money-back guarantee.

☐ **Yes!** Send me the products I've specified above, I'm enclosing $_____

Ship To:

PLEASE PRINT!

Name _____

Address _____
(If possible, please write a street address, not a P.O. Box)

City/State/Zip _____

Daytime Phone _____

Please send check or money order with this order form to:
Capital Search Systems, P.O. Box 4518, Hempstead, NY 11550

Thank You!

If you're ordering the **Deluxe version** of the *Prepayment Tracking Book,* please provide below: the borrower *name* and *address* to show on the payment slips and stubs, the *mortgage* or *loan number*, and the *lender name.*

Information for placement on mortgage payment slips and stubs in **Deluxe version** of the *Prepayment Tracking Book:*

Borrower Name: _____

Address: _____

City/State/Zip: _____

Mortgage Number: _____

Lender Name: _____

AMORTIZATION SCHEDULE INFORMATION FORM

Attach this form to your order

Type of Mortgage: ☐ *Fixed*   ☐ *Other (Please, specify on reverse side)*

Number of Payments Required By The Bank Per Year: ☐

1	Original Loan Amount:	
2	Original Term	*Years:*
3	Original Interest Rate:	%
4	Original Periodic Payment: *(Principal & Interest Only)*	*(If paid monthly, Periodic Payment is a **Monthly Payment**)*
5	Number of Payments Made: *(To Date)*	
6	*Current* Loan Balance:	
7	*Current* Remaining Term	*Years:* *Months:*
8	*Current* Interest Rate	%
9	*Current* Periodic Payment *(Principal & Interest Only)*	*(If paid monthly, Periodic Payment is a **Monthly Payment**)*
10	Last Payment Date: Next Payment Date:	
11	Balloon Payment Due In: ___ *years*	*(Leave blank if you do not have a balloon payment)*

12 *Prepayment Method To Use*
(Pick ONE from the following)

See other side for *Comparative Amortization* information area

☐ **None**
(For regular amortization)

☐ **Increasing Prepayment**

☐ **Fixed Prepayment**   *Base Prepayment:*

☐ **Term-Based Prepayment**   *Base Prepayment:*   *Years To Cut:*

☐ **Extra-Annual Payment**   ☐ *With ANNUAL*   ☐ *With SEMI-ANNUAL*
(Pseudo Bi-Weekly)   *Prepayments*   *Prepayments*

INFORMATION AREA FOR *OTHER MORTGAGE TYPE*

Use this area only to specify the type of your mortgage, if it's not a FIXED RATE mortgage. For example, if you have a *variable rate* mortgage, **check** the box, then specify the **index rate**, **margin,** adjustment period in **years**, the **interest rate caps, maximum interest rate decrease**, and the monthly payment cap, if any.

☐ **Variable Rate**

Index rate:	%
Margin:	%
Adjustment **period:**	Check ONE: ρ *years or* ρ *months*
Interest rate **Cap** per adjustment period:	%
Lifetime interest rate **Cap:**	%
Maximum Interest rate **DECREASE:**	%
Monthly Payment **Cap:** $	

☐ **Graduated Payment**

Graduation **period:**	*years*
Annual **rate of graduation:**	%

☐ **Growing Equity**

Annual **growth rate** of payments:	%

INFORMATION AREA FOR
COMPARATIVE AMORTIZATION SCHEDULE

Use this area only to specify parameters for a **second** amortization schedule to be run in comparison with the first one requested on the other side, if you're ordering a *Personalized Comparative Amortization Report.* Otherwise, leave it blank

13 | *Prepayment Method To Use*
(Pick ONE from the following)

Use this side for *Comparative Amortization* information

☐ None
(For regular amortization)

☐ Increasing Prepayment

☐ Fixed Prepayment   ***Base Prepayment:***

☐ Term-Based Prepayment   ***Base Prepayment:***   ***Years To Cut:***

☐ Extra-Annual Payment   ☐ *With ANNUAL*   ☐ *With SEMI-ANNUAL*
(Pseudo Bi-Weekly)   *Prepayments*   *Prepayments*

SHORT-TERM DEBT ELIMINATION PROJECTION INFORMATION FORM

Attach this form to your order
(See explanation of column headers on reverse)

Total Initial Booster Cash $ [   ]   *Initial Booster Cash Percentage to **Short-term Debt*** [%]   *Percentage to **Mortgage*** [%]

☐ Please, apply the ***booster cash percentage to mortgage*** I specified above to an amortization schedule as *additional* fixed prepayments. I'm providing the amortization information in the data area on the other side

No.	Description	Initial Balance	Initial Monthly Payment	Initial Expected Duration (Months)	Estimated Start Date
1					
2					
3					
4					
5					
6					
7					
8					
9					
10					
11					
12					
13					
14					
15					

Amortization Schedule Information Area

> Use the area below only to specify parameters for an amortization schedule to be run in conjunction with the **Short-term Debt Elimination Projection**, *if you so indicated on the other side.* Otherwise, leave it blank

1   *Current* Loan Balance: [ ]

2   *Current* Remaining Term   *Years:* [ ]   *Months:* [ ]

3   *Current* Interest Rate: [ ] %

4   *Current* Periodic Payment: [ ]   *(If paid monthly, Periodic Payment is a **Monthly Payment**)*
(Principal & Interest Only)

5   Last Payment Date: [ ]   Next Payment Date: [ ]

6   Balloon Payment Due In: [ ] *years*   *(Leave blank if you do not have a balloon payment)*

7   **Prepayment Method To Use**
(Pick ONE from the following)

Increasing booster prepayments will be gradually added to the method you pick below.

❐   Fixed Prepayment   ***Use Booster Cash as ONLY Base Prepayment***

❐   Fixed Prepayment   ***Base Prepayment:*** [ ]

❐   Term-Based Prepayment   ***Base Prepayment:*** [ ]   ***Years To Cut:*** [ ]

❐   Extra-Annual Payment   ❐ ***With ANNUAL Prepayments***   ❐ ***With SEMI-ANNUAL Prepayments***
(Pseudo Bi-Weekly)

Explanation of Column Headers
(In Short-term Debt Elimination Information Form)

Column Header	Explanation
No.	Sequence number of bill in this list. The order does not matter. Just list the items as you find them.
Description	Name of the bill or creditor. Examples: *VISA, Student Loan, Prudential Car Loan, etc.*
Initial Balance	Balance you expect at the time you start the program.
Initial Monthly Payment	Regular monthly payment or average minimum monthly payment.
Initial Expected Duration (Months)	Number of months you expect this bill to last normally.
Estimated Start Date	Date you expect to put this program into operation. *You could actually start on the first bill **before** you get the report back. So, specify the date you plan to start.*